ADVANCED MICROECONOMICS

ADVANCED MICROECONOMICS

Volume I

K.R. Gupta

ATLANTIC
PUBLISHERS & DISTRIBUTORS (P) LTD

Published by

ATLANTIC

PUBLISHERS & DISTRIBUTORS (P) LTD

7/22, Ansari Road, Darya Ganj,
New Delhi-110002
Phones : 23273880, 23275880, 23280451
Fax : 91-11-23285873
Web : www.atlanticbooks.com
E-mail : info@atlanticbooks.com

Branch Office
5, Nallathambi Street, Wallajah Road,
Chennai-600002
Phones : +91-44-64611085, 32413319
E-mail : chennai@atlanticbooks.com

Printed in India at Nice Printing Press, A-33/3A, Site-IV, Industrial Area, Sahibabad, Ghaziabad, U.P.

Preface

When I published *Macroeconomics* three decades ago, there was a demand that I should also publish a book on microeconomics. But because of my other engagements I could not do that. Now I am glad to put in the hands of the readers, the book *Advanced Microeconomics*.

My objective in writing *Advanced Microeconomics*, has been to present modern economics in a simple and easily comprehensible style so that it can be used even by those students who have had no prior exposure to the subject. As for the applications in the book, they have been carefully related to the text's basic theoretical concepts, so that students can see how the concepts can be used to explore new areas of concern as they arise. This book brings forth many problems that urge the students to think more broadly about what they are learning. I have adopted the verbal method of presenting the material covered, with extensive use of diagrams and mathematics to illustrate the verbal exposition. Mathematical proofs have been provided wherever they are necessary.

The book proceeds in a very standard way through demand, supply, and market structure. It also covers factor markets, capital and time, asymmetric information, and externalities. I have adopted partial equilibrium analysis approach in this book. The behaviour of buyers and sellers in a particular industry has been examined in isolation from the conditions prevailing in other industries (markets).

The interaction of industries as studied by various general equilibrium methods has also been discussed.

In this book I have also included the theory of games and the linear programming model of optimal decision-making. Here, I have attempted to give these theories their due place in the theory of microeconomics. It is hoped that the comprehensive treatment of the material covered and the inclusion of the main 'recent' developments in the theory of the firm will provide the students with the necessary modern tools and general theoretical framework with which to approach and analyse with more realism the complex phenomena of the contemporary business world. It is an exhaustive and elaborate presentation of all the concepts along with various theories and laws.

This book is designed as a textbook which can be used in undergraduate and postgraduate courses as well as for the courses in which microeconomics is taught as a specialised subject. It will also be useful to the students of M.B.A., C.A., I.C.W.A., C.S., those preparing for competitive examinations such as Indian Administrative Services, Indian Economic Services, etc. and for the examinations where economics is a special paper.

K.R. Gupta

Contents

Volume II

Methods of Economics

1

Every science follows certain methods for the formulation of its laws, principles and theorems. Broadly speaking, there are two methods of investigation, viz. (i) deductive method and (ii) inductive method. The deductive method deduces conclusions from certain fundamental assumptions or axioms established through other methods by logical processes of reasoning. In this method, we proceed from the general to the particular. We start from certain principles which are either self-evident or based on strict observation and carry them down as a process of pure reasoning to the consequences which they implicitly contain. This method is known as 'hypothetical' method because some of the methods may not correspond to facts. They may, however, come so near to facts that they can be used as premises for reasoning and deriving conclusions. The inductive method, which is also sometimes called historical method, is based on prior examination of facts. It attempts to generalise from the observed facts or collected data. Thus, while the deductive method involves reasoning from the general to the particular, the inductive method implies generalisation from the particular to the general.

In the latter half of the 19th century, there was a great controversy between the Classical School of Britain and the Historical School of Germany on the relative merits and demerits of the deductive and inductive methods. The Classical School advocated deduction while the Historical School was in favour of induction. The controversy was finally settled by Marshall who was of the opinion that the two methods were not competitive but complementary to each other. He approvingly cited Schmoller as saying that, "Induction and deduction are both needed for scientific thought, as the right foot and the left foot are both needed for walking”. [1]

Deductive Method

The deductive method of reasoning was perfected in the able hands of Ricardo and the later English economists drew inspiration mostly from him. Following Ricardo, the deductive method was further developed by Nassau William Senior, J.S. Mill, J.E. Cairnes and Walter Bagehot.

Merits of Deductive Method

The deductive method is extremely simple. Several inferences can be drawn from a few basic facts of human nature. This method does not involve the difficult task of collecting, classifying and interpreting statistical data. The inductive method is complicated, time consuming and very costly.

The economic phenomenon is of a very complex nature and often the cause and effect are so much intertwined with each other that it is almost impossible to separate the two. The inductive method is not very suitable for studying such phenomenon. Further, as compared with other sciences, economics, which deals with social behavior, is less amenable to experimentation. In such a situation the economists have naturally to resort to deductive reasoning.

The deductive method leads to precise and exact generalisations provided the axioms and assumptions from which they are deduced are correct. Since it makes use of logic and mathematics, there is less probability of deduced inferences going wrong. The deductive method has to its credit some contributions not only in Economics but even in physical sciences. Einstein’s *Theory of Relativity*, for instance, was formulated through deduction.

Demerits of Deductive Method

We mentioned above the merits of deduction. But the method has also serious limitations. In the first place, the generalisations reached through the method of deduction would be true only if the assumptions on which they are based hold good. But these assumptions many times turn out to be only partially true and as such the inferences drawn from them are not fully valid. It is now generally accepted that the assumptions made by the classical economists were far removed from reality. The result was that the entire body of economic theory built by them did not much relevance to the real world. Prof. Gide aptly remarks, "the mistakes of the classical school did not consist in too frequent use of the abstract method but in having too often mistaken the abstraction for the reality". Even if a definite fact is used as a premise, the inferences drawn therefrom would have only limited application because economic conditions are continuously undergoing change over time and place and as such the conclusions drawn by deduction would not be applicable at another time and place where these premises do not hold true. The deductive method is very dangerous when universal validity is claimed for generalisations based on imperfect or incorrect assumptions, and when efforts are made to use these generalisations as guides for formulating practical policies for the country.

It is often difficult to test the generalisations arrived at through deduction. Sometimes the economic phenomenon is so complicated that testing of generalisations is more or less impossible. The generalisations which cannot be tested and confirmed would have only limited value.

Inductive Method

The Historical School represents a reaction against the deductive approach. The reaction was particularly marked in Germany and represented by economists like Roscher, Hilnebrand and Frederick List. In England the reaction to deductive approach came from economists like Richard Jones, Ashley and Cliff Leslie. They advocated a method which has come to be known as Historical, Inductive or Realistic. This method insists on examination of facts and then laying down general principles. In this method we proceed from 'particulars' to 'generals' while in case of deductive method we proceed from 'generals' to 'particulars'.

The advocates of the inductive method—the German Historical School—believed that the national economy of every country, the nature, amount, distribution and consumption of wealth was the result of a long evolution and it could best be studied with reference to the history and the general laws of social evolution. They, therefore, first collected material through the study of history or of contemporary events and then proceeded to form generalisations from a number of particular cases.

The inductive method generally takes two forms, viz. (i) experimentation and (ii) statistical form. The first is concerned with testing the validity of laws or generalisations arrived at as a result of deductive reasoning by resorting to the study of actual facts. The second is concerned with the formulation of laws and generalisations on the basis of facts collected from the various sectors of the economy. The method of experimentation—which is the most important one in physical and natural sciences—does not have much applicability in the field of Economics. The economic phenomenon is so complex and complicated that it is not amenable to controlled experimentation. The economic movements are so closely intermined and intertwined that it is almost impossible to segregate them for the purpose of experimentation. So many things are happening in the economic field at a time that it is not possible to isolate economic phenomenon for experimentation. The above, however, should not be taken to mean that experimentation has no place whatsoever in Economics. It certainly has some scope in economics, though a modest one. It can, for instance, be employed for testing validity of some laws of economics like the law of diminishing returns. The statistical approach, on the other hand, has much wider application in the field of Economics and this method is commonly followed by the economists.

Merits of Induction

The economic laws or generalisations arrived at through the process of induction from carefully collected facts generally lead to precise and reliable conclusions. Since they are based on very sure and realistic foundation, their validity is not open to challenge. The exponents of the inductive method have done a lot to check and verify the conclusions of the old deductive economists.

The chief merit of this method is to show the complexity of economic phenomenon and to emphasize the important fact that any generalisation will have validity only under certain conditions and circumstances. It stresses the importance of relativity. An economic generalisation which is the result of a particular historical situation and which holds at a particular time cannot be equated to an absolute truth which has universal validity.

Limitations of Induction

There is the risk that hurried conclusions may be drawn from inadequate facts. This risk is particularly marked when the investigator lacks a balanced and discriminating judgement.

Collection of adequate and reliable facts is not an easy job. The economic phenomenon being highly complex and complicated, the facts bearing on it are bound to be complex and intermingled. Isolation of economic from non-economic facts would require, besides a good knowledge of theoretical apparatus of Economics, a degree of competence and understanding.

Induction above will not deliver the goods unless it is supplemented by deduction. To cite Prof. Durbin, "Facts do not speak for themselves. It is only by analysis, comparison, hypothesis and prophecy that they can be made to speak at all". In the absence of a hypothesis (a working explanation to direct the enquirer) to guide them in their study, the exponents of the inductive method were likely to be lost in a maze of facts and this was what actually happened with the earlier members of the Historical School. But the later writers of this School avoided these difficulties by employing a well-thought-out hypothesis.

Conclusion

In fact, the two methods are complementary rather than being competitive. Different methods are required for studying different problems. To cite Marshall, "It is to be hoped that these two schools will always exist; each doing its own work thoroughly, and each making use of the work of the other".[2] Today there is consensus of opinion that the two methods must be combined together for economic analysis and investigation.

NOTES

1. Marshall, *Principles*, p. 29.
2. *Ibid*., p. 30.

Static and Dynamic Economics

2

The terms 'static' and 'dynamic' have different meanings in Economics from those in physical sciences. In physical sciences, the term 'static' indicates a position of rest, or, in other words, an absence of movement of any type. In contrast, in Economics, the term does not mean an absence of motion. The economy is certainly moving but the movement is constant, regular, smooth and certain. There is no uncertainty. There are no sudden jerks and shocks. The movement takes place at even or uniform rates so that the economic process simply reproduces itself. In other words, the various quantities used remain constant and with the help of these constant quantities, the economy reproduces itself regularly. To cite Pigou, "Of course, stationariness in this sense does not mean frozen fixity; individual drops composing the waterfall are continually in movement, though the waterfall itself remains."[1] According to J.M. Keynes, the static economics "is based on the assumption of what has been called a *stationary state,* that is to say, a state in which there occurs no essential modification of the general conditions under which production and consumption, distribution and exchange, are carried on. In other words, in a static enquiry, the effects of changes of a specific kind are considered, but the general, social and economic conditions are supposed fixed; it is assumed that no fundamental changes take place in the general character of social wants, that no invention leads to the introduction on a large scale of new methods of production, that no sudden dimunition of population is caused by war or famine, that there is no progressive exhaustion of sources of supply, and so forth."[2]

Economic dynamics have been defined differently by different authors. According to Hicks, dynamics refers "to that part of economic theory in which all quantities must be dated". According to Harrod, dynamics is the study of an "economy in which the rates of output are changing". Samuelson says, "It is the essence of Dynamics that economic variables at different points of time are functionally related." Mrs. Joan Robinson says that economic dynamics "cannot explain how an economy behaves, in given conditions, without reference to past history while static analysis purports to describe a portion of equilibrium which the system will reach no matter where it started from". According to Prof. Baumol, economic dynamics is "the study of economic phenomena in relation to preceding and succeeding events." In the words of Ragnar Frisch, "the essential characteristic of a dynamic theory is that we consider the magnitude of certain variables in different points in time and we introduce certain equations which embrace at the same time several of these magnitudes belonging to different instants".

All the above definitions emphasise one common thing, that is, the *time-element*. Dynamics is, therefore, the study of movement and change in economic systems. Values of economic variables at any particular time depend partly on their values at past moments of time. Economic processes are traced over a time-path made up of a sequence of periods with the use of appropriate lags. Some economists define dynamics as the study of the processes through which the final position of equilibrium is reached through a series of adjustments over time. The dynamic economics in this sense can be divided into two types. The first studies the manner in which the various economic phenomena change from time to time on the assumption that no change takes place in the original data, while the second type studies changes in the economic phenomena when the original data also undergoes a change. In fact, it is the second type which can really be termed 'dynamic economics', the first type being only 'development economics'.

Thus, dynamic economics is concerned with a period of time while static economics deals with the situation at any given point of time. In static economics, we determine only the final equilibrium position while in dynamic economics, we determine various positions of equilibrium at successive moments of time.

Scope of Static Economics

Static economics, according to Hicks, includes much of the more important part of the traditional economics (viz. theories of rent, comparative cost, monopolistic exploitation) which can be studied without involving the element of time. But it cannot study the problem of capital or interest or the problem of business cycles, or even the problem of money because in the study of these problems it is absolutely essential to date the economic quantities. Tinbergen is of the opinion that static analysis can be applied to the study of those cases in which the interest lies in the long run tendencies—determination of the ultimate results—and in which the movements generated by the changes in data are damped and the data itself does not undergo any change.

Normally expectations tend to be associated with dynamics. But this is not entirely correct. A once-for-all change in the expectations does not differ from a once-for-all change in tastes. The static analysis is, therefore, quite adequate to deal with problems arising from a once-for-all change in expectations.

Value of Static Analysis

Static analysis presents the working of an economy in an extremely simplified manner and thus helps the beginners in understanding the subject. Just as it becomes easy to understand the laws of motion if a person first studies the laws of rest, so also it becomes easy to understand dynamic economics if a person first understands the principles of static economics.

The main weakness of static economics is its unrealistic character. It is based on certain assumptions (e.g. perfect knowledge and perfect foresight) which do not hold true in the actual world. In the words of Hicks, "Although some notable economists have been content to mould their thought in such a frame as this, it (statics) leaves out far too much of the real problem to be a secure resting place."[3]

Value of Dynamics

There are many problems in economics which cannot be tackled in terms of static analysis. The problems of partial equilibrium, for instance, can be studied only in terms of dynamic analysis. Economic statics can study change from one equilibrium position to another equilibrium position. But it cannot study the problems of transition from one equilibrium position to another. It is only dynamic economics which can trace the path of forces of stability which are active during transition and which ultimately assist in restoring equilibrium.

Dynamic analysis presents a fairly realistic picture of such complex economic phenomena as business cycles and economic growth. It is highly flexible and an infinite number of models can made to explore all possibilities. Most of the modern business cycle theories are based on dynamic models of Ragnar Frisch and Paul A. Samuelson and explain cyclical oscillations as endogenous movements of a self-propelling system.

No doubt, dynamic economics is more comprehensive and realistic, it has its own limitations. Dynamic analysis is very difficult and complicated and involves the use of a good deal of mathematics. As such it is beyond the understanding of a common man.

Comparative Statics

Comparative statics studies the evolutionary process in a series of equilibria and compares the new equilibrium position with that of the old. It, however, ignores the transitional period from one position of equilibrium to another. It deals only with the final position of the equilibrium and jumps over the transitional developments. Ricardo was an advocate of comparative statics. In a letter to Malthus, he wrote, "You always have in mind the immediate and temporary effects.... I fix my whole attention on the permanent state of things which result from them."[4] He was of the opinion that the transitional developments were not of much importance and could be ignored. He believed that the "transitional developments have no effect on the final position of the equilibrium" and as such did not present any interesting problems to the economists.

Henry Ludwell Moore, an American Economist, was a great exponent of the method of comparative statics. His work *Synthetic Economics* (1929) is recognised as a great landmark in the development of comparative statics. But Sismondi was a great critic of the method of comparative statics. While admitting that a new equilibrium would emerge when change in a single datum is introduced, he wrote, "the road to it (new equilibrium) may be so long and lead through such upheavals—'terrible sufferings'—as to make it practically impossible for the analyst to deal cavalierly with the incidental phenomenon". Sismondi attached great importance to the transitional developments between the old and the new equilibrium.

Development of Dynamic Economics

Though most of the rigorous dynamic analysis has been developed only in recent years, the elements of dynamic analysis are not completely missing in the writings of the earlier economists. The use of geometric progression in the Malthusian theory of population provides an important example of the dynamic analysis in the classical Economics. J.M. Clark's principle of acceleration and Aftalion's theory of trade cycles provide examples of dynamic analysis in the writings of economists before 1925. It was, however, only after 1925 that important developments occurred in dynamic Economics. The pioneers in this field were Frisch, Roos, Tinbergen, and Kalecki. In the field of national income analysis, the use of dynamic analysis was emphasised by economists like Robertson, Haberler, Harrod, Kapp, Hansen, Machlup, Myrdal, Bertil Ohlim, Lindhal and Lundberg. In recent years, a lot of work based on dynamic analysis has been done in the field of the theory of trade cycles. As a result of these developments in the field of aggregative theory, in recent years, Macro-dynamics has emerged as a distinct branch of economic theory.

Statics

According to Hicks, statics is concerned with stationary situations which are completely devoid of changes and, therefore, do not bear any relation to past or future. In a stationary situation, the future can be conveniently predicted with the help of present facts. According to him, it is only a change in the system which makes the analysis dynamic. He says that change will cause things to be different at different dates and this is enough to give the analysis a dynamic character.

Hicksian definition has been criticised on the ground that it includes in dynamics many problems which can be tackled with the help of static analysis. A comparative study of two phenomena does not require dynamic analysis. Such a study can be made with the help of comparative statics. Criticising Hicksian definition, Harrod writes, "Mr. Hicks appears to be analysing the effects of a once over change in fundamental conditions. There is no recognition that a different technique may be required for analysing the effects of continuing changes." This shows that Harrod wants to base the definition of dynamic economics on continuing changes as against once-for-all changes in economic variables. In his book entitled *Towards a Dynamic Economics*, Harrod remarks, "A once-over-change is the same thing as a once-over-change in taste. The determinant in a dynamic system will not be the existence of a certain expectation or a once over a change in that expectation. This, of course, may itself be determined by a rate of change in some other fundamental condition. The effects of a once-over-change in expectation are likely to continue to be handled by the technique of static economics."

According to William J. Baumol, economic dynamics enables us to answer such questions as "Here are the facts about yesterday, what will happen to-day as a result? Its essence is, thus, prediction not simply in the sense of forecasting stock exchange prices, for example, but also in the general sense of relating an event to the events which preceded it."[5] He further writes, "Economic dynamics is the study of economic phenomena in relation to preceding and succeeding events."[6]

Baumol makes a distinction between 'dynamic economy' and 'dynamic analysis'. A dynamic economy is one which is changing. The dynamic analysis refers to the analysis of change in the 'economy'. According to Baumol, the basis of dynamics economics is predictability while Ragnar Frisch considers it to be the analysis of a process. The definitions of Hicks and Harrod lay stress on the contents of dynamic economics. In fact, Hicksian approach to dynamics is not dynamics as he claims it to be but 'statics involving time'. Hicks wrongly says that different values of an economic variable at different periods of time are studied in dynamic economics. In fact, dating is necessary not for dynamics but for comparative statics. Economic dynamics is concerned with the influences of past events on the likely future events and as such time slices do not constitute the subject of dynamic study.

Harrod's approach to dynamic economics differs from that of Hicks to the extent the former says that dynamic analysis is concerned with the study of an economy in which the rate of change of income or output is changing. It is continuously changing acceleration or retardation which Harrod calls dynamics. The entire marginal analysis would fall in the field of statics or at best in that of comparative statics.

In order to settle the controversy, Samuelson has defined economic dynamics as follows: "It is the essence of dynamics that economic variables at different points of time are functionally related including velocities, acceleration or higher derivatives". Samuelson's definition is a sort of compromise between the definitions of Hicks, Harrod, Frisch, and Baumol. The important contributors to economic dynamics include Timbergen, Kalecki, Frisch, Harrod, Domar, Hansen, Kahu, Hicks, Large, Klein and Samuelson.

NOTES

1. A.C. Pigou, *The Economics of Stationary State* (1935), p. 8.
2. J.M. Keynes, *The Scope and Method of Political Economy* (4th ed.), p. 147.
3. J.R. Hicks, *Value and Capital*, p. 6.

4. *Ricardo's Notes on Malthus' Principles*, ed. by Prof. Hollander, p. xxxviii (1928).
5. William J. Baumol, *Economic Dynamics*, p. 4.
6. *Ibid.*

Nature and Scope of Economics

3

There is a vast variety of definitions of Economics. John Maynard Keynes appropriately remarks that "Political Economy is said to have strangled itself with definitions".[1] We examine below some of the important definitions put forward from time to time.

Wealth Definition

Adam Smith and his eminent followers—the classical economists—defined economics as the science of wealth. According to Adam Smith, economics was concerned with "An Enquiry into the Nature and Causes of Wealth of Nations". J.B. Say, a distinguished French disciple of Adam Smith, wrote that "Political economy...makes known the nature of wealth: from the knowledge of its nature deduces the means of its creation, unfolds the order of its distribution and the phenomena attending its destruction".[2] Nassau William Senior, perhaps the best exponent of the classical school in regard to the nature, scope and methodology of economics, defined economics as follows: "The subject treated by the Political Economist...is not Happiness but Wealth; his premises consist of a very few general propositions, the result of observation, or consciousness and scarcely requiring proof or even formal statement;...and his inferences are nearly as general and if he has reasoned correctly as certain as his premises".[3] Thus, Senior very much narrowed the scope of economics and made it an abstract and deductive science. J.S. Mill defined economics as the "science which traces the laws of such of the phenomena of society as arise from the combined operations of mankind for the production of wealth in so far as these phenomena are not modified by the pursuit of any other objects".

At a time when religious sentiments were strong and spiritual values held sway over men's minds, the idea of wealth, owing to the pampered and degenerating ways of the rich, only led to a repulsion in the enlightened mind. It called forth indignation from men of letters like Carlyle and Ruskin. The early economists were, therefore, looked down upon. Economics was dubbed as the "science of bread and butter", the "Gospel of Mammon", the science that taught selfishness and love of money, a dark and dismal science. Ruskin characterised economics as "a bastard science, the science of getting rich" and he referred to Adam Smith as "the half-bred and half-witted Scotchman who taught the deliberate blasphemy: Thou shalt hate the Lord, thy God, damn his laws and covet his neighbour's goods".

Welfare Definition

Marshall deserves credit for lifting economics from the morass into which it had fallen towards the end of the nineteenth century. He shifted emphasis from 'wealth' to 'welfare'. He considered wealth not the end but only a means to an end, the end being human welfare. According to him, Economics is "on the one side a study of wealth; and on the other, and more important side, a part of the study of Man". [4] He defined economics thus: "Political Economy, or Economics is a study of mankind in the ordinary business of life; it examines that part of an individual and social action which is most closely connected with the attainment and with the use of the material requisites of well-being". [5]

Marshall deliberately restricted the scope of economics by saying that economics was concerned only with those forces which could be measured in terms of money. According to him, economics studied only those activities which were "most closely connected with the attainment and with the use of the material requisites of well-being". A person may have several aspects of his life, e.g. social, political, religious, etc. Economics is concerned only with the economic aspect and not with the social, political and religious aspects of life. Marshall excluded the latter aspects because they were not amenable to quantitative measurement with the help of measuring rod of money. In this he was considerably influenced by the classical economic thought which held that the economics should try to become an exact, precise and universal science. Following Marshall, Pigou defined economics as a study of economic welfare which is "that part of social welfare that can be brought directly and indirectly into relation with the measuring rod of money".[6] According to Edwin Cannan, "The aim of Political Economy is the explanation of the general causes on which the material welfare of human beings depends".[7] According to Beveridge, "Economics is the study of the general methods by which men cooperate to meet their material needs".[8]

Criticism of Welfare Definitions

The 'material welfare' definitions of Marshall, Pigou and others were widely accepted and were considered to have settled all controversies in regard to the scope of economics. But the forceful criticism of these definitions by Lionel Robbins again revived these controversies. We study below the major criticisms of these definitions.

In the first place, welfare definitions of economics distinguish between two types of human activities, viz. economic activities and non-economic activities. The economic activities are concerned with the attainment and use of material requisites of well-being. Non-economic activities are those political, social and religious activities which are not concerned with wealth and cannot be measured with the rod of money. Economics is concerned only with economic activities. Robbins criticised Marshall's distinction between economic and non-economic activities on the ground that all human activities have an economic aspect. In the words of Robbins, "an economic problem will arise wherever and whenever scarce means such as time and money are involved in the satisfaction of certain ends". Earlier Wicksteed had pointed out that economic problem is by no means limited to market alone and all human activities have an economic aspect, that is, the aspect of choice where the scarce means have to be apportioned between competing ends. His interesting example of cutting short the family prayers to enable the host to see off the parting guest at the railway station shows the great generality of economic principles.

This criticism, however, does not carry much weight if we study Marshall's ideas carefully. Marshall wanted to make economics a precise science which had universal application. Precision and certainty can be attained only through quantitative measurement. Marshall, therefore, insisted that economics should be concerned only with those activities which are closely related to wealth and can be measured with the measuring rod of money. Advocating exclusion of other human activities from the scope of economics, Marshall wrote, "If the matter is important let us take account of it as far as we can. If it is one as to which these exist divergent opinions such as cannot be brought to the test of exact and well-ascertained knowledge; if it is one on which the general machinery of economic thought cannot get any grip, then let us leave it aside in our purely economics studies; the attempt to include it would lessen the certainty and exactness of our economic knowledge without any commensurate gain".[9] Thus, if the economics is to be made an exact science, its scope would have to be limited and cannot be made wide to cover all human behaviour as suggested by Robbins.

Secondly, Marshall treats economics as a social science rather than as a human science. In other words, economics studies an individual as a member of society. It is not concerned with the problems of an isolated individual like Robinson Crusoe. A human science, in contrast, will study the problems of every human being whether he is living as a member of the society or as an isolated individual. As the basic laws of economics apply to all persons regardless of whether they are living as members of organised societies or as isolated individuals, economics should be treated more of a human science than a social science.

Thirdly, welfare definitions of economics restrict the scope of economics only to those activities which aim at increasing material welfare. Examples, however, can be cited of activities which have economic significance but have hardly to do anything with material welfare. A certain commodity may contribute to material welfare at one time under one set of circumstances and not at another time under another set of circumstances. Whether under any circumstances a commodity or service has economic significance or not entirely depends on whether or not it commands a price in the market. A commodity would command a price only if it possesses two characteristics, viz. (i) influence on human behaviour and (ii) relative scarcity. These two factors should be considered together and not in isolation. Thus, whether or not a commodity or service has economic significance does not depend only on whether or not it contributes to material welfare. Robbins, therefore, remarks that "whatever Economics is concerned with, it is not concerned with the causes of material welfare as such".[10]

Fourthly, Robbins criticises the relation between 'economics' and 'welfare' which the material welfare definitions try to establish. According to him, economics includes in its scope several commodities which may not be conducive to economic welfare. Intoxicants like opium and alcoholic drinks, for instance, command a price in the market and are considered wealth but by no stretch of imagination can they be regarded as conducive to human welfare. In other words, they have economic significance, though they do not promote welfare. Robbins says, "why talk of welfare at all? Why not throw away the mask altogether?"

Fifthly, the ideas of welfare differ from individual to individual, from country to country and from age to age. The concept of welfare is very vague, uncertain and indefinite and, therefore, can provide a sound foundation for building up a respectable science.

Professor Robbins considers materialistic definitions as incomplete because they leave a good deal of economic activities outside their scope. Take, for instance, the case of wages. If they are paid to a worker who produces goods which are conducive to material welfare, they fall within the scope of economics but if the wage are paid to opera singers they will not come within the scope of economics because they do not contribute to material welfare and provide only a sense of pleasure which is non-material welfare.

According to material welfare definitions 'Economics of War' will not come under the scope of economics because war does not contribute to material welfare. But, of late, 'Economics of War' has gained great importance in economic studies because it tells a country how the war can be successfully fought financially.

A certain activity may be conducive to material welfare at one time and not so at another time. If a doctor attends patients in the hospital where he is employed on wages, his services have an economic significance but if he renders the same service to his children at home, the service will not be considered as one having an economic aspect.

Scarcity Definition

Rejecting the material welfare definitions of economics, Robbins gave his own definition which is as follows: "Economics is the science which studies human behaviour as a relationship between ends and scarce means which have alternative uses". Robbins definition has three fundamental propositions which constitute the main structure of economic science. These three fundamental propositions are: (i) ends, (ii) scarce means and (iii) their alternative applications. We briefly study these below one by one.

Ends: Ends refer to wants. As is well known, human beings have unlimited wants. Since all wants cannot be satisfied, one has to choose between more urgent and less urgent wants.

Scarce Means: Though the wants are unlimited, the means available at the disposal of any person to satisfy those wants are strictly limited. It is this thing which gives rise to economic problems. If the means of satisfaction were unlimited, there would be no economic problem.

The term scarcity is used in a relative sense. Scarcity is in relation to requirements. A commodity (say rotten apples) may exist in a small quantity and may yet not be scarce because there does not exist much demand for it. In contrast, another commodity (say foodgrains) may be available in large quantities and may yet be scarce because the demand for it exceeds its supply. Thus, the scarcity is determined by supply in relation to demand and not by demand alone.

Alternative Uses of Scarce Means: The third proposition in Robbins' definition is that scarce means are capable of alternative uses. If a commodity can be used only for one purpose and none else, it will not give rise to any economic problem. In fact, most of the commodities can be put to several alternative uses of varying importance. Some of the uses are more urgent than others. This gives rise to the problem of choosing between different uses to which the commodity is to be put.

No economic problem will arise unless all the three conditions mentioned above are present. Multiplicity of wants alone, for instance, will not involve an economic problem if the resources for satisfying these wants are available in plenty. Again scarcity of means would not involve an economic problem if the means are not capable of alternative uses. "But when time and means for achieving ends are limited and capable of alternative application, and the ends are capable of being distinguished in order of importance, then behaviour necessarily assumes the form of choice",[11] which has an economic aspect.

Robbins claims his definition to be superior to the earlier definitions. It widens the scope of economics. It is more scientific. It lays down a maxim which is true of all times and places. To cite Wicksteed, "Its laws are the laws of life and are applicable to fields that have no connection whatever with business or production of wealth".[12] When economics is defined like this, it is freed from the criticism of sordidness or preaching of Mammonism. It cannot be called a 'dismal' science because it assumes no responsibility for selecting the ends. The ends may be socially desirable or otherwise, it is not the concern of economics.

But Robbins' definition is not free from criticism. It has been criticised on or number of grounds. We briefly mention below the important criticisms of the definition.

In the first place, Robbins' concept of economics, though more scientific, is colourless, impersonal, and neutral as regard to ends. If economics is to serve as an engine of social betterment, it cannot absolve itself of all normative significance. To cite Thomas, "the function of the economist is not only to explain and explore but also to advocate and condemn".

Secondly, economic problems do not always arise from scarcity. They can also arise from abundance. The problems created by the Great Depression of the thirties arose not from scarcity but from overproduction and abundance. Similarly, the problem faced by most of the underdeveloped countries is not of scarcity of manpower but of surplus manpower.

Thirdly, it is said that Robbins has reduced economics merely to valuation theory. To cite Fraser, "Economics is more than a value theory or equilibrium analysis or resource allocation". In economics we study not only how scarce resources are allocated but also many other probably more important things like the determination of national income and employment, business cycles, etc.

Fourthly, Robbins considers the productive resources as given and is concerned only with their allocation. His definition, therefore, does not adequately cover economic growth or economic development. The major problem for developing countries is not a better allocation of existing productive resources but the increase in the productive resources like capital, skills, raw materials, etc.

Fifthly, individual choices having no social implications are not of much economic significance. As Professor Cairncross has pointed out, we study choices if they have social repercussions.

Sixthly, Robbins' definition has been criticised on the ground that it lacks human touch. To cite Ely, "Economics is something more than a science, a science shot through with the infinite variety of human life, calling not only for systematic thinking but for human sympathy, imagination and in an unusual degree for the saving grace of common sense".[13]

No-Definitionists

There is another school of economic thought among the present-day economists which does not look favourably to any attempt at defining economics or delimiting its subject matter. On being asked to define Economics, Professor Jacob Viner replied "Economics is what economists do". In fact it is very difficult to delimit the scope of economics. With the passage of time, there are new developments; new topics might come up which need to be included in the subject-matter of Economics and some old ones might have to be excluded from it. Any definition which appears suitable today might become unsuitable after some time because of the emergence of new problems. Criticising the attempts to precisely define the subject-matter of Economics, Murice Dobb writes, "The search for logically concise definitions of one's subject-matter, which is so popular today must generally be barren, and when pushed to an extreme, must result in emptying ideas of real content and attaining little but an arid and scholastic dogmatism".[14] Similarly Myrdal writes, "Such definitions are both unnecessary and undesirable. They are unnecessary for one concept which an economist need not define precisely in Economics. No argument can possibly be affected by such a definition, just as no chemist can draw any scientific conclusions from a definition of the concept 'chemistry'".[15]

The relation between economic and non-economic activities is so close and intimate that it is not possible to precisely define the subject-matter of Economics. Even if it were possible to precisely define the subject-matter of Economics, such a definition would not be of much help in the formulation of the laws of Economics.

The definitionists, in contrast, point out that the absence of a specific definition of Economics may lead to the bringing in of all sorts of extraneous things and thereby endangering the very identity and individuality of the subject. Prof. Robbins advocates definition of the scope of Economics so as to safeguard against "the preoccupation with the irrelevant—the multiplication of activities having little or no connection with the solution of problems strictly germane to his (economist's) subject".[16] The non-definitionists' reply to this is that it is very difficult to separate the 'relevant' from the 'irrelevant' and such an attempt may even prove detrimental to the subject. It may create artificial barriers between different social sciences which is not desirable and may harm the larger interests of social and economic research.

Economics—A Positive or Normative Science

Before we study the controversy as to whether Economics is a *positive* or *normative* science, let us be clear about the meaning of the two terms. J.M. Keynes brings out the distinction between the two very clearly. "A positive science may be defined as a body of systematised knowledge concerning *what is*; a normative science or a regulative science is a body of systematized knowledge relating to criteria of *what ought to be*; and concerned with the *ideal* as distinguished from the actual.... The objective of a positive science is the establishment of uniformities; of a normative science the determination of ideals".[17] A positive science is concerned with *things as they are*; it explains their causes and effects. It remains strictly *neutral* in regard to ends and abstains from passing moral judgements. A normative science, in contrast, deals with *things as they ought to be*. It does not abstain from discussing the moral rightness or wrongness of things or, in other words, of passing moral judgements.

The English Classical School was of the opinion that it was none of the functions of the economist to pass judgement on the rightness or wrongness of an economic situation. Senior was of the view that the economist should not add even a single word of advice. Cairns held the view that Political Economy stood neutral in regard to ends as mechanics stands neutral between rival schemes of railway construction. In recent years Robbins has reaffirmed this neutrality. According to him, Economics is a pure and positive human science whose objective is to establish cause and affect relationship in human behaviour. Economists are not concerned with ends as such.

If the economist tries to suggest how social welfare can be maximised, he would have to deal with subjective non-measurable, non-comparable, indefinite and vague considerations of welfare. To cite Robbins, "The role of the economist is more and more conceived of as that of the expert who can say what consequences are likely to follow certain actions but who cannot judge as an economist the desirability of these actions". In other words, the economist is to explore and explain and not to advocate and condemn. Robbins says that the economist should simply study how the rate of interest is determined by the equilibrium of demand and supply conditions. He should not be concerned with the desirability or otherwise of the high rate of interest. Robbins believes that if Economics is made to possess a normative aspect, it will have to be associated with ethics. He does not consider it desirable to fail in recognising the essential difference between Ethics and Economics. To cite Robbins, "Economics deals with ascertainable facts; Ethics with valuations and obligations. The two planes of enquiry are not on the same plane of discourse".[18] He disagrees with Hawtrey's view that "Economics cannot be disassociated from ethics". Thus, Professor Robbins holds the opinion that there is obviously no case for economics being considered to have any normative aspect at all. He limits Economics to be only a pure and positive science. It may be mentioned that Robbins is not the only economist to consider Economics a positive science. This view is held by many classical as well as modern economists. To cite Professor Stigler, "The philosopher and not the economist, attempts to decide whether a consumer should prefer recitals of the modern dance to spiked bear; strictly speaking words like ought and bad cannot occur in economic discussions".

Following may be mentioned among the important arguments generally put forward in support of maintaining the positive character of Economic Science:

In the first place, great confusion would be created in the minds of enquirers if the inquiries as to *what is* are linked with the inquiries as to *what ought to be*. It would not be possible to maintain the scientific foundation of Economics if the two types of inquiries were not separated.

Secondly, the progress of Economics would be hampered if it is not made strictly a positive science. There is not much scope for differences of opinion in inquiries regarding *what is* because such inquiries are concerned simply with facts as they are. In contrast, there is great scope for differences of opinion in inquiries regarding *what ought to be*. To cite Robbins, "Shut Mr. Hawtrey in a room as Secretary of a committee composed of Bentham, Buddha, Lenin and Head of the United States Steel Corporation, set up to decide upon the ethics of usury and it is improbable that he could produce an agreed 'document'. Set the same committee on the role of discount and it ought not to be beyond human ingenuity to produce unanimity—or at any rate a majority report with Lenin perhaps dissenting".[19] Thus, the introduction of ethical considerations in pure economics would increase the scope for disagreement.

Thirdly, mixing of inquiries regarding *what is* and inquiries regarding *what ought to be* would put the economist in a very awkward position and make his task more complicated. Further, where the economist does not censure or condemn, he shall naturally be considered to approve or at least to excuse. This would expose the economist to the risk of being misunderstood.

Having examined the arguments of those economists who want Economics to be only a positive science, let us now study the views of those economists who desire Economics to be both a positive as well as a normative science. It may be mentioned that there is no controversy in regarding Economics as a positive science; the differences of opinion exist only in regard to its normative character.

Among those who want Economics to be a positive as well as a normative science the important are Professor Pigou, Marshall, Fraser, Mrs. Barbara Wooten, etc. According to them, Economics is something is more than a mere value theory or a science studying choice making decisions only. The objective of Economics is to maximise social welfare which can be attained only when the concern themselves not only with what is going on but also with what ought to be. The positive and normative aspects are interrelated. To cite Professor Pigou, "Economics is chiefly valuable neither as an intellectual gymnastic nor as a means of winning truth for its own sake but as a handmaid of Ethics and servant of practice". The modern economic theory is both a value theory and a welfare theory which implies that it has positive as well as normative aspects. Hawtrey says, "Economics cannot be dissociated from ethics". Fraser says, "Economics is something more than mere value theory or equilibrium analysis". Wolfe remarks, "A non-psychological Economics must, therefore, be regarded as either superficial figment or as positively non-scientific. It is Hamlet with Hamlet left out". Paul Streeten writes, "Economics cannot and should not refrain from making value judgements if their studies are to be more than a purely formal technique of reasoning, an algebra of choice".[20] Having analysed, for instance, the causes of the maldistribution of wealth, there is no reason why an economist should feel shy of saying that it ought to be better distributed. Mrs. Barbara Wooten has aptly remarked, "It is very difficult for economists to divest their discussions completely of all normative significance". The position is very well summed up by Cairncross:[21]

> However reluctant economists may be to introduce the brittle thread of ethics (so often snapped by disagreement) into their analysis, they cannot offer the guidance which is so urgently sought of them unless they do. They can explain how the economic system works without putting the mantle of philosophy over the rather drab working clothes of economic science. But they cannot say how the system can be made to work *better*. They can *offer* light, but not fruit; and it is the fruit for which most people turn to Economics. Immediately the economist does venture to offer counsel—as is expected of him—he appears in the role of sheep in wolf's clothing, economist turned philosopher. This is a role which he must play consciously—not sheepishly, as if there were no wolf's

> clothing there!—if his conclusions are to command attention and respect.

From the above discussion, we can safely conclude that Economics is both a positive as well as a normative science.

NOTES

1. J.M. Keynes, *Scope and Methods of Political Economy* (1930), p. 153.
2. *A Treatise on Political Economy*, trans., C.R. Princep (Boston: 1821), p. XVIII.
3. Nassau William Senior, *An Outline of the Science of Political Economy.*
4. Marshal, *Principles of Economics* (8th Edition), p. 1.
5. *Ibid.*
6. A.C. Pigou, *The Economics of Welfare* (4th ed. Reprint 1938), p. 11.
7. E. Cannan, *Wealth*, p. 17.
8. Beveridge, *Economics as a Liberal Education.*
9. Marshall, *Principles*, p. 23.
10. Robbins, *An Essay on the Nature and Significance of Economic Science*, p. 9.
11. Robbins, *Nature and Significance of Economic Science* (1945), p. 14.
12. *The Common Sense of Political Economy.*
13. Ely and Others, *Outline of Economics* (1930), p. 4.
14. Maurice Dobb, *Political Economy and Capitalism*, p. 173.
15. Gunnar Myrdal, *The Political Elements in the Development of Economic Theory* (1953), p. 155.
16. Robbins, *An Essay on the Nature and Significance of Economic Science*, p. 3.
17. J.M. Keynes, *Scope and Method of Political Economy*, p. 16.
18. Robbins, *Nature and Significance of Economic Science.*
19. *Ibid.*
20. Paul Streeten, "Economics and Value Judgements", *Quarterly Journal of Economics* (1950), p. 595.
21. Cairncross, *Introduction to Economics* (1944), p. 9.

Utility and Welfare

4

Utility refers to the quality possessed by a commodity to satisfy a human want. In other words, it is the satisfaction obtained from the consumption of a commodity. According to Prof. Jevons, it indicates "that abstract quality whereby an object serves our purposes, and becomes entitled to rank as a commodity". The concept of utility, though apparently simple, has given rise to a lot of controversy among economists. The controversy has two aspects. In the first place, utility is identified with welfare and the question arises as to whether the utility can be measured in a way which makes possible additions and interpersonal comparisons of utility. The second aspect of controversy is that of consumer's demand. In discussion of consumer's demand, utility is divorced of any ethical content, that is, it is not necessarily identified with welfare. It is used only to explain consumer's behaviour.

Different economists have different views regarding utility theory. All the views can be split into two camps:

(a) Those who believed the concept of cardinal, measurable utility.

(b) Those who have thrown over the cardinal concept but have dispensed with the utility concept as well and have substituted an analysis based on indifference curves.

Cardinal theory of utility is based on the psychological magnitudes which cannot be measured due to lack of objectively extensive unit—a necessary requisite of measurement. Also the actual choice cannot demonstrate any form of measurable utility; it can only demonstrate one alternative being preferred to another. That is why the cardinalist approach has been abandoned.

The ordinalist concept took into consideration the very concept of marginal utility along with measurability. This concept was essential for the mathematical representation of utility. If utilities can be subjected to the arithmetical operation of subtraction, and can be differentiated and integrated, then the concept of marginal utility must imply cardinally measurable utilities. A typical error on the concept of marginal utility is a recent statement by Professor Kennedy that "the word 'marginal' presupposes increments of utility" and hence measurability. But the word "marginal" presupposes not increments of utility, but the utility of increments of goods, and this need have nothing to do with measurability.

Professor Lionel Robbins, in the course of defense of ordinalism, raised a problem. Accepted doctrine, he declared, states that if difference between utility rankings can be judged by the individual, as well as the rankings themselves, then the utility scale can, in some way, be measured. Yet, Robbins says, he can judge difference. For example, among three paintings, he can say that he prefers a Rembrandt to a Holbein far less than he prefers a Holbein to a Munnings. How, then, can ordinalism be saved? Is he not conceding measurability? Yet Robbins' dilemma had already been answered twenty years earlier in a famous article by Oskar Lange. Lange pointed out that in terms of what we would call demonstrated preference, only pure rankings are revealed by acts of choice. "Difference" in rank is not so revealed, and is therefore mere psychological, which, however interesting, is irrelevant to economics. To this, we need only add that difference of rank can be revealed through real choice, whenever the goods can be obtained by money. We need only realise that money units, which are characteristically highly divisible, can be lumped in the same value-scale as commodities.

Money and units of various goods can be ranked on one value scale is the consequence of Mises's money—regression theorem, which makes possible the application of marginal utility analysis to money.

The Hicksian Revolutionaries replaced the cardinal utility concept with the concept of indifference classes. The consequence of the demonstrated preference approach is that the entire indifference-class concept, along with the complicated superstructure erected upon it, must fall to the ground. Indifference can never be demonstrated by action. Every action necessarily signifies a choice, and every choice signifies a definite preference. Action specifically implies the contrary of indifference. The indifference concept is a particularly unfortunate example of the psychological error. Indifference classes are assumed to exist somewhere underlying and apart from action. This assumption is particularly exhibited in that discussion that tries to "map" indifference curves empirically by the use of elaborate questionnaires. A person is really indifferent between two alternatives, then he cannot and will not choose between them. Indifference is, therefore, never relevant for action and cannot be demonstrated in action. The concept of "indifference" may be important for psychology, but not for economics. In psychology, we are interested in finding out intensities of value, possible indifference, and so on. But in economics, we are only interested in values revealed through choices. It is immaterial to economics whether a man chooses alternative A to alternative B because he strongly prefers A. The fact of ranking is what matters for economics, not the reasons for the individual's arriving at that rank.

In recent years, the indifference concept has been subjected to serve criticism. Professor Armstrong pointed out that under Hick's curious formulation of "indifference", it is possible for an individual to be "indifferent" between two alternatives and yet chooses one over the other. Little has some good criticism of the indifference concept, his analysis is vitiated by his eagerness to use faulty theorems in order to arrive at welfare conclusions, and by his radically behaviourist methodology. If the concept of the individual indifference curve is completely fallacious, it is quite obvious that Baumol's concept of the "community indifference curve", which he purports to build up from individual curves, deserves the shortest possible shrift.

John von Neumann and Morgenstern gave a neo-cardinalist, quasi-measurement theory of utility which has the psychological advantage of being garbed in a mathematical form. This theory had the further advantage of being grounded on the most recent and fashionable developments in the philosophy of measurement and the philosophy of probability. The Neumann-Morgenstern thesis was adopted by the leading mathematical economists and has gone almost unchallenged to this day. The chief consolation of the ordinalists has been the assurance by the neo-cardinalists that their doctrine applies only to utility under conditions of uncertainty, and therefore does not shake the ordinalist doctrine too drastically.

The Neumann-Morgenstern theory can be briefly described as follows: an individual can compare not only certain events, but also combinations of events with definite numerical probabilities for each event. Then, if an individual prefers alternative A to B, and B to C, he is able to decide whether he prefers B or a 50:50 probability combination of C and A. If he prefers B, then his preference of B over C is deduced as being greater than his preference of A over B. In similar fashion, various combinations of probabilities are selected. A quasi-measurable numerical utility is assigned to his utility scale in accordance with the indifference of utilities of B as compared with various probability combination of A or B. The result is a numerical scale given when arbitrary numbers are assigned to the utilities of two of the events.

This theory can be criticised on the following grounds:

(a) None of the axioms can be validated on demonstrated preference grounds, since all of the axioms can be violated by the individual.

(b) The theory leans heavily on a constancy assumption so that utilities can be revealed by action over time.

(c) The theory relies heavily on the invalid concept of indifference of utilities in establishing the numerical scale.

(d) The theory rests fundamentally on the fallacious application of a theory of numerical probability to an area where it cannot apply. Richard von Mises has shown that numerical probability can be assigned only to situations where there is a class of entities, such that nothing is known about the members except they are members of this class, and where successive trials reveal an asymptotic tendency toward a stable proportion, or frequency of occurrence, of a certain event in that class. There can be no numerical probability applied to specific individual events.

In human action, precisely the opposite is true. Here, there are no classes of homogeneous members. Each event is a unique event and is different from other unique events. These unique events are not repeatable. Therefore, there is no sense in applying numerical probability theory to such events.

(e) The neo-cardinalists admit that their theory is not even applicable to gambling if the individual has either a like or a dislike for gambling itself. Since the fact that a man gambles demonstrate that he likes to gamble, it is clear that the Neumann-Morgenstern utility doctrine fails even in this tailor-made case.

Ordinal Utility Measurement

When utility is conceived in terms of greater or less, it is said to be expressed ordinally. The concept of ordinal utility means that any set of welfare propositions can be arranged in a unique and consistent order of ascending preference.

Ordinal Utility and Welfare Economics

A person's welfare does not necessarily increase when he is able to shift to a higher indifference curve. Little contends that it is quite possible for a person to be on a higher indifference curve and still obtain a smaller amount of satisfaction. When a person tries to reach the highest possible indifference curve, he is attempting to maximise 'something' but that 'something' may not necessarily be welfare. In positive economics, the principle of maximisation can well explain consumer's behaviour irrespective of whether the consumer is maximising utility or something else. But in welfare economics one must know what it is that the individual is trying to maximise. To say that he is trying to maximise welfare requires making of some value judgement. In view of this difficulty, some economists, like Professor Friedman, refuse to attach any 'welfare content' to their definition of utility. They believe that a person choosing among different alternatives acts as if he is pursuing or trying to maximise a single end. The different alternatives from which he is making a choice must possess some common property which makes comparisons among them possible. This property may be called 'utility' which does not necessarily have any welfare content. The utility function simply describes a man's hypothetical choices. It enables us to predict a man's behaviour but does not necessarily tell us anything from the point of view of welfare. Therefore, when a person reaches a higher indifference curve, he is said to be in a chosen position. There are, however, reasons why an individual's welfare may not increase even when he is not in a chosen position. These "reasons may be briefly summed up by saying that people are not independent of each other in respect of welfare, and that they do not always know what would give them most satisfaction".[1] In spite of the weaknesses of the ordinal analysis of welfare, Little and others have not given up faith in it. So long as we consider a 'representative' individual whose economic behaviour is consistent, we may assume that his welfare has increased when he is in a chosen position.

Some economists like Dr. Graaff also translate individual welfare in terms of conjectural choices. But they do not seek an explanation for choices. To say that 'the utility of A is greater than the utility of B' is simply a way of saying that A would be chosen. Explanation of such choices involves the problem of measuring utility and the problem of interpersonal comparisons. If such explanation is not sought, the question whether utility can be measured or not, or whether it exists at all, does not arise. The only requirement for this type of behaviouristic approach is to assume 'utility' as an ordinal quantity which can be measured up to a monotone transformation.

Ordinal Analysis of Social Welfare

A very important problem in welfare economics relates to obtaining a social maximum derived from individual tastes. There are two important ways in which ordinal analysis can help in solving this problem. One is to decide the list of situations open to society, to ask each member of the society to order them according to his preferences, and then to reduce these various orders to a single community order through the method of committee voting. The social optimum then is the situation highest on the community order.

But obtaining social choices through the process of aggregating the tastes of many individuals may lead to contradictory and inconsistent results. Though each individual member of the community behaves in a rational manner, the overall decision of the majority may not be rational. To illustrate this, Professor Arrow[2] considers a committee of three individuals each faced with three individuals (A, B and C). Each individual is assumed to arrange the alternatives in a consistent manner, that is, if he prefers A to B and B to C he must A to C. This is also called the rule of transitivity. Now let us assume that individual I prefers A to B and B to C (and therefore A to C), individual II prefers B to C and C to A (and therefore B to A), and individual III prefers C to A and A to B (and therefore C to B). As a committee of three, the individuals decide the social order of preference by the majority rule. Now it is obvious that a majority prefers A to B, and a majority prefers B to C; the committee, therefore, prefers A to C. Another majority, however, prefers C to A. Thus, this way of passing from individual to collective tastes does not satisfy the principle of 'rationality'. The behaviour of the committee is not rational in so far as it prefers C to A after it has expressed a preference for A to C.

Another method has been proposed by Prof. Bergson and later adopted by Samuelson and Lange. This involves the formulation of a social welfare function of the type $W = W(U_1, U_2, U_3, \ldots, U_n)$, where U represents the ordinal utility functions of the individuals constituting the society and W represents their ethical judgements in regard to the manner in which their various levels of indifference contribute to social welfare. For an optimum in welfare economics, W has to be a given function, though still ordinal. In case the individual utility functions have cardinal properties, ethical judgements have still to be made in order to evaluate their contribution to social welfare.

Cardinal and Ordinal Interpretations of Utility

The idea of a social welfare function is part of normative economics. There are several plausible formulations of normative economics, but almost all of normative economics begins with the fundamental idea of utility as a conception or measure of the good. Regarding utility there are several different ideas. One of the important differences is between ordinal and cardinal interpretations. The former consists of a rank ordering of possible states of affairs for an individual while the later yields a real-number value for each possible state of affairs.

The distinction between cardinal and ordinal utilities is potentially important for utilitarianism. As a theory of evaluation, utilitarianism is the view that an action is the best action if and only if the action maximises utility when compared with all possible alternative actions. Utilitarianism requires both cardinality and full interpersonal comparability which are related to the history of welfare economics, the explicitly normative branch of economic theory. But both cardinality and interpersonal utility comparisons are problematic. It is difficult to measure cardinal utilities for even a single individual. Therefore, the challenge for welfare economics was to develop a methodology that yields robust evaluations but does not require the cardinal interpersonally comparable utilities.

In the history of moral philosophy, utilitarianism is strongly associated with two historical figures, Jeremy Bentham and John Stuart Mill. Mill's views are important and deeply interesting, but they are also extremely difficult to sort out properly. Jeremy Bentham, however, provides a wonderful entrée into the world of utilitarian moral and political philosophy. Utilitarianism is just one member of a more general family of moral theories, which we might call "consequentialist". Consequentialism is the view that morality is about consequences of decisions. Utilitarianism is a particular form of consequentialism, but not the only form. Consequentialism is sometimes contrasted to deontology, where deontological moral and political theories maintain that there are moral rules or principles, the violation of which cannot be justified on the ground that good consequences would result. Thus, a consequentialist might believe that one may tell lies, break promises, or injure innocent persons in order to accomplish a greater good, whereas a deontologist might believe that such actions are forbidden—even if good consequences will result.

There are three versions of utilitarianism:

(a) **Hedonistic Utilitarianism**—According to Bentham, utility is pleasure and the absence of pain. Now suppose that it is possible to measure and quantify pleasures and pain. Then we might call one unit of pleasure a positive "hedon" and one unit of pain a negative "hedon". Maximising utility then would simply be to maximise the sum of hedons.

(b) **Eudaimonistic Utilitarianism**—In this version of utilitarianism, rather than maximise pleasure, we might instead maximise "happiness"—eudaimonia in ancient Greek. Happiness may be related to pleasure, but it includes more abstract satisfactions. For example, climbing a mountain may involve much more pain than pleasure, but this activity may still contribute to the happiness of the climber.

(c) **Preference Satisfaction Utilitarianism**—If we consider happiness a better measure than pleasure, there are difficulties with the proposition that the law should maximise "happiness". Happiness is difficult to define, and different persons have different views about what makes for a happy life and it is also difficult to measure directly. To overcome this difficulty economists have substituted preference for happiness. Preferences can be measured in a variety of ways. For example, we can ask individuals to simply rank order their preference among various states of affairs, giving us an ordinal utility function for the individual. This rank order can be transformed into numerical values. Thus, we can construct a cardinal utility function for an individual. Since preference-satisfaction is measurable, economists use a preference-based conception of utility.

Now we have learned some concept of utility. Our next step is to know the decision that is supposed to maximise utility. Different forms of utilitarianism give different answers to the scope of decision question. Following are the some examples.

(a) *Act Utilitarianism*: Here we suppose that each individual action should maximise utility. On this basis utilitarianism can be formulated as "Act so that your action maximises utility as opposed to any alternative action that you could perform".

(b) *Rule Utilitarianism*: Here the scope of decision shifts from individual actions to general rules. Thus, although the individual actions might maximise utility of individual as compared to the alternative, the general rule might produce more utility than the alternative rules, but only when there is nothing better to do. This rule has three important sub-variants: (i) Ideal Rule Utilitarianism—It says that you should act in accordance with the set of ideal rules that would maximize utility if everyone were actually to act in conformity with the rules. (ii) Actual Rule Utilitarianism—It says that you should act in accord with the set of actual rules that would maximise utility if it were adopted as the moral code of a real society in which persons will sometimes fail to live up to the requirements of the moral code. (iii) Legal Rule Utilitarianism—It responds to an obvious fact about the application of utilitarianism to the law. The law is concerned with individual acts, but it is also concerned with rule creating acts.

(c) *Utilitarian Generalisation*: It says that one should act on the basis of principles that would produce the greatest utility if they were generalised.

There is another ambiguity about utilitarianism that is really important to its application. What does it mean to maximise utility? This is a complex question. To solve this question we have following concepts.

(a) *Classical Utilitarianism*: The classical answer to the above stated question is "add them up" which implies that individual utilities should be summed up.

(b) *Average Utilitarianism*: This states that we could average rather add which implies that we could take the sum of individual utilities and divide by the number of persons.

(c) *Bernoulli-Nash John Nash*: Here we multiply rather than add utilities and it makes more sense if our utility values for individuals are relative rather than absolute.

Preference Intensity

Economists like Ozga, Alchian and others have examined the question as to whether, under certain conditions, ordinal utility can also be considered as measurable. A single axiom, known as the basic axiom of ordered preferences, is adequate to express the ordinal concept of utility. According to this axiom, any set of welfare situations can be arranged in an order of ascending utility. Suppose that an individual prefers C to B and B to A, that he is indifferent between D and C, and that he prefers E to D. Then if his behaviour is consistent, he must prefer C to A, D to A as well as B, and so on. The utility levels can be expressed as:

$$U_a < U_b < U_c = U_d < U_e$$

Speaking in geometrical terms, C and D are on the same indifference curve which lies below that on which E lies but above that on which B lies and still higher than that on which A lies.

Now this fundamental axiom of ordered preferences can be extended so as to make ordinal utility measurable. This can be done by introducing another axiom, that is, increments of utility or preference intensities can be ordered. Or in other words, $(U_b - U_a)$, $(U_c - U_b)$... can be arranged in ascending order of preference as well as U_a, U_b, U_c.... Now a situation B can be considered as lying between A and C in the list of ordered preferences so that the increment $(U_b - U_a)$ is considered equal to the increment $(U_c - U_b)$.

Hence,

$$U_b - U_a = U_c - U_b \text{ or } U_b = ½ (U_a + U_c)$$

This relation means that B lies precisely half-way and not simply somewhere between A and C and that its utility is half the sum of utilities of A and C. In this sense, the utility becomes measurable, subject only to an arbitrary origin and unit of measurement.

Thus, utility becomes measurable with the help of two axioms on consistent ordering of preferences—one relating to the ordering of original preferences and the other to the ordering of increments. The first axiom implies that U is an ordinal function having the general form $\varphi(U)$ so that when an increase takes place in U, there also occurs an increase in φ. The second axiom suggests that the utility can be measured cardinally in the sense that any such measure depends on the origin and unit of measurement. In other words, ordered utility is measurable up to a monotonic transformation while cardinal utility can be measured up to a linear transformation.

The above method, however, has its own weaknesses. While the first axiom can be easily verified against observation, the same is not true of the second axiom. From the empirical point of view, any check on the equal ranking of preference intensities is generally neither possible nor justifiable. In other words, from the practical point of view, the idea of preference intensity does not have much meaning.

Pigovian Welfare Economics

Professor Pigou's *Economics of Welfare* represents the culmination of the great neo-classical tradition and yet makes a departure from it. Pigou has attempted to give a systematic shape to his predecessor's *ad hoc* approach to welfare economic problems and arrived at a concept of the general optimum. His concept of the optimum, however, is not as logical and rigorous as that of Pareto. It represents an intermixture of the concrete particular approach of the English economists and the formal general approach of the continental economists.

The neo-classical element in Pigou's approach is evident from a strong admixture of the ideas which originate in the classical physical level of analysis. Though Pigou defines economic welfare subjectively as the amounts of satisfaction which can be brought into relation with the measuring rod of money but he adds that "economic causes act on the economic welfare of any country, not directly, but through the making and using of that *objective* counterpart of economic welfare which the economists call the national dividend or national income".[3] The influence of the classical physical approach becomes clear from the way he defines national dividend. He defines it as the flow of goods and services annually *produced* in contrast to Prof. Fisher's definition of national dividend as the flow of goods and services *actually consumed* during the year.

The departure from neo-classical tradition in Pigou's analysis takes place in two ways. In the first place, instead of Marshall's surplus analysis which deals with "chunks of economic welfare", Pigou introduces the marginal analysis which is concerned with balancing the advantages and disadvantages of very small variations of output in different industries. Secondly, instead of studying particular cases, in an *ad hoc* manner, of exception to *laissez-faire* as the neo-classical economists had done, Pigou systematically analyses all such possible conflicts between the private and social interest under his generalised concept of the marginal social product curves. Thus, instead of the earlier case-by-case approach and the partial surplus analysis, Pigou formulated a more systematic general welfare analysis built round the concept of the optimum which requires the equality of the marginal social product of resources in all uses throughout the economic system.

Economic Policy Under Pigovian Welfare

In this section we are going to identify and explore the role of selective perception, sentiment and valuation in the formation of economic policy under the Pigovian welfare economics. We shall proceeds in three steps. First, we identify certain background condition. Second, we present an argument with regard to the economic role of government. Finally, we apply the argument to Pigovian welfare economic reasoning, showing, first the equivalence of Pigovian and Paretian reasoning under particular assumptions and their non-equivalance under more realistic conditions, and then how the latter results give rise to selective perception, sentiments and valuation in the formation of economic policy.

Two approaches to analysing the economic role of government may be contrasted. One is the technical and the other is the ideological. The technical approach is pursued by the administrative or managerial mentality. It encompasses the perception of problems and the application of technical skills to working out solutions. The ideological approach encompasses the reaction to putative problems on the basis of ideological litmus tests. In the former case, success is achieved if expertise works out a program deemed likely to succeed. In the latter case, success is achieved if policies are adopted which comport with the ideology being applied. These are two polar extremes. In reality, decision-makers represent combinations of the two. And there are other approaches, one of which may be designated the pragmatic. It is the method of immersion, in which the decision-maker immerses himself or herself into the issues and materials and somehow intellectually arrives at a conclusion as to what the problem is and how to solve it. All approaches include selective perception, sentiment, and valuation by individual actors and analysts.

The nature and significance of economic policy and the making of that policy must be understood against the background of certain conditions. It is these conditions which generate the human meaning of economic policy. The conditions are illustrated below:

(a) The economy is a product, a changing product, of human social construction. Much of this product is a result of non-deliberate decision-making, the operation of the principle of unintended and unforeseen consequences, due to the interaction and integration of diffused decision-making. The social construction of economic reality, with that principle, among others, as a qualifier, renders the economic role of government important as a contributor to that construction.

(b) Coupled with the actions and choice of individuals and sub-groups, the legal-economic nexus is the complex and recondite source of both legal rights of economic significance and their change. Given that decision-making always exists within an inherited set of arrangements, the critical issue is always change of law through law, or simply legal change, and not the intrusion of government into a situation in which it has hitherto been absent. The issue is not government versus no government, but the interest to which government is to lend its protection and the change of the interests to which it gives its protection. What emerges from the legal-economic nexus is a product of many things, including jockeying for position to have one's interest be the one protected by government, or to capture government to put it to one's own use.

(c) No unique Pareto optimal solution exists. Rather, a set of Pareto optimal solutions exists, each solution more or less specific to initial structure of power/rights/entitlements.

(d) Institutions represent the means of organised living; the definitions of reality in terms of which we think and form personal and social interests, and the ways in which individuals are both constrained and enhanced through collective action. In particular, institutions are both the source and the consequence of the rights which take place in the legal-economic nexus and are the basis on which the actually realised Pareto optimal solutions are achieved.

(e) Society is a vast valuational process. It is a process in which the articulation, juxtaposition, assessment and effective choice of values takes place.

(f) Society, especially the legal-economic nexus, is a process. Although individual participants contribute their own more or less socialised values and judgments, often as if these were conclusively correct, society as a process is a process of working things out. The result may appear odd and awkward as well as inconsistent and incoherent from the perspective of any particular participant or line of reasoning, the result represents a temporary balancing of interests, perceptions and sentiments.

Mankind in general seeks conclusively dispositive answers to questions and solutions to problems. This quest generally reflects a widespread desire for determinacy and closure. In economics the quest takes the form of generating mechanistic, unique, determinate, optimal equilibrium solutions, a quest reinforced by a certain conception of science.

For the most part, the problems facing mankind in general and economists in particular are antinomian in nature and are incapable of complete and permanent solution. The ubiquity of opportunity costs is combined with selective perception and sentiment in a world of continuing tension over specification of problems and their solution. One person's, or one interest's, solutions and benefits are another's problem and costs both logically and as a matter of perception. Each party seeks in various ways to acquire more benefits and to shift or otherwise avoid costs.

The problem of order, analytically and neutrally formulated, posits the continuing constituent problems of reconciling freedom with control, hierarchy with equality, and continuity with change. The overriding facts are that all social and economic systems are inexorably simultaneous systems of freedom and control, hierarchy and equality, and continuity and change, and that these elements are both multifaceted and capable of selective perception and sentimental attachment or identification.

On a different but not unrelated front are individualism and collectivism, each of which can be defined in various ways. They are largely (albeit not entirely) sentimental categories, not least in their selective recognition and emphasis of freedom and control and of legal change of rights. All of this takes place in a world in which, as Pareto himself concluded (Samuels, 1974), power, knowledge and psychology combine in a system of mutual manipulation and in which belief is manipulated by power through the manipulation of psychology. Pareto's world is one in which selective perception and sentiment, while always subject to manipulation by power, reign supreme as a principal characteristic of policy.

The social construction of economic reality, the operation of the legal-economic nexus, and the conduct of economic analysis, are laden with, perhaps even driven by, selective perception and sentimental attachments. Selective perception and sentimental attachments apply to topics and areas such as taxation, regulation, social policy, welfare policy, and so on. This applicability exists not only substantively but also logically. In the latter respect it exists because choice must be made on the basis of explicit and/or implicit values, and one mode of valuation is the application of selective perception and sentiments.

Actual economic results, including the goods and the bads, are a function of numerous factors and forces. The identifications of these factors, forces, goods and bads are themselves matters of selective perception and sentiment. Both the market and government are given alternately credit and blame for results whose origins are often vastly complex and generated elsewhere. Some of these selective perceptions are influenced by vast efforts at manipulating public opinion (Pareto's manipulation of psychic states). Some are a function of experience and of expectations, but even these are a function of selective perception and expectation.

Pigovian welfare economics approaches the achievement of maximised or optimised welfare from the standpoint of a set of equivalences: welfare is optimised if marginal social costs and marginal private costs are equated, and if marginal social benefits and marginal private benefits are equated. In such a case no externalities exist. Absent the equivalences, opportunity exists for governmental corrective action. The problems here are that the elements of the equations are not self-defining and self-measuring: externalities are ubiquitous and reciprocal in character, and government somehow has to choose which of these externality problems it will try to solve—necessarily doing so only by incurring the opposite reciprocal externality. Despite the ostensible ubiquity of externalities and the nature of Pigovian welfare economics as constituting a philosophy of reform (redress of externality grievances), the principal and indeed overriding gravamen of Pigovian welfare economics is an affirmation of a market economy and market solutions to allocative problems. The present point is that the affirmation of market solutions, the recognition of externalities, and the call for and conduct of externality policy are all laden with selective perception and sentiment.

Whereas Paretian welfare economics takes a different approach to welfare optimisation. It affirms that welfare is optimised when all gains from trade are exhausted through voluntary exchange. Thereby, it also affirms market solutions. The problems with Paretian welfare economics are that it gives effect to the structure of existing markets and to the existing distribution of wealth, rights and entitlements. These also are matters of selective perception and sentiment, inasmuch as they too involve determinations of whose interest should count in, for example, legal rules. Indeed, Pigovian welfare economics, insofar as it affirms markets, is subject to the same point. It is now widely recognised that because of differences in initial wealth distributions and because of the differences between zero transaction cost and various positive transaction cost systems, there are no unique Pareto optimal results; institutions, including rights, matter.

Both Pigovian and Paretian welfare economics make a rebuttable presumption in favor of markets. The difference between them is that the psychodynamics of Pigovian welfare economics is reformist and that of Paretian welfare economics is antithetical to reform. Fundamentally, however, both of these approaches, and the operationalisation of the attendant concepts of market failure, government failure, freedom, coercion, and so on, have considerable room for selective perception and sentiment. The role of selective perception and sentiment is to provide inputs into the social valuational process in the process of working things out. Neither Pigovian nor Paretian welfare economics, nor any other mechanical mode of reasoning, can avoid the role of instrumental valuation in the social construction of reality. Neither approach can conclusively dispose of the issues to which they are usually addressed without additional normative premises—and these are valuations ensconced within selective perceptions and sentiments.

The final irony is that redefining the economic role of government largely involves only a change of the interests government supports. The ultimate selective perception, sentiment and valuation involves treating analytically equivalent uses as different; some as government interference if not coercion, and some as government enhancement of freedom. The difference typically is only one of selective perception, sentiment and valuation, and typically involves only a change of the interest to which government gives its support.

While there are a number of fronts along which one could contrast the Pigovian and Paretian approaches to policy analysis, we will take as our case study the analysis and resolution of externality problems under these respective approaches. As the supposed optimality or non-optimality (depending on the side being argued) of each of these approaches has been debated extensively in the literature, this particular application offers an excellent illustration of the themes elaborated above.

The Pigovian and Paretian approaches to dealing with externality problems generate identical allocations of resources. That is, the Pigovian and Paretian equivalences are satisfied at the same allocative solution. It is thus a matter of indifference, from an allocative perspective, whether one analyses and/or pursues externality policy from one line of thinking or the other. The Paretians have no argument against the Pigovians because the outcome generated by the Pigovian remedy is equivalent to that which the parties would have bargained for of their own accord. Similarly, the Pigovians have no argument against the Paretians because the desired equivalences between private and social benefits and costs are achieved within the bargaining process and the consequent optimal allocation is obtained. Additionally, we should note the fact that externalities are reciprocal in nature has no allocative policy implications here because the outcome is invariant under alternative policy mechanisms.

There are costs associated with the operation of government; that is, resources are used by the government in the execution of its tasks. As such, the application of Pigovian remedies through the aegis of government impacts the allocation of resources in markets beyond those in which the externalities obtain or filter through, owing to the costs of gathering data (valuing damages, monitoring externality levels, etc.), carrying out the program, monitoring compliance, etc. Moreover, to the extent that these governmental activities are financed through distortionary taxes—as is the case with a subsidy, a regulatory scheme, or a Pigovian tax which does not generate revenue sufficient to cover associated bureaucratic costs—the allocation of resources is further impacted. To this, one can add the costs associated with lobbying, etc. as this legislation is put into place or as affected parties seek to alter it subsequent to its imposition. Thus, even if the Pigovian instrument can generate the optimal allocation in the market directly affected by the externality, the various costs associated with implementing and carrying out the policy introduce allocative distortions in other markets.

A potentially more serious problem arises from the presence of imperfect information within the governmental decision-making process. The Pigovian instrument will generate the optimal allocation of resources only so long as the tax or subsidy rate is equal to marginal damage at the efficient level of output. The determination of such requires that the government possess a degree of omniscience that few would be willing to grant. In the case of pollution, estimates of total (to say nothing of marginal) damage vary drastically, and firm-specific emissions data is woefully inadequate. The determination of private and social net benefit more than a short distance away from the status quo point—requiring detailed information on potentially significant ranges of both firm-level demand curves and marginal cost curves—is fraught with difficulties. All in all, we are left with little reason for confidence in the applicability of the Pigovian approach, literally interpreted. We do not know how to calculate the required taxes and subsidies and we do not know how to approximate them by trial and error.

The presence of various other distortions within the system—from other tax or subsidy instruments, monopoly power, etc.—further complicate this situation. Nevertheless, the Pigovian theoretical framework (particularly, but not solely, the textbook treatments at all levels) continues to gloss over many of these qualifications.

The equivalence of Pigovian and Paretian remedies is also negated by the presence of costs associated with the transacting process. Given the presence of transaction costs, parties will bargain over rights so long as the expected gains from the bargain exceed the expected costs, which include the costs of transacting. We will assume for convenience that marginal transaction costs (MTC) are constant for both parties.

Suppose that A has the right to undertake its activity so that, in the absence of some agreement between A and B, Q = [Q.sub.0]. A will only agree to reduce the level of its activity if the bribe from B covers both the reduction in net marginal benefit and the costs of transacting. Similarly, the amount that B will be willing to pay to avoid damage is now reduced owing to the transaction costs. The resulting output will be some amount [Q.sub.1] [greater than] [Q.sup.*] and, if transaction costs are sufficiently high, no alteration of output will take place because the expected costs of bargaining will exceed the expected gains.

The same results hold, but in the opposite direction, if B is given the right to be free from the harm caused by A's activity. Here, transaction costs reduce the amount that A is willing to pay in order to secure the right to produce and increase B's reservation price for giving up the right. As a result, the agents arrive at an output level [Q.sub.2], where [Q.sub.2] [less than] [Q.sup.*].

Of course, income effects, endowment effects, etc.—implicitly assumed to be zero in the above discussion—will have a similar influence on outcomes attained under alternative initial assignments of rights.

The previous illustrations assume, at least implicitly, that such information as the parties are able to acquire is perfect. Suppose, instead, that information is imperfect—that the parties cannot know with certainty whether the information they have acquired is indeed correct. This opens the door to various forms of strategic behaviour, including the attempt by A to over-represent its net marginal benefit and by B to over-represent the marginal damage it incurs. The effect of these actions, too, is to push the outcome away from [Q.sup.*] and, potentially, to exacerbate the divergence already caused by the presence of the types of transaction costs described above.

The identity and optimality of the Pigovian and Paretian solutions to externalities on the blackboard is—like much of blackboard economics—both useful and misleading. It is useful in that the Pigovian approach demonstrates the power of governmental incentives and regulations to enhance efficiency, while the Paretian approach demonstrates the inclination of individuals toward (and the ability of market-like mechanisms to facilitate) that same end. On the other hand, by obfuscating the forces that stand in the way of achieving this result, they are both misleading (in their blackboard forms) as to the possibilities of government and markets, and obfuscatory with regard to the essential subjective element underlying their implementation.

It was noted above that both the Pigovian and Paretian approaches are market-affirming—the former arguing that the government at times needs to guide the market and the latter holding that government should simply let the market work. Yet, as the foregoing discussion makes clear, there is no inherent distinction between these respective positions. The market does not work of its own volition, but, rather, functions in this way or that depending upon (among other factors) the rights underlying it—and these are determined by government—and selective perception, sentiment and valuation. Thus, the Pigovian-Paretian debate is not about government versus the market, as is often believed. Rather, it is about the form that the governmental-cum-market process should take. Pareto (1935) himself recognised the multiplicity of potential optimal solutions, the contingency of any one of them on the initial system of relations between individuals, and the necessity—indeed inevitability—of bringing in extra-economic, non-positive, considerations or premises to guide the determination of these relations.

None of this meshes terribly well with the economist's desire to derive determinate optimal solutions to problems of economic policy. Following Shackle, however, the application of economic theory to social life necessitates a process of naming and framing—a process in which selective perception, sentiment, and valuation are inherent—where the output is a direct function of the input, or, at least, the lens through which it is filtered. If the determination of the appropriate economic role for government is not a matter of selective perception and valuation, why is it that there are two, often divergent, approaches to welfare economics?

NOTES

1. I.M.D. Little, *A Critique of Welfare Economics* (Oxford, 1957), p. 47.
2. Arrow, *Social Choice and Individual Values*, pp. 1-3.
3. Pigou, *Economics of Welfare*, 4th ed., p. 31.

Theory of Consumer Behaviour

5

CONSUMER DEMAND

Demand—whether the demand for a service like metro service or the demand for a good like garments—has a very specific meaning. Demand is a multivariate relationship, that is, it is determined by many factors simultaneously. Some of the most important determinants of the market demand for a particular product are its own price, consumer's income, price of other commodities, consumer's tastes, income distribution, total population, consumer's wealth, credit availability, government policy, past levels of demand, and past level of income.

Consumer demand is the mainspring of all economic activity. The most successful producers are those who quickly shift their productive resources with the shifts in demand. The resources are withdrawn from those industries the demand for whose products is declining and employed in industries the demand for whose products is rising.

Adam Smith and, following him, other classical economists, while realising that the value of a commodity is determined by the demand and supply, explained it only in terms of cost of production and ignored demand as a factor determining value. Adam Smith's conclusion that utility was not a factor determining value was related to his famous 'diamond-water paradox'. Smith argued that in spite of the fact that water is more useful than diamonds, the latter are costlier than the former. Smith posed to himself a question: if the value were determined by utility, how could this happen? In this way, he dropped demand (utility) as a factor determining the value of a commodity though it was a pre-requisite for any commodity to command price. Beginning in the seventies of the last century, development of the utility approach was spread almost over a century. The utility approach was developed simultaneously in England, France and Austria by William Stanley Jevons, Leon Walras and Carl Menger respectively. The theory was further developed and refined by Marshall, Clark and Fisher.

The theory of demand as developed over time can be classified into (i) cardinal utility analysis, (ii) indifference curve analysis, (iii) revealed preference analysis, and (iv) cardinal utility analysis of risky choices. We shall begin below with the first, that is, cardinal utility analysis.

Cardinal Utility Analysis

According to cardinalist school of thought, utility can be measured. Various suggestions have been made for the measurement of utility out of which measurement in monetary units has been considered by some economists. It is the amount of money that the consumer is willing to sacrifice for another unit of a commodity. And according to some other economists the utils can be considered as the subjective units of measurement of utility.

Assumptions underlying the analysis

(a) The consumer is supposed to be a rational person who aims at the maximisation of his utility subject to the constraint imposed by his given income.

(b) Utility is measurable and the most convenient measure is money. It is measured by the monetary units that the consumer is ready to pay for another unit of the commodity.

(c) Marginal utility of money is constant. If it changes as income changes the measuring scale for utility becomes inappropriate for measurement.

(d) The utility gained from successive units of a commodity diminishes. This is the axiom of diminishing marginal utility.

(e) The total utility of a basket of goods depends on the quantities of the individual commodities. If there are n commodities in the bundle with quantities x_1, x_2, x_3,..., x_n, the total utility is given by

$$U = f(x_1, x_2, x_3, \ldots, x_n)$$

(f) The total utility from a basket of goods is additive, i.e.

$$U = U_1(x_1) + U_2(x_2) + U_3(x_3) + \ldots\ldots\ldots\ldots + U_n(x_n)$$

This assumption is unrealistic and unnecessary for the cardinal theory because additivity implies independent utilities of various commodities in a bundle. Therefore, it was dropped in later version of the cardinal utility theory.

Equilibrium Condition

Let the utility function be

$$U = f(q_x)$$

where utility is measured in monetary units and the price is P_x. If the consumer buys q_x his total expenditure is q_xP_x. The problem of consumer is to maximise his utility which is the difference between his utility and his expenditure.

$$U - P_xq_x$$

The necessary condition for maximisation is

$$\frac{\partial U}{\partial q_x} - \frac{\partial(P_xq_x)}{\partial q_x} = 0$$

i.e. $$\frac{\partial U}{\partial q_x} = P_x \text{ or } MU_x = P_x$$

Here we have considered that the utility derived from spending an additional unit of money must be the same for all commodities.

Demand

By demand is meant the various quantities of a given commodity which consumers would buy in one market in a given period of time at various prices, or at various incomes, or of various prices of related goods. Distinction may be made between three kinds of demand, viz. (i) price demand, (ii) income demand, and (iii) cross demand.

Price Demand: This demand refers to the various quantities of a commodity or service which a consumer would buy at a given time in a given market at various hypothetical prices. It is supposed that other things like consumer's income, his tastes, prices of inter-related commodities, etc. remain unchanged.

Income Demand: This demand refers to the various quantities of a commodity or service which a consumer would buy at different levels of income. It is assumed that other things such as the price of the commodity or service, prices of inter-related goods, tastes of the consumer, etc. remain unchanged. Thus, while the price demand expresses a relation between prices and quantities demanded, the income demand shows the relationship between income and quantities demanded.

Cross Demand: It refers to the various quantities of a good which a consumer would buy with reference to changes in the prices of other inter-related goods. These other goods are either substitutes or complementary goods. A change in the price of coffee, for instance, will affect the demand for tea. Similarly, a change in the price of hockey sticks will affect the demand for balls.

Demand Schedule: A list of the quantities demanded at various prices is known as demand schedule. Let us consider the demand for DVD rentals. The following table represents a demand schedule for DVDs. It shows the number of DVDs that a consumer would be willing and able to rent at each price during a year, everything else held constant. As the price of the DVD gets higher relative to the prices of other goods, consumer would be willing and able to rent fewer DVDs.

Combination	Rent per DVD	Quantity Demanded per Week (Constant quality units)
A	Rs. 10	10
B	Rs. 8	20
C	Rs. 6	40
D	Rs. 4	60

It represents a functional relationship between the price and the amount demanded. The important factors which determine the demand schedule of an individual are: (i) income of the individual, (ii) his tastes, habits and preferences,

(iii) price level, (iv) prices of substitutes and complementary goods, and (v) social customs. The demand schedule for the entire market is known as Market Demand Schedule. It is obtained by adding the quantities demanded by all prospective buyers at various prices.

Demand Curve

A demand schedule can be represented in the form of a curve, which is known as demand curve. The demand curve, as shown below, normally slopes downwards from left to the right, indicating that the amount demanded increases with every decline in the price and conversely.

Demand Curve for DVDs

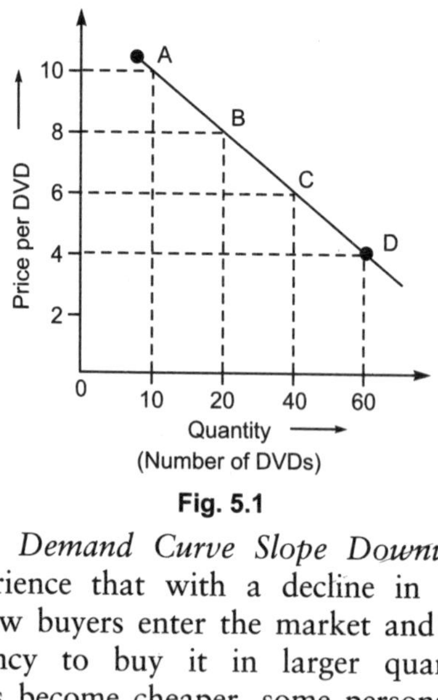

Fig. 5.1

Why Does Demand Curve Slope Downwards?: It is a common experience that with a decline in the price of a commodity, new buyers enter the market and the old buyers have a tendency to buy it in larger quantities. As the commodity has become cheaper, some persons will buy it in preference to other commodities. A commodity tends to be put to more uses when it becomes cheaper. Further, with the decline in price, the purchasing power of money rises and as such the consumers can afford to buy more.

But let us go a little deeper to find out as to why the demand increases with decline in price. As the marginal utility derived by a consumer declines with an increase in consumption of any given commodity, the consumer can be induced to purchase more of this commodity only if its price is reduced so as to compensate the decline in its marginal utility. The increase in demand for a commodity with a decline in its price can be explained in another way also. Every consumer aims at maximising his utility from a given amount of money possessed by him. The law of equi-marginal utility tells us that a consumer would attain maximum satisfaction only when he spends his limited amount of money over various commodities in such a way that the marginal utility of each commodity bought is in the same ratio to price. Other things being equal, if the price of a commodity declines, its ratio between marginal utility and price will be higher than that of any other commodity. The consumer can, therefore, obtain from it a greater marginal utility in relation to the price paid for it. In order to maximise his utility, he will, therefore, shift expenditure from other commodities whose marginal utility-price ratio is comparatively lower to the commodity whose price has declined and as such whose marginal utility price ratio is relatively high. This process will continue till the marginal utility of this commodity falls into the same relationship with its price as that of other commodities. Similarly, if the price of a commodity rises, its marginal utility-price ratio will be lower than that of other commodities. In order to maximise his utility, he will now shift his expenditure from that commodity to other commodities. As such, the rise in the price of a commodity will reduce the amount demanded of that commodity. This explains why the demand curve slopes downwards from the left to the right.

Axiom of diminishing marginal utility is used to derive the demand curve. We know that the marginal utility of commodity x is given by a line with a negative slope (Fig. 5.2 (a)) and geometrically the marginal utility of x is the slope of the total utility function $U = f(q_x)$. The total utility increases, but at a decreasing rate, up to quantity x, and then starts declining (Fig. 5.2(b)).

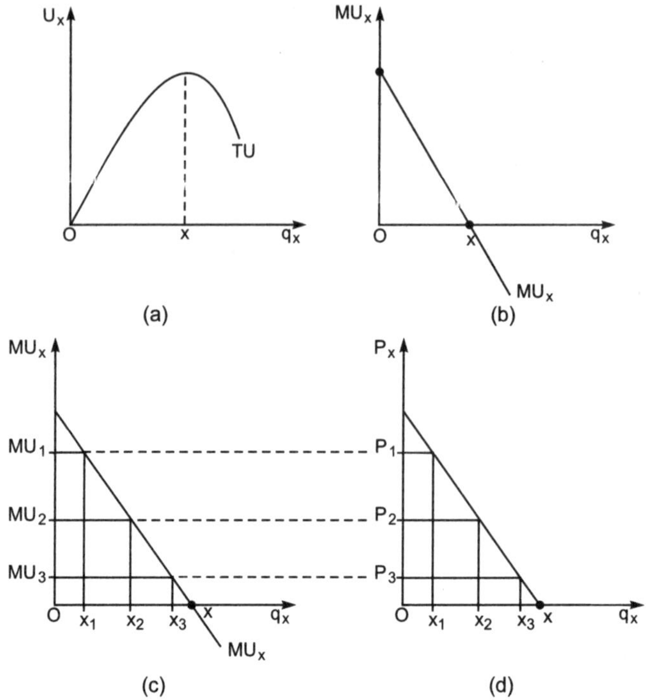

Fig. 5.2

If we measure the marginal utility in monetary units the demand curve for x is identical to the positive segment of the marginal utility curve. At x_1 the marginal utility is MU_1 (Fig. 5.2(c)) and is equal to P_1 by definition. Thus, the consumer demands x_1 quantity at price P_1 (Fig. 5.2(d)). Similarly at x_2 the marginal utility is MU_2, which is equal to P_2. Hence, x_2 will be bought at price P_2 and so on. Since quantity cannot be negative therefore negative section of the MU curve does not form part of the demand curve.

Law of Demand

The law of demand expresses the relationship between the quantity demanded of a commodity and its price. It states that demand varies inversely with price, though not necessarily proportionately. In other words, other things remaining unchanged, a rise in the price of a commodity is followed by a decline in demand and a decline in price by an increase in demand. The law holds true only under certain assumptions which are covered under our phrase "other things remaining unchanged". Important of such assumptions are: (i) that people's income remain unchanged, (ii) that there is no change in consumers' tastes, (iii) that the prices of substitutes and complementary goods remain unchanged, (iv) that no further change in price is expected, (v) that no new substitutes for the commodity have been discovered, and (vi) that the commodity is not one which confers distinction.

Why Does the Law of Demand Operate?: In the first place, the law of demand operates because of the working of the law of diminishing marginal utility. As the consumer buys more and more of a commodity, his marginal utility from the additional units goes on decreasing. This would obviously limit his purchases of the commodity unless its price is corresponding reduced. Thus, the consumer can be induced to buy more only if the price of the commodity is reduced.

Secondly, the law operates because most of the commodities have several uses, some of which are more important than others. When the price of the commodity is high, its use would be limited to the most important purposes. If the price of the commodity declines, the buyers would tend to use it for less important purposes also and thus the demand for the commodity would rise.

Thirdly, the law operates because incomes differ from person to person. The rich men can afford to pay more for a commodity than the poor people. If the supply of the commodity is small, the entire amount can be sold to the rich people who can afford to buy it at a high price. But if the supply is large and some quantities have also to be sold to the poor people, it will be necessary to lower the price to induce the poor people to buy the commodity.

Fourthly, the intensity of demand for a commodity differs from person to person. The persons with more intense demand will be willing to pay a higher price than the price which people with less intense demand are ready to pay. If the supply of the commodity is small, the entire amount can be sold to the people with more intense demand who are ready to pay a higher price. But if the supply is large and some quantities have to be sold to the people with less intense demand, it would be necessary to reduce the price to attract such buyers.

The working of the law can also be explained in terms of the Income Effect and Substitution Effect.

Income Effect: A decline in the price of a commodity amounts to an increase in the consumer's real income. With the increase in his real income, the consumer can obviously afford to buy a larger quantity. On the other hand, a rise in the price of a commodity amounts to a decline in the consumer's real income which would compel him to cut his purchases.

Substitution Effect: The decline in the price of a commodity makes it more attractive against its substitutes whose prices remain unchanged. As such the consumers would tend to substitute the former for the latter commodities. On the other hand, rise in the price of a commodity would make it unattractive against its substitutes whose prices remain unchanged and thus lead to a decline in the demand for it.

Generally the income effect is weaker than the price effect. Since the consumer normally spends only a small part of his income on any individual commodity, the change in its price is not likely to appreciably affect his real income. The income effect would, however, be quite strong if the consumer spends a considerable amount of his income on the commodity concerned. The substitution effect, however, is generally stronger than income effect because normally the consumers tend to substitute cheaper goods for the expensive goods. Further the income effect is positive only in case of a superior commodity. With the decline in the price of such a commodity, the consumer's real income rises and he would naturally tend to buy more of the commodity concerned. The income effect will, however, be negative in case of an inferior commodity. With the decline in the price of such a commodity, the consumer's real income rises and he would naturally buy less of the commodity concerned.

Exceptions to the Law of Demand

The law of demand is a general statement. There are, however, a few exceptions to this general statement which are mentioned below:

The Giffen Paradox: In case of inferior goods, a rise in price tends to extend demand while a decline in price tends to reduce demand. Take, for illustration, the case of a poor man who spends a substantial portion of his income on inferior foodgrains and as such is able to spend only a small portion of income on other goods. Now suppose that the price of inferior foodgrains rises while the prices of other goods remain unchanged. This would result in a decline in his real income. If he spends the same amount of money on inferior foodgrains, he would be able to obtain a smaller quantity of foodgrains and thus face starvation. He can avoid starvation only by readjusting his expenditure in such a way that he reduces expenditure on other items so as not only to maintain but actually to increase the quantity of foodgrains which he buys. On the contrary, if the price of inferior foodgrains declines, his real income would rise and as such he would be able to buy better quality goods. Thus, he would spend more on better quality goods and less on inferior foodgrains. The above analysis shows that in case of inferior goods, the demand extends with a rise in price and contracts with a decline in price. The phenomenon was observed for the first time by Sir Robert Giffen and is, therefore, know after his name. He found that faced with a rise in the price of bread, the poor labouring families were forced to cut their consumption of meat and spend more money on bread. It may, however, be mentioned that, from the point of view of the aggregate demand for a commodity, the Giffen paradox may not be very significant. The reason being that a commodity which is inferior for some people may not be so for others and as such the aggregate demand for the commodity may extend with a decline in price and contracts with a rise in price.

Prestige Goods: A commodity may sometimes be demanded not because of its intrinsic quality but because its possession confers a social distinction on its possessor.

Diamonds and precious stones, for instance, are bought by the rich people mainly because of the prestige which they confer on them. If the price of such a commodity falls to the extent that even poor people can afford to buy it, it will no longer confer any prestige value and as such the rich people may cease buying it altogether. But, barring very exceptional cases, this may not lead to a decline in the aggregate demand for the commodity because many others, who could not afford it earlier, may now start buying it.

Speculation: If after a certain increase in price, the consumers expect the price to rise still further, they would tend to buy more at the higher price than they bought before. This particularly holds in case of essential commodities. But such a phenomenon should more appropriately be treated as a rightward shift in the demand curve as a whole than its movement upwards to the right. In another sense, the phenomenon of increased quantity bought at a higher price, when further price increases are expected, may even be treated as a confirmation of the Law of Demand: the consumers buying more at the higher price only to be able to buy less when the price rises still higher.

Ignorance: Sometimes people may buy more at a higher price in sheer ignorance.

The above discussion shows that the exceptions to the Law of Demand are quite weak and not of much significance from the quantitative point of view. By and large, it would not be wrong to say that, other things remaining unchanged, more of a commodity would be bought at a lower price and less at a higher price, though some consumers may not act in this generalised manner on certain occasions.

Determinants of Demand Curve

We have seen above that in case of price demand the quantity of a commodity demanded depends upon its price. But the demand schedule for a commodity depends upon a number of factors. Important of such factors are mentioned below:

Demand for various commodities depends upon the intensity of consumer preference for them. The consumer preferences depend on a number of factors like tastes, fashions, habits, customs, etc. Changes in relative preferences for different commodities lead to a shift in demand schedules for them. Consumer preferences can be influenced by effective publicity and salesmanship.

Level of income and wealth of the consumers is another factor which affects the height of the demand curve. Changes in incomes of consumers lead to changes in the amounts of various goods demanded, the extent of change varying with different types of goods. The demand for some commodities (e.g. necessities) does not change much in response to changes in demand while that for some other commodities (e.g. luxuries) changes substantially with the changes in income. The impact of a change in income on the quantity demanded may not be felt immediately and generally the demand is influenced not only by changes in current income but also by accumulated income of the preceding periods.

The demand for a commodity is affected by changes in the prices of related goods. If the price of a substitute declines, the demand for the commodity will decline. Similarly, if the price of a substitute rises, the demand for the commodity will increase. A decline in the price of a commodity will lead to an increase in the demand for complementary goods and conversely. A decline in the price of milk, for instance, will lead to an increase in the demand for sugar.

The demand for a commodity is influenced by expectations in regard to the future price of the commodity concerned as well as those in regard to the future prices of the related goods. If the consumers expect the price of a commodity to rise, they would tend to buy large quantities in anticipation of the increase in price and thus shift the demand curve upwards. It may, however, be mentioned that these expectations can change frequently and as such their effect on demand may be only temporary.

The demand for a commodity depends upon the size of the population. An increase in the size of the population, for instance, will increase the demand for any commodity.

Lastly, the demand for a commodity may change by exogenous factors (the factors over which the consumers or producers have no control) like changes in season, changes in social structure of the community, etc.

Change in Demand

We have been stating above that a change in price brings about a *change in quantity or amount demanded*, but not a *change in demand*. This is an important distinction. On a demand curve, we can read different amounts which would be demanded at different prices. Thus, a change in quantity demanded as a consequence of the change in price alone can be represented by a movement up or down a given demand curve and does not involve drawing a new demand curve. Changes in the amount demanded as a result of changes in price are known as extensions or contractions as the case may be. A decline in price, other things remaining unchanged, results in an extension in demand, while a rise in price, other things remaining unchanged, is followed by a contraction in demand. Thus, the 'amount demanded' changes only in response to variations in price.

'Demand', however, changes without a change in price. In fact, to study such changes in demand, it is assumed that the price remains unchanged. The demand can change, without a change in price, as a result of changes in incomes, tastes, fashions, prices of related commodities, etc. Such a change in the demand curve can be represented by a shift in the entire demand curve. The demand curve will shift to the right in case of an increase in demand and to the left in case of a decrease in demand. When the curve shifts to the right, the consumers buy a larger quantity at the old price and conversely if the curve shifts to the left. Thus, an 'increase' in demand takes place when the consumer buys a larger quantity at the same price. Similarly a 'decrease' in demand takes place when the consumer buys a smaller quantity at the same price.

Graphical Representation of Change in Demand

Shift in demand curve can be attributed to various sources such as consumers' preferences, consumers' information, consumers' incomes, the number of consumers in the market, consumers' expectations of future prices, price of related goods, etc. And a movement along the demand curve occurs when the quantity demanded changes as a result of a change in the price of the good.

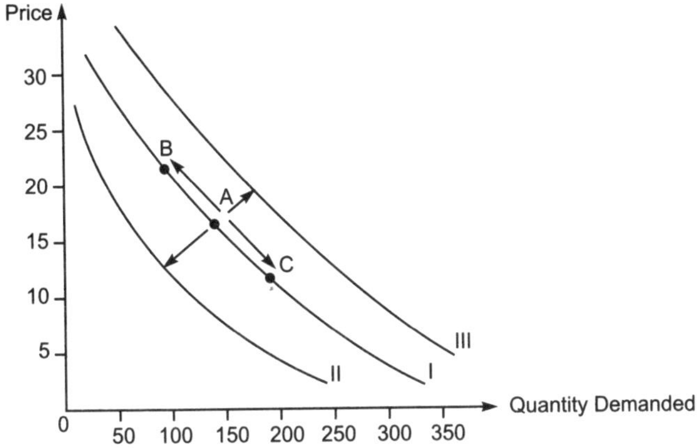

Fig. 5.3

Let point A represents the initial position of the consumer. A movement from point A to B or from A to C is due to change in price of the good. An increase in price decreases the quantity demanded and a decrease in price increases the quantity demanded. A shift in demand curve from I to III indicates an increase in demand and a shift from I to III indicates a decrease in demand.

Defects of Utility Analysis of Demand

The utility analysis was developed in the nineteenth century by economists like Jevons, Walras and Menger. Three important observations may be made in regard to their utility analysis. In the first place, they defined utility as the capacity of a commodity to yield pleasure and represented disutility by the pain involved. Secondly, as the pleasure or pain is experienced by the mind, the term utility or disutility has to be a psychological concept. In other words, the utility can only be experienced and not measured. In spite of this, these economists expressed the utility of a commodity in terms of units of utility. They never explained how the utility can be measured when it is purely a mental phenomenon. Thirdly, the utility of a commodity was treated as a function of its supply or quantity. In other words, the utility of a commodity was considered to be independent of the quantities of other related commodities.

Marshall brought about several improvements in the utility analysis as developed by Jevons, Walras and Menger. In the first place, he dropped the hedonistic approach of his predecessors and instead used the word 'satisfaction' for 'pleasure' and 'effort and sacrifice' for pain. Secondly, he librated the term utility from its ethical content. In other words, he considered the commodity to possess utility if it satisfied a want, irrespective of whether the want was morally good or bad. Tobacco, for instance, would possess utility in spite of the fact that it satisfies a want which is not considered moral by society. Thirdly, Marshall maintained that utility can be measured, of course, only indirectly. The satisfaction which a consumer derives from the consumption of a commodity cannot be measured directly because it is a psychological phenomenon. But it can be measured indirectly by the amount of money which the consumer is ready to pay for it. Thus, Marshall believed that the money could provide a measuring rod for utility.

In spite of the improvements affected by Marshall, the utility analysis has been criticised on a number of grounds. Important of such criticisms are mentioned below:

In the first place, money does not provide a satisfactory rod for measuring utility because its own value is not stable and continues changing.

Secondly, the fundamental weakness of the utility analysis arises from the fact that the utility cannot be measured, in terms of numerical units. The utility analysis is based on the cardinal number system and not on the ordinal number system. According to the cardinal number system, the utility of a commodity can be measured in some type of units. The utilities can also be added up and subtracted. In other words, the utility analysis assumes that the consumer not only knows his preferences but can also give them numerical value. According to the ordinal system, the consumer can only indicate his preference for a particular good but cannot express the extent of his in concrete numerical terms. The consumer, for instance, can say that he prefers an apple to an orange but he cannot say how much he prefers an apple to an orange. The cardinal utility system has been criticised on the ground that it is imaginary and unrealistic and it has been maintained that the utility cannot be measured in terms of numerical units.

Thirdly, the utility analysis does not make a distinction between the *income effect* and *substitution effect* of a decline in the price of a commodity. The utility analysis tells us that a decline in the price of a commodity would lead to a larger demand for the commodity. But it does not tell how much of the total increase in the amount demanded in due to income effect and how much is due to substitution effect.

The utilitarian approach studies the demand for a commodity independent of the demand for other commodities. In other words, the utility of a commodity depends on the quantity of that commodity alone. In fact, the marginal utility of a commodity depends not only on its quantity but also on the quantities of other related commodities. The marginal utility of tea, for instance, would change without any change in the quantity of tea possessed by a consumer if his stock of coffee undergoes a change. By ignoring the cross effects, the utility analysis subjected itself to the criticism of being unrealistic and escapist. Marshall replied this criticism by saying that the analysis would become very complicated if the cross effects were taken into account. Marshall appears to have obtained simplicity in analysis at the cost of realism.

While studying the effect of a change in price on the amount demanded by an individual consumer, the utility analysis assumes that the marginal utility of money remains unchanged. Marshall supports this assumption by saying that the income of an individual does not change in the short period; as such the marginal utility of money also remains constant in the short period. The utility analysis ignores the fact that a decline in the price of a commodity itself releases some money and, as such, the marginal utility of money does not remain unchanged. The increase in money with the consumer resulting from a decline in the price of a commodity is bound to lower the marginal utility of money for that consumer.

The utility analysis suffers from the weakness that it does not explain the demand for indivisible commodities like a television set, a refrigerator, a washing machine, etc. Since the consumer normally buys one such commodity at a time, it is not possible to draw his demand curve; nor is it possible to find out his diminishing marginal utility.

Indifference Curve Analysis

6

In the last chapter we saw the weakness of the utility analysis. To avoid the shortcomings of the utility analysis, an alternative approach has been developed which is known as the indifference curves analysis. The idea of indifference curves appears to have first been conceived by Edgeworth.[1] He employed the technique to show the possibilities of exchange between two persons (i.e. exchange under conditions of bilateral monopoly) and did employ it to the theory of consumer demand. In 1882, Fisher also independently found the technique of indifference curves.[2] Fisher attempted to formulate the theory of consumer equilibrium with the help of indifference curve analysis but could not go beyond discussing the question of substitutes and complementary goods. The technique was further developed by Vilfredo Pareto who tried to build his own theory of value with the help of indifference curve analysis in 1906. He was followed by the Russian economist, Slutsky, who in his article published in 1915 further improved the technique of indifference curves. Slutsky's paper, however, remained unnoticed outside Italy. In 1934, two noted English economists, J.R. Hicks and R.G.D. Allen, presented a scientific treatment of the indifference curves approach in their famous article "A Reconsideration of the Theory of Value". Later in 1939, Hicks presented a detailed treatment of the indifference curve analysis in his book *Value and Capital.* Since then the technique of indifference curves has been further elaborated and employed in analysing many economic problems.

The indifference curve analysis is based on the assumption that every consumer has a scale of ordered preferences which enables him to compare any combination of two or more goods and decide whether or not a given combination of any two goods, say X and Y, is preferred, not preferred or equivalent to any other combination of X and Y. There would be some combinations of X and Y which the consumer would prefer over a given combination of X and Y while there would be some others which he would reject in favour of this given combination of X and Y. There would be some other combinations of X and Y which the customer would consider equal to this combination of X and Y. An indifference curve can be defined as the locus of all those different combinations of goods X and Y which give the same satisfaction to the consumer. A family or collection of indifference curves showing different levels of satisfaction is known as an indifference map.

The indifference curve analysis is not concerned with the absolute magnitude of the satisfaction which the consumer obtains from a certain combination of goods. As already seen, this type of analysis considers the absolute magnitude of satisfaction that a consumer derives from a commodity as immeasurable and as such quantitative considerations do not enter into it. The analysis only says that the consumer obtains a greater (smaller or the same) satisfaction from a certain combination of goods as compared with that he obtains from another combination of goods.

The indifference curve analysis retains some of the important assumptions of the old cardinal utility analysis. In the first place, it assumes, like the utility analysis, that the consumer possesses 'complete information' about all the relevant aspects of economic environments in which he finds himself, e.g. the prices of goods, the markets in which they are available, the satisfactions to be obtained from them, etc. Secondly, it is assumed that the consumer behaves in a rational manner in the sense that, given the prices of goods and money income, he would choose the combination from the various possible combinations which provides him maximum satisfaction. Thirdly, the indifference curve analysis retains the assumption of continuity which means that the consumers are capable of ordering or ranking all conceivable combinations of goods according to the satisfaction they yield.

According to the advocates of the indifference curve analysis, utility is a psychic entity and as such cannot be measured in quantitive terms. The concept of cardinal utility, therefore, is untenable. In contrast, they consider the assumption of ordinal utility to be quite reasonable and realistic. According to the ordinal utility analysis, while the consumer is unable to indicate the precise magnitudes of the utilities which he obtains from commodities or any combination of them, he can judge whether the satisfaction obtained from a good or a combination of goods is equal to, lower than, or higher than another. For formulating the theory of consumer behaviour, it is enough to assume that the consumer is able to rank his preferences in a consistent manner. According to cardinal utility analysis, the consumer cannot go beyond stating his preference or indifference. If the consumer prefers a certain combination of goods, say A, to another combination of goods, say B, he cannot tell by *how much* he prefers A to B. In other words, the consumer cannot tell the quantitative difference between various levels of satisfaction; he can only tell whether one level of satisfaction is higher than, lover than, or equal to another. The advocates of the indifference curve analysis believe that for deriving the laws of consumer behaviour it is not necessary to know by how much one combination of goods is preferred to another. It is enough to assume that the consumer is able to tell whether one combination of goods gives equal to, or greater or lesser than, another combination of goods.

It may be mentioned that the consumer formulates his scale of preferences independently of the market prices of goods; he takes into consideration only the satisfaction which he expects obtain from various combinations of the goods. Further the indifference curve analysis assumes that the preference and indifference relations are 'transitive'. The transitivity of preference or difference relations means that if the consumer prefers A to B and B to C, he would also prefer A to C and similarly, if he is indifferent between A and B and between B and C, he will also be indifferent between A and C.

The indifference curve analysis is based on the *weak-ordering* form of preference hypothesis. The weak-ordering means that there is the possibility of the consumer being indifferent between two combinations. The weak-ordering recognises the relation of preference as well as of indifference. In other words, the consumer may prefer A to B or B to A or may be indifferent between A and B. In contrast, *strong ordering* means that the relation can only be of preference. In other words, the consumer may prefer A to B or B to A but cannot be indifferent between A and B.

Nature of Indifference Curves

Since the income of the consumer is limited and he desires to buy so many goods, he has to pick and choose between different goods and their quantities in a way that maximises his total satisfaction. While making choices, he comes across some combinations of any two goods which give him the same amount of satisfaction. If all such combinations are plotted on a graph paper, we get a curve which is known as indifference curve. Different points on the same indifference curve indicate the same amount of satisfaction. Suppose a consumer is asked to indicate all those combinations of the two goods X and Y which yield him the same amount of satisfaction. Further suppose that the combinations indicated by him are as below:

Combination	X	Y	MRS of Y to X
A	14	0	–
B	10	1	1·4
C	7	2	1:3
D	5	3	1:2
E	4	4	1:1

If the five combinations in the table given above are plotted, we get an indifference curve as shown below. The curve is known as indifference curve because it implies that the consumer is indifferent about the selection of a particular combination of X and Y because all of them yield the same amount of satisfaction. The smoothness and continuity of an indifference curve means that the goods in question are assumed to be perfectly divisible.

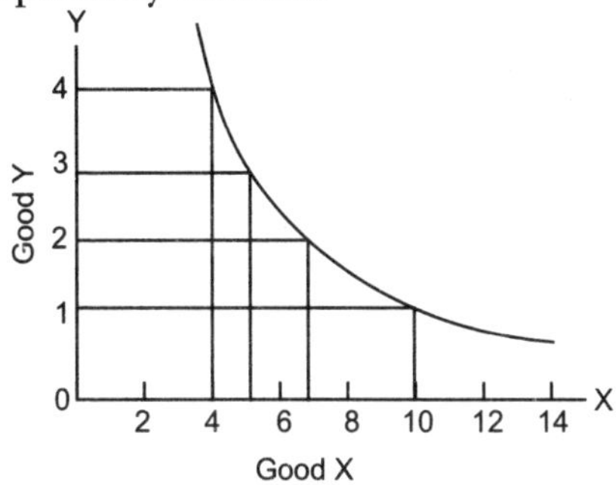

Fig. 6.1

A given indifference curve indicates a given amount of satisfaction and a separate indifference curve would be required to indicate a smaller or a greater amount of satisfaction. Any combination on a higher indifference curve will be preferred to any combination on a lower indifference curve. Thus, an indifference curve which is higher than and which lies to the right of another indifference would indicate a larger amount of satisfaction. Similarly, the indifference curve lying lower and to the left of another would indicate a smaller amount of satisfaction.

A complete description of consumer's tastes and preferences can be represented by an 'indifference map' which consists of a set of indifference curves. Since the field in the two dimensional diagram contains an infinite number of points each indicating a combination of goods X and Y, there would be an infinite number of indifference curves each passing through combinations equally acceptable to the consumer. Shown below is an indifference map of a consumer containing four indifference curves.

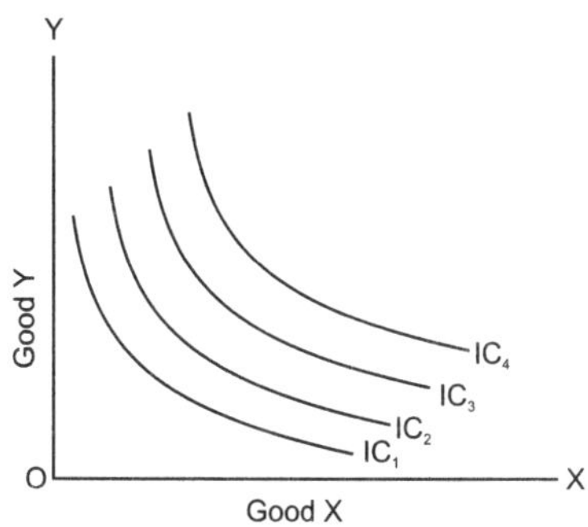

Fig. 6.2

All combinations on indifference curve I (IC_1) are equally desirable for the consumer. Similarly, all combinations on indifference curve II (IC_2) yield the same satisfaction but level of satisfaction on IC_2 would be higher than that on IC_1. Similarly, IC_3 and IC_4 indicate higher and higher levels of satisfaction.

An indifference map depicts consumer's scale of preferences. It replaces Marshall's utility schedule. So long as there is no change in consumer's tastes and preferences, the entire indifference map would remain unchanged. If there is a change in the tastes and preferences of the consumers, a new indifference map corresponding to new tastes and preferences will have to be drawn. If the consumer, for instance, develops a greater taste for Y, he would be prepared to offer a greater quantity of X for a unit of Y, therefore, the shapes of all the indifference curves would change and the entire indifference map will have to be redrawn.

As the indifference curve is an iso-utility curve, it means that the total utility or the level of satisfaction remains unchanged along it as the amounts of the two goods possessed by the consumer undergo a change. In algebraic language, it means $\Delta Y = 0$. Algebraically, an indifference curve is defined by the equation given below:

$$\Delta U = u'_x \, \Delta X + u'_y \Delta Y = 0$$

According to this equation change in the total utility caused through changes in the quantities of goods X and Y, which is equal to the marginal utility of X, when Y is assumed constant, or (u'_x) times the change in quantity X plus the marginal utility of Y, assuming X to be constant, or (u'_y) times the change in the quantity Y, is equal to zero, i.e. the total utility remains unchanged. This is possible only when the value of the terms $u'_x \Delta X$ and $u'_y \Delta Y$ is equal and the signs are opposite. In other words, when the quantity of one good increases the quantity of the other must decline along an indifference curve in such a way that the total satisfaction obtained by the consumer remains unchanged.

Indifference curve maps might be used to reflect particular kinds of preferences. Following figures show four special cases.

(a) An Economic Bad

Figure 6.3(a) shows an indifference curve map for food and houseflies. Holding food consumption constant at 20, utility declines as the number of houseflies increases. Because additional houseflies reduce utility, an individual might even be willing to give up some food in exchange for fewer houseflies.

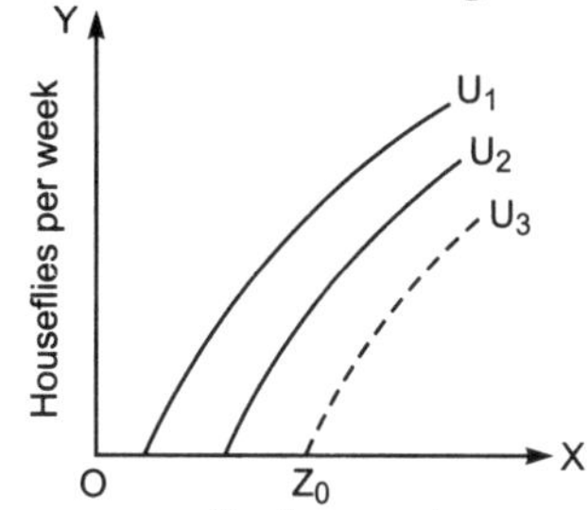

(a)

Fig. 6.3

(b) A Useless Good

Figure 6.3(b) shows an indifference curve map for food and smoke grinders. Because smoke grinders are completely useless, increasing purchases of them does not increase utility. Only by getting more food does this person enjoy a higher level of utility.

(c) Perfect Substitutes

Figure 6.3(c) shows an indifference curve map for tea and coffee which can be perfect substitutes to each other.

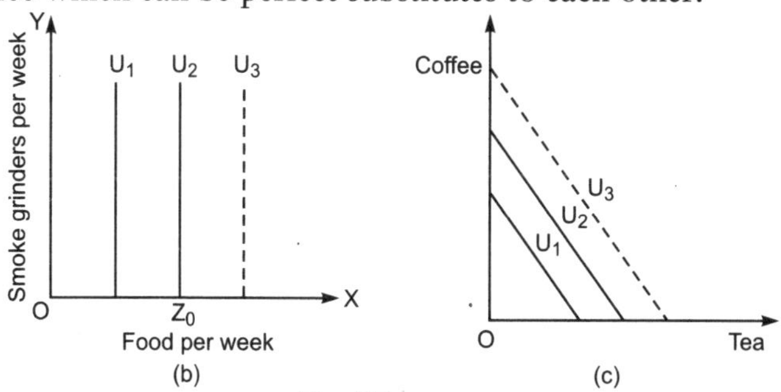

Fig. 6.3

(d) Perfect Complements

Figure 6.3(d) shows an indifference curve map for perfect complements good, i.e. right shoes and left shoes. The consumer prefers to consume left shoes and right shoes in pairs. If, for example, he has two pairs of shoes, additional left shoes provide no more utility. Similarly, additional right shoes alone provide no additional utility. On the other hand, an extra pair of shoes increases utility (from U_2 to U_3).

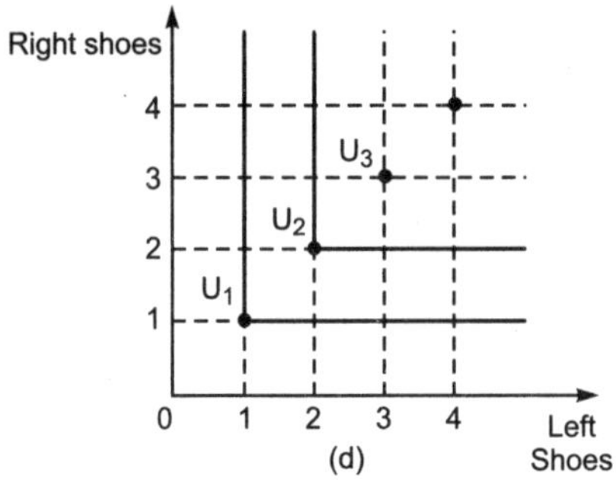

Fig. 6.3

Marginal Rate of Substitution

The concept of marginal rate of substitution is an important tool in the modern theory of consumer demand. It is defined as the rate at which a consumer is prepared to exchange successive units of one commodity for another. If in the beginning, for instance, the consumer has a large amount of X and a small amount of commodity Y, he would be prepared to give up a large amount of X for an additional unit of Y. As his stock of X increases, he would be prepared to part with successively smaller quantities of X for an additional unit of Y. Marginal rate of substitution (MRS) is thus the ratio between the marginal quantities of the commodities X and Y. In other words, MRS of Y for X indicates the amount of X which the consumer has to give up to obtain an additional unit of Y so that his level of satisfaction remains the same.

The marginal rate of substitution can move in three directions. It may decline, remain constant or rise. We examine these three possibilities below. Figure 6.4 shows that as the consumer obtains more and more Y, he is prepared to part with a smaller and smaller member of X for every additional unit of Y. The reason is obvious. As the stock of Y goes on increasing, its significance in terms of X goes on declining. In other words, as his stock of Y increases, every additional unit of Y becomes to him less and less important in terms of X. That is why he is willing to offer a smaller and smaller number of X for every additional unit of Y. This is known as the principle of diminishing marginal rate of substitution.

How to measure the marginal rate of substitution on an indifference curve?

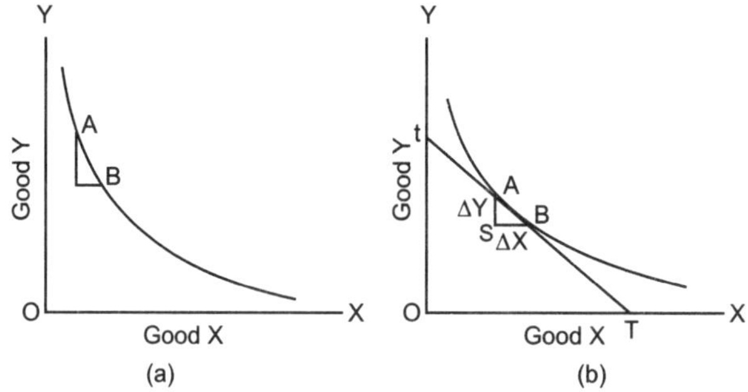

Fig. 6.4

In Fig. 6.4(a) above, when the consumer moves from point A to point B, he surrenders SA of Y and obtains SB of X and remains on the same indifference curve. The marginal rate of substitution of X for Y(MRS_{xy}), therefore, is $\frac{SA}{SB}$. A small change in the amount of Y such as SA along an indifference curve can be written as ΔY and a similar change in X as ΔX. Thus, ΔY indicates the quantity which the consumer has to surrender for ΔX increase in X if he is to remain on the same indifference curve. From above it follows:

$$MRS_{xy} = \frac{SA}{SB} = \frac{\Delta Y}{\Delta X}$$

Now, let us suppose that the points A and B are very close to each other so that it can be assumed that both of them lie on the same tangent tT as shown in Fig. 6.4(b). In the right-angled triangle ASB, $\frac{SA}{SB}$ is equal to the tangent of the angle ABS. Thus,

$$MRS_{xy} = \frac{SA}{SB} = \frac{\Delta Y}{\Delta X} = \text{tangent } \angle ABS$$

In Fig. 6.4(b) $\angle ABS = \angle tTO$

Hence, MRS_{xy} = tangent of $\angle tTO$

But the tangent of $\angle tTO$ is equal to $\frac{Ot}{OT}$.

The tangent of $\angle tTO$ indicates the slope of the tangent line drawn to the points A or B on the indifference curve. In other words, the slope of the indifference curve on point A or B is equal to the tangent tTO.

Hence, MRS_{xy} = tangent of $\angle tTO$ = slope of the indifference curve on A or B = $\frac{Ot}{OT}$

It is obvious from the above that for finding out MRS_{xy} at any point on the indifference curve what we have to do is just to draw the tangent to that point on the indifference curve and then measure the slope finding out the value of the tangent of the angle which the tangent line makes with the X-axis.

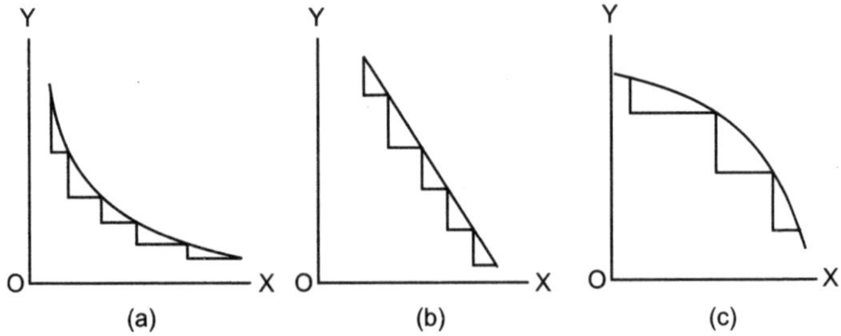

Fig. 6.5

Diminishing marginal rate of substitution is shown in Fig. 6.5(a). It means that the slope of the indifference curve must decline as we move along it from left to the right. We have drawn a staircase along the indifference curve which descends to the right. The steps of this staircase are of equal width but their height declines as we move from left to right. This is because of the fact that the number of X units in the indifference schedule continues to increase at the rate of one unit of X in the various combinations, the number of units of Y continues to decline at a progressively diminishing rate. Figure 6.5(b) shows the case of constant marginal rate of substitution. In this case, one unit of X exchanges for one unit of Y. A constant marginal rate of substitution is shown in the form of a straight diagonal indifference curve making a 45 degree angle. The steps of the staircase in this case are of equal width as well as height. Figure 6.5(c) shows the case of increasing marginal rate of substitution. An increasing marginal rate of substitution is indicated by an indifference curve which bulges towards the right or is concave to the origin. The steps of the staircase in this case are equal in width but their height increases as we move from the left to the right. This is because of the fact for every additional unit of X the consumer is prepared to surrender an increasing number of units of Y.

The case of constant MRS is a limiting case and can take place only when one commodity is a perfect substitute of the other. R.G.D. Allen points out that this is not only a limiting but also an impossible case. To say that one commodity is a perfect substitute of another means that the two commodities are not different but simply different lots of the same commodity. A constant MRS, therefore, is only an imaginary situation. Similarly, the case of increasing MRS is impossible because it indicates an abnormal behaviour on the part of the consumer. Normally, as the consumer's stock of commodity X increases, its significance in terms of commodity Y must decline. He would, therefore, be willing to part with a diminishing and not increasing number of units of commodity Y for every additional unit of commodity X. As such the shape of an indifference curve would normally be convex and not concave to the origin.

The law of diminishing MRS is a better and more reliable basis of the theory of consumer behaviour than the old law of diminishing marginal utility. The latter law establishes a simple relation between the quantity of a commodity and its marginal utility. It does not trace the effect on the marginal utility of a commodity (say tea) of a change in the quantity of some other related goods (say coffee). The law, thus, does not take into consideration the *cross effects* on the marginal utility of tea. Experience tells us that the marginal utility of tea is affected not only by the quantity of tea but also by the quantity of coffee which is a close substitute of tea. To the extent the principle of MRS takes into consideration the *cross effects*, it is superior to the law of diminishing marginal utility.

The concept of marginal utility is implicit in the definition of the MRS, since it can be proved that the marginal rate of substitution (the slope of indifference curve) is equal to the ratio of the marginal utilities of the commodities involved in the utility function:

$$MRS_{x,y} = \frac{MU_x}{MU_y} \quad \text{or} \quad MRS_{y,x} = \frac{MU_y}{MU_x}$$

Let us prove the above statement:

The slope of a curve at any one point is measured by the slope of the tangent at that point. The equation of a tangent is given by the total derivative or total differential, which shows the total change of the function as all its determinants change.

The total utility function for two commodities can be given by

$$U = f(x, y)$$

The equation of an indifference curve is

$$U = f(x, y) = k$$

where k is a constant.

The total differential of the utility function is given by

$$dU = \frac{\partial U}{\partial y}dy + \frac{\partial U}{\partial x}dx = (MU_y)\,dy + (MU_x)\,dx$$

It shows the total change in utility as the quantities of both commodities change. The total change in U caused by changes in y and x is equal to the change in y multiplied by its marginal utility, plus the change in x multiplied by its marginal utility.

Along any particular indifference curve the total differential is by definition equal to zero. Thus, for any indifference curve

$$dU = (MU_y)dy + (MU_x)dx = 0$$

Thus, we get

either $-\dfrac{dy}{dx} = \dfrac{MU_x}{MU_y} = MRS_{x,y}$ or $-\dfrac{dx}{dy} = \dfrac{MU_y}{MU_x} = MRS_{y,x}$

Substitutability and Complementarity

We have already seen above that if the two goods are a perfect substitute for each other, the marginal rate of substitution would be constant and the indifference curve would take the form of a straight diagonal line making a 45 degree angle. Let us now take the case when there is complete complementarity between two goods. Complete or perfect complementarity means that one unit of one good requires a certain specified number of units of another good for the combination to be of any use at all. There exists, for instance, complete complementarity between the right and left shoes. The right shoe would be useless without the left shoe and vice versa. In case of perfect complementarity, the marginal rate of substitution would be zero. The indifference curve in this case takes the form of two straight lines, each running parallel to one of the axes and meeting each other vertically. The curve would have, as shown in Fig. 6.6, a sharp kink in its slope towards the origin.

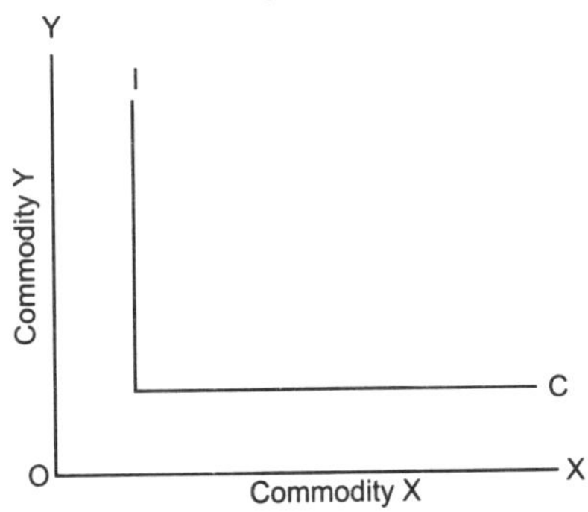

Fig. 6.6

We have seen above that complete substitutability is indicated by a straight diagonal, indifference curve making a 45 degree angle and complete complementarity by an indifference curve parallel to each axis and making a 90 degree angle. These are the limiting cases. In actual practice, the indifference curve would lie somewhere between these two limits. The flatter is the indifference curve, the larger would be the degree of substitutability, and the greater the bend in the indifference curve, the larger would be the degree of complementarity between the two goods.

We defined the marginal rate of substitution of Y for X (MRS_{xy}) as the ratio of marginal quantities of two goods.

$$MRS_{xy} = -\frac{\Delta Y}{\Delta X}$$

It can also be expressed as a ratio of the marginal utilities of X and Y. Earlier we defined an indifference curve as

$$\Delta U = u'_x \Delta X + u'_y \Delta Y = 0$$

$$u'_x \Delta X + u'_y \Delta Y = 0$$

$$u'_x \Delta X = -u'_y \Delta Y$$

Dividing both sides by $u'_y \Delta X$ we get

$$\frac{u'_x}{u'_y} = -\frac{\Delta Y}{\Delta X}$$

Since the term $-\frac{\Delta Y}{\Delta X}$ is nothing but the marginal rate of substitution, it follows that the marginal rate of substitution can also be expressed as a ratio of the marginal utilities of X and Y.

$$\frac{u'_x}{u'_y} = -\frac{\Delta Y}{\Delta X} = -MRS_{xy}$$

What are the reasons for the diminishing marginal rate of substitution? There are two principal reasons for the diminishing marginal rate of substitution.

In the first place, since the want for a particular good is satiable, as the consumer obtains more and more of a good, the intensity of his want for that good goes on diminishing. Owing to a decline in the intensity of want for the good, say X, with the increase in the consumer's stock of this good, he would be prepared to part with a smaller and smaller quantity of another good, say Y, for every additional unit of X.

Secondly, the goods are imperfect substitutes for each other. If the two goods are perfect substitutes for each other, an increase in the quantity of one and a decline in that of other would not make any difference in the marginal significance of the goods and as such there would be no decline in the marginal rate of substitution.

Assumptions of Indifference Curves

Before we go to discuss the characteristics of indifference curves, it would be useful to briefly mention the assumptions about the psychology of the consumer which are generally made (at least implicitly) in indifference curves analysis.

In the first place, it is assumed that a consumer would always prefer a larger quantity of a good to a smaller quantity of that good provided the quantities of other goods at his disposal remain unchanged. This is quite a reasonable and realistic assumption. This assumption implies that the consumer is not over-supplied or over-satiated with a good. When a consumer is over-supplied with a good, he would prefer a smaller amount to a larger amount of that good. In other words, it is assumed that the consumer has not reached the point of satiety in the consumption of any good.

Secondly, it is assumed that the consumers behave in a consistent manner. For illustration, suppose there are three combinations of goods: A, B and C. If the consumer is indifferent between A and B and also between B and C, it is assumed that he would be indifferent between A and C also. This assumption is known as the assumption of transitivity.

Thirdly, it is assumed that there operates the principle of diminishing marginal rate of substitution. We have already discussed this principle in detail above.

Properties of Indifference Curves

The first characteristic of indifference curves is that they slope downwards from left to the right. The reason for this is obvious. When the consumer desires to obtain the same amount of satisfaction by getting a larger quantity of good Y, he will have to surrender some amount of the good X. Since, by definition, an indifference curve indicates an equal amount of satisfaction throughout its length, obtaining a larger quantity of good Y naturally means taking a smaller quantity of good X and vice versa. The substitution of one good for the other results in the indifference curve sloping downwards from the left to the right. We illustrate this point below diagrammatically.

Figure 6.7(a) shows that the consumer has to give up N_2N_1 quantity of Y to obtain M_1M_2 additional quantity of X. It appears quite reasonable to assume that the consumer would be getting the same amount of satisfaction if he gets a larger quantity of X only by surrendering some quantity of Y.

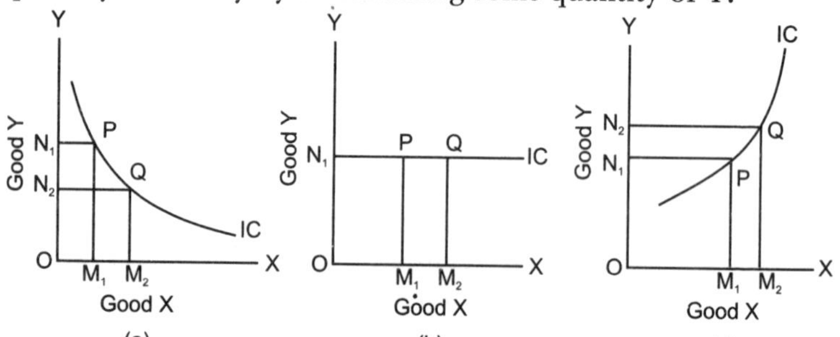

Fig. 6.7

In Fig. 6.7(b), the two combinations are indicated by the points P and Q. The combination at the point P includes OM_1 of X and ON_1 of Y. The combination at the point Q includes OM_2 of X and ON_1 of Y. Since ON_1 of Y is common in the two combinations and OM_2 is greater than OM_1, the total satisfaction at Q would be greater than the satisfaction at P. It is obvious that when one of the two points indicates a greater volume of satisfaction, the two points cannot be on the same indifference curve. This means that the indifference curve cannot be parallel to X-axis. Similarly, it is shown that an indifference curve cannot be parallel to Y-axis.

Let us now consider an upward sloping indifference curve as shown in Fig. 6.7(c) and see if it can be consistent with the definitions of an indifference curve. In the figure, the combination at the point P includes OM_1 of X and ON_1 of Y and that at point Q includes OM_2 of X and ON_2 of Y. Since OM_2 is greater than OM_1 and ON_2 is greater than ON_1, the combination at point Q would include a greater quantity of both X as well as Y than at point P. This means the total satisfaction at point Q would be greater than at point P, which is inconsistent with the definition of an indifference curve. Thus, the indifference curve cannot slope upwards from left to right. The above leads to the conclusion that the only possible shape of the indifference curve consistent with its definition is that of downward sloping from left to right as shown in Fig. 6.7(a).

The second important characteristic of the indifference curves is that they are convex to the origin of axes. This property follows from the law of diminishing marginal rate of substitution, which we have already studied above. We have already seen that the MRS neither increases nor does it remain constant. And if the MRS diminishes, the indifference curve will necessarily be convex to the origin of axes.

Sometimes the marginal significance of one good in terms of another good may go on increasing instead of diminishing and in this case the indifference curve would be concave instead of being convex to the origin. But such an increase in the marginal significance of a good is only temporary and lasts over a small range. If it were to increase indefinitely, the consumer should spend his entire income on that particular good. In actual practice, we cannot find even a single consumer who spends his entire income on a particular item. It would, therefore, be wrong to assume that the marginal significance of any good can increase indefinitely.

But the possibility of a temporary increase in the marginal significance of a commodity cannot be ruled out. Such a situation is represented in Fig. 6.8.

In Fig. 6.8, the indifference curve is convex from A to B, then takes a concave form B to C and once again becomes convex from C to D. The small range BC over which the marginal significance is increasing is known as the 'Bump of Concavity' or 'Wobble'.

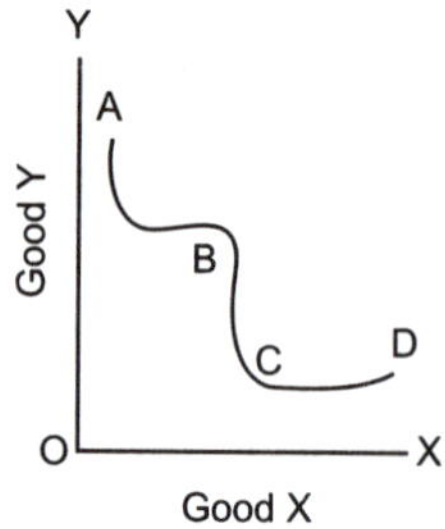

Fig. 6.8

It may, however, be mentioned that the consumer cannot be in an equilibrium position so long as he remains on the concave range of the indifference curve. Since the marginal rate of substitution in terms of X is increasing, it will not be profitable for him to go on giving up more and more of X units. The 'bump of concavity', therefore, is a temporary phase. As such it will not be wrong to assume that the indifference curves are convex to the origin.

The third important property of the indifference curves is that the two indifference curves cannot intersect each other. Let us assume for the time being that the two indifference curves intersect each other at point A as shown in Fig. 6.9 and see what happens.

Now, as the points A and B are on the same indifference curve IC_2, the amount of satisfaction at A = the amount of satisfaction at B. Similarly, since the points A and C are on the same indifference curve IC_1, the amount of satisfaction at A = the amount of satisfaction at C. Since

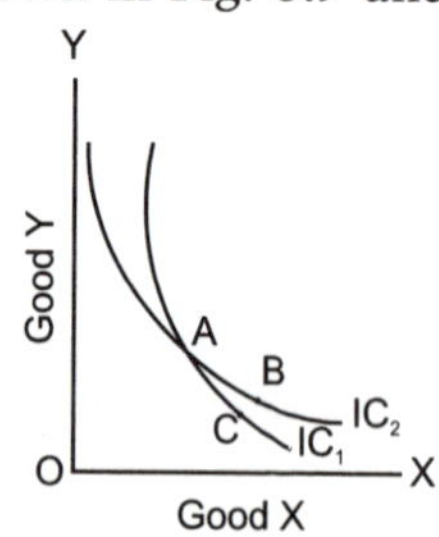

Fig. 6.9

A is common in both these equations, the amount of satisfaction at B would be equal to the amount of satisfaction at C. But, in fact, since points B and C are on two different indifference curves, the amounts of satisfaction at these two points cannot be equal. This shows that the assumption that two indifference curves intersect each other is wrong.

The fourth characteristic of indifference curves is that they need not be parallel to each other. There are two reasons for this. In the first place, the indifference curves are not based on the cardinal measurability of utility. Secondly, the rate of substitution between two commodities need not be uniform in all indifference schedules.

Fifthly, a higher indifference curve indicates a higher level of satisfaction than a lower indifference curve. Consider indifference curves IC_1 and IC_2 in Fig. 6.10.

IC_1 is higher indifference curve than IC_2. Combination B has been taken on a higher indifference curve IC_2 and combination A on a lower indifference curve IC_1. Combination B on the higher indifference curve IC_2 would provide the consumer greater satisfaction than combination A on the lower indifference curve IC_1 because combination B contains greater quantities of both goods X and Y than combination A. Hence, B combination is valued more than combination A. Since all points on an indifference curve represent equal satisfaction, any point on IC_2 would be preferred to any point on IC_1. Thus, a higher indifference curve indicates a higher level of satisfaction than a lower indifference curve.

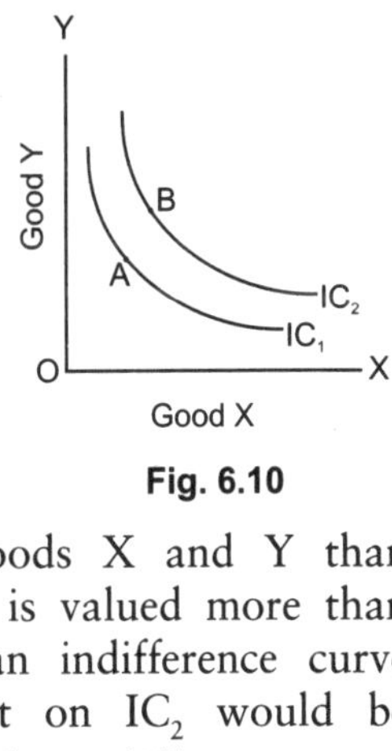

Fig. 6.10

Total Outlay Curve

We have so far been considering what different combinations of the two goods the consumer would like to have, given his tastes and preferences. But what combination he can obtain depends on the respective prices of the two goods and his income. These are known as his 'opportunity factors' and on their basis we can draw his budget line or the line of attainable combinations, which would indicate the different combinations which he can actually obtain. Let us assume that the money per unit of time at his disposal is M. With this money, given the two prices, he can purchase either OB of commodity X and nothing of commodity Y or OA of commodity Y and nothing of X. The line AB is called the price line or the budget line. It is also called 'budget restraint', 'consumption possibility line', 'expenditure line', 'outlay line' and 'price income line'. In what follows, however, for the sake of brevity and simplicity, we shall use the term 'price line'. If we know the income of the consumer and the various quantities of the goods he can purchase with this income, it is very easy to find out the prices of the two goods. If, for instance, the income of the consumer is M and with this he can purchase only OB of good X or only OA of good Y, the price of good X would be M/OB and that of good Y would be M/OA. The price line AB indicates that the consumer can purchase both the goods in any combination represented by the points either on or below it. If he purchases the two goods in such a combination that can be indicated by a point, say E, which lies left to the price line, it would mean that he is saving a part of his income. In case the combination purchased by him is indicated by a point lying on the price line, it would mean that he is spending his entire income on the purchase of goods. But if the combination is indicated by a point, say D, which lies beyond or to the right of price line AB, it would mean that the consumer's income is not adequate to buy it and, therefore, he cannot actually purchase this combination. The ratio between the prices of two goods X and Y would be OB/OA, i.e. the slope of the price line.

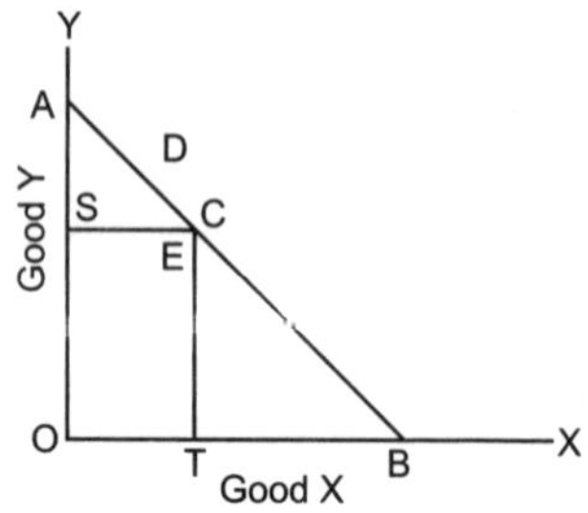

Fig. 6.11

The position of the price or budget line depends upon the consumer's money income. If his income increases, the prices of the two commodities remaining unchanged, he would be able to buy larger quantities of both the goods. In this case, the new price or budget line will be to the right of and parallel to the original price line. On the other hand, if the income declines, the prices of the two goods remaining unchanged, the consumer will be able to buy smaller quantities of both the goods. In this case, the new price line will be to the left and parallel to the original price line.

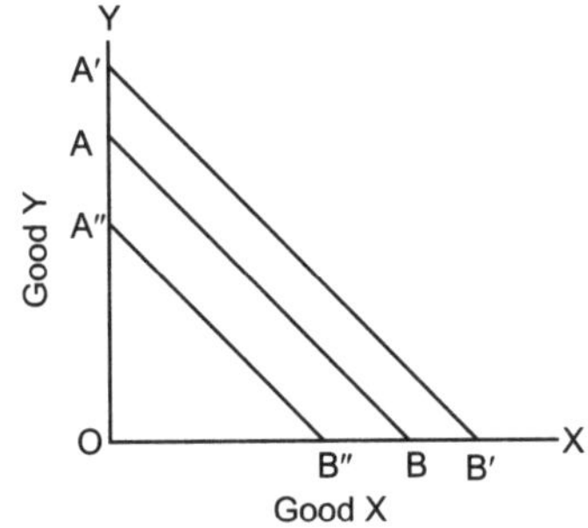

Fig. 6.12

In Fig. 6.12, AB is the original price line. The prices of the two goods remaining unchanged, an increase in income shifts it towards the (i.e. A′B′) while decline in income shifts it towards the left (i.e. A″B″). Thus, a change in income shifts the price line to a new position which is parallel to the position of the old price line.

While the position of the price depends upon the size of the consumer's income, its slope is determined by the price structure of the two goods.

Let us see how the slope of the price line is affected by a change in the price of one of the goods. Suppose that the price of good Y remains unchanged and the price of good X decline so that with the same income the consumer can now buy OB′ of good X, if he were to spend his entire income on good X alone.

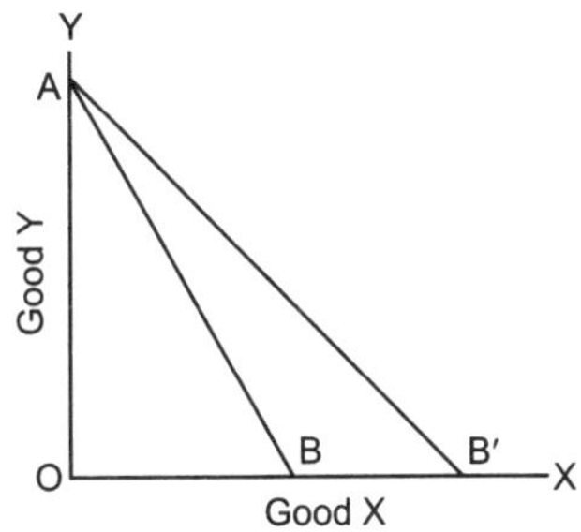

Fig. 6.13

To indicate a decline in the price of good X, a new price line would have to be drawn touching the X-axis at point B′ instead of B. Since there is no change in the price of good Y, it would continue touching the Y-axis at the old point A. Thus, the decline in the price of good X, the price of good Y remaining unchanged, would be represented by the line AB′. In case the price of good X rises, the price of good Y remaining unchanged, the new price line would be towards the left of the original price line. Thus, while income determines the position, price determines the slope of the price line.

As in case of indifference curves, we can have a family of price or budget lines. There is, however, a basic difference between the indifference curves and the price lines. While the price line shows the various combinations of the two goods which the consumer can buy, given his income and the prices of the two commodities, the indifference curve indicates the tastes and preferences of the consumer independent of his income and the prices of the goods. While the price line shows the objective and measurable quantities, the indifference curve indicates simply the subjective preferences and tastes of the consumer. It may also be pointed out that the indifference map and the price line are quite independent of each other. The indifference map is not affected by the prices. Similarly, the prices under competitive conditions are given and are not influenced by the behaviour of an individual consumer.

Consumer Equilibrium

Previously we discussed consumer's equilibrium in terms of Marshallian utility analysis. Now we shall see how a consumer reaches the equilibrium position with the aid of indifference curve analysis. While explaining the consumer's equilibrium, we make the following assumptions.

(i) The consumer has an indifference map indicating his scale of preferences for combinations of the goods in question.

(ii) The scale of preferences imprinted on his mind remains unchanged throughout the analysis.

(iii) The consumer possesses a limited amount of money which, if he does not spend on the good in question, will certainly be spent on some other good or goods.

(iv) He is one of the numerous buyers and knows the prices of all goods. All prices remain constant until a new equilibrium position is to be attained.

(v) All good are homogeneous and divisible.

(vi) The consumer behaves in a rational manner and aims at maximising his satisfaction.

We have now at our disposal both the sets of tools basic to indifference curves analysis: iso-utility curves and total outlay curves. The former alone cannot determine a consumer's behaviour because they show neither his income nor the commodity prices. In the absence of this information, it is not possible to know how much of the two commodities the consumer will buy. The indifference map enables the consumer to put various sets of combinations in a certain imaginary order of preference. But, by itself, it does not tell him as to which particular combination to buy. On the other hand, the outlay map simply indicates the different groups of the two commodities which the consumer can buy at different income levels, with given prices. It does not tell which particular combination of the commodities he will prefer most.

By combining the iso-utility map and total outlay curves, we can determine the combination of the two goods which will provide maximum satisfaction to the consumer. Let us assume that the amount of money which the consumer has at his disposal is M and the prices of the two goods X and Y are P_x and P_y respectively.

With the money possessed by him, the consumer can buy any combination from A to B on the price line in the above diagram. But any combination on indifference curves 1 and 2 would give the consumer a smaller amount of satisfaction than a combination on indifference curves 3. Thus, though the consumer can afford all combinations from A to B, he would actually choose only E, which includes OL of good X and OM of good Y. E, being a unique point on the highest curve to which his money income can take him, provides him the maximum possible satisfaction. He cannot choose any other point on curve 3, say H, even though it will provide him the same amount of satisfaction as E. This is because any other point on curve 3 is above AB and as such he cannot afford it. Thus, at the equilibrium point, the outlay line must be tangent to the highest indifference curve which the consumer can reach. In Fig. 6.14, E, the point of tangency is common to both the outlay line and the indifference curve. As such, the two curves must have the same slope at this point. The slope of the outlay curve, however, is constant throughout and is equal to OA/OB. But since OA = M/P_y and OB = M/P_x, the slope of the price line can also be expressed as $M/P_y/M/P_x$ or P_y/P_x. In other words, the slope of the price line can be expressed by P_y/P_x at the point E. Similarly, the slope of the indifference curve 3 can be represented by MRS_{yx} at the point E. Now MRS_{yx} must be equal to P_y/P_x at the point E. Thus, the slope of the price line must be equal to the slope of indifference curve 3 at the point E. The consumer will attain maximum satisfaction only at the point where the slopes of the price line as well as the indifference curve are equal to each other. This equality between the slopes of the two curves is possible only at the point of tangency. The consumer, for instance, cannot obtain maximum satisfaction at the points C, D, F or G because at all these points the price line intersects the indifference curves. All points of intersection are on lower indifference curves. There is no point higher than the point of tangency, which, by definition, is on the highest curve.

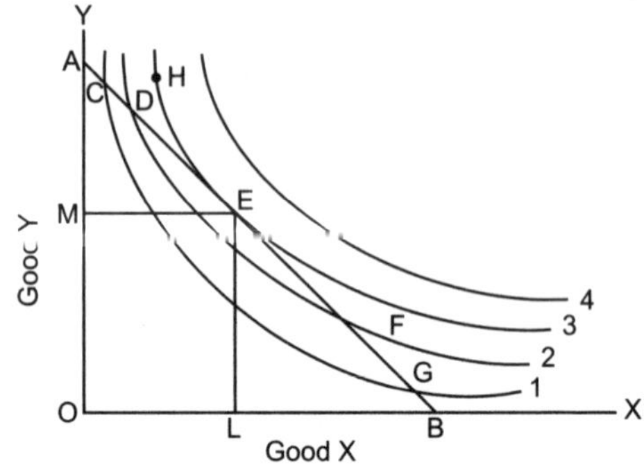

Fig. 6.14

The question may be raised as to why the consumer attains maximum satisfaction at point E and at no other point. The reason is that it is only at this point that the slope of the price line is equal to the slope of the indifference curve 3. At any point like D, the numerical value of the slope of the indifference curve is greater than that of the outlay curve. In other words, at the point D, the MRS of the consumer is greater than the price ratio (P_y/P_x) or the market rate of exchange. This means that at the point D, the consumer is prepared to surrender a larger number of units of good Y or for an additional unit of good X than is warranted by the current market rate of exchange. Since at this point he has only a few units of good X, their marginal significance to him in terms of good Y is greater than the market rate of exchange. But because of the existence of the market system, he need not give up all the units of good Y he is willing to surrender for a unit of good X. Suppose he is ready to surrender four units of Y for a unit of X to remain at indifference curve 2. But if in the market he can obtain one unit of X for only three units of Y, he will certainly do so and thus reach a higher indifference curve 3. D, therefore, cannot be a point of equilibrium.

Similarly, it can be shown that a point like F or G also cannot be an equilibrium point. At point F, for instance, the numerical value of the consumer's MRS is less than P_x/P_y. He possesses too many units of good X here and their marginal significance to him in terms of good Y has declined. He is prepared to offer a smaller number of units of Y for a unit of X at this stage than he has to offer at the market rate of exchange. As such no one will accept his offer. In such a situation, he may like to reduce his stock of good X and to buy more units of good Y. If he does so, he would get better terms in the market. His attempts to buy more units of Y will take him back to the point E at the higher indifference curve 3. F, therefore, cannot be a point of equilibrium. Similarly, C and G cannot be points of equilibrium. Thus, only E can be the point of maximum satisfaction for the consumer. At this point, consumer's MRS and the price-ratio (P_y/P_x) are equal. He has, therefore, no incentive for substituting one good for the other.

The tangency condition between the budget line and an indifference curve, though a necessary condition, is not a sufficient condition for the consumer to reach the equilibrium position. In other words, it means that while it is not possible to attain a position of consumer equilibrium without the tangency condition being fulfilled, the tangency condition by itself does not ensure equilibrium. For the equilibrium to be reached, in addition to the existence of tangency between the budget line and the indifference curve, it is also necessary that at the equilibrium point the MRS of good Y for good X must be declining. In case the latter condition is not fulfilled, the equilibrium attained will not be a stable one.

In Fig. 6.15, for instance, the indifference curve is concave to the origin around the point D. The price line AB is tangent to the indifference curve at point D and MRS_{xy} is equal to the price ratio P_x/P_y. But D cannot be a point of stable equilibrium because here the volume of satisfaction would not be maximum. The indifference curve being concave at the tangency point D, there are some points on the given price line AB such as L and M, which will be on indifference curve higher than IC_1. Thus, the consumer by moving along the given price line AB can go to points like L and M and obtain greater satisfaction than at D. To conclude, the following two conditions are necessary for the consumer to reach a position of stable equilibrium:

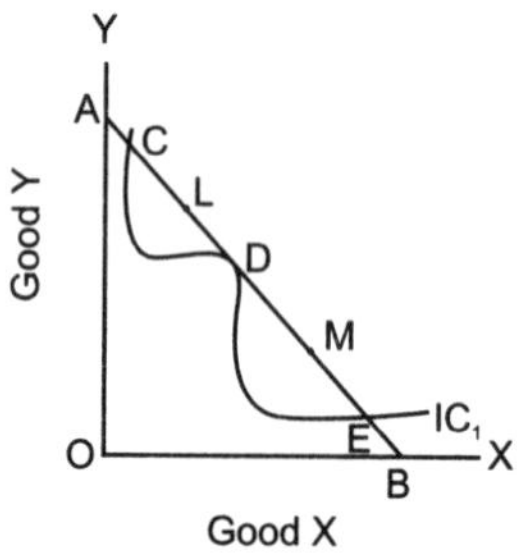

Fig. 6.15

(i) A given price line must be tangent to an indifference, or the marginal rate of substitution of X for Y (MRS_{xy}) must be equal to the price ratio between the two goods $\left(\frac{P_x}{P_y}\right)$.

(ii) Indifference curve must be convex to the origin at the point of tangency.

This is a very important conclusion. It helps us to understand, in terms of indifference curve analysis, as to why and by how much the consumer's demand for a commodity changes as a result of a given change in price or his income. In other words, with the help of this analysis, we can obtain the consumer's demand curve (price-quantity relationship) for a commodity or his Engel curve (income-quantity relationship) for it.

Mathematical Derivation of the Consumer Equilibrium

Given the market prices and his income, the consumer aims at the maximisation of his utility. Let us assume that there are n commodities available to the consumer, with given market prices $P_1, P_2, \ldots, P_n$ and his money income is Y which he spends on the available commodities.

The problem may be stated as follows:

Maximise $U = f(q_1, q_2, \ldots, q_n)$

subject to $\sum_{i=1}^{n} q_i P_i = q_1 P_1 + q_2 P_2 + \ldots + q_n P_n = Y$

We use the 'Lagrangian multipliers' method for the solution of this constrained maximum.

Let us write the constraint in the form

$$(q_1 P_1 + q_2 P_2 + \ldots + q_n P_n - Y) = 0$$

Multiplying the constraint by the Lagrangian multiplier λ we get

$$\lambda (q_1 P_1 + q_2 P_2 + \ldots\ldots + q_n P_n - Y) = 0$$

Subtracting the above constraint from the utility function we get the composite function as

$$\phi = U - \lambda (q_1 P_1 + q_2 P_2 + \ldots\ldots + q_n P_n - Y)$$

It can be shown that maximization of the composite function implies maximisation of the utility function.

First Order Condition of Maximisation

The first order condition of maximisation of a function is that its partial derivatives be equal to zero. Differentiating ϕ with respect to $q_1, q_2, \ldots, q_n$ and λ, and equating to zero we find

$$\frac{\partial \phi}{\partial q_1} = \frac{\partial U}{\partial q_1} - \lambda (P_1) = 0$$

$$\frac{\partial \phi}{\partial q_2} = \frac{\partial U}{\partial q_2} - \lambda (P_2) = 0$$

....

....

$$\frac{\partial \phi}{\partial q_n} = \frac{\partial U}{\partial q_n} - \lambda (P_n) = 0$$

$$\frac{\partial \phi}{\partial \lambda} = -(q_1P_1 + q_2P_2 + \ldots. + q_nP_n - Y) = 0$$

From the above equations we obtain

$$\frac{\partial U}{\partial q_1} = \lambda P_1$$

$$\frac{\partial U}{\partial q_2} = \lambda P_2$$

....

....

$$\frac{\partial U}{\partial q_n} = \lambda P_n$$

But $\frac{\partial U}{\partial q_1} = MU_1, \frac{\partial U}{\partial q_2} = MU_2, \ldots, \frac{\partial U}{\partial q_n} = MU_n$

Substituting and solving for λ we find

$$\lambda = \frac{MU_1}{P_1} = \frac{MU_2}{P_2} = \ldots. = \frac{MU_n}{P_n}$$

Alternatively, we can obtain

$$\frac{MU_x}{MU_y} = \frac{P_x}{P_y} = MRS_{x,y}$$

We observe that the equilibrium conditions are identical in the cardinalist approach and in the indifference curve approach. In both the theories we have

$$\frac{MU_1}{P_1} = \frac{MU_2}{P_2} = \ldots\ldots = \frac{MU_x}{P_x}$$

$$= \frac{MU_y}{P_y} = \ldots\ldots = \frac{MU_n}{P_n}$$

Cardinality of utility is not required in the indifference curve approach while the MRS require knowledge of the ratio of the marginal utilities. Hence, the first order condition for two commodities can be written as

$$\frac{MU_x}{MU_y} = \frac{P_x}{P_y} = MRS_{x,y}$$

Hence, the concept of marginal utility is implicit in the definition of the slope of the indifference curves, although its measurement is not required by this approach. What is needed is a diminishing marginal rate of substitution, which does not require diminishing marginal utilities of the commodities involved in the utility function.

Derivation of the Demand Curve using the Indifference Curve Approach

Graphical Derivation

As the price of a commodity, for example, of X falls the budget line of the consumer shifts to the right, from its initial position AB to a new position AB′ due to the increase in the purchasing power of the given money income of the consumer. Now the consumer can buy more of X (and more of Y). The new budget line is tangent to a higher indifference curve. The new equilibrium occurs to the right of the original equilibrium (for normal goods) showing that as price falls more of the commodity will be bought. If we allow the price of X to fall continuously and we join the points of tangency of successive budget lines and higher indifference curves we form the price consumption line from which we derive the demand curve for commodity X. At point e_1 the consumer buys quantity x_1 at price y_1. At point e_2 the price y_2, is lower than y_1, and the quantity demanded is increased to x_2, and so on. We can plot the price-quantity pairs defined by the points of equilibrium on the price-consumption line to obtain a demand curve, as shown below:

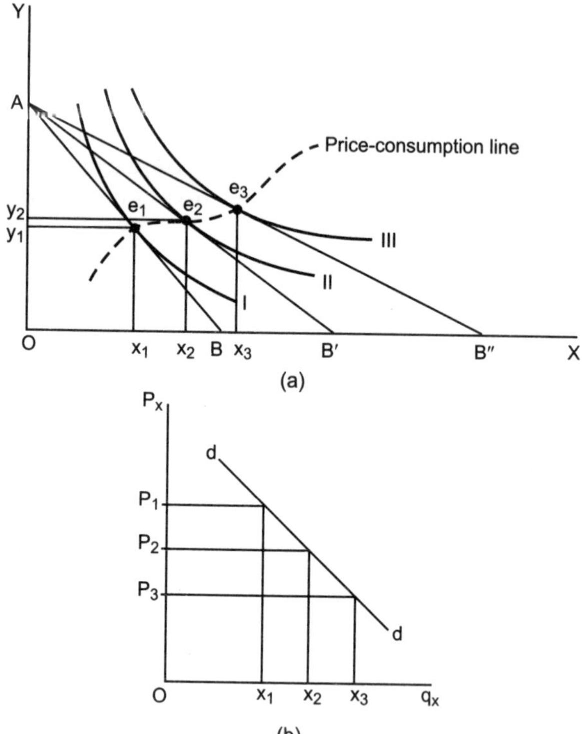

Fig. 6.16

The demand curve for normal goods will always have a negative slope denoting the law of demand, i.e. the quantity bought increases as the price falls.

Mathematical Derivation

The demand curve can be derived from the equilibrium condition

$$\frac{MU_x}{P_x} = \frac{MU_y}{P_y} = \ldots\ldots\ldots\ldots\ldots = \frac{MU_n}{P_n}$$

And he budget constraint

$$Y = \sum_{i=1}^{n} p_i q_i$$

Let us assume that there are only two commodities and that the total utility function is multiplicative of the form

$$U = \frac{1}{4} q_x q_y$$

The marginal utilities of x and y are

$$MU_x = \frac{\partial U}{\partial q_x} = \frac{1}{4} q_y$$

And

$$MU_y = \frac{\partial U}{\partial q_y} = \frac{1}{4} q_x$$

Substituting the marginal utilities in the equilibrium condition we get

$$\frac{1}{4} \frac{q_y}{P_x} = \frac{1}{4} \frac{q_x}{P_y}$$

Or $$q_y P_y = q_x P_x$$

We can derive the demand for commodity x by substituting $q_y P_y$ in the budget constraint:

$$q_y P_y + q_x P_x = Y$$

$$2q_x P_x = Y$$

$$q_x = \frac{1}{2P_x} Y$$

Thus, the demand for x is negatively related to its own price P_x and positively to income Y. Similarly the demand for y is obtained by substituting $q_x P_x$ in the budget constraint:

$$q_y = \frac{1}{2P_y} Y$$

Income Effect

The effect of a change in consumer's income on his total satisfaction is called *income effect*. Assuming that the prices of the goods purchased by the consumer remain unchanged, he would be able to enjoy a greater or a smaller volume of satisfaction with an increase or a decline in his income respectively. The income effect may thus be defined as the effect on the purchases of the consumer caused by changes in income, the prices of goods remaining unchanged. An increase in consumer's income would improve his position and take him to a higher indifference curve. Similarly, a decline in income deteriorates his position and pulls him down to a lower indifference curve. The income-consumption curve traces the income effect. We explain below the meaning and technique of drawing a income-consumption curve.

We had studied above consumer's equilibrium on the assumption that the consumer had a given income and the prices of the goods remained constant. Now it would be assumed that while the prices of the two goods remain unchanged, the income of the consumer changes. Obviously, an increase in consumer's income will shift his price line towards the right because with an increase in income he can purchase more of both the goods. But since the prices of the two goods remain unchanged, the slope of the new price line would be the same as that of the old one. In other words, the new price line will be parallel to the old one. The new price line would, however, be tangent to a higher indifference curve. Similarly, if there takes place a decline in income, the new price line will be parallel to but below the old price line. It would also be tangent to a lower indifference curve. This is shown in Fig. 6.17.

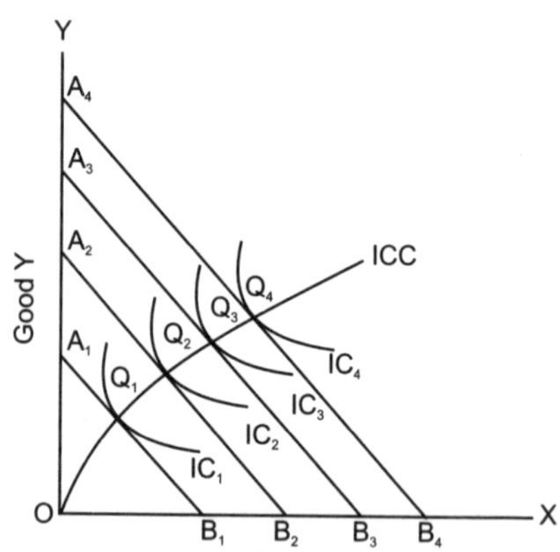

Fig. 6.17

The initial income of the consumer is indicated by the income line A_1B_1. The consumer is in equilibrium at point Q_1. Now suppose his income increases so that the new income line is A_2B_2. Now the consumer would be in equilibrium at the point Q_2. A further increase in income will take the consumer to be in equilibrium on a higher indifference curve (i.e. IC_3) at the point Q_3. If all the equilibrium points (viz. Q_1, Q_2, Q_3, etc.) are joined, we get a curve which is known as "Income Consumption Curve" (ICC). The curve indicates the relation between changes in the money income of the consumer and the consumption of the two commodities on the assumption that the prices of the two commodities remain unchanged. The income-consumption curve normally slopes upwards to the right indicating that with an increase in income the consumer would buy greater quantities of the two commodities. This, however, need not be so in all cases. The shape of the particular income-consumption curve throws a good deal of light on the manner the consumer divides his increasing (or decreasing) income for the purchase of different goods.

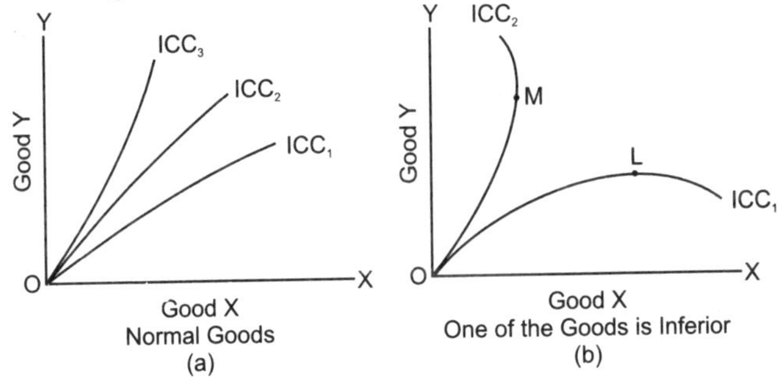

Fig. 6.18

The three income-consumption curves shown in Fig. 6.18(a) above, for example, indicate that both the commodities concerned are 'normal' goods, i.e. with an increase in consumer's income, he purchases more of both the goods. ICC_2 indicates a more or less proportionate increase in expenditure on the two goods. ICC_1 indicates that the expenditure on commodity X increases but less than proportionately. This happens, for instance, with expenditure on food. ICC_3, in contrast, indicates that the expenditure on good X increases more than proportionately. This is the case, for instance, with expenditure on items like recreation.

It is quite possible that with an increase in income the consumer's expenditure on a particular good, instead of increasing, may actually decline. This is the case with inferior goods. Such goods are consumed in larger quantities at a lower income and in smaller quantities at a higher income. This happens because with an increase in income, the consumer can afford to shift to better quality goods. This phenomenon, popularly known as the Giffen Paradox, is shown in Fig. 6.18(b). Curve ICC_1 indicates that after point L good X becomes an inferior good. Curve ICC_2 indicates that after point M good Y becomes an inferior good.

In case with an increase in income the consumer does not change the amount of the good purchased, the income effect would be zero. In the real world, it is very unlikely to find zero income effect over a considerably long range of income.

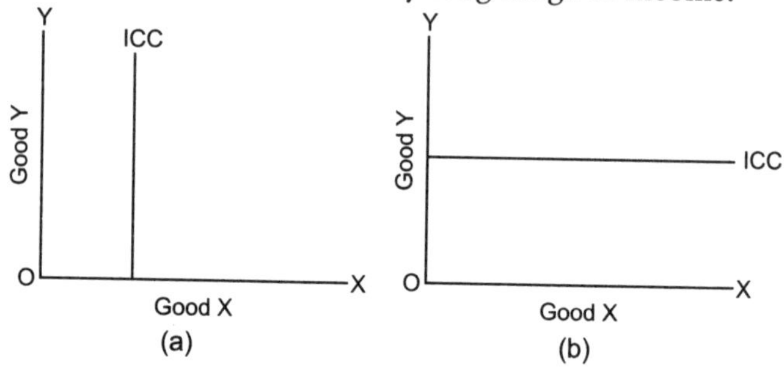

Fig. 6.19

In Fig. 6.19(a), with an increase in income, the consumer buys more and more of good Y and an unchanged amount of good X. This represents a case of positive income effect in case of good Y and zero income effect in case of good X. In Fig. 6.19(b), on the other hand, with an increase in income, the consumer buys more and more of X but the same amount of Y. This indicates a case of positive income effect in case of good X and zero income effect in case of good Y.

To sum up, we can say that when the income consumption curve slopes upwards to the right, the income effect would be positive for both the goods. If it slopes downwards, the income effect is negative for Y but positive for X. In case it slopes backwards to the left, the income effect is negative for X but positive for Y. The income effect is positive for Y and zero for

X if the income consumption curve is vertical in shape and the reverse of that when the curve takes a horizontal form.

Substitution Effect

The 'substitution effect' occurs when the relative prices of the two goods change in such a way that the consumer is neither better off nor worse off than before but is obliged to rearrange his purchases according to the changed relative prices. When the price of a good changes, the real income of the consumer also changes. To keep the real income of the consumer unchanged so that the effect of a change in the relative prices alone is known, the change in price is compensated by a simultaneous change in income. For instance, if the price of a good, say X, declines, it would cause an increase in the consumer's real income. If we want to find out the substitution effect, i.e. change in the amount of X purchased resulting from a change only in its relative price, the consumer's money income must be reduced by an amount so as to counteract the increase in real income which results from a decline in the price of good X. In regard to the change in the money income which should be brought about so as to cancel the change in real income of the consumer caused by a change in the price of good X, two slightly different concepts have been developed by Hicks and Allen and by Slutsky. The substitution effect developed by Hicks and Allen is known as *Hicks-Allen Substitution Effect* and that formulated by E. Slutsky is called *Slutsky Substitution Effect.*

According to Hicks-Allen substitution effect, a change in price is accompanied by so much change in money income that the consumer is neither better off nor worse off than before. In other words, money income of the consumer is changed to the extent that the consumer remains on the same indifference curve on which he was before the change occurred in the price of the good X. Thus, Hicks-Allen substitution effect occurs on the same indifference curve. The amount by which the money income of the consumer is changed so that the consumer is neither better off nor worse off than before is called *Compensating Variation in Income*. Figure 6.20 represents Hicks-Allen substitution effect.

With a given money income and given prices of the two goods as indicated by the price line AB, the consumer is in equilibrium at point Q on the indifference curve IC. At this point he purchases OL of good X and OM of good Y. Now suppose that the price of good X declines, the price of Y remaining unchanged, so that the price line shifts to AB′. The decline in the price of X would raise the real income of the consumer. In order to find out the substitution effect, this increase in real income should be counteracted by reducing the money income of the consumer to the extent that he remains on the same indifference curve IC. When some money is taken away from the consumer to counteract the increase in his real income, the price line which shifted to AB′ will now shift downward but will be parallel to AB′. In Fig. 6.20, price line PK has been drawn at such a distance from AB′ that it touches the indifference curve. It means that the consumer's income is reduced by an amount PA (in terms of Y) or B′K (in terms of X) so as to keep him on the same indifference curve. PA or B′K is just enough to offset the rise in real income resulting from a decline in the price of X. PA or B′K is thus the compensating variation in income.

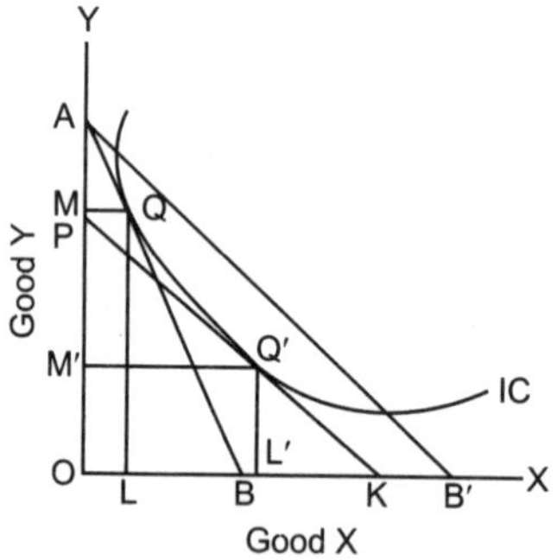

Fig. 6.20

The price line PK indicates the new relative prices of goods X and Y because it is parallel to the price line AB′ which was obtained when the price of good X had declined. As compared to the price line AB, the price of X is now comparatively lower. The consumer would, therefore, has a tendency to rearrange his purchases of X and Y in a way so as to substitute X for Y.

Since the X is now relatively cheaper and Y relatively dearer, the consumer would a larger quantity of X and a smaller quantity of Y. The price line PK represents the changed relative prices and a smaller amount of income than that indicated by AB′ because the income has been reduced by compensating variation in income.

With the new price line PK, the consumer is in equilibrium at the point Q′. At this point he buy OL′ of X and OM′ of Y. This increase in the purchase of X by LL′ and decline in the purchase of Y by M′M is entirely owing to a change in the relative prices of goods X and Y because the effect of increase in real income resulting from a decline in the price of X has been cancelled out by an equivalent reduction in the consumer's income. Thus, the movement from point Q to Q′ represents the substitution effect. The substitution effect on X is the increase in its quantity purchased by LL′ and that on Y is the decline in its quantity purchased by M′M. Thus, the substitution effect leaves the consumer on the same indifference curve but there is a shift in the equilibrium point.

The strength of the substitution effect depends upon the extent of the convexity of the indifference curve. The more convex the indifference curve, the weaker would be the substitution effect and conversely. As we have already seen, the indifference curve is less convex in case of goods which substitutes for each other, e.g. tea and coffee. As such the substitution effect in very strong in case of such goods.

Slutsky Substitution Effect

The substitution effect formulated by Slutsky is slightly different. According to this when the price of a good declines and the real income or purchasing power of the consumer increases, his income is reduced by an amount equal to the change in its purchasing power which takes place as a consequence of the decline in price. In other words, the purchasing power is changed by an amount equal to the change in the price multiplied by the number of units of the good which the consumer was purchasing at the old price. According to Slutsky's approach, income is changed by an amount which leaves the consumer to be just able to purchase the same combination of goods, if he so desires, which he was buying at the previous price. In other words, the income is changed by the difference between the cost of the amount of good X bought at old price and the cost of the same amount of X at the new price. This change in income is called *cost difference*. Thus, while according to Hicksian approach income is changed by compensating variation, according to Slutsky's approach income is changed by the cost difference.

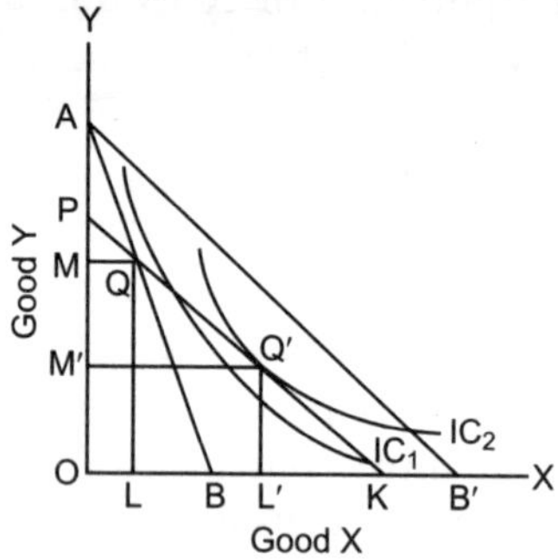

Fig. 6.21

Figure 6.21 illustrates the Slutsky substitution effect. With a given money income and the given prices of the two goods as indicated by the price line AB, the consumer is in equilibrium at point Q. At this point he buys OL of good X and OM of good Y. Now suppose the price of X declines while the money income of the consumer and the price of good Y remains unchanged. The decline in the price of X will shift the price line to AB′ and the real income of the consumer will rise. In order to find out the Slutsky substitution effect, the money income of the consumer has to be reduced by the cost difference or, in other words, by an amount which would leave him to be just able to buy the previous combination Q, if he so desires. This is indicated by the price line PK which is parallel to AB′ and passes through the point Q. The means that the consumer is deprived of income equivalent to AP in terms Y or KB′ in terms of X and as a consequence he can buy the combination Q, if he so likes, because Q also lies on the price line PK. In actual practice, he will not purchase combination Q because now X has become relatively cheaper and Y relatively dearer. The change in relative prices will induce the consumer to rearrange his purchases so as to substitute X for Y. In Slutsky substitution case, the consumer would not move along the previous indifference curve IC_1 because the new price line PK, on which the consumer has to remain owing to the price-income situation, is at no place tangent to the indifference curve IC_1. The price line PK is tangent to the indifference curve IC_2, at point Q′. The consumer will, therefore, be in equilibrium at point Q′ at a higher indifference curve IC_2. The movement from Q to Q′ represents Slutsky substitution effect according to which the consumer moves not on the same indifference curve but from one indifference curve to another. At point Q′ the consumer buys OL′ of X and OM′ of Y. LL′ of X has been substituted for M′M of Y.

The difference between the Hicksian substitution effect and the Slutsky substitution effect arises entirely from the amount of money income by which income is to be changed to cancel out the change in real income resulting from a change in the price of X. While Hicksian approach just restores to the consumer his previous level of satisfaction, the Slutsky approach 'overcompensates' the consumer by taking him to a higher indifference curve. Hicks points out that the method of compensating variation "has the merit that the two parts into which the whole effect of the price-change is divided are parts that have special economic significance. For on this interpretation, the substitution effect measures the effect of the change in relative prices, with *real income constant*; the income effect measures the effect of the change in real income. Thus, the analysis which is based upon the compensating variation is a resolution of the price change into two fundamental economic 'directions'; we shall not encounter a *more fundamental distinction upon any other route*".[3] (Italics in original)

Slutsky method, however, possesses the advantage that it is very easy to find out the amount of income equivalent to the "cost difference" by which income of the consumer is to be changed. In contrast, it is extremely difficult to find out the compensating variation in income. The cost difference method has the merit that it depends on observable market data whereas the method of compensating variation requires a knowledge of indifference curves (or tastes and preferences) of the consumer between different combinations of goods. Hicks himself recognises this merit of Slutsky approach: "The difference between the two methods is solely a matter of the magnitude of the rise in income, which leads to the income effect; and on this point the method of cost-difference has a distinct advantage. For while the magnitude of the compensating variation is quite a problem..., the magnitude of the cost-difference raises no problem at all. It can be read off at once from the data of the situation under discussion".[4]

The two approaches have their own merits. While the law of demand can be easily and adequately established by the method of cost difference, method of compensating variation is highly useful for analysis of consumer's surplus and welfare economics. To cite Hicks again, "The merit of the cost-difference method is confined to the property...that its income effect is peculiarly easy to handle. The compensating variation method does not share in this particular advantage; but it makes up for its clumsiness in relation to income effect by its convenience with relation to the substitution effect. The higher reaches of demand theory...are mainly concerned with further study of the substitution effect; thus they are for the most part more easily investigated by the method of the compensating variation than by its rival".[5]

Price Effect

The effect of a change in the price of a commodity on its quantity bought is called *price effect*. The most common factor disturbing the consumer's equilibrium is a change in price without compensating variation of the substitution effect. Unlike the substitution effect, the consumer may be better off or worse off than before. In the real world, there may be no compensatory relation between changes in the prices of X and Y and the changes may be absolutely independent of each other irrespective of what happens to the satisfaction of the consumer. Though the prices of both X and Y may change, for the sake of the simplification of the analysis, we assume that it is only the price of X that changes and that too in the downward direction. What will be the effect of a decline in the price of X? In the first place, as seen above, it will shift the consumer's outlay or price line towards the right indicating that with the same money income the consumer can now buy a larger quantity of good X. Secondly, the decline in the price of X means an increase in the real income of the consumer, his money income remaining unchanged. With the increase in real income, the consumer can buy more of good X or more of other goods, if he so likes. This, as we have seen, is known as income effect. Thirdly, a decline in the price of X vis-à-vis Y will induce the consumer to substitute X for Y. This is known as substitution effect. Thus, the consumer's demand for X increases owing to the combined operation of the *income effect* and the *substitution effect.*

Figure 6.22 shows the price effect. With every decline in the price of X, the price line shifts towards the right. In other words, as the price of X declines, the price line rotates anti-clockwise with its focal point at A. Similarly, if the price of X starts rising, the price line will shift towards the left or, in other words, rotate clockwise with its focal point at A. With every change in the price of X, the consumer attains a new equilibrium position. If all such equilibrium points (viz. Q, Q_1, Q_2, etc.) are joined, we obtain a curve AQQ_1Q_2 which is known as Price Consumption Curve (PCC).

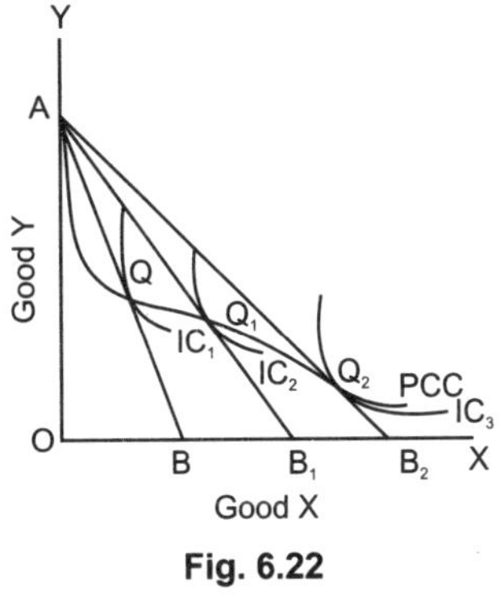

Fig. 6.22

In the figure, the price consumption curve slopes downwards to the right which means that as the consumer moves to higher levels of satisfaction, he buys larger and larger quantities of X and smaller and smaller quantities of Y. But a downward (or negatively) sloping price-consumption curve is not the only type of curve. There are other types of curves also with varying slopes. A discussion of the various types of the price-consumption curves is important because it throws light on the nature of the good to which it relates—whether the good is superior, inferior or neutral.

Figure 6.23(a) represents an upward-sloping price consumption curve. An upward sloping price-consumption curve for X means that when the price of good X falls, the amount demanded of both goods X and Y rises. Figure 6.23(b) portrays a backward-sloping price consumption curve for X, which means that with a decline in the price of X, its quantity purchased falls. This is the case with inferior goods known as *Giffen Goods*. This happens because the negative income effect is stronger than the positive substitution effect. Figure 6.23(c) shows a horizontal price-consumption curve, which means that with a decline in the price of X, its quantity bought increases proportionately but the quantity bought of Y remains unchanged. The price-consumption curve can also take a vertical shape as shown in Fig. 6.23(d). In this case with a decline in the price of X, the quantity of X purchased remains unchanged. This happens because the negative income effect just counteracts the substitution effect. While income effect can be positive (in case of superior goods), negative (in case of inferior goods), or zero (in case of neutral goods), the substitution effect is always positive.

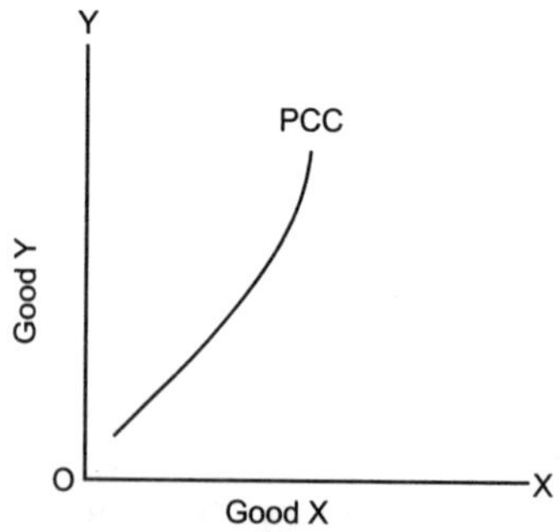

(a)

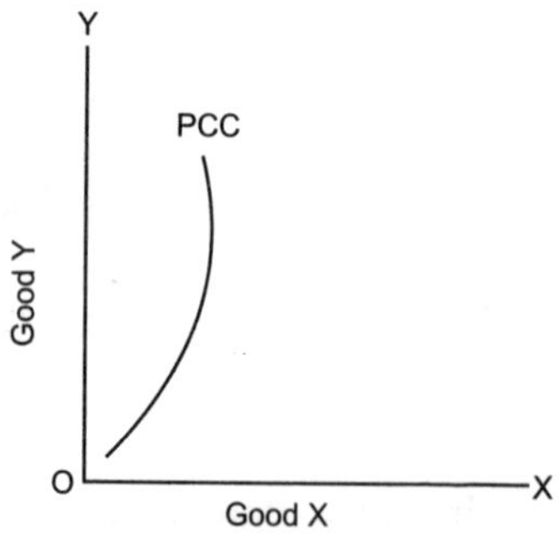

(b)

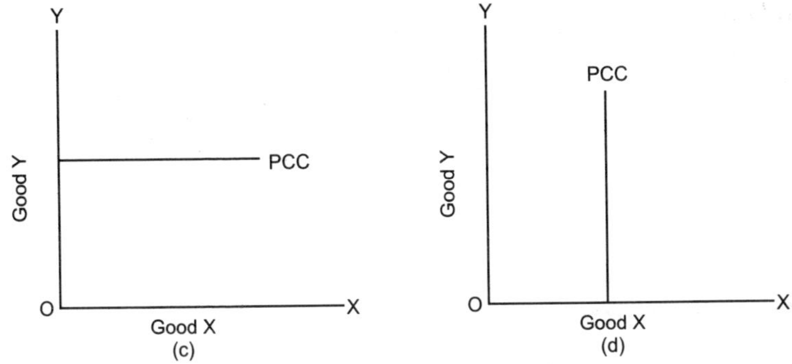

Fig. 6.23

Decomposition of Price Effect into Substitution Effect and Income Effect

In the previous section we have discussed the over all effect of change in price of a good. In this section we shall decompose that effect into two components—a substitution effect and an income effect.

Let us suppose the consumer buys two goods, food and clothing, the both goods have a positive marginal utility, and that the price of food decreases.

If the price of good decreases and the prices of all other goods remain the same, all individuals who consume that good will experience an increase in their real income even though their money income will remain constant. By an increase in real income, we simply mean the ability to reach a higher level of preference—a capability that obviously exists if the price of one good decline and all other prices remain constant. An increase in the consumer's real income will have an effect on the rate at which he or she wishes to consume a particular good; we refer to this effect as the *income effect.*

An increase in real income will cause an increase in the desired consumption of a normal good and a decrease in the desired consumption of an inferior good. In the case of a normal good, the income effect is said to be *positive*; in the case of an inferior good, the income effect is *negative*.

Independent of the income effect is the fact that a decrease in the price of one good will reduce the price of that good *relative* to the price of *all* other goods, if all other prices remain constant. This makes it less costly to substitute the good whose price has declined for other goods and, as we will see, always has the effect of increasing the consumption of the good that is cheaper. This effect is referred as the *substitution effect.*

The substitution effect is always negative because, if we consider only this effect, a decrease (increase) in price causes an increase (decrease) in desired consumption.

The Substitution Effect

The substitution effect is the amount of additional food the consumer would buy to achieve the same level of utility. Following figure shows three optimal choice diagrams that illustrate the steps involved in finding the substitution effect associated with this price change.

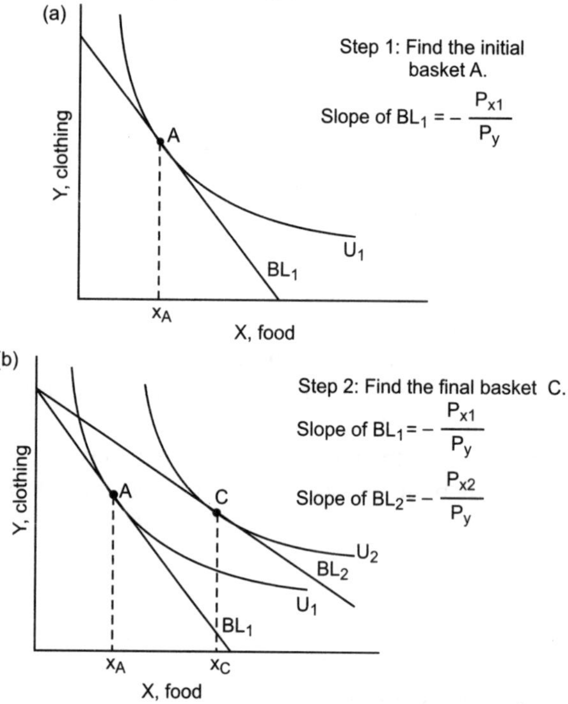

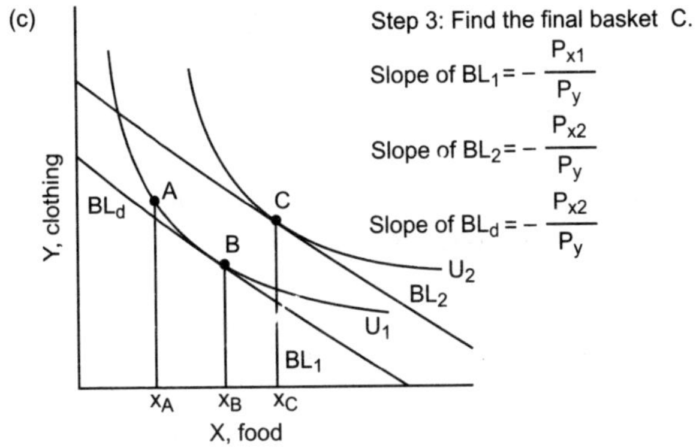

Fig. 6.24

When the price of good is P_{x1}, the consumer faces budget line BL_1 and maximises utility by choosing basket A on indifference curve U_1. The quantity of food purchased at this point is x_A (Fig. 6.24(a)).

When the price of food falls to P_{x2}, the budget line rotates outward to BL_2, and the consumer maximises utility by choosing basket C on indifference curve U_2 (Fig. 6.24(b)).

At this point x_C amount of food is purchased. Thus, the overall effect of the price change on the quantity of food purchased is $x_C - x_A$. Thus, the consumer realises a higher level of utility as a result of the price decrease, as shown by the fact that the initial basket A lies inside the new budget line BL_2.We have to find an intermediate decomposition basket that will enable us to identify the portion of the change in quantity due to the substitution effect. To find out this basket we have to keep in mind two things: First, the decomposition basket reflects the price decrease, so it must lie on a budget line that is parallel to BL_2. Second, the decomposition basket reflects the assumption that the consumer achieves the initial level of utility after the price decrease, so the basket must be at the point where the budget line is tangent to indifference curve U_1. From Fig. 6.24(c) we find that these two conditions are fulfilled by basket B on budget line BL_d (the decomposed budget line). At basket B, the consumer purchases the quantity of food x_B. Thus, the substitution effect accounts for the consumer's movement from basket A to basket B—that is, the portion of the overall effect on the quantity of food purchased that can be attributed to the substitution effect is $x_B - x_A$.

The Income Effect

Let us assume that the income of the consumer is I. When the price of food is P_{x1}, he can buy any basket on BL_1, and when the price of food is P_{x2}, he can buy any basket on BL_2. From Fig. 6.24(c) we find that the decomposition budget line BL_d lies inside BL_2, which means that the income I_d that would be needed to buy a basket on BL_d is less than the income I needed to buy a basket on BL_2. We also see that baskets A and B are on the same indifference curve U_1 which means that the consumer would be in different between the following two situations: (a) having a higher income I when the price of food is higher at P_{x1} and (b) having a lower income I_d when the price of food is lower at P_{x2}.

Now let's us find the income effect, the change in the amount of a good consumed as the consumer's utility changes. The movement from basket A to basket B doesn't involve any change in utility, and this movement can be viewed as the result of a reduction in income from I to I_d as the price falls from P_{x1} to P_{x2}. In reality, however, the consumer's income doesn't fall when the price of food decreases, so his level of utility increases, and we account for this by restoring the lost income. When we do this , the budget line shifts fro BL_d to BL_2, and the consumer's optimal basket shifts from basket B to basket C. Thus, the income effect accounts for the consumer's movement from the decomposition basket B to the final basket C—that is , the portion of the overall effect on the quantity of food purchased that can be attributed to the income effect is $x_C - x_B$.

To sum up , when the price of food falls from P_{x1} to P_{x2}, the total change on food consumption is $(x_C - x_A)$. This can be decomposed into the substitution effect $(x_B - x_A)$ and the income effect $(x_c - x_B)$. When we add the substitution effect and the income effect, we get the total change in consumption.

NOTES

1. Edgeworth, *Mathematical Physics*, 1881.
2. Fisher, *Mathematical Investigations in the Theory of Value and Prices*, 1892.
3. J.R. Hicks, *A Revision of Demand Theory* (London, 1956), p. 62.
4. *Ibid.*, p. 64.
5. *Ibid.*, p. 69.

Revealed Preference Theory of Demand

7

We have seen that the Marshallian utility analysis is purely subjective. It attempts to explain observed consumer behaviour in terms of motivation and psychological valuation. The indifference curves analysis takes the observed behaviour as an ultimate fact but does not try to explain it.[1] It thus frees the theory of consumer's choice from psychological implications. But until a satisfactory method of deriving quantitative counterparts of indifference functions from empirical analysis is discovered, the indifference curves remain a sort of psychological postulate. The desire among economists to have a 'scientific' (meaning 'behaviouristic' as against 'psychological') explanation of consumers' behaviour gradually led to the emergence of a technique which tries to derive the demand theorem from observed consumer behaviour.

The new technique is based on a hypothesis put forward by Samuelson in 1938 and more recently used by him and others for several economic formulations. The hypothesis consists of an assumption that 'choice' reveals 'preference'. 'Preference Hypothesis' means that when a consumer is observed to choose a combination A out of various alternative combinations open to him, he reveals his preference for combination A over all other alternative combinations which he could have bought. In other words, when a consumer chooses a combination A, it means that he considers all other alternative combinations that he could have bought inferior to A. Still in other words, it means he rejects all other alternative combinations available to him in favour of the chosen combination A. The hypothesis of 'choice reveals preference' enables us to obtain definite information about the preferences of a consumer from the observation of his behaviour in the market.

Samuelson's revealed preference hypothesis is based on the following assumptions:

(i) The consumer's tastes remain unchanged.

(ii) The consumer's choice reveals his preference.

(iii) The consumer prefers a combination of more goods to that of less goods in any situation.

(iv) The consumer must choose only one combination in any given price-income situation.

(v) No two observations of choice behaviour can conflict with regard to an individual consumer's preferences.

The revealed preference theorem observes the reactions of the consumer to price changes in the market and from them draws its conclusions about the preferences of the consumer. We graphically explain below the preference hypothesis.

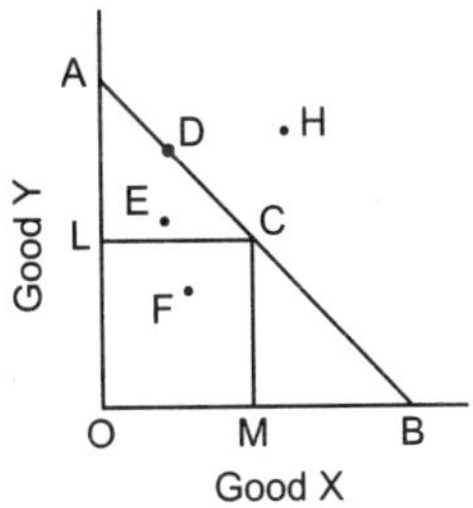

Fig. 7.1

Given the prices of two commodities X and Y and the income of the consumer, the price line AB is drawn in Fig. 7.1. The price line AB indicates a given price-income situation. Given the price-income situation as indicated by AB, the consumer can buy or choose any combination lying within or on the triangle OAB. In other words, all combinations lying on the line AB like C and D and those lying below the line AB, like E and F, are alternative combinations open to the consumer from among which he has to make a choice. If he chooses combination C out of all the combinations open to him in the given price-income situation, it means he reveals his preference for C over all other combinations open to him. When the consumer chooses combination C, he buys OM of commodity X and OL of commodity Y.

Any other combination of commodities X and Y like D, which lies on the same price-income line AB is as costly as C. Any other combination like E or F lying below the line AB indicates smaller quantities of both the commodities X and Y and is cheaper than the combinations C and D. If in spite of the fact that combination E is cheaper, the consumer buys combination C, it is evident that he reveals his preference for combination C over combination E. Any combination of the two commodities like H which lies above or to the right of price-income line AB indicates larger quantities of both the commodities and is costlier than the combinations C or D. If the consumer buys combination C, it does not mean that he reveals his preference for C over H.

The formulators of the revealed preference theory do not bother about the sequence of events by which choice becomes preference. The 'inference' that choice is preference thus becomes axiomatic and may be considered as an implicit underlying assumption of the theory.

Samuelson's revealed preference theory is based on the strong form of the preference hypothesis. Strong ordering preference hypothesis means that there is a *definite ordering* of various combinations in the consumer's scale of preferences and as such the choice of a combination by the consumer reveals his definite preference for that combination over all alternative combinations open to him. Thus, it rules out the relation of indifference between various alternative combinations. In Fig. 7.1, the consumer is shown to prefer combination C to all other alternative combinations 'in or on the triangle'. Prof. J.R. Hicks, in his *Revision of Demand Theory*, does not consider the assumption of strong ordering as satisfactory and instead makes use of weak ordering hypothesis. Under weak ordering hypothesis, the chosen combination A is preferred to all alternative combinations that lie within the triangle OAB and will be either preferred or indifferent to other combinations on the price-income line AB.

The revealed preference theory assumes consistency or transitivity of consumer behaviour. The consistency assumption means that if A is preferred to B in one situation, B cannot be preferred to A in another situation. This is Hicks' Direct Consistency Test under strong ordering. Transitivity assumption, on the other hand, refers to three-term consistency. It means that if the consumer prefers A to B and B to C, he must prefer A to C. This assumption is necessary for the revealed preference theory if the consumer is to make a consistent choice from given alternative situations.

The consistency postulate in the revealed preference theory is the counterpart of the utility maximisation assumption in both the Marshallian utility analysis and the Hicks-Allen indifference curve analysis. The assumption that the consumer aims at maximising his utility or satisfaction is known as rationality assumption. It is said that a rational consumer aims at maximising his utility or satisfaction. The utility maximisation assumption has, however, recently been challenged by some economists, who hold that in actual practice the consumers do not always try to maximise their utility. The revealed preference theory is superior to the other two analyses to the extent that its rationality assumption can be easily realised in actual practice. The rationality assumption of the revealed preference theory only requires that the consumer should behave in a consistent manner. Consistency of choice is a less restrictive assumption than the utility maximisation assumption.

It may be pointed out that Samuelson's revealed preference is not a statistical concept. It derives its entire meaning from a single-choice situation in which the consumer chooses a particular combination of goods, C, of all the alternative combinations available to him. The concept can be given a statistical form only if the consumer has an opportunity to exercise his choice several times in similar circumstances. When the consumer is given a single choice, he cannot reveal his indifference for any other combinations of goods in his market behaviour. Thus, Samuelson's theory implies rejection of indifference. To cite Tapas Majumdar, "The rejection of indifference in Samuelson's theory is therefore not a matter of convenience but dictated by the requirements of his methodology".[2]

The revealed preference hypothesis can also be translated into index-number form. If in a given situation, Q_1 and Q_2 are the two combinations of goods and a price level P_1 prevails, the statement that the consumer chooses Q_1 over Q_2 can be expressed by the formula, $\Sigma P_1Q_1 \geq \Sigma P_1Q_2$. Since ΣP_1Q_1 represents the total expenditure on the combination of goods Q_1 and ΣP_1Q_2 the total expenditure on combination of goods Q_2, the condition $\Sigma P_1Q_1 \geq \Sigma P_1Q_2$ shows that the consumer could have bought Q_2 with the amount of expenditure he incurs for buying Q_1 but the fact that he chooses Q_1 rather than Q_2 reveals his preference for Q_1 over Q_2. The index-number formulation, however, is simply tautological and conveys no additional economic meaning. It may, of course, be more convenient for some construction.

The revealed preference hypothesis is a sort of fundamental on which several propositions of demand theory as well as welfare economics can be based. Professor Samuelson has employed this hypothesis to derive the Marshallian law of demand—A rise in the price of a commodity, assuming income and prices of other commodities remain unchanged, must lead to a decline in the quantity demanded of this commodity. His theory is based on a logical deduction that positive income elasticity implies negative price elasticity. Samuelson states his 'Fundamental Theorem of Consumption Theory' as follows: "Any good (simple or composite) that is known always to increase in demand when money income alone rises must definitely shrink in demand when its price alone rises".[3] The geometric proof of this theorem is illustrated below.

Let us suppose that the consumer spends his entire income on two goods, X and Y. We further assume that his income in terms of good X is OB and in terms of Y is OA. Thus, AB is his original price-income situation. All the combinations of goods X and Y lying within or on the triangle OAB are open to the consumer for purchase. Let us assume that the consumer is observed to choose the combination R. By choosing the combination R, the consumer reveals his preference for this combination over all other combinations open to him in or on the triangle OAB.

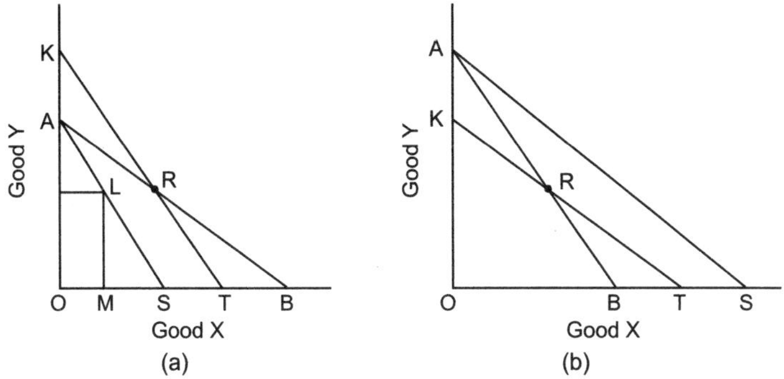

Fig. 7.2

Now suppose that the price of good X rises while that of good Y remains unchanged. This shifts the price-income line to the new position AS in Fig. 7.2(a). Now we have to prove that consumer buys good X in a quantity which is smaller than the quantity of good X bought by him at the original price line. Let us 'overcompensate' the consumer by giving him enough extra money income to enable him to buy exactly the same quantity of good X which he would have bought before the rise in the price of X. This is indicated by the amount AK in terms of good Y. After the 'overcompensation effect' has occurred, the new price-income line KT must pass through A and be parallel to price-income line AS. This gives us OKT as the consumer's triangle of choice. Since prior to the rise in the price of X, R was chosen in preference to all alternatives available in or on the triangle OAB, the alternatives lying on the RT portion of the price-income line KT must be considered as rejected in favour of R which means the consumer's choice lies on RK. It is evident that any point on RK reveals that the consumer buys a smaller quantity of X, excepting the limiting case of point A where he buys the same quantity as before. It is very probable that the consumer will decrease his consumption of X because X has become relatively costlier after the rise in its price. Thus, the consumer will buy either the combination at R or any other combination in the triangle AKR. In order to distinguish this type of 'substitution effect' from the Hicks-Allen kind of 'substitution effect', Samuelson calls it the 'overcompensation effect'. The 'overcompensation effect' like the Slutsky 'substitution effect' permits the consumer to shift to a higher indifference curve. The Hicks-Allen 'substitution effect', in contrast, as seen earlier, takes place along a given indifference curve.

Now, to move to second stage of the Theorem, if the 'gift of extra money income' is withdrawn, while the rise in the price of good X continues, the consumer will buy a combination to the left of R on the price-income line AS, say at point L where he buys OM of X. This conclusion will hold good only if the income-elasticity of demand for X is positive. Since the Fundamental Theorem is based on the assumption of positive income elasticity of demand, no theoretical difficulty is involved here. This second stage can be legitimately compared to the 'income-effect' in the Hicks-Allen theory.

The Fundamental Theorem can also be established when the price of good X declines. In this case the new price-income line AS shifts to the right of the original price-income line AB and KT is drawn parallel but to its left as shown in Fig. 7.2(b). After the decline in the price of X, the consumer chooses a combination below R in the triangle RBT. When he buys more of X in the new situation, the Fundamental Theorem is again established that positive income elasticity means negative price elasticity of demand.

Superiority of Revealed Preference Theory

Samuelson's revealed preference theory is considered to be superior to the alternative Marshallian utility theory and the Hicks-Allen indifference curve theory on several counts. It does not require any psychological or introspective information about the behaviour of the consumer. Instead, it provides a behaviouristic analysis based on observed consumer behaviour in the market. The behaviouristic approach is considered to be more scientific than the introspective approach. But it suffers from the handicap that it cannot go as far as the introspective approach can. To cite Majumdar, "Behaviourism certainly has great advantages of treading only on observed ground: it cannot go wrong. But whether it goes far enough is the question. It may also be claimed for the method of introspection that operationally it can get all the results which are obtained by the alternative method, and it presumes to go further, it not only states, but also explains its theorems".[4]

Samuelson's revealed preference theory avoids the much discredited 'utility maximisation' assumption involved in Marshallian utility approach and the Hicks-Allen indifference curve approach. The 'consistency' assumption employed by Samuelson in deriving his demand theorem is much less restrictive and more realistic.

The revealed preference theory also drops the assumption of continuity involved in the indifference curve analysis. Indifference curves are continuous curves on which lie all conceivable combinations, whether or not they are available in the actual market. The price line may be tangent to an indifference curve at a point that represents a combination which is not available in the actual market. Thus, the continuity assumption is not realistic. The real economic world is marked by discontinuity. Following Samuelson, Hicks in his *Revision of Demand Theory* abandons the assumption of continuity and substitutes in its place 'strong and weak ordering'.

The 'overcompensation effect' in Samuelson's Fundamental Theorem, like the Slutsky substitution effect, is more realistic as an explanation of consumer behaviour than the Hicksian substitution effect. It permits the consumer to shift to a higher price-income situation with a rise in the price of X and conversely. It is superior to Hicksian 'compensating variation'. Following Samuelson, Hicks in his *Revision of Demand Theory* abandons the principle of compensating variation and substitutes in its place the principle of 'cost-difference' which is the same thing as 'compensating variation'.

Derivation of the Demand Curve

Let us assume that the consumer has a budget line AB and choose the collection of goods denoted by the point Z on the budget line which revealed his preference for the basket of goods. Again let us consider that the price of the good X falls so that the new budget line for the consumer is AC. The following graph shows the situation of the consumer.

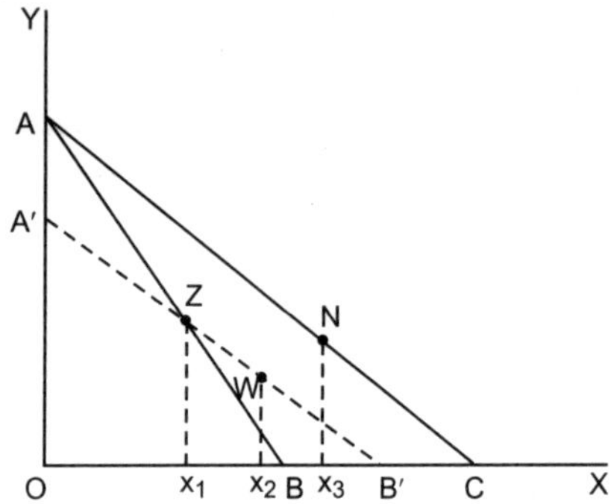

Fig. 7.3

First we consider the compensating variation of the income which consists in the reduction of income so that the consumer has just enough income to enable him to continue purchasing Z if he so wishes. The compensating variation can be shown by a parallel shift of the new budget line so that the compensated budget line A′B′ passes through Z. Since the collection Z is still available to him, he will not choose any bundle to the left of Z on the segment A′Z, because his choice would be inconsistent because all points in the segment A′Z are inferior to Z. Hence, the consumer will either continue to by Z or he would prefer to choose a bundle from ZB′ like W. Secondly, if we allow the consumer to move on the new budget line AC, he will choose a bundle such as N to the right of W. The new position N includes a larger quantity of X resulting from the fall in price of X. Thus, the revealed preference axiom and the implied consistency of choice open a direct way to the derivation of the demand curve: as price falls, more of X is purchased.

Derivation of the Indifference Curves

In Samuelson's revealed preference theory, the consumer needs not to rank his preferences or to give any other information about his tastes. By using this theory, we can construct the indifference map of the consumer, just by observing his behaviour at various market prices provided that (a) he has a consistent choice, (b) his tastes are independent of his choice over time and do not change and (c) that the consumer is rational in the Pareto sense, means he prefers more goods to less.

Let the AB be the initial budget line of the consumer and he chooses the bundle Z. All other points on the budget line and below it denote inferior bundles to Z. Let us depicts this condition of the consumer through Fig. 7.4.

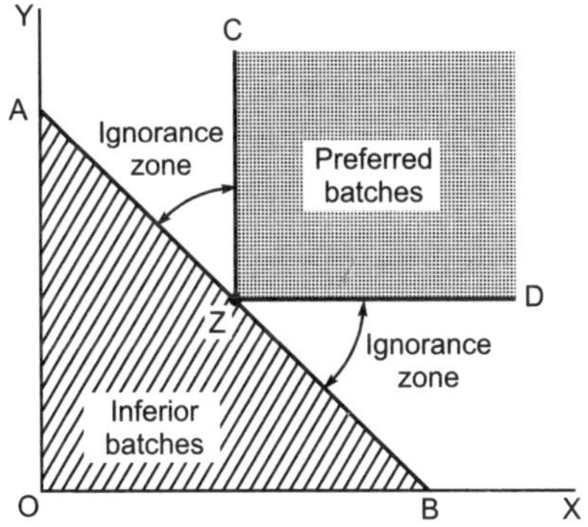

Fig. 7.4

If we draw perpendicular through Z, CZ and ZD, all the bundles on these lines, and in the area defined by them to the right of Z, are preferred to Z because they contain more quantity of at least one commodity. Bundles of the goods in the remaining area are still not ordered. But we can rank them relative to Z by using the following procedure.

Let us consider the fall in price of X. Now the new budget line EF passes below Z.

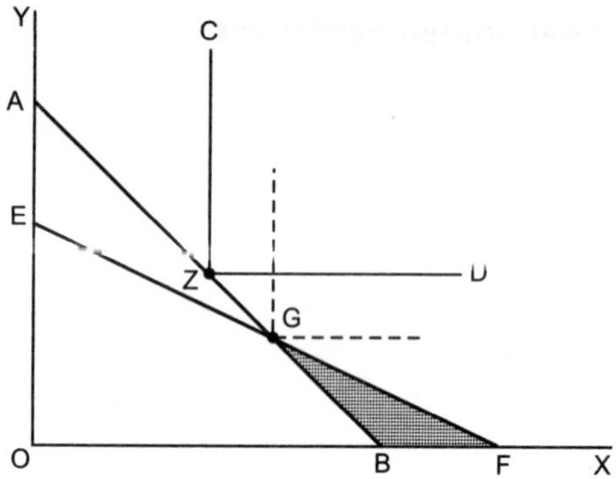

Fig. 7.5

The consumer will choose either G or a point to the right of G, since points on EG would imply inconsistent choice because it is below the original budget line and hence inferior to G. Let us assume that the consumer chooses G. Using the transitivity assumption we have

$$Z > G \quad \text{and } G > (GBF)$$

Hence $$Z > (GBF)$$

In this way, all the bundles in GBF can be ranked relative to Z. By repeating this procedure through drawing budget lines below Z we can find the lower ignorance zone that is inferior to Z. Similarly we can find upper ignorance zone. For example, let us assume that the price of X increases and the new budget line KL passes through Z. This can be shown in Fig. 7.6.

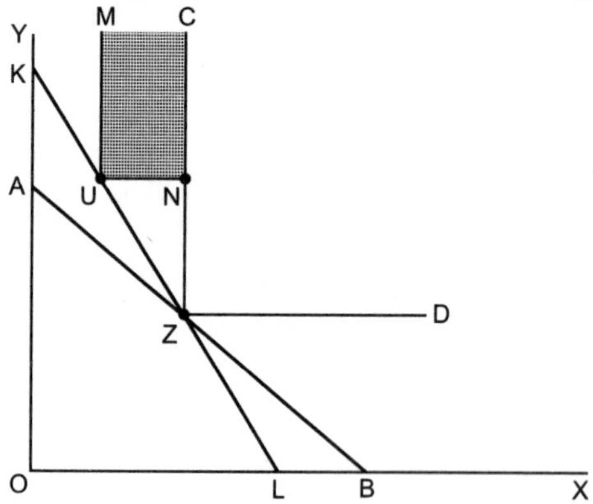

Fig. 7.6

Now the consumer will either stay at Z or choose a point such as U on KL. Using the rationality assumption we find

$$(MUN) > U$$

From the revealed preference principal

$$U > Z$$

And from the transitivity postulate

$$(MUN) > Z$$

In this way we can rank the bundles in MUN as preferred to Z. Thus, by repeating this procedure we may gradually narrow down the ignorance zone until we locate the indifference curve within as narrow a range as we wish. Hence, the revealed preference axiom permits us to derive the indifference curve from the behaviour of the consumer in various market situations.

We can also prove the convexity of the indifference curve graphically. Let us consider Fig. 7.7.

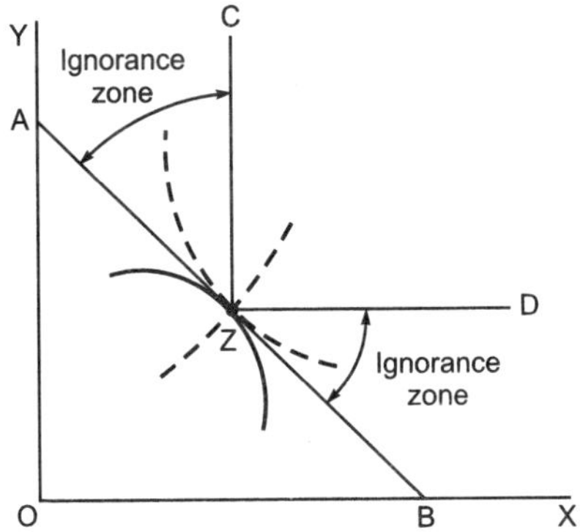

Fig. 7.7

From Fig. 7.7, we observe that the indifference curve through Z must be somewhere in the ignorance zone and must be convex, because it cannot have any other shape. The indifference curve cannot be the straight line AB because the choice of Z shows that all the other points on AB are inferior to Z. It cannot be a curve or line cutting AB at Z, because the point below Z would imply indifference of the consumer, while he has already revealed his preference for Z. Finally, the indifference curve cannot be concave through Z, because all its points have already been ranked as inferior to Z. Hence, the only possible shape of the indifference curve is to be *convex to the origin*.

Criticism of Revealed Preference Theory

Samuelson's revealed preference theory, though an improvement over utilitarian analysis and indifference curve analysis, is not without flaws. In the first place, it does not take into consideration the possibility of indifference in consumer behaviour, which is contrary to common experience. The possibility of indifference is ruled out because of Samuelson's strong ordering hypothesis and because according to him preference is to be revealed by a single act of choice. But if the consumer's preference is to be judged from a large number of observations, there would arise the possibility of indifference.

If it is assumed that an individual is able to compare his ends, which is quite a realistic assumption about an individual's behaviour, there arises the possibility of indifference, or in other words, remaining at the same level of satisfaction by giving up some quantity of a commodity for a certain quantity of another commodity. Evaluating Samuelson's revealed preference theory from the point of view of welfare, Tapas Majumdar states, "It may be remembered that in all forms of welfare theory, indeed in any integral view of human activity, we have to assume that the individual can always compare his ends. If this axiom is not granted, the whole of welfare economics falls to the ground. And if this axiom is granted, then the idea of remaining on the same level of welfare while sacrificing something of one commodity for something else of another will emerge automatically."

Armstrong is of the opinion that there are points of indifference on every side of a given chosen point. The combination actually chosen by the consumer may be one of the few between which the consumer is indifferent. If this possibility is accepted, the proof which Samuelson's theory offers to establish the Fundamental Theorem of consumption theory breaks down. This is illustrated with the help of Fig. 7.8.

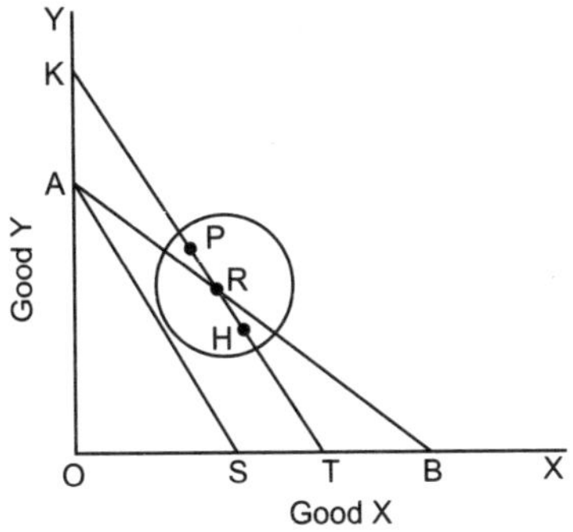

Fig. 7.8

Let us assume that (i) AB is the original price-income line, (ii) in this price-income situation the consumer actually chooses combination R, (iii) AS is the new price-income line after rise in the price of good X, and (iv) AK is the gift of money income to enable the consumer to continue buying combination R if he so chooses. Let us now suppose that the consumer is indifferent between combinations lying in the encircled area. Now in the price-income situation KT, the consumer can choose a point like H below R on RT. The choice of S instead of R, or P or any other point in the circle is not inconsistent with his previous choice because he is indifferent between points R, H, P, etc. But the choice of combination H in price-income situation KT means that the consumer buys a larger quantity of good X now when its price has risen (as KT is parallel to AS, it indicates a higher price of X as indicated by AS). Thus, if Armstrong's view of points of indifference around the chosen point is conceded, Samuelson's Fundamental Theorem breaks down.

Secondly, according to Prof. Hicks, since the revealed preference hypothesis is based on strong ordering, it is not possible to assume that "all the geometrical points which lie within or on the triangle (OAB in Fig. 7.8) represent effective alternatives. A two-dimensional continuum cannot be strongly ordered. We have therefore no alternative but to assume that the commodities are only available in discrete units, so that the diagram is to be thought of as being drawn on squared paper and the only effective alternatives are the points at the corners of the squares. The point R itself must evidently lie at a square corner".

Thirdly, since Samuelson's theory argues deductively from positive income elasticity to negative price elasticity, it can take into consideration only the income-effect resulting from a certain change in price. As the response of an individual to a change in price is a composite of income and substitution effects, it follows that Samuelson's theory provides only a partial explanation a change in demand as a result of a change in price. From the empirical point of view, however, the neglect of substitution effect can be justified on the ground that on the plane of observation, it is not possible to distinguish between income and substitution effects.

Fourthly, Samuelson's Fundamental Theorem is conditional and not universal. It is based on the postulate that the positive income elasticities imply negative price elasticities. It cannot establish the demand thereom when the income elasticity is negative. Samuelson is able to establish the demand theorem in the case in which, in terms of Hicksian indifference curve analysis, substitution effect is fortified by positive income-effect of the price change. When the income elasticity of demand is negative, Samuelson's revealed preference theory does not enable us to know the direction of change in demand as a result of a change in price. From this it follows that the 'Giffen Paradox', so much fussed about in the study of demand, cannot be accounted for in Samuelson's theory. The 'Giffen Paradox' arises when the income-effect is negative and this negative income-effect is so strong that it outweighs the substitution effect. For Giffen goods, the demand varies directly with price. Since Samuelson's theorem is based on the assumption of positive income elasticity, it cannot include the Giffen case. According to Samuelson, the only valid theorem in the demand theory is one which establishes an inverse relation between income and price elasticity. In regard to Giffen Paradox, the position taken by Samuelson is as follows: "But the phenomenon of Giffen's Paradox reminds us that the Marshallian proposition is not a true theorem, and it is rather to a theory's credit than discredit if it refuses to enunciate a false theorem".[5] It may, however, be pointed out that though there may not exist many Giffen goods in the real world, but the possibility of their existence cannot be ruled out altogether. Samuelson's Fundamental Theorem is, therefore, is less inclusive than the Hicks-Allen law of demand which provides an integrated explanation of 'income' and 'substitution' effects as well as Giffen's Paradox.

Lastly, the revealed preference theory is applicable only to an individual consumer. With the help of this theory we can draw a negatively inclined demand curve for each consumer, assuming that other things remain unchanged. But the theory does not enable us to draw the market demand curve. A decline in the price of X in the market is likely to affect the prices of other goods and thereby alter the distribution of real income in the community. The Hicks-Allen approach has the advantage over the revealed preference theory that it can derive both the individual and market demand curves from the price consumption curves.

In view of the weaknesses of Samuelson's revealed preference analysis mentioned above, it is doubtful if this approach is superior to the Hicks-Allen indifference curve approach. Some economists are, however, of the view that certain welfare propositions can be better expressed in terms of observable consumer behaviour and to this extent Samuelson's approach has rendered valuable service to the welfare economics.

NOTES

1. H.K. Manmohan Singh, *Demand Theory and Economic Calculation in a Mixed Economy* (London, 1963), pp. 64-76.
2. Tapas Majumdar, *Measurement of Utility*.
3. P.A. Samuelson, "Consumption Theorems in Terms of Overcompensation...", *Economica*, February, 1953, p. 1.
4. Tapas Majumdar, *op. cit.*
5. P.A. Samuelson, *op. cit.*, p. 2.

Elasticity of Demand

8

The concept of the elasticity of demand, though generally associated with the name of Alfred Marshall who did much to develop it, was formulated much earlier by economists like Cournot and Mill. The term elasticity refers to the degree of responsiveness of demand to variations in the price of a commodity. It is the rate at which quantity demanded varies in response to a change in price. According to Marshall, "the elasticity (or responsiveness) of demand in a market is great or small according as the amount demanded increases much or little for a given fall in price, and diminishes much or little for a given rise in price".[1] A more precise definition is given by Mrs. Joan Robinson, "the elasticity of demand, at any price or at any output, is the proportional change of amount purchased in response to a small change in price, divided by the proportional change of price".[2]

We have seen earlier that the demand is influenced not only by changes in price but also by changes in a number of other factors like the prices of related goods, incomes of the consumers, their tastes and habits, etc. In other words, the demand for a commodity is a function of its price, the prices of related goods, incomes of the consumers, their tastes and habits, fashion, etc. Whenever there occurs a change in any one or more of these factors, the amount demanded of the commodity would change. If factors other than the price of the commodity concerned are assumed to remain unchanged, the quantity demanded of the commodity would be directly related to its price. Marshall used the concept of elasticity only with reference to changes in price. His concept of elasticity is known as *price elasticity*. In addition to this, today, we have several other concepts like *income elasticity*, *cross elasticity*, *substitution elasticity*, etc.

Price Elasticity of Demand

The price elasticity of demand is defined as the relative responsiveness of quantity demanded to changes in price. More precisely speaking, it is the ratio of proportionate change in the quantity demanded of a commodity to a given proportionate change in its price. In regard to the degree of responsiveness of demand to price, the price elasticity has been divided into five types which are briefly described below:

(i) *Perfectly Elastic Demand*: It refers to the situation where an infinitesimal rise in price causes the amount demanded to fall to zero and an infinitesimal decline in price leads to an infinite increase in quantity demanded. This represents a case of infinite elasticity of demand. Such cases, however, are normally not found in actual practice and are, therefore, of hardly any practical value.

(ii) *Perfectly Inelastic Demand*: The demand is said to be perfectly inelastic when the amount demanded of a commodity does not vary at all even when its price is raised or lowered substantially. This represents a case of zero elasticity of demand. Such cases again are exceptionally rare in actual practice, and are, therefore, not of much practical value.

(iii) *Relatively Elastic Demand*: It refers to a situation where a given proportionate decline in the price of a good causes a relatively larger proportionate increase in the quantity demanded and conversely. This represents a case of more than unity elasticity.

(iv) *Relatively Inelastic Demand*: It refers to a situation where a given proportionate decline in price of a commodity causes a relatively smaller proportionate increase in the quantity demanded and conversely. This represents a case of less than unity elasticity.

(v) *Unitary Elastic Demand*: It refers to a situation where a given decline or rise in the price of a commodity causes equi-proportionate increase or decrease in the quantity demanded. It represents a case of unity elasticity.

Normally, a demand curve does not have the same elasticity throughout its length.[3] The degree of elasticity varies from point to point on the same curve. It would, therefore, be more appropriate to talk of elasticity.

Measurement of Elasticity

There are three main methods of measuring elasticity of demand, viz. (i) Total Outlay Method, (ii) Point Method, and (iii) Arc Method. We briefly describe these methods below one by one.

Total Outlay Method: One of the methods suggested by Marshall for measuring the price elasticity of demand is to consider the change in the price of a commodity and the resultant change in the total amount of money spent on it. If, after the change in price, the total amount of money spent (or total outlay) remains unchanged, the elasticity of demand is said to be unity. If with a rise in price, the total outlay declines, the elasticity of demand is said to be more than unity. This is because the increase in price has caused the amount demanded to decline to such an extent that, in spite of the higher price being paid per unit, the total outlay declines. The elasticity of demand is less than unity if with the rise in price, the total outlay also rises. This is because the rise in price causes so small a decline in the amount demanded that, in spite of a smaller amount being purchased, the total outlay increases. To sum up, If, after a change in price, the total outlay remains unchanged, the elasticity of demand is equal to unity. In case the price and total outlay move in opposite directions, the elasticity of demand is more than unity. If they move in the same direction, elasticity is less than one.

The major weakness of this method is that with it we can not obtain a precise numerical measure of the elasticity. It only classifies elasticity into three types, viz. (i) unity, (ii) more than unity, and (iii) less than unity.

Point Method: This method enables us to find the precise degree of elasticity when the change in price and that in quantity are extremely small. Let us derive the algebric formula for this measure of elasticity. We have already defined the elasticity (E) as below:

$$E = \frac{\text{Proportionate Change in Quantity Demanded}}{\text{Proportionate Change in Price}}$$

If q is the original quantity and q_1 the changed quantity, the proportionate change in quantity demanded = $\frac{q_1 - q}{q}$.

Similarly, if p is the original price and p_1 the new price, the proportionate change in price = $\frac{p_1 - p}{p}$.

Then $\quad E = \frac{q_1 - q}{q} \div \frac{p_1 - p}{p}$

Let the absolute change in quantity, $q_1 - q$, be represented by Δq and the absolute change in price, $p_1 - p$, by Δp. Since a rise in price causes a decline in the amount demanded and a decline in price causes an increase in it, Δp and Δq must have opposite signs. Substituting Δq for $q_1 - q$ and Δp for $p_1 - p$ in the above measure of elasticity, we obtain

$$E = -\frac{\Delta q}{q} \div \frac{\Delta p}{p} = -\frac{\Delta q}{\Delta p} \times \frac{p}{q}$$

Since our main interest is in finding out the magnitude of response of amount demanded to the change in price, we normally do not bother about the sign and take into consideration only the numerical value of the elasticity. The conventional measure of elasticity, therefore, is written as:

$$E = \frac{\Delta q}{\Delta p} \times \frac{p}{q}$$

Diagrammatic Representation: The measurement of elasticity, $E = \frac{\Delta q}{\Delta p} \times \frac{p}{q}$, can be employed only if the relevant demand schedule is available. It has to be given a new form if the elasticity is to be measured on a demand curve. This is done with the help of diagram given below:

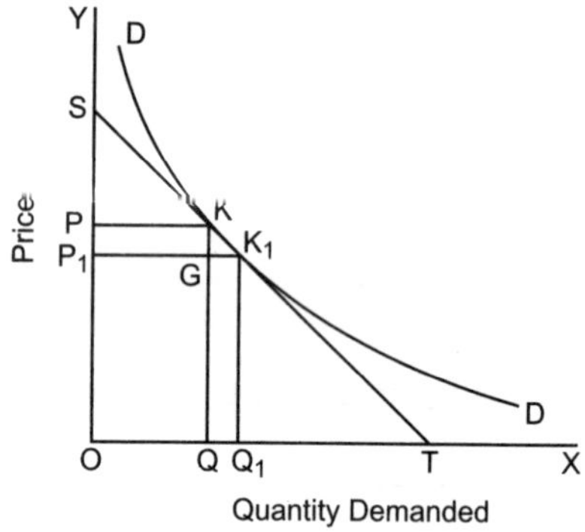

Fig. 8.1

In Fig. 8.1, the price declines from OP to OP_1 and as a result the amount demanded increases from OQ to OQ_1. The corresponding points on the demand curve are K and K_1. Let us draw a straight line through these points to cut the X-axis at T and the Y-axis at S. The change in price is represented by PP_1 and the resultant change in quantity demanded by QQ_1. Then, ignoring the sign,

$$E = \frac{OP}{OQ} \times \frac{QQ_1}{PP_1} = \frac{OP}{OQ} \times \frac{GK_1}{GK}$$

Since triangles KGK_1 and KQT are similar

$$\frac{GK_1}{GK} = \frac{QT}{KQ(=OP)}$$

Therefore, $$E = \frac{OP}{OQ_1} \times \frac{GK_1}{GK} = \frac{OP}{OQ} \times \frac{QT}{OP} = \frac{QT}{OQ}$$

But $$OQ = PK$$

$\therefore$ $$\frac{QT}{OQ} = \frac{QT}{PK}$$

Again since triangles SPK and KQT are similar

$$\frac{QT}{PK} = \frac{TK}{KS}$$

Therefore, $E = \frac{TK}{KS}$

In Fig. 8.1, points K and K_1 are far part from each other on the demand curve. As the change in price becomes smaller and smaller, K_1 starts coming closer and closer to K. When the change in price is considered to be extremely small, K_1 will be on K and the straight line ST, which was passing through both the points, will become tangent to the demand curve at K. Two important conclusions follow from this:

(i) To measure the elasticity of demand at a point on the demand curve, we have just to draw a tangent to DD at that point, and let it meet both the axes. The portion of the tangent below the point divided by the portion above it would provide the magnitude of elasticity at that point.

(ii) In case the demand curve takes the form of a straight line, it is still simpler to measure elasticity of demand. It should just be extended both ways to meet the two axes and then the elasticity can be measured in a manner similar to the above.

It may be pointed out that even on a straight line which has a uniform slope throughout, elasticity of demand will be different at different points. This is illustrated with the help of Fig. 8.2.

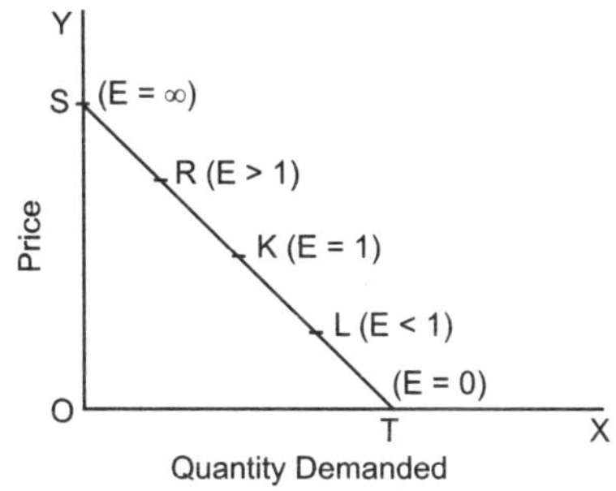

Fig. 8.2

Take a straight line demand curve ST. Consider a point K which lies precisely at the middle of this straight line ST. The distance KS will be equal to KT. The elasticity which is equal to $\frac{TK}{KS}$ would, therefore, be equal to one. Now, take another point R which lies above the middle point on the straight line demand curve ST. Evidently, distance RT is greater than the distance RS. As such the elasticity of demand at R, which is $\frac{TR}{RS}$, is more than one. Further the elasticity will go on increasing as the point R moves towards S and at point S, the elasticity would be equal to infinity. This is because as we move towards S, the lower segment goes on decreasing and the upper segment goes on increasing. At the point S the lower segment is entire TS and the upper segment becomes zero. Therefore, the elasticity at point S = TS/0 = infinity. Similarly, it can be shown that elasticity at any point which lies below the middle (say point L) would be less than one. Further, it would go on declining as we move down towards point T and it would become zero at point T. To sum up, the elasticity of demand on a straight line demand curve would be unity at the middle point, more than unity at any point above the middle point, less than unity at any point below the middle point, infinity at the point where the demand curve meets the Y-axis and zero at the point where the demand curve meets the X-axis.

The point method of measuring elasticity is very useful when there are very small changes in the price and quantity demanded of a commodity. It also helps us to understand the important fact that the elasticity of demand is different at different points on a straight line demand curve even though such a demand curve has uniform slope throughout its length.

Making use of the point method of measuring elasticity of demand, Mrs. Joan Robinson measures elasticity of demand in terms of average revenue and marginal revenue.

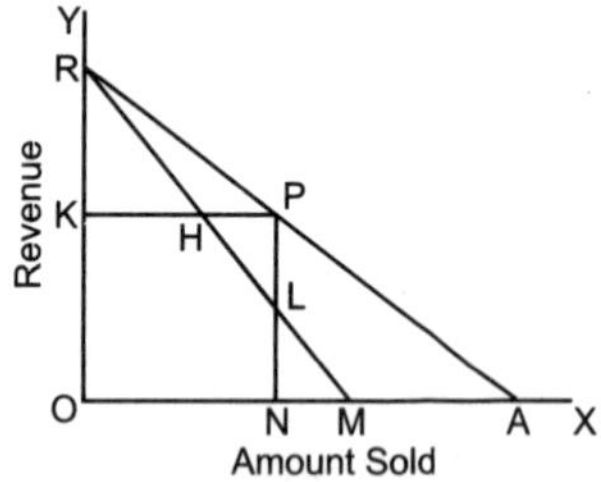

Fig. 8.3

In Fig. 8.3, AR is average revenue curve and MR the marginal revenue curve. The amount sold is ON and the elasticity of demand for this amount is

$$E = \frac{AP}{PR} = \frac{NP}{KR} \quad (\because \Delta\, KRP \text{ and } \Delta\, NPA \text{ are equiangular})$$

Since triangles KRH and HPL are congruent (i.e. equal in all respects)

$$KR = LP$$

$$\therefore \quad E = \frac{AP}{PR} = \frac{NP}{KR} = \frac{NP}{LP} = \frac{NP}{NP - NL}$$

It is evident from the figure that NP is the average revenue and NL the marginal revenue at output ON which corresponds to the point R on the average revenue curve. Therefore,

$$\text{Elasticity at R} = \frac{\text{Average Revenue}}{\text{Average Revenue} - \text{Marginal Revenue}}$$

If the elasticity of demand is represented by e, average revenue by A and marginal revenue by M, then

$$e = \frac{A}{A - M}$$

Thus, if we know the average revenue and the marginal revenue, we can easily find out the elasticity of demand. Similarly, if we know the average revenue and the elasticity of demand, we can easily find out the marginal revenue. The formula required for this is derived as:

$$e = \frac{A}{A - M}$$

$$eA - eM = A$$

$$eM = eA - A$$

$$M = A\left(\frac{e-1}{e}\right)$$

Similarly if we know the marginal revenue and the elasticity of demand, we can easily find out the average revenue. The formula required for this is derived as:

$$e = \frac{A}{A - M}$$

$$eA - eM = A$$

$$eA - A = eM$$

$$A(e - 1) = eM$$

$$A = M\left(\frac{e}{e-1}\right)$$

The above formulae, though derived in case of straight lines curves, also hold true when the curves do not take the form of straight lines.

Arc Elasticity: The concept of point elasticity that we have studied above is of considerable theoretical importance. But since demand schedule giving minute changes in price and the corresponding changes in the amount bought are not available, the concept is not of much practical value. In actual practice, the elasticity has to be measured not at a point but between two points lying at a reasonable distance from each other. What is required, therefore, is not a measure of point elasticity but of arc elasticity. For measuring the elasticity of an arc, we do not require a new formula and have only to modify the formula for measuring the elasticity at a point.

In case the change in price is significant, the magnitude of the percentage change will depend on whether it is taken in relation to the old price or the new price. If, for example, the price declines from Rs. 100 to Rs. 90 per unit, the decline will be 10 per cent in relation to the old price and 11.1 per cent in relation to the new price. This gives rise to the question as to which price should be chosen. The best way out would be to choose neither the new nor the old price but to take an average of the two prices, i.e. $\frac{p_1 + p}{2}$, and consider the absolute change as a percentage of this.

In this way the percentage change in price will be

$$\frac{p_1 - p}{\frac{p_1 + p}{2}}$$

where p_1 stands for the new price and p for the old price.

Similarly, the percentage change in the quantity bought will be

$$\frac{q_1 - q}{\frac{q_1 + q}{2}}$$

where q_1 stands for quantity bought after the change in price and q for original quantity bought.

Therefore,

$$\text{Arc Elasticity} = \frac{q_1 - q}{\frac{q_1 + q}{2}} \div \frac{p_1 - p}{\frac{p_1 + p}{2}} = \frac{q_1 - q}{q_1 + q} \div \frac{p_1 - p}{p_1 + p}$$

Arc elasticity thus is an average elasticity or elasticity at the point midway between the two points under consideration.

While the concept of arc elasticity of demand is more realistic than that of the point elasticity of demand, the former concept is not as precise as the latter one.

Slope and Elasticity

The foregoing analysis shows that the slope of the curve and elasticity are not one and the same thing. The slope of the curve, for instance, may remain constant and yet the elasticity may vary from point to point on the demand curve. In case of a straight line demand curve, while the slope is uniform, the elasticity keeps on changing throughout the length of the curve. In case of perfectly elastic and perfectly inelastic demand curves, however, the slope as well as the elasticity are similar and uniform. But these are exceptional cases and not of much practical importance. Normally the slope and elasticity are not one and the same thing. In the case of a rectangular hyperbola demand curve, while the elasticity is uniform throughout the length of the curve, its slope keeps on changing. Thus, it would be wrong to draw any inference about elasticity by simply looking at the slope of the curve.

The above, however, should not be taken to mean that the slope of the curve at the relevant point has nothing to do with the elasticity at that point. Cast a look at the elasticity formula again:

$$E = -\frac{\Delta q}{\Delta p} \times \frac{p}{q}$$

E is the product of two ratio, i.e. p/q and $\frac{\Delta q}{\Delta p}$. The latter ratio is the reciprocal of the slope of the demand curve at a particular point. But it is only one of the factors determining elasticity of demand at that point. The other is the ratio of price to quantity, $\frac{p}{q}$. In the case of a straight line demand curve, for instance, the slope of the curve (and hence its reciprocal) remains constant. But the elasticity varies from point to point because $\frac{p}{q}$ remains changing. It is only in the case of a horizontal demand curve and a vertical demand curve that the elasticity is determined by the slope alone. In case of a horizontal demand curve, as $\frac{\Delta q}{\Delta p}$ approaches infinity, the value of E also approaches infinity. In case of a vertical demand curve, on the other hand, whatever the change in price, $\frac{\Delta q}{\Delta p}$ remains zero and this reduces E to zero.

Factors Influencing Elasticity of Demand

The degree of elasticity of demand for a commodity depends on a number of factors, important of which are briefly studied below:

Extent of Necessity: Normally the demand is less elastic for necessaries and more elastic for luxuries. The reason is that necessities must be bought irrespective of their prices because we cannot keep alive without them. For instance, the people would consume more or less the same amount of foodgrains irrespective of whether the price rises or falls. In contrast, comforts and luxuries can be more easily dispensed with. The demand for such goods, therefore, would be more responsive to changes in price. More people, for instance, would go to see movies if ticket is reduced and a smaller number would go if the ticket is raised.

The above should not, however, be taken to mean that the demand for necessities is completely inelastic. In poor countries like India, even the demand for necessities is somewhat elastic. In India in 1923, the doubling of the salt duty reduced the demand for it. Similarly, a change in the price of foodgrains may not affect the demand for these of the upper and middle classes but it certainly affects that of the poor classes. Again the demand for luxuries may not always be elastic. The demand for very costly luxuries like diamonds may not be very elastic because their price is already so high that a small decline or rise in it will not matter for their buyers.

Existence of Substitutes: The more and better the substitutes for a particular good, the more elastic will be the demand for it. Goods with few and poor substitutes—salt, for example—will normally have a low price elasticity. On the other hand, goods with many and fairly good substitutes will generally have a more elastic demand. For instance, the total demand for toothpaste may be less elastic but the demand for any particular brand of toothpaste is likely to be more elastic because different brands of toothpaste provide good substitutes for each other. In this connection we may point out the influence of habit on elasticity of demand. People often become habituated to the use of certain particular brands of goods and do not like frequent shifting to other brands. As such changes in prices may not have appreciable effect on demand in the short period. But people do adjust their consumption of different goods to changes in their prices in the long run. The price elasticity of demand, therefore, is more in the long run than in the short run.

Proportion of Consumer's Income Spent on the Commodity: Demand for goods that account for a large amount of the consumer's income is likely to be more elastic than demand for goods which take only a small portion of the consumer's income. Goods like refrigerators which require a considerable amount of expenditure make consumers price-conscious and substitute-conscious. Demand for such goods, therefore, is highly responsive to changes in their prices. In contrast, the demand for goods like salt or spices, which take only a very small part of consumer's income, does not respond much to changes in their prices.

Number of Uses of Commodity: The wider the range of uses for a commodity, the more elastic is likely to be the demand for it. The larger the number of uses for a commodity the larger is the possibility of variations in demand for it in response to changes in its price. Coal provides an example of such a commodity. It can be used for a number of purposes like cooking, heating, generation of power, etc. When its price falls, it will be used for more and more purposes. On the other hand, if its price rises, it will be used only for urgent purposes and a smaller quantity will be purchased.

Postponement of Consumption: The demand for goods the consumption of which can be postponed is elastic. The consumption of furniture or refrigerator can be postponed if their prices go up but the same is not possible in case of foodgrains. The demand for furniture or refrigerator, therefore, would be more elastic than the demand for foodgrains. It may, however, be pointed out that the scope for postponement of consumption exists only in case of luxury and semi-luxury goods and not in case of necessities like foodgrains.

Range of Prices: The demand tends to be less elastic for goods which are either very expensive or very cheap. Very expensive goods are bought only by the rich people for whom a small rise or decline in price does not matter. On the other hand, if the good is very cheap, people would have already bought as much as they wanted and any decline in price will not raise their demand for it. Thus, it can be said that the demand is less elastic for very expensive and very cheap goods and more elastic for moderately priced goods. In this connection, Marshall remarks, "The elasticity of demand is great for high prices, and great, or at least considerable, for medium prices; but it declines as the price falls; and gradually fades away if the fall goes so far that satiety level is reached. This rule appears to hold with regard to nearly all commodities and with regard to the demand of every class...."[4]

Time Element: Demand is more elastic in the long-period than in the short-period. Demand takes time to respond to a change in price. As already stated above, the consumers take time to change their habits. It also takes time for the consumers to be aware of a change in price. In case where a product is used in conjunction with some more durable product, the response of demand to change in price will depend on the adjustment of the stock of the more durable complementary product. For instance, if the price of electricity declines, demand for it will not increase till the consumers are in a position to buy electric appliances like electric stove, iron, refrigerator, radio, etc. The consumer may not find it worthwhile to purchase an electric stove till the oil stove which he already possess wears out.

Level of Incomes: The demand of the poor people is more sensitive than that of the rich to changes in prices. To derive maximum satisfaction out of their meagre incomes, the poor people have to be very alert to adjust their purchases to changes in prices. The rich people, in contrast, do not bother much about small changes in prices and continue buying the same quantities. The poor people have to be on the lookout for cheaper substitutes while the rich people do not feel such need.

Income Elasticity of Demand

Income elasticity of demand shows the change in demand in response to a change in consumer's income, price of the commodity concerned and the prices of related goods remaining unchanged. In other words, it shows the responsiveness of consumer's demand for a particular good to a change in his income. It may be defined as the ratio of proportionate change in the quantity demanded of the commodity concerned to a given proportionate change in income of the consumer. The algebraic formula for measuring income elasticity of demand can be obtained from the arc elasticity formula, replacing the price data by income data.

$$E_y = \frac{q_1 - q}{q_1 + q} \div \frac{y_1 - y}{y + y_1}$$

where E_y stands for income elasticity of demand, q_1 and q for quantities after the change in income and before the change in income respectively, and y_1 and y for the new and old incomes respectively. We assume here that the prices of all goods remain unchanged and that the change occurs only in consumer's money income. We have already seen that income effect is positive for all normal or superior goods and as such income elasticity of demand is positive. In other words, the change in consumer's money income and the resultant change in his expenditure on any particular commodity are normally in the same direction. Income elasticity of demand, therefore, is normally positive, though it can also be zero or negative.

Similar to the five types of price elasticity of demand, we can distinguish between five types of income elasticity of demand.

(i) *Zero Income Elasticity of Demand*: This refers to the situation where a given increase in consumer's money income does not lead to any increase in the quantity demanded of the commodity. In other words, the expenditure on the commodity remains unchanged in spite of an increase in the consumer's income.

(ii) *Negative Income Elasticity of Demand*: This refers to the situation where a given increase in consumer's money income results in an actual decline in the quantity demanded of the commodity. In other words, the expenditure on the commodity declines in spite of an increase in the consumer's income. This, as we have seen earlier, generally happens in case of inferior goods.

(iii) *Unitary Income Elasticity of Demand*: This refers to the situation where the proportion of consumer's income spent on the commodity concerned is exactly the same before as well as after the change in his income.

(iv) *Income Elasticity of Demand Greater than Unity*: This refers to the situation where the consumer spends a greater proportion of his money income on the commodity concerned with an increase in his income. This is the case generally with luxuries and comforts.

(v) *Income Elasticity of Demand Less than Unity*: This refers to the situation where the proportion of consumer's money income spent on the commodity concerned declines with an increase in his income. This is the case generally with the necessities, expenditure on which increases in a smaller proportion with the increase in consumer's income.

Income Sensitivity

The concept of income sensitivity refers to the proportionate change in expenditure on a particular commodity in relation to the proportionate change in income. The difference between the income elasticity and the income sensitivity is that while the former establishes a relation between the relative change in physical units of the commodity concerned and the relative change in the consumer's income, the latter establishes a relation between the relative change in money expenditure on the commodity concerned and the relative change in consumer's income. Income sensitivity can be measured by the formula given below:

$$S_y = \frac{\text{Proportionate Change in Expenditure on Good X}}{\text{Proportionate Change in Income}}$$

It may be mentioned that in actual practice it is very difficult to measure the co-efficient of income sensitivity because it is almost impossible to separate the effects of changes in income from those of changes in prices and tastes.

Income Elasticity of Demand and Propensity to Consume

The income elasticity of demand can be expressed in terms of the average and marginal propensities to consume. As already stated above, income elasticity of demand can be defined as the ratio of proportionate change in consumption expenditure to proportionate change in income, the formula being:

$$E_y = \frac{\text{Proportionate Change in Consumption Expenditure}}{\text{Proportionate Change in Income}}$$

Algebraically it can be expressed as.

$$E_y = \frac{\Delta C}{C} \div \frac{\Delta Y}{Y} = \frac{\Delta C}{\Delta Y} \times \frac{Y}{C}$$

where C and Y stand for original consumption and original income respectively and ΔC and Δy for change in consumption and income respectively. Now $\frac{\Delta C}{C}$, which is the ratio of incremental consumption expenditure to incremental income, is simply the marginal propensity to consume (MPC) and $\frac{Y}{C}$, which is the ratio of total income to total consumption expenditure, is simply the inverse of average propensity to consume $\left(\text{i.e. } \frac{1}{APC}\right)$. Income elasticity of demand can, therefore, be expressed as the ratio of marginal propensity to consume to the average propensity to consume, the formula being,

$$E_y = \frac{MPC}{APC}$$

Cross Elasticity of Demand

Cross elasticity of demand measures the extent of relationship between different commodities. The relationship between two commodities, say X and Y, can be either substitutive or complementary or of neutrality. In other words, the two goods can either be substitutes of each other, or complementary to each other, or completely independent of each other. The cross elasticity of X with respect to Y equals the proportionate change in quantity of X bought divided by the proportionate change in the price of Y. The formula for the measurement of cross elasticity of demand is as follows:

$$\text{Cross Elasticity of Demand} = \frac{\text{Proportionate Change in Quantity Demanded of X}}{\text{Proportionate Change in Price of Y}}$$

In algebraic terms, the formula can be written as:

$$E_c = \frac{\Delta q_x / q_x}{\Delta p_y / p_y} = \frac{\Delta q_x}{\Delta p_y} \times \frac{p_y}{q_x}$$

The cross elasticity would be negative if the two goods are complementary to each other. Take, for instance, the case of demand for hockey sticks and balls. A decline in the price of hockey sticks would expand the demand for them which would in turn increase the demand for balls. The change in the price of hockey sticks is accompanied by a change in the demand for balls in the opposite direction. The cross elasticity of demand will, therefore, be negative. Cross elasticity is negative in case of jointly-demanded goods.

The cross elasticity of demand, on the other hand, would be positive if the two goods are substitutes for each other. Take, for instance, the case of tea and coffee. An increase in the price of coffee would make people consume more tea. The change in the price of coffee is accompanied by a change in the demand for tea in the same direction and hence, the cross elasticity of demand is positive. If the two goods, say X and Y, are perfect substitutes for each other, the cross elasticity of demand will be infinity. It means that a small change in the price of X would be accompanied by a very large change in the demand for Y and conversely. On the other hand, if the two goods cannot be substituted for each other at all, the cross elasticity will be zero. It means that change in the price of one will not affect the quantity demanded of the other. The higher would be the cross elasticity of demand, the greater is the degree of substitutability between the two goods. The cross elasticity of demand would be infinity if the two goods are perfect substitutes for each other.

Thus, the cross elasticity of demand can be positive, zero, and negative. It is positive when the two goods are substitute of each other. It is zero when there exists no relation between the two goods, or in other words, when the goods are neither substitutive nor complementary. It is negative when the two goods are complementary to each other.

The concept of cross elasticity of demand has often been employed to define the boundaries of an industry. Its use in this respect, however, leads to certain complications. High cross elasticities indicate close relationships or goods belonging to the same industry. Low cross elasticities indicate remote relationships or goods belonging to different industries. A commodity whose cross elasticity is low with respect to all other commodities is sometimes considered to be in an industry by itself. A group of commodities with high cross elasticities within the group but low cross elasticities with respect to other commodities is often said to constitute an industry. Different types of men's shoes will have high cross elasticities among each other, but low cross elasticities with other articles of men's clothing. Thus, we have a basis for separating out a men's shoe industry.

An important difficulty in employing cross elasticity as a method of determining industry boundaries is that of deciding how high must cross elasticities among commodities be if they are to be put in the same industry. Cross elasticities among some foods are quite high, e.g. between frozen peas and frozen green beans. On the other hand, cross elasticities among some foods are quite low, e.g. frozen vegetables and frozen meat. Can we then talk of a frozen food industry? There can be no unequivocal answer to this question. Some wider economic problems can best be tackled by considering all frozen foods in the same industry. More specific economic problems would require a more narrow industry groupings—a frozen vegetable industry or probably even a frozen peas industry. Cross elasticities thus provide only a guide and not a hard and fast rule for determining the boundaries of an industry.

Another problem relates to the chains of cross relationships. Cross elasticities may be high between passenger cars and station wagons, and between station wagons and pick-up trucks but may be low between passenger cars and pick-up trucks. Should we consider passenger cars and pick-up trucks in the same industry or in separate industries? Again the type of problem we want to solve would provide a guideline to the proper definition of industry boundaries.

NOTES

1. Alfred Marshall, *Principles* (8th ed.), p. 86.
2. Joan Robinson, *The Economics of Imperfect Competition* (1945), p. 18.
3. An exceptional case is of a rectangular hyperbola demand curve which has a unitary elasticity throughout its length. This type of demand curve never meets the two axes and the product of the vertical and horizontal distances from all points on the demand curve to the axes is constant. The other exceptional cases are of perfectly elastic and perfectly inelastic demand curves. But these three types of exceptional cases are rarely found in actual practice.
4. Alfred Marshall, *op. cit.*, p. 87.

Hicks' Revision of Demand Theory

9

In his book *A Revision of Demand Theory*, Hicks presents a revised version of his demand theory earlier presented in the first three chapters of this famous book *Value and Capital* published in 1939. The new version goes deeper into the 'foundations' and is very patient in its 'elaborations'.[1] The major reasons which impelled Hicks to undertake this revision include emergence of Samuelson's revealed preference theory, certain developments in the mathematical theory of 'strong' and 'weak' ordering, the discovery of a more closely reasoned derivation of the law of demand from a few simple propositions of logic, and realisation of some mistakes in his earlier analysis of consumer's surplus and complementarity.

In his revision of demand theory, Professor Hicks stresses the econometric approach to the demand theory. According to him, the demand theory which is useful for econometric purposes is certainly superior to the one that cannot serve econometric purposes. "For whatever we may think of the results that the econometrists have attained, there can be no doubt that econometrics is now a major form of economic research; a theory which can be used by econometrists is to that extent a better theory than one which cannot."[2] Though a beginning in this direction was made in his book *Value and Capital* but yet the demand theory presented in that book had a serious defect that the econometric reference was not made more explicit. According to Hicks, in Samuelson's revealed preference theory, reference to econometrics is made explicit. But Hicks was not satisfied with the extent upto which

Samuelson went in this direction and, therefore, wanted to go beyond this. "In Samuelson the whole form of the theory is allowed to be dictated by the reference to econometrics. Great and beautiful simplifications follow. But I am not convinced that even in Samuelson the econometric reference is quite as it should be, so that the present work, deeply influenced by Samuelson as it is, will not follow him at all exactly. In technique we shall keep quite close to him, but our methodology will be more explicitly econometric even than this."[3]

Hicks rejects cardinal utility analysis at the very outset. "...the special properties of a cardinal index are irrelevant to the econometric theory of consumers' behaviour. Concepts derived from these properties contain an element which is incapable of being used for the analysis of the market data with which the econometrist is concerned. A theory which is to provide the econometrist with tools which he can use, which is to ask questions which he is to have some hope of being able to answer, must, if it is based upon cardinal utility, extrude these cardinal properties before it reaches its conclusions. There would accordingly appear to be some presumption in favour of setting them on one side from the start."[4] Hicks rejects the cardinal hypotheses that the utilities of different commodities are independent of each other and that the marginal utility of money remains unchanged. He is of the view that in more elementary parts of the theory the assumption of cardinal utility neither helps nor hinders but, "in the more difficult branches cardinal utility becomes a nuisance".[5] If one rejects, as one probably is compelled to by rather simple reflection, the hypothesis of independent utilities, and if one admits the usefulness and possibility of dividing the effects of price changes into those of substitution and changes in income, one has in effect eliminated cardinalism from the argument.

Hicks also gives up use of indifference curves because this geometrical method involves several disadvantages. "In the first place, geometry is fully effective as a means of demonstration only in quite simple cases, especially those in which the choice concerns quantities of two commodities only.

As soon as we want to generalise, we have to fall back upon rather elaborate mathematics, which often tends to conceal the economic point of what is being done."[6] "Another disadvantage of the geometrical method is that it forces us, at the start, to make assumptions of continuity, a property which the geometrical field does have, but which the economic in general does not."[7] Neither of these disadvantages, however, provide enough justification for Hicks to give up indifference curves method which he believes has its own merits and which economists have become accustomed to use. The consideration which makes Hicks in favour of preference hypothesis method is "its greater effectiveness in clarifying the nature of the preference hypothesis itself. The demand theory, which is based upon the preference hypothesis, turns out to be nothing else but an economic application of the logical theory of ordering; if we begin from the logic of ordering itself, instead of starting from the geometrical application of it, we begin by getting to our credit a number of distinctions, which will be of much use to us, and will save us from falling into some notorious pitfalls, later on".[8]

After rejecting the utilitarian and indifference curve approaches, Hicks develops an empirical approach to the theory of demand. The econometrist, who wants to study demand, has at his disposal some factual data, generally in the form of a time-series, showing the quantities of some commodity (commodities) bought by a particular group of people during certain specified periods of time. The quantities bought are affected by a number of factors. In the first place, there are non-price factors like changes in population, age-distribution of population, social habits on account of developments in housing and education, and so on. Such factors, though not unimportant, are less susceptible to economic analysis. The second category of factors consists of price-explanations or explanations in terms of prices. This includes both price (and prices) of the commodity (or commodities) under consideration and the prices of other commodities—as well as the incomes of consumers. In regard to the prices to be taken into consideration, Hicks restricts himself to current prices, i.e. prices ruling during the same period as that in which the commodities are bought. The third category includes explanations in terms of deferred or lagged effects of price changes, which are particularly important in case of durable goods. Hicks, though fully aware of the importance of factors falling in the first and third categories, confines himself to the factors included in the second category. The task before the econometrist is to estimate the effects on empirical demand data which are owing to change in current prices and incomes. But to make such estimates, the econometrist needs a technique for separating out the current price-effects from the others. "The econometric purpose of the theory of demand is to give assistance in making this separation."[9] The theory which is required for this purpose is one which will tell us something about the ways in which consumers are likely to react if changes in current prices and incomes were the only causes of changes in consumption. Such a demand theory proceeds by assuming an *ideal consumer* who by definition is affected only by current market conditions and asks how he should be expected to behave.

In order to obtain an answer to this question, some assumption has to be made about the principles governing consumer's behaviour. "The assumption of behaviour according to a scale of preferences comes in here as the simplest hypothesis, not necessarily the only possible hypothesis, but the one which, initially at least, seems to be the most sensible hypothesis to try. Its status is identically the same as that of well-known class of hypotheses in natural sciences, hypotheses which cannot be tested directly, but which can be used for the arrangement of empirical data in meaningful ways, and which are accepted or rejected according to their success or failure as instruments of arrangement.... Until we have alternative that is equally usable, the Preference Hypothesis has to be (provisionally) accepted."[10]

Professor Hicks explains action according to a scale of preferences as follows. "The *ideal consumer* (who is not affected by anything else than current market conditions) chooses that alternative, out of the various alternatives open to him, which he most prefers, or ranks most highly. In one set of market conditions he makes one choice, in others other choices; but the choices he makes always express the same ordering, and must therefore be consistent with one another. This is the hypothesis made about the behaviour of the ideal consumer."[11]

It may be mentioned here that the demand theory presented by Hicks in his book *Value and Capital* was also based on preference hypothesis but there the given scale of preferences was expressed in the form of a set of indifference curves. In his book, *A Revision of Demand Theory*, as already seen, Hicks gives up the technique of indifference curves because of the several disadvantages involved in it and begins from the logic of ordering itself rather than starting from the geometrical application of it.

Hicks draws a distinction between 'strong ordering' and 'weak ordering' and then bases his demand theory on weak ordering preference hypothesis. A set of items is strongly ordered if "...it is such that each item has a place of its own in the order; it could, in principle, be given a number, and to each number there would be one item, and only one item, which would correspond".[12] In contrast, a set of items is weakly ordered if the items are clustered into groups but none of the items within a group can be put ahead of others. "A weak ordering consists of a division into groups, in which sequence of groups is strongly ordered, but in which there is no ordering within the groups."[13]

The indifference curve approach is based on weak ordering, with all the positions on the same indifference curve representing a non-ordered group. On the other hand, Samuelson's revealed preference approach is based on strong ordering in as much as the choice of a combination reveals consumer's preference for it over all other alternative combinations open to him. The concepts of strong ordering and weak ordering are illustrated in Fig. 9.1.

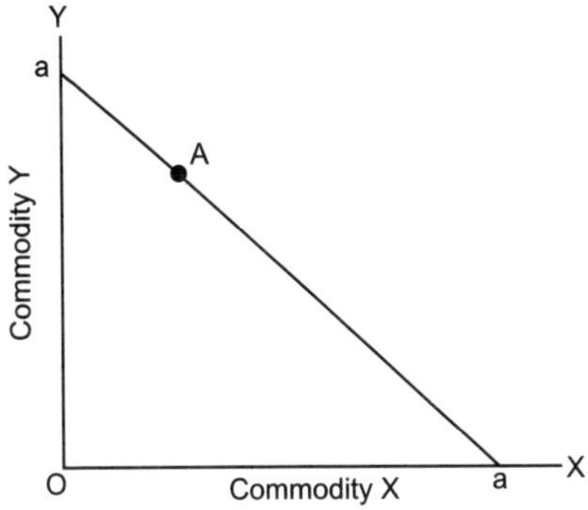

Fig. 9.1

If the consumer is confronted with the price-income situation aa, he can choose any combination that lies in or on triangle aOa. Let us suppose that the consumer chooses combination A. In case the alternative combinations open to the consumer are strongly ordered, the choice of combination A means that the consumer prefers A over all other available alternatives.

Strong Ordering

Professor Hicks criticises strong ordering. "If we interpret the preference hypothesis to mean strong ordering, we cannot assume that all the geometrical points, which lie within or on the triangle aOa, represent effective alternatives. A two-dimensional continuum of points cannot be strongly ordered. We have therefore no alternative but to assume that the commodities are only available in discrete units, so that the diagram is to be thought of as being drawn on squared paper, and the only effective alternatives are the points at the corners of the squares. The point A itself must evidently lie at a square-corner."[14] Since in the real world the commodities are usually sold in discrete units, strong ordering hypothesis does not present any difficulty. While actual commodities are available in integral number of units, the same is not true of the composite commodity money (M), which is usually measured on the Y-axis, while studying the demand for a single commodity measured along X-axis. Hicks considers money to be finely divisible. "If every one of the actual commodities into which M can be exchanged is itself only available in discrete units, then (in a sense) M is only available in discrete units; but if the number of such commodities is large, there will be a large number of ways in which a small increment of M can be consumed by rearrangement of consumption among the individual commodities, whence it will follow that the units in which M is to be taken to be available must be considered as exceedingly small. And as soon as any individual commodity becomes available in units that are finely divisible, M must be regarded as finely divisible. In practice, we should usually think of M as being money, held back for the purchase of other commodities than X; though money is not finely divisible in a mathematical sense, the smallest monetary unit (farthing or cent) is so small in relation to the other units with which we are concerned that the imperfect divisibility of money is in practice a thing of no importance. For these reasons, while it is a theoretical improvement to be able to regard the actual commodity X as available in discrete units, it is no improvement at all to be obliged to impute the same indivisibility to the composite commodity M. It is much better to regard M as finely divisible."[15]

When the choice is between any commodity which is available in discrete units and money which is finely divisible, the strong form of the preference hypothesis cannot be maintained. In such a situation the alternatives are represented not by square-corners but by a series of parallel lines or stripes as shown in Fig. 9.2.

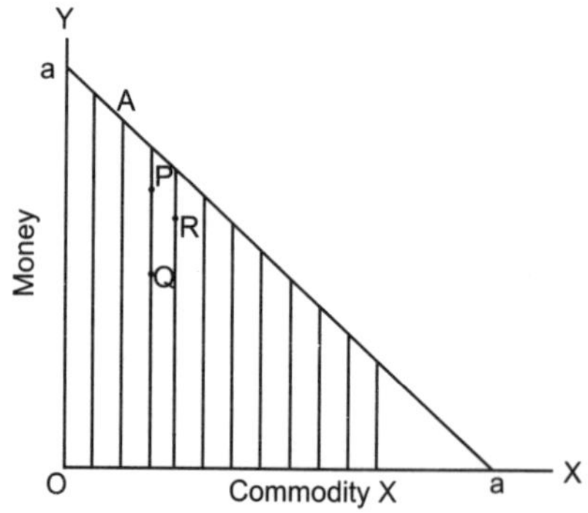

Fig. 9.2

Any point on any of these stripes represents an effective alternative. "Now such alternatives as these cannot be strongly ordered, unless the *whole* of one stripe was preferred to the *whole* of the next stripe, and so on; which means that the consumer would always prefer an additional unit of X, whatever he had to pay for it—though he would prefer a larger amount of M to a smaller, if the amount of X which he had was unchanged. This assumption is nearly nonsensical, and can be ruled out. If, on the other hand, there are two points P, Q on the same stripe, which are such that P is preferred to R on another stripe, while R is preferred to Q, we could always find a point between P and Q which was indifferent to R, so that we could not maintain strong ordering. As soon as we introduce the smallest degree of continuity (such as is introduced by the 'striped' hypothesis), strong ordering has to be given up."[16]

Weak Ordering

According to Hicks, one of the most awkward of the assumptions into which the indifference curve approach appears to be impelled by its geometrical analogy is that "the consumer is capable of ordering all conceivable alternatives that might possibly be presented to him—all the positions which might be represented by points on his indifference map. This assumption is so unrealistic that it was bound to be a stumbling block."[17] In contrast, all that the revealed preference hypothesis assumes is that the consumer "can order those alternatives which he does actually have to compare in the situations under discussion—or, at the most, those which we might present to him, by a kind of hypothetical experiment, in the course of our argument".[18] This approach, therefore, is superior to the indifference curve approach to the extent it enables us to restrict our assumption. Though Hicks concedes this weakness of the indifference curve approach, he does not give up its use. "The older theory (indifference curve approach)[19] may have exaggerated the omnipresence of indifference; but to deny its possibility is surely to run to the other extreme. It is surely the case that actual consumers do sometimes find themselves confronted with alternatives between which they are indifferent, if the ideal consumer is made incapable of being faced with such alternatives he is being made more unlike an actual consumer than he need be. If it is asked just what he will do when he is confronted with such alternatives, the answer must surely be that he will make a decision, but he will make it on grounds that have been excluded from consideration; his choice may depend, for instance, upon what he was doing *previously*. From the standpoint of a static theory, such as ours, such decision is a matter of chance. But chance, in this sense, is not a thing which ought to be excluded. I am therefore of the opinion that demand theory, even in its new guise, ought to remain based upon weak ordering—chiefly for the reason that weak ordering is the less restrictive assumption."[20]

Thus, Hicks bases his theory of demand on weak ordering hypothesis. Under weak ordering, the choice of a particular combination A does not show or reveal that A is preferred to any rejected position within or on the choice triangle. It only shows that other possible alternative combinations within or on the choice triangle cannot be preferred to the chosen combination. It is quite possible that some of the rejected combinations may be indifferent to A. The weak ordering hypothesis, however, yields so little information about the consumer's behaviour that the basic propositions of demand theory cannot be derived from it. Hicks, therefore, feels the necessity of supplementing this hypothesis with an additional hypothesis so as to be able to derive the basic propositions of demand theory. The additional hypothesis is simply that "the consumer will always *prefer* a large amount of M to a smaller amount of M, provided that the amount of X at his disposal is unchanged."[21] It may be pointed out that this additional hypothesis would not be necessary if strong ordering form of preference hypothesis is adopted. But this additional hypothesis is quite reasonable and has often slipped into economic analysis without having been explicitly stated.

What is the effect of supplementing the weak ordering hypothesis with this additional assumption? This is shown in Fig. 9.3.

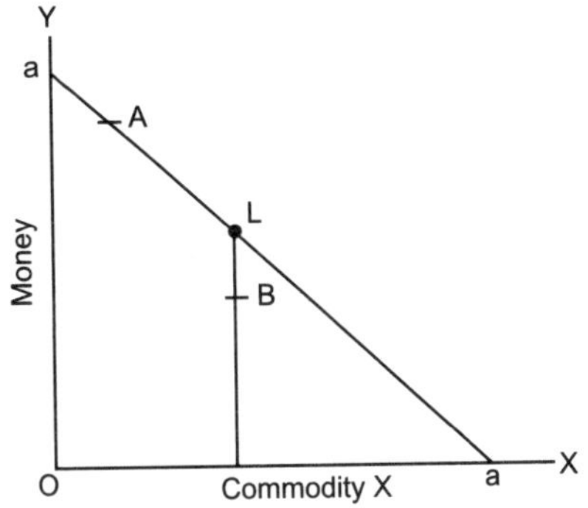

Fig. 9.3

The consumer chooses combination A from all the available combinations in and on the triangle aOa. Under weak ordering hypothesis, the choice of combination A instead of combination B, which lies within the triangle, does not in itself show that A is preferred to B. All that it tells us is that B is not preferred to A. In other words, under weak ordering, the choice of A rather than B means that either A is preferred to B, or A and B are indifferent. Now consider a point L which lies where the stripe through B meets the line aa. Under the assumptions we are making, L is a possible alternative. By the additional hypothesis made, L is preferred to B because L includes a larger amount of money than B, the quantity of X being the same in both the positions. If A and B are indifferent, it follows from the transitivity of weak ordering that L is preferred to A. But L is one of the combinations which has been rejected in favour of A. As such, though L can be indifferent to A, it cannot be preferred to A. Thus, the possibility of A and B being indifferent must be ruled out. In this way, when the weak ordering fortified by the additional hypothesis is adopted, it is possible to prove that the combination actually chosen is preferred to any other combination which lies within the choice triangle. What cannot be shown, by this reasoning, is that A is preferred over L, or in other words, that the chosen combination is preferred over another combination which also lies on the line aa. "The difference between the consequences of strong and weak ordering, so interpreted, amounts to no more than this: that under strong ordering the chosen position is shown to be preferred to all other positions *in* and *on* the triangle, while under weak ordering it is preferred to all positions *within* the triangle, but may be indifferent to other positions on the same boundary as itself."[22]

The difference between the effects of the two hypotheses is, of course, very small. It merely affects a class of limiting cases, i.e. positions lying on the triangle. The weak ordering theory has a larger tolerance and deals with the limiting cases rather better. Apart from this, we obtain a much wider benefit from a recognition of the fact that there are these two alternative approaches, and from an exact appreciation of the assumptions upon which each is based. "If we take the strong ordering approach, we are committing ourselves to discontinuity; not merely to the indivisibility of the particular commodity, demand for which is being studied, but also to indivisibility of the composite commodity used as background. If, on the other hand, we take the weak ordering approach, we are committing ourselves to some degree of continuity—but divisibility of the background commodity is itself quite sufficient to ensure that the weak approach is practicable. We have, however, also learned that the weak approach requires an additional assumption, to which there is no parallel in the strong case: we have to assume that marginal units of the background commodity are positively desired—or, as the older theory would say, that the background commodity has a positive marginal utility. We have further to assume that the preference order is transitive...."[23] Hicks believes that these assumptions are not at all hard to swallow and represent a fair price for the benefits which flow from them.

Direct Consistency Test

Following Samuelson, Hicks also assumes consistency of choice behaviour on the part of an ideal consumer whose scale of preferences remains unchanged with changes in prices of goods and his income. In deriving laws about consumer's demand, Hicks applies the consistency test which has been applied by Samuelson in his revealed preference approach. Hicks calls consistency test as the Direct Consistency Test, which is nothing else but the economic expression of the two-term consistency condition of the theory of logic of order.

Samuleson's consistency test is quite simple. But Hicks elaborates the consistency idea by considering the consisting or inconsistency involved in several alternative cases. As before, let the commodity X (with variable price) be measured along X-axis and the composite commodity M (which represents all other commodities) along the Y-axis. The price of X and the income of the consumer being given, the alternative combinations open to the consumer are represented by points in or on the triangle aOa in Fig. 9.4.

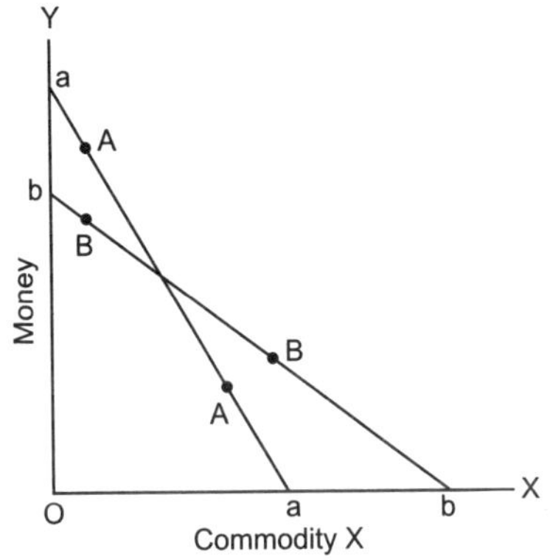

Fig. 9.4

The point A on the line aa represents the actual combination chosen by the consumer. Under preference hypothesis (in its strong ordering form), A is shown to be preferred to all other available positions in and on the triangle aOa. Under weak ordering (with the additional hypothesis which then becomes called for) all that is implied is that A is preferred to all combinations within the choice triangle and is either preferred or indifferent to other combinations on the line aa.

Now consider another market situation in which the price of X is different while the income of the consumer may or may not be different. The various alternative combinations available to the consumer in the new situation are represented by points in or on the triangle bOb. Point B on the line bb represents the combination actually chosen in the new situation. Similar type of preferences, as in situation A, will follow in situation B under strong and weak forms of preference hypothesis.

If the consumer is acting according to the same scale of preferences in both situations, the preferences shown by him in the two situations must be consistent with each other. Since the comparison is only between two situations, the only type of consistency which is relevant is two-term consistency. Transitivity cannot yet enter in. What is meant by two-term consistency under strong and weak ordering type of preference hypothesis? Under strong ordering, the consumer's behaviour will be inconsistent if he reveals his preference for combination A over combination B in situation A and for combination B over combination A in situation B, when both combinations A and B are available in both situations. Under weak ordering, the possibility of indifference has also to be taken into consideration.

The various possible cases can be classified in the following manner. In the first place, it is possible that one of the two opportunity lines lies completely outside the other; say aa lies completely outside bb. In this case, B must lie within the triangle aOa; as such, in the A situation, A is preferred to B under strong as well as under weak ordering. In the B situation, A is not an available alternative. Therefore, there is no inconsistency when the consumer chooses A in the A situation and B in the B situation.

Secondly, if one of the opportunity lines does not lie completely outside the other, the two must intersect; say aa lies outside bb on the left of the cross (so that it represents a higher income) and lies inside bb on the right of the cross. In this situation, there are four main possibilities:

(i) Both points, A and B, lie to the left of the cross. In this case, as before, under weak as well as under strong ordering, B is rejected in favour of A in the A situation; since A is not an available alternative in the B situation, there is no inconsistency when the consumer chooses A in the A situation and B in the B situation.

(ii) Both points, A and B, lie to the right of the cross. In this case, under weak as well as under strong ordering, A is rejected in favour of B in the B situation and B is not an available alternative in the A situation. In this case also, preference of B over A does not involve any inconsistency in consumer's behaviour.

(iii) The two points lie outside the cross, A to the left and B to the right of it. In this case, A is not an available alternative in the B situation and same is the case with B in A situation. Nothing, therefore, can be said, under weak as well as under strong ordering, about preference of one over the other.

(iv) The two points lie inside the cross; say B to the left and A to the right. In this case, there is inconsistency, both under strong and weak ordering because B is rejected in favour of A in the A situation and A is rejected in favour of B in the B situation.

Finally, there is a group of special cases when the two price-income lines intersect each other and one of the two points lies at the cross while the other lies either outside the cross or inside the cross. In the case in which the other point lies outside the cross, there is no inconsistency under weak as well as under strong ordering because it is not an available alternative in one of the two situations. But there arises inconsistency if the other point lies inside the cross. Let us suppose that A lies at the cross and B lies inside the cross. In this case, position B lies within the triangle aOa. The choice of A in the A situation, therefore, shows, even under weak ordering, that A is preferred to B. But in the B situation, the choice of B, under weak ordering, shows that either B is preferred to A or B is indifferent to A (A also lies on the line bb), either of which is inconsistent with definite preference for A over B. Thus, when one point lies at the cross and other lies inside the cross, there is inconsistency of choice in consumer's behaviour.

The above analysis shows that, whether we adopt weak or strong ordering hypothesis, we reach the same conclusion in all cases from the direct consistency test. On either assumption, there is inconsistency in the following two cases: (i) when both points A and B lie within the cross and (ii) when one point lies at the cross and the other inside the cross.

Though the weak and strong forms of preference hypothesis give the same result in regard to the consistency tests, it may be stressed that the arguments by which they attain the result are different. The identity of result under weak and strong ordering, therefore, will not occur when we generalise, or in other words, when we consider more commodities besides X and composite money M and permit the price of more than one commodity to vary.

Law of Demand

From the logic of weak ordering (along with the two additional assumptions) and the theory of direct consistency test based upon it, Hicks proceeds to derive all major propositions of the theory of consumer's demand. Hicks first derives the demand for a single commodity, i.e. for the behaviour of a consumer "confronted with a market in which the price of no more than one good is liable to change".[24] The primary task is to derive the law of demand, i.e. "the principle that the demand curve for a commodity is downward sloping".[25] The technique adopted by Hicks is that of dividing the effects of a price change into two parts, viz. (i) income effect and (ii) substitution effect. "The substitution effect is the effect of the change in price under consideration, combined with the effect of an appropriate change in income—which is chosen in such a manner that the effect of the combined change (the substitution effect) has definite properties that can be deduced from consistent theory. The income effect is the *remainder* of the actual change that has taken place. Since the change in prices has already been allowed for in the substitution effect, the income effect is limited to the effect of a change in income without change in prices."[26] The substitution effect can be deduced from the consistency theory. The income effect is based on empirical evidence. "It follows that in strictness the law of demand is a hybrid; it has one leg resting on theory, and one on observation. But, in this particular instance, the double support happens to be quite exceptionally strong."[27]

The real task in deriving the law of demand is to separate out the substitution effect. The substitution effect can be separated from the income effect by two methods, viz. (i) the method of compensating variation, and (ii) the method of the cost difference. We explain below the separation of the substitution effect from the income effect by means of these two methods and the derivation of the law of demand.

Derivation of Law of Demand by Method of Compensating Variation

Let us consider the demand for a commodity X which is measured along X-axis in Fig. 9.5.[28] The composite commodity M is measured along Y-axis. Given a certain price of the commodity and income of the consumer, the opportunity line (or price-income line) aa is drawn. We assume that in this initial price-income situation, the consumer chooses the combination A on aa.

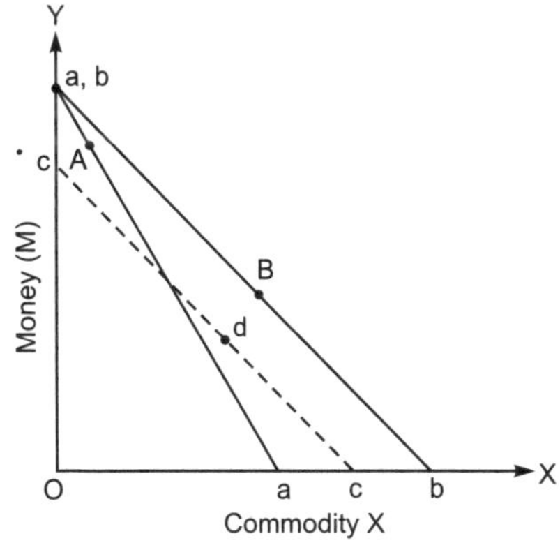

Fig. 9.5

Now suppose the price of commodity X declines, the money income of the consumer remaining unchanged. Since money income as well as the price of M remain unchanged, the quantity of M which can be obtained, if no X is bought, would remain unchanged. As such, the new opportunity-line (bb) will pass through the same point on the vertical (M) axis as aa. Since the price of X has declined, bb will otherwise lie outside aa. It follows from the consistency theory that, so long as some amount of X is being consumed in both situations, any position on line bb (say B) must be preferred to A because A lies within the triangle bOb. But this is all the consistency theory tells us when applied to these two positions. It is perfectly consistent for there to be a rise, or a decline, or no change, in the consumption of X between A and B.

It can, however, be shown, from the consistency theory, that if the decline in the price of X is accompanied by an appropriate decline in income, the consumption of X must rise or remain unchanged; it cannot decrease. Thus, it is possible to construct a position or which is (in a certain sense) intermediate between A and B, and which is such that the consumption of X must 'tend to increase'[29] between A and d; while the movement from d to B is the result of a pure change in income, which is called income effect.

Since the income is reduced between A and d, it must be increased between d and B. There is no theoretical rule to prove that an increase in income must 'tend to increase' the consumption X. But the empirical evidence tells us that this does happen barring the exceptional cases of 'inferior goods' in which income effect is negative. Barring the exceptional cases of inferior goods, it can be said definitely that a decline in the price of X (income constant) must tend to increase the demand for X through income effect and substitution effect together. In order to prove this, we have to make a suitable selection of an intermediate position. This can be done by two different methods, viz. (i) method of Compensating Variation adopted by Hicks in his book *Value and Capital* and (ii) method of Cost Difference put forward by Samuelson. Hicks believes that both the methods have their own merits and need to be preserved.

According to the first method, we construct a position d which will be taken up by the consumer when the price of X declines but his income is reduced to an extent that wipes out the gain in real income which would have accrued to the consumer from the decline in price. Income is then said to be reduced by a compensating variation; the position d, taken up at the B price but with this lower income, is indifferent to A. "This particular selection of the intermediate position d has the merit that the two parts into which the whole effect of the price-change is divided are parts that have special economic significance. For on this interpretation, the substitution effect measures the effect of the change in relative prices, with *real income constant*; the income effect measures the effect of the change in real income. Thus, the analysis which is based upon the compensating variation is a resolution of the price-change into two fundamental economic 'directions'; we shall not encounter a more fundamental distinction upon any other route."[30]

If the intermediate position can be obtained by the method of compensating variation, it is easy to show, from the consistency theory, that it has the properties that are required. Since the price of X is the same in the intermediate situation as indicated by the line bb, the opportunity line cc on which the intermediate position d lies must be parallel to bb. Since the consumer is indifferent between the positions A and d, the opportunity line cc must intersect the line aa; for if it lays wholly outside aa, d would be shown to be preferred to A; and if lays wholly inside aa, A would be shown to be preferred to d. The same reasoning shows that it is impossible for A and d to lie both to the left, or both to the right, of the cross of the lines on which they lie. Further, if they both lay within the cross, or one at the cross and other within the cross, there would occur inconsistency of choice. Thus, the only alternatives left are (i) that positions A and d both lie at the cross, (ii) that one lies at the cross and the other outside the cross, and (iii) that both lie at the cross. These are the only possible cases if A and d are to be indifferent. In any of these cases, the consumption of X either increases or remains unchanged between A and d. Thus, in all cases when X is not an inferior good, it follows that the consumption of X must increase or remain unchanged between A and B. In other words, as a consequence of substitution effect, the quantity demanded of good X whose price declines will increase or at least remain unchanged.

The substitution effect analysed above is only one part of the price effect. The other part of price effect is the income effect. Let the money income which was taken away from the consumer by the amount of compensation variation be now given back to him. Empirical evidence tells us that with the increase in income, barring the exceptional cases of inferior goods, the consumer tends to increase his consumption of commodity X.

The above analysis shows that the demand for a commodity increases with a decline in its price owing to substitution effect and income effect. This proves the fundamental law of demand.

Derivation of Law of Demand by Cost Difference Method

The method of cost difference has the advantage of being more convenient for the purpose of deriving the law of demand. Under this method, we consider the effect of a decline in the price of X, when it is accompanied by a reduction in income which is such as will leave the consumer just able to purchase the A collection of goods, if he so likes. Thus, income is reduced by the difference between the cost of his previous (i.e. A) consumption of X at the old and the new price.

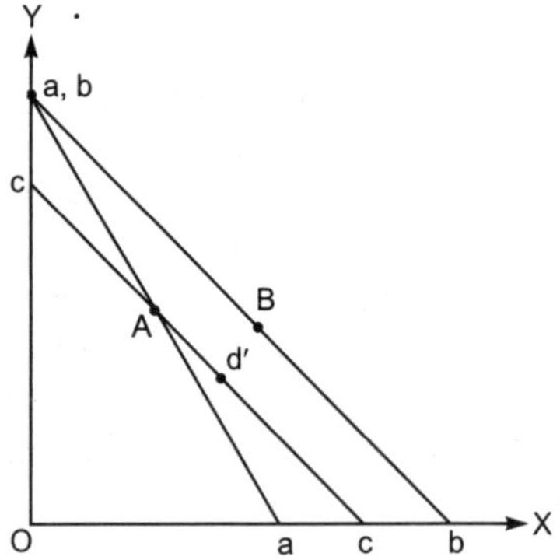

Fig. 9.6

The intermediate opportunity line cc will remain parallel to bb; but instead of passing below A (as in Fig. 9.5), it will pass, by definition, through A as shown in Fig. 9.6. The new intermediate position (d′) is that which would be chosen by a consumer, with the given wants, faced with this particular opportunity-line Ad′. It can easily be shown that d′, like d, has the properties which are required for the establishment of our proposition.

Let us compare, in the light of the consistency theory, the situations in which A and d′ are taken up. Now the two opportunity lines are aa and Ad′. Since one of the two positions (A) now lies at the cross of the two opportunity lines, the number of possible cases in which consistency tests have to be applied are much reduced. The position d′ cannot lie to the left of A because that would involve inconsistency. The only possible cases which remain are (i) that d′ lies to the right of A, and (ii) that d′ and A coincide. In case (i) the consumption of X will increase between A and d′ and in case (ii) the consumption of X will remain unchanged. Thus, as a result of substitution effect, the consumption of X must increase or remain unchanged; it cannot decline. Now, if the income taken away from the consumer is returned to him, barring the exceptional cases of inferior goods, he would further increase his consumption of X. Thus, the position B will lie to the right of d′ showing the increase the consumption of X between d′ and B as a result of the income effect.

The above shows that the choice of an intermediate position through the cost difference method provides an alternative method of dividing the effect of a price change into income effect and substitution effect. Though the intermediate positions obtained through these two methods are not exactly the same, the parts into which they break-up the price effect have more or less similar properties. "Whichever division we make, it remains true that the substitution effect of a fall in the price of X must tend to increase the consumption of X, by a necessary consequence of the preference hypothesis; and it remains true in each case that the income effect of the same price-change is the pure effect of a rise in income. The difference between the two methods is solely a matter of the magnitude of the rise in income, which leads to the income effect; and on this point the method of cost-difference has a distinct advantage. For while the magnitude of the compensating variation is quite a problem..., the magnitude of the cost difference raises no problem at all. It can be read off at once from the data of the situation under discussion."[31]

In case the consumer is initially spending only a small portion of his income on X, even a large proportional decline in the price of X will not generate a cost difference which is more than a small proportion of his income. In such a situation, unless the consumption of X is abnormally responsive to variations in income, or in other words, unless the income elasticity of demand for X is abnormally high, the income-effect of the price-change would be very small in relation to previous consumption. But the same need not necessarily be true of the substitution effect. Consider, for instance, the case where no X was being bought before the decline in its price. In this case, the cost difference and hence the income-effect would be zero. But it is quite possible that the decline in the price of X may have a large effect in inducing the consumer to substitute X for other commodities. In other words, when the income-effect is low, it is quite possible that the substitution effect may be large. Normally, in case of the demand for a single commodity of a consumer whose consumption is fairly diversified, the major effect of the price-change will be substitution effect and the income-effect would be relatively small.

Inferior Goods

It is not necessary that an increase in income should tend to increase the demand for every commodity in the consumer's budget It is quite possible that the demand for some commodities may decline with a rise in consumer's income because they are replaced by superior substitutes which the consumer could not afford to buy before the rise in his income. The simplest example of this phenomenon is where the commodity involved is of inferior quality in the physical sense. It is for this reason that commodities with negative income elasticity are often called *inferior goods*. It is, however, not necessary that the goods which are replaced with a rise in income should be inferior in the physical sense; similarly, the substitutes which replace the so-called inferior goods need not necessarily be superior goods in the physical sense. It is not even necessary that the 'wants' which are served by the two types of goods should be in any recognisable sense the same. "Consider the case in which a person is induced, by a small rise in income, to run a car; he will then be obliged to economise on several of his previous lines of expenditure. For the particular rise in income which has taken place, all these ordinary forms of consumption will have become 'inferior goods'."[32]

Depending on consumer or market indifference curves the amount of a good bought can either increase, decrease, or stay the same when income increases. In Fig. 9.7, good X is a normal good since the amount purchased increases from x_1 to x_2 as the budget constraint shifts from BC_1 to the higher income BC_2. Good Y is an inferior good since the amount bought decreases from y_1 to y_2 as income increases.

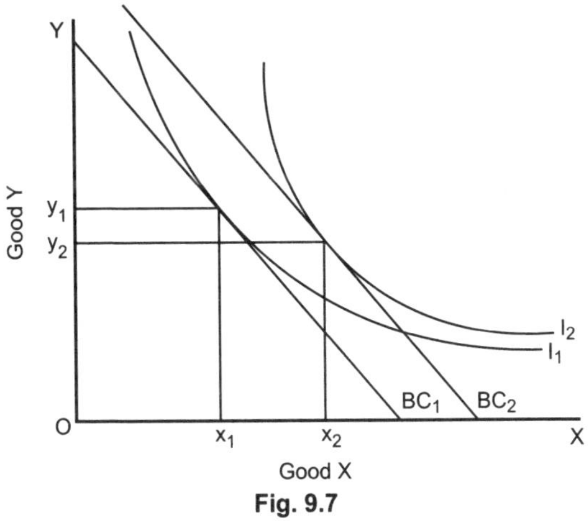

Fig. 9.7

Let us now analyse the effect of change in price of an inferior commodity on the demand for it. We have already seen that the substitution effect of the decline in the price of a commodity always tends to increase the demand for it. But the income effect of the decline in price of an inferior good diminishes the demand for it. Thus, in case of inferior goods, the income effect and the substitution effect work in opposite directions. We have also seen above that normally the income effect in case of a single commodity is small. Therefore, in case of inferior goods, although the income effect operates in the opposite direction, it is not likely to outstrip the substitution effect. Thus, though the law of demand does not necessarily hold true in the case of inferior goods, in actual practice, it is likely to hold true. The law would not hold in case of an inferior good if the income effect is substantial and outweighs the substitution effect. The income effect can be substantial if the income elasticity of demand is very high and also the proportion of income spent on the commodity is quite large. According to Hicks, for a commodity to be an exception to the general law of demand, which maintains an inverse relationship between the price and quantity demand of a commodity, three conditions are necessary:[33] (i) the commodity must be an inferior good, with a negative income elasticity of significant size, (ii) the substitution effect must be small, and (iii) the proportion of income spent upon the inferior good must be large. There are not likely to be many inferior goods in whose case all these conditions would be satisfied. To cite Hicks, "Although exceptions to the law of demand are theoretically possible, the chance of their occurrence is in practice negligible."[34]

Elasticities of Demand

In this section we shall try to understand the elasticity approach in demand. We are always interested to know how a change in one variable affects some other variable. For example, how much does a change in price of a good affect the quantity of it demanded or how a change in income affect total spending on a particular good does. The problem in summarising these kinds of effect is that goods are measured in different ways. When two goods are measured in different units, we cannot make a simple comparison between the demands for them · to determine which demand is more responsive to change in its price. To solve this problem, the concept of elasticity is used. In economics, elasticity is a measure of how sensitive one variable is to another. In case of demand, elasticity measures how sensitive the quantity of a good that people demand, is to the price of good or the income of the consumer or the price of other goods. There are three main kinds of elasticity of demand: (a) the price elasticity, (b) the income elasticity and (c) the cross elasticity.

(a) The Price Elasticity of Demand

The price elasticity of demand measures how much the quantity demanded of a good changes when its price changes. It can also be stated as the percentage change in quantity demanded divided by the percentage change in price or price elasticity of demand is a measure of the relative change in quantity demanded of a good in response to a relative change in its price. If the changes in price are very small we use the point elasticity of demand and if the change in price is not small we use the arc elasticity of demand as the relevant measure.

$$\text{Price Elasticity of Demand} = \frac{\%\text{change in quantity demanded}}{\%\text{ change in price}}$$

$$= \frac{\text{Proportionate change in quantity demanded}}{\text{Proportionate change in price}}$$

$$= \frac{\dfrac{\text{Change in quantity demanded}}{\text{Quantity demanded}}}{\dfrac{\text{Change in price}}{\text{Price}}}$$

Let us first consider *point elasticity of demand*. The point elasticity of demand is defined as the proportionate change in the quantity demanded resulting from a very small proportionate change in price. Symbolically, we have

$$e_p = \frac{dQ}{Q} \bigg/ \frac{dP}{P}$$

Or $$e_p = \frac{dQ}{dP} \cdot \frac{P}{Q} \qquad \text{(i)}$$

where

e_p = Price elasticity of demand
Q = Quantity demanded
P = Price

If the demand curve is liner, we can write

$$Q = b_0 - b_1P \tag{ii}$$

Differentiating equation (ii) with respect to price we get

$$\frac{dQ}{dP} = -b_1 = \text{Slope of demand curve} \tag{iii}$$

Substituting the value of $\frac{dQ}{dP}$ from (iii) in (i) we get

$$e_p = -b_1 \cdot \frac{P}{Q}$$

this implies that the elasticity changes at the various points of the linear demand curve. Graphically the point elasticity can be shown as in Fig. 9.8.

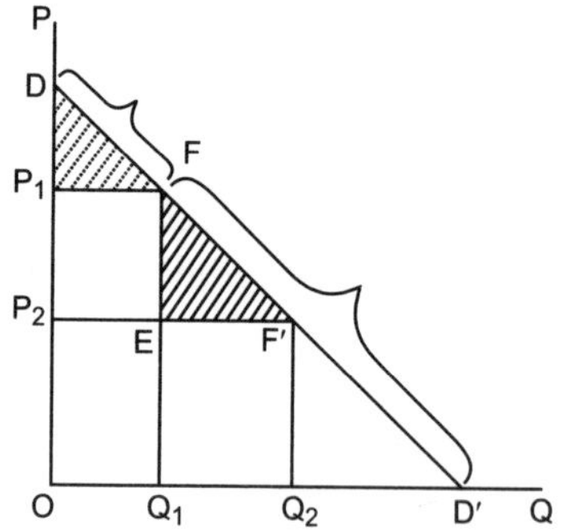

Fig. 9.8

In the figure, the elasticity of the linear demand curve at point F is given by the ratio $\frac{FD'}{FD}$.

Proof:

From the figure we have

$$\Delta P = P_1P_2 = EF$$

$$\Delta Q = Q_1Q_2 = EF'$$

$$P = OP_1 \text{ and } Q = OQ_1$$

If we consider very small changes in P and Q, then we have $\Delta P \approx dP$ and $\Delta Q \approx dQ$. Substituting in (i) we have

$$e_p = \frac{Q_1Q_2}{P_1P_2} \cdot \frac{OP_1}{OQ_1} = \frac{EF'}{EF} \cdot \frac{OP_1}{OQ_1}$$

From the figure we also have

$$\frac{EF'}{EF} = \frac{Q_1D'}{FQ_1} = \frac{Q_1D'}{OP_1}$$

since $\Delta FEF'$ and $\Delta FQ_1D'$ are similar due to equality in corresponding angle.

Thus, $$e_p = \frac{Q_1D'}{OP_1} \cdot \frac{OP_1}{OQ_1} = \frac{Q_1D'}{OQ_1}$$

Also, $\dfrac{Q_1D'}{FD'} = \dfrac{P_1F}{FD} = \dfrac{OQ_1}{FD}$ since ΔDP_1F and $\Delta FQ_1D'$ are similar.

From above expression we get

$$\frac{Q_1D'}{OQ_1} = \frac{FD'}{FD}$$

Thus, the price elasticity at point F is given by

$$e_p = \frac{Q_1D'}{OQ_1} = \frac{FD'}{FD}$$

Economic factors determine the size of price elasticity for individual goods: elasticities tend to be higher when the goods are luxuries, when substitutes are available, and when consumers have more times to adjust their behavior. The more the possible uses of a commodity the greater its price elasticity will be. The price elasticity is always negative because the change in quantity demanded is in opposite direction to the change in price. But by convention negative sign is ignored. The range of values of the elasticity is

$$0 \leq e_p \leq \infty$$

If $e_p = 0$, the demand is perfectly inelastic it means quantity demanded is completely insensitive to price.

If $e_p = 1$, the demand has unitary elasticity it means percentage increase in quantity demanded is equal to percentage decrease in price.

If $e_p = \infty$, the demand is perfectly elastic it means any increase in price results in quantity demanded decreases to zero and any decrease in price results in quantity demanded increase to infinity.

If $0 < e < 1$, the demand is inelastic it means quantity demanded is relatively insensitive to price.

If $1 < e < \infty$, demand is elastic it means quantity demanded is relatively sensitive to price.

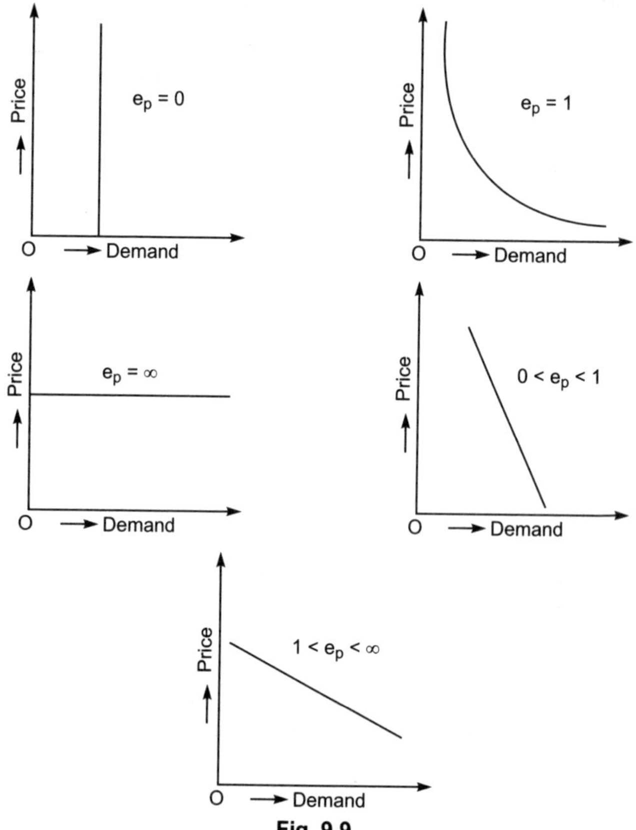

Fig. 9.9

Now we consider the *arc elasticity of demand*. The point method for measuring price elasticity is applicable when the change in price is infinitesimally small. But when the price change is large we use the formula for the arc elasticity of demand. In this method the price is measured as an average of the original price and changed price and similarly quantity is also measured by taking an average of the original quantity and the changed quantity.

Let us consider the following figure.

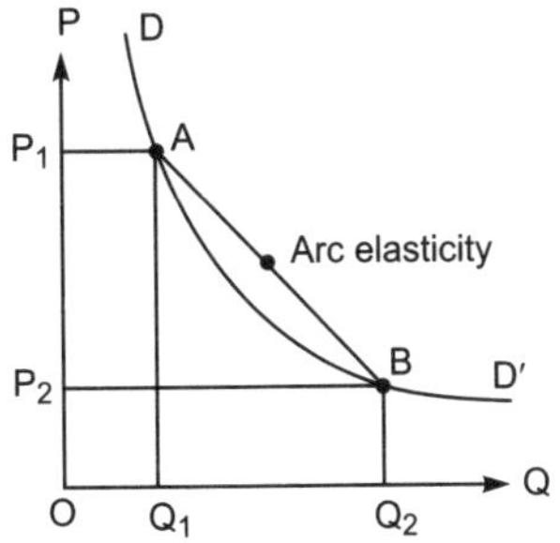

Fig. 9.10

P_1 is the original price and P_2 is the price after change, then the average price = $\frac{P_1 + P_2}{2}$

Similarly, the average quantity = $\frac{Q_1 + Q_2}{2}$

where Q_1 = Original quantity

Q_2 = Quantity after change in price

Now the formula for the arc elasticity of demand can be given by

$$e_p = \frac{\Delta Q}{\Delta P} \cdot \frac{\frac{P_1 + P_2}{2}}{\frac{Q_1 + Q_2}{2}} = \frac{\Delta Q}{\Delta P} \cdot \frac{(P_1 + P_2)}{(Q_1 + Q_2)}$$

The arc elasticity is the elasticity at the mid-point of the chord that connects the two points A and B on the demand curve defined by the initial and the new price levels. The measure of the arc elasticity is an approximation of the true elasticity of the section AB of the demand curve, which is used when we know only the two points A and B from the demand curve, but not the intermediate ones.

Elasticity and Slope of Demand Curve

The elasticity of the demand curve is not the same as the slope of the demand curve. Because the demand curve's slope depends upon the changes in P and Q, whereas the elasticity depends upon the percentage change in P and Q. The only exceptions are the polar cases of completely elastic and inelastic demands. Now let us consider the straight line demand curve as shown in Fig. 9.11.

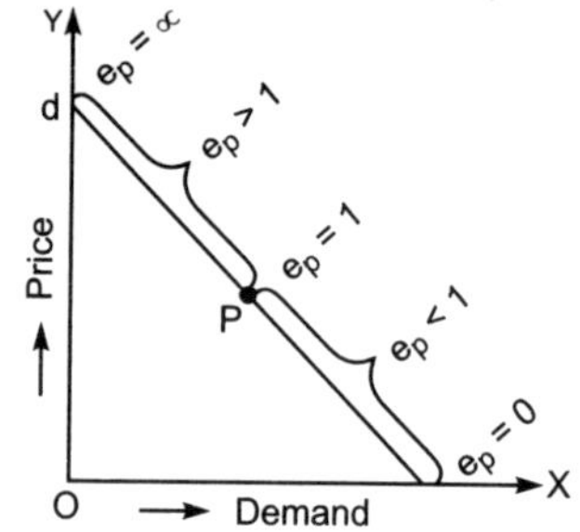

Fig. 9.11

All points on the straight line demand curve have the same slope. But above the mid-point, demand is elastic; below it, demand is inelastic; at the mid-point, demand is unit-elastic. Only in the case of vertical or horizontal curves we can infer the price elasticity from slope alone.

Elasticity and Revenue

We all are interested to know whether raising price will raise or lower the revenue. This question is of strategic importance for businesses like hotels, airlines and magazines, which must decide whether it is worthwhile to raise prices and whether the higher prices make up for lower demand.

Because revenue is defined as price times quantity, an increase or a decrease in the price has an effect on revenue. There are two opposite effects. Let us consider an increase in the price. When the price increases, people pay more for each item, and this increases revenue; but they buy fewer items, and this decreases in the quantity demanded reduces revenue. Here the work of the elasticity is to determine which of these two opposite effects dominates.

If we know the price elasticity of demand, we can find out what will happen to total revenue when price changes:

(a) When demand is price-inelastic, a price decrease reduces total revenue.

(b) When demand is price-elastic, a price decrease increases total revenue.

(c) In the borderline case of unit-elastic demand, a price decrease leads to no change in total revenue.

Revenue and the elasticity of a straight line demand curve may be shown in Fig. 9.12.

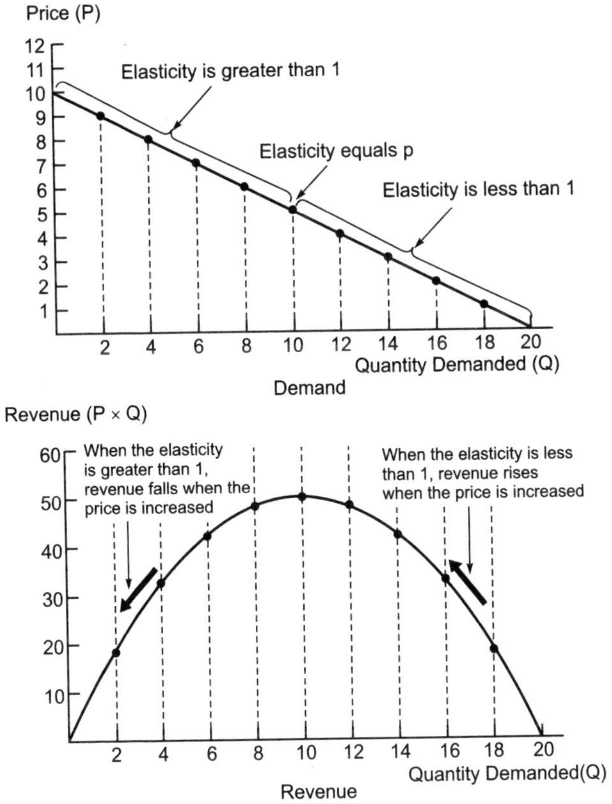

Fig. 9.12

Along the straight line demand curve at the top, the price elasticity ranges from above 1 (to the left) to below 1 (to the right). When the price elasticity is greater than 1, an increase in the price will reduce revenue, as shown in the lower panel.

The total revenue is the product of the quantity sold and the price

$$TR = P.Q$$

And the marginal revenue will be equal to the price of the extra unit sold minus the loss from selling all previous units at the new lower price.

That is $$MR = P_{n+1} - (P_n - P_{n+1})Q_n$$

where Q_n is the quantity sold before the fall in price.

Mathematically, the MR can be derived from the TR function:

$$MR = \frac{d(TR)}{dQ} = \frac{d(P.Q)}{dQ}$$

Or $$MR = P + Q.\frac{dP}{dQ}$$

Let us consider the linear demand curve

$$Q = b_0 - b_1P$$

Dividing both side of the above equation by b_1 and solving for P we get

$$P = a_0 - a_1Q$$

where $$a_0 = \frac{b_0}{b_1} \text{ and } a_1 = \frac{1}{b_1}$$

Substituting P in the total revenue function we get

$$TR = PQ = a_0Q - a_1Q^2$$

Now the MR can be given by

$$MR = \frac{d(TR)}{dQ} = a_0 - 2a_1Q$$

Thus, we find that the MR curve begins from the same point (a_0) as the demand curve, and is a straight line with a negative slope twice as steep as the slope of the demand curve.

The Relationship between Marginal Revenue and Price Elasticity

Let us assume the demand function be

$$P = f(Q)$$

The total revenue is

$$TR = PQ = [f(Q)]Q$$

The MR can be given as

$$MR = \frac{d(PQ)}{dQ} = P\frac{dQ}{dQ} + Q\frac{dP}{dQ} = P + Q\frac{dP}{dQ}$$

The price elasticity of demand is defined as

$$e = -\frac{dQ}{dP} \cdot \frac{P}{Q}$$

$$-e\frac{Q}{P} = \frac{dQ}{dP}$$

$$-\frac{P}{eQ} = \frac{dP}{dQ}$$

Substituting the value of $\frac{dP}{dQ}$ in the expression of the MR we find

$$MR = P + Q\frac{dP}{dQ} = P - Q\,\frac{P}{eQ} = P - \frac{P}{e}$$

$$MR = P\left(1 - \frac{1}{e}\right)$$

At e = 1, the total revenue curve reaches its maximum level because at this point its slope, i.e. the MR, is equal to zero.

At e > 1 the total revenue curve has a positive slope, i.e. it is still increasing and hence has not reached its maximum point given that

$$P > 0 \text{ and } \left(1 - \frac{1}{e}\right) > 0\text{; hence, MR} > 0$$

At e < 1 the total revenue curve has a negative slope which implies it is falling.

i.e. $$P > 0 \text{ and } \left(1-\frac{1}{e}\right) < 0, \text{ hence, } MR < 0$$

(b) The Income Elasticity of Demand

We already know the difference between a shift in the demand curve and a movement along the demand curve. A shift in the demand curve occurs when there is a change in the quantity people are willing to buy due to a change in anything except the price—for example, a change in income. Therefore, the concept of elasticity can also be applied in the case of change in income and this elasticity must be distinguished from the price elasticity of demand.

The income elasticity of demand is the ratio of the percentage change of quantity demanded to the percentage change of income, holding price and all other determinants of demand constant. That is,

$$\text{Income Elasticity of Demand} = \frac{\%\text{ change in quantity demanded}}{\%\text{ change in income}}$$

Symbolically this can be written as

$$e_y = \frac{dQ}{Q}\bigg/\frac{dY}{Y} = \frac{dQ}{dY}\cdot\frac{Y}{Q}$$

The main determinants of income elasticity are:

(a) the nature of the need that the commodity covers,

(b) the initial level of income and

(c) the time period, because the consumers adjust their consumption pattern with a time-lag to changes in income.

Thus, income elasticity is positive for normal goods because increase in income lead to increase in purchase of the good. In the case of inferior good income elasticity would be negative, implying that increase in income leads to decrease in quantity purchased. A good is considered to be a 'luxury' if its income elasticity is greater than unity. On the other hand, if income elasticity is less than unity then the good under consideration is 'necessity'.

(c) The Cross Price Elasticity of Demand

This concept of elasticity is based upon the fact that some goods have close substitutes due to which the consumer can use one for another. For example, if the fair of buses increases, people would opt for train. Thus, the demand for train goes up not because the fair for train has gone down, but because the price of a close substitute, i.e. bus has gone up. In case of a complementary good, a person cannot use one without the use of another at a time. For example, if the price of tea goes up, the demand for sugar would fall and vice versa.

Thus, the cross elasticity of demand is defined as the proportionate change in the quantity demanded of x resulting from a proportionate change in the price of y. Symbolically, we can write

$$e_{xy} = \frac{dQ_x}{Q_x} \Big/ \frac{dP_y}{P_y} = \frac{dQ_x}{dP_y} \cdot \frac{P_y}{Q_x}$$

If the two goods are substitutes, the cross price elasticity of demand will be positive because the price of one good and the quantity demanded of the other good will move in the same direction.

If two goods in question are complements, the cross price elasticity will be negative, showing that the price of one good and the quantity of the other good move in opposite directions.

The main determinant of the cross elasticity is the nature of the goods relative to their uses. If two goods can satisfy equally the same need, the cross elasticity is high, and vice versa.

NOTES

1. Fritz Machlup, "Professor Hicks' Revision of Demand Theory", *American Economic Review* (March, 1957), reprinted in William Briet and Harold M. Hochman (ed), *Readings in Microeconomics* (New York, 1968), p. 89.
2. J.R. Hicks, *A Revision of Demand Theory* (Oxford, 1956), p. 3.
3. *Ibid.*, p. 4.
4. *Ibid.*, p. 9.
5. *Ibid.*

6. *Ibid.*, p. 18.
7. *Ibid.*, pp. 18-19.
8. *Ibid.*, p. 19.
9. *Ibid.*, p. 17.
10. *Ibid.*, pp. 17-18.
11. *Ibid.*, p. 18.
12. *Ibid.*, p. 19.
13. *Ibid.*
14. *Ibid.*, pp. 39-40.
15. *Ibid.*, p. 41.
16. *Ibid.*
17. *Ibid.*, p. 20.
18. *Ibid.*
19. Words within parenthesis added.
20. J.R. Hicks, *op. cit.*, p. 21.
21. *Ibid.*, p. 42.
22. *Ibid.*, p. 43.
23. *Ibid.*, p. 44.
24. *Ibid.*, p. 47.
25. *Ibid.*, p. 59.
26. *Ibid.*
27. *Ibid.*
28. Following Hicks we do not show the horizontal axis in the diagram. As this diagram is usually drawn, it shows the consumer spending a preposterously large proportion of his income on the commodity concerned. This defect can be removed, without inconvenience in drawing, if we suppose the horizontal axis to be removed to a distance so that the reader is left to imagine it to be somewhere at the bottom of the page. It is in fact the top end of the diagram which we need and this is shown here, drawn on a large scale.
29. Hicks uses the term 'tend to increase' to mean 'increase or possibly remain constant' and 'tend to diminish' in the corresponding sense. This makes for brevity and does not cause any ambiguity in a static theory.
30. J.R. Hicks, *op. cit.*, p. 62.
31. *Ibid.*, p. 64.
32. *Ibid.*, p. 66.
33. *Ibid.*, pp. 66-67.
34. *Ibid.*, p. 67.

Marshallian Utility Analysis vs. Indifference Curves Analysis

10

Having studied the Marshallian utility analysis as well as the indifference curves analysis, we are now in position to compare and contrast the two types of analyses. First of all, we note below the similarities in the two types of analysis.

Similarities Between Marshallian Utility Analysis and Indifference Curves Analysis

In the first place, both the analyses assume that the consumer behaves in a rational manner and aims at maximising his utility or satisfaction. The indifference curve analysis assumes that the consumer tries to maximise his satisfaction by reaching the highest possible indifference curve. In the similar way, Marshallian utility analysis assumes that the consumer tries to maximise his utility.

Secondly, both the approaches make use of psychological or introspective method. In the introspective method, we attribute a certain psychological feeling to the consumer by looking into and reaching from our own mind. In Marshallian analysis, the observed law of demand is explained by the psychological law of diminishing marginal utility which involves introspection. Though some attempts have been made recently to derive indifference curves from the observed data of consumer's behaviour, much success has not been obtained in this direction. By and large indifference curves are based on hypothetical experimentation. Thus, the indifference curves analysis, like the Marshallian utility analysis, is basically psychological and introspective. To cite Tapas Majumdar, "The basic methodological approach of Hicks-Allen is same as in the Marshallian marginal utility hypothesis: It is, that is to say, mainly introspective".[1]

Thirdly, both analyses are based on some form of the diminishing marginal utility. The convexity of the indifference curves means that the marginal rate of substitution of X for Y declines as more and more of X is substituted for Y, which is equivalent to the Marshallian law of diminishing marginal utility.

Finally, in Marshallian utility analysis, the condition of consumer's equilibrium is that the marginal utilities of various goods are proposition to their prices. Algebraically the condition of consumer equilibrium can be written as:

$$\frac{\text{MU of X}}{\text{Price of X}} = \frac{\text{MU of Y}}{\text{Price of Y}} \text{ and so on.} \qquad \text{(i)}$$

In terms of indifference curves analysis, the consumer is in equilibrium when the marginal rate of substitution between two goods equals price ratio. Algebraically this can be written as

$$MRS_{xy} = \frac{\text{Price of X}}{\text{Price of X}} \qquad \text{(ii)}$$

It can be easily shown that the condition of consumer's equilibrium is the same in both the analyses. According to Hicks, the MRS of X for Y is the ratio between their marginal utilities. Therefore,

$$\text{MRS of X for Y} = \frac{\text{MU of X}}{\text{MU of Y}} \qquad \text{(iii)}$$

From (ii) and (iii) we get

$$\frac{\text{MU of X}}{\text{MU of Y}} = \frac{\text{Price of X}}{\text{Price of Y}}$$

which can be put as

$$\frac{\text{MU of X}}{\text{Price of X}} = \frac{\text{MU of Y}}{\text{Price of Y}}$$

The above shows that the condition of consumer's equilibrium is the same in both analyses.

Superiority of Indifference Curves Analysis

The indifference curves analysis makes greater insight into the effect of a price change on demand for a commodity by splitting up the price effect into two parts, viz. (i) substitution effect and (ii) income effect. By assuming constant marginal utility of money, Marshall ignore the income effect of a price change. To cite Tapas Majumdar, "The efficiency and precision with which the Hicks-Allen approach can distinguish between the 'income' and 'substitution' effects of a price change really leaves the cardinalist argument in a very poor state indeed".[2]

An important advantage of splitting up the effect of price change into income and substitution effects is that it enables us to enunciate a more general and more inclusive law of demand than the Marshallian law of demand. In case of normal goods, the income effect as well as the substitution effect operate in the same direction, i.e. they tend to expand the quantity demanded of a good when its price declines. This leads to an inverse relationship between the price of a commodity and the demand for it. The same relationship is established by the Marshallian law of demand.

But if a certain good is considered to be an inferior good by the consumer, an increase in his income would be accompanied by a decline in his purchases of that good. Thus, when the price of an inferior good declines, the income effect and the substitution effect generated by it, would operate in the opposite directions. If the inferior good does not account for a substantial proportion of consumer's total income, the income effect will not be strong enough to outweigh the substitution effect. The net result would be that the decline in the price of the good expands the demand for it. Thus, the relationship between price and quantity demanded established by the Marshallian law of demand holds good even for most of the inferior goods which do not account for large portion of the consumer's income.

For some inferior goods, however, the income effect of a price-change may be more powerful than the substitution effect and as such the net effect of a decline in price of the good may be decline in demand for it. These goods are known as Giffen goods for which the Marshallian law of demand does not hold good. Marshall was not able to explain 'Giffen Paradox' because, by assuming constant marginal utility of money, he ignored the income effect of a change in price. In contrast, the indifference curve analysis, by splitting up the effect of a price change into income effect and substitution effect, provides explanation for the 'Giffen Paradox'.

Thus, by splitting up the price effect into income effect and substitution effect, the indifference curve analysis enables us to formulate a more general and inclusive law of demand in the following composite form:[3]

(i) The demand for a commodity various inversely with price if the income elasticity of demand for the commodity is zero or positive.

(ii) The demand for a commodity varies inversely with price if the income elasticity is negative but the income effect of the price-change is smaller than the substitution effect.

(iii) The demand for a commodity varies directly with price if the income elasticity is negative and the income effect of the price-change is greater than the substitution effect.

Thus, the indifference curve analysis, though based upon fewer as well as restrictive assumptions, enables us to state the law of demand in a more general form, which covers Giffen goods also.

Another important advantage of indifference curves analysis is that it enables us to translate the welfare consequences of a change in price into those of a change in income. The decline (rise) in the price of a commodity enables the consumer to shift from a lower (higher) to a higher (lower) indifference curve and therefore to a higher (lower) level of welfare. This means that a decline (rise) in price causes a change in consumer welfare similar to that caused by the rise (decline) in income. This basic relation remains obscure in cardinal utility analysis with its single commodity model and the assumption of constant marginal utility of money. To cite Tapas Majundar, "The equivalence of a given change in price to a suitable change in income is a major discovery of ordinal utility analysis".[4] This discovery has enabled Hicks to rehabilitate and extend the concept of consumer's surplus. Marshall's concept of consumer's surplus is based on the assumptions that the utility is cardinally measurable and that the marginal utility of money remains unchanged with a change in the price of a commodity. With the help of indifference curves analysis, Hicks has freed the concept of consumer's surplus from these assumptions.

The indifference curves analysis does not go into the psychological causes of preference. Marshallian utility analysis inquires why the consumer prefers commodity X to commodity Y. It explains consumer's preferences in terms of utility. The consumer prefers commodity X to commodity Y because he derives greater utility from the former commodity than from the latter. The utility analysis goes behind consumer's preference and inquires into the psychological causes responsible for it. Thus, while studying the preferences of the consumer, it enters the domain of psychology. The indifference curves analysis, in contrast, takes consumer's preferences for granted without going into their psychological causes. It concerns itself only with the external behaviour of the consumer and does not bother about the psychological causes of that behaviour.

The Marshallian utility analysis assumes that the utilities of different commodities are independent. In other words, it assumes that the utility of every commodity is a function of the quantity of that commodity alone and is not influenced by the quantities of other commodities. Jevons, Menger, Walras and Marshall believed alike that the utilities of different commodities could be combined by simple arithmetic addition. According to them, if $x_1, x_2, \ldots, x_n$ are the commodities, the total utility function can be written as

$$U = V_1(x_1) + V_2(x_2) + ... + V_n(x_n)$$

Marshall made this assumption in spite of the fact that he was fully aware of the existence of competitive goods (e.g. tea and coffee, beef and mutton, etc.) and complementary goods (e.g. pen and ink, etc.). Marshall brought the latter type of commodities under the concept of joint demand. About the former type of commodities he believed that the difficulty could be overcome by grouping two competitive commodities under a common demand schedule. Edgeworth, who fully shared the view that utility was cardinally measurable, did not accept the view that the utilities of different commodities could be combined by simple arithmetic addition. In his *Mathematical Psychics* (1881) he adopted the generalized utility function in which utility to the individual was made a function of all commodities that enter the individual's budget. He wrote the utility function as:

$$U = Q(x_1, x_2,..., x_n)$$

where Q is a joint function of all commodities.

Demand analysis based on the assumption of independent utilities does not take into consideration the complementary and substitution relations between different commodities. In contrast, the indifference curve analysis, by adopting more than one commodity model and recognising interdependence of utilities, is in a better position to deal with related goods.

Criticism of Indifference Curves Analysis

The superiority of indifference curves analysis over the Marshallian utility analysis has, however, been challenged by some economists, important among whom are Prof. D.H. Robertson, F.H. Knight, W.E. Armstrong, etc. The indifference curves analysis has been criticised on a number of grounds.

It is argued that the indifference curves analysis avoids the difficulties involved in a quantitative measurement of utility by making the unrealistic assumption that the consumer possesses complete knowledge of all his scale of preference or indifference map. It is almost impossible for a consumer to possess complete knowledge of all the combinations of two goods which provide him equal satisfaction. While the consumer might be supposed to possess a somewhat accurate knowledge of a few combinations of the two goods in the neighbourhood of his actual purchases, it would be too much to expect him to know the satisfaction yielded by all the possible combinations of the two goods. In other words, while the consumer may have knowledge of a part of his preference schedule or indifference curve, he cannot be expected to know his entire preference schedule. Hicks himself realised this weakness of the indifference curves analysis. While revising his demand theory, he remarks that "one of the most awkward of the assumptions into which the older theory appeared to be impelled by its geometrical analogy was the notion that the consumer is capable of ordering all conceivable alternatives that might possibly be presented to him—all the positions which might be represented by points on his indifference map. This assumption is so unrealistic that it was bound to be a stumbling block".[5]

The indifference curves analysis can effectively analyse consumer behaviour only in simple cases, particularly when the choice is to be made between the quantities of two commodities only. If the choice is extended to three commodities, three-dimensional diagrams would be required to handle the analysis, which are difficult to draw and understand. When the choice is extended to more than three goods, the geometry becomes incapable of handling the analysis and resort has to be taken to completed mathematics which often has a tendency to conceal the economic point of what is being done. Prof. Hicks realises this drawback of the indifference curve analysis.

The indifference curves analysis has the drawback that its geometrical nature is based on the assumption of continuity "a property which the geometrical field does have, but which the economic in general does not". The real economic world exhibits discontinuity and it would be unrealistic not to take note of it. This drawback of indifference curve analysis was admitted by Hicks and as a result be dropped the assumption of continuity in his book *Revision of Demand Theory*.

Prof. W.E. Armstrong, a great critic of indifference curves analysis, is of the view that in most cases in which the consumer's indifference is noticed is owing to the consumer's lack of ability to judge the difference between alternative combinations of goods. If this view of consumer's indifference is accepted, the relation of indifference becomes non-transitive. Further, since, in Armstrong's view, the underlying utility relation is quantitative, the relation of indifference can remain symmetrical only when utility difference is zero; otherwise it becomes asymmetrical. Armstrong's argument can be explained in Fig. 10.1.

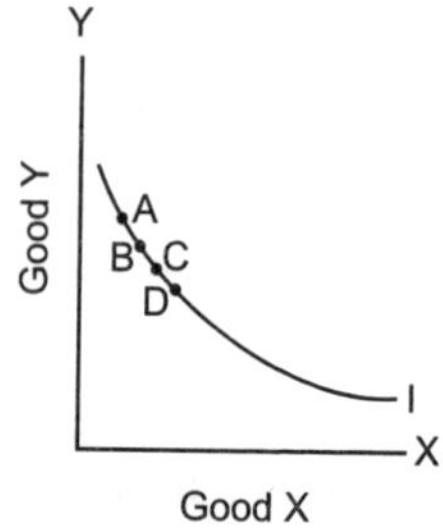

Fig. 10.1

Consider four points A, B, C and D, lying continuously on curve I. Each of these points indicates a combination of the two commodities X and Y which is different from the other three. Further suppose that the relation of indifference holds between any pair of two points taken consecutively (A and B, B and C, and C and D)—the usual case of an indifference curve. According to Armstrong's interpretation, the consumer is indifferent between A and B not because the total utility of combination A is equal to the total utility of combination B but because the difference in the total utilities of A and B is so small that it is imperceptible to the consumer. However, if we compare A to C (or D), the imperceptible difference between total utilities of A and B and B and C (or D) might accumulate to an extent that becomes perceptible. If this happens, the consumer will prefer A to C or C to A. The relation of indifference which held true (owing to the difference being imperceptible to the consumer) between A and B and between B and C does not hold true between A and C. Once the intransitivity of indifference is accepted, the entire system of indifference curves breaks down.

Prof. D.H. Robertson is of the view that indifference curves technique is simply "the old wine in a new bottle". It simply substitutes new concepts and equations in place of the old ones but the basic approach of the two types of analysis is the same.

It substitutes the concept of preference and the scale of preference for the concept of utility. It substitutes introspective ordinalism in place of introspective cardinalism, i.e. it uses ordinal number system of first, second, third and so on to indicate the order of consumer's preferences instead of the cardinal system of one, two, three and so on which measures the amount of utility derived by the consumer. It replaces marginal utility by the marginal rate of substitution and the law of diminishing marginal utility by the principle of diminishing marginal rate of substitution. Instead of Marshall's proportionality rule of consumer's equilibrium, which expresses the ratio of the marginal utility of a good to its price with that of another good, the indifference curve technique equates the marginal rate of substitution of one good for another to the price ratio of two goods.

Prof. Robertson is of the view that the concept of marginal rate of substitution involves the concept of marginal utility from the back door. He holds that the use of marginal rate of substitution implies the presence of cardinal element in indifference curve technique. In moving from one combination to another on an indifference curve, the consumer is supposed to be able to tell what constitutes his compensation in terms of a good for the loss of a marginal unit of another good. In other words, the consumer is supposed to be able to tell his marginal rate of substitution of one good for another. Now, the marginal rate of substitution has here defined by Hicks and others as the ratio of the marginal utilities of the two goods $\left(\text{i.e.}\, MRS_{xy} = MU\,\text{of}\,X / MU\,\text{of}\,Y\right)$. But the ratio cannot be measured unless the two marginal utilities concerned are measurable at least in principle. It has thus been argued that the concept of marginal rate of substitution necessarily involves an admission that the utility is quantifiable in principle.

But Hicks contends that in order to know the marginal rate of substitution, it is not necessary to assume that marginal utilities are measurable in principle. According to him, "All that we shall be able to measure is what the ordinal theory grants to be measurable—namely the ratio of the marginal utility of one commodity to the marginal utility of another". If a consumer, for instance, is ready to accept 3 units of commodity Y for the loss of one marginal unit of X, marginal rate of substitution of X for Y is 3:1. Thus, we can directly derive the ratio indicating the marginal rate of substitution by offering the consumer how much compensation in terms of commodity Y he would accept for the loss of one marginal unit of X without actually measuring the marginal utilities of the two commodities.

Robertson and Armstrong are further of the view that it is not possible to arrive at the Hicksian principle of diminishing marginal rate of substitution without making use of the concept of marginal utility and the principle of diminishing marginal utility. The question is asked as to why the marginal rate of substitution of X for Y diminishes as more and more of X is substituted for Y. It is held that the marginal rate of substitution diminishes and the indifference curve becomes convex to the origin because as the quantity of commodity X possessed by the consumer increases, the marginal utility of X declines and that of Y rises. The critics, therefore, hold that the principle of diminishing marginal rate of substitution cannot be derived without making use of the law of diminishing marginal utility. This criticism of the principle of diminishing marginal rate of substitution, however, does not appear to be valid. As we have already seen the derivation of the marginal rate of substitution does not depend upon the actual measurement of marginal utilities. While the law of diminishing marginal utility is based upon the cardinal utility hypothesis (i.e. the utility is quantifiable and measurable), the principle of marginal rate of substitution is based upon the ordinal utility hypothesis (i.e. utility is simply orderable). As a consumer obtains more and more units of commodity X, the strength of his desire for it (which, of course, cannot be measured) will go on declining and as such he would be prepared to give up a smaller and smaller quantity Y for obtaining an additional unit of X. Thus, the principle of diminishing marginal rate of substitution depends upon purely ordinal hypothesis and is derived independently of cardinal concept of marginal utility. Hicks, therefore, is right when he says that "the replacement of the principle of diminishing marginal utility by the principle of diminishing marginal rate of substitution is not a mere translation. It is a positive change in the theory of consumer's demand".

The indifference curves analysis has been criticised for its low empirical content. The indifference curves are hypothetical because they are not subject to direct measurement. Though consumer choices are grouped in combinations on an ordinal scale, no operational method has been devised so far to draw the actual indifference curves. To cite Hicks, "...from a practical standpoint we are not much better off when drawing purely imaginary indifference curves than we are when speaking of purely imaginary utility functions".

Some attempts at experimental measurement of indifference curves have been made by psychologists and economists. Though a limited success has been attained, it may be pointed out that all these experiments were made under controlled conditions. The subjects were asked to choose from hypothetical rather than actual combinations of goods. From the economist's point of view, the indifference curves, therefore, still remain imaginary.

Prof. Knight contends that the observed market behaviour cannot be explained objectively with the help of the indifference analysis. As the individual thinks and acts subjectively, it is wrong not to base the analysis of consumer's demand on the cardinal utility theory. The income and substitution effects, for instance, cannot be separated from the observed data. What the empirical data shows is the composite price effect. Similarly, the concepts of complementaries and substitutes based on the principle of marginal rate of substitution cannot be derived from the observed data.

The indifference curves analysis, like the utility analysis, is based on the assumption that the consumer acts in a rational manner. He is assumed to be of a calculating mind who carries innumerable combinations of different commodities in his head, substitutes one for the other and makes a rational choice between various combinations of goods. This is too much to expect from a consumer who has to act under several social, economic and legal disabilities. Boulding remarks in this connection, "In seeking to cover the whole of field of potential preference, they (indifference curves) seem to state more than what actually exists in the mind. We make choices in particular situations, we do not contemplate making choices in an indefinitely large number of situations". Further, the consumer may be carried away by advertisement, impulses and sentiments, resulting in an irrational behaviour on his part. The consumers are also slaves of customs and habits to a great extent. They continue buying the various goods in the same ratio even after prices of some of them have changed.

It may be pointed out, however, that while examining the question as to whether or not the consumer acts on the maximisation principle, the theory should not be stretched too far. Though an average consumer may not be aware of the maximisation principle, he does react to significant changes in prices in a way so as to roughly equate the marginal rate of substitution of money for a good with the price of the good. The consumer may not be able to precisely equate the marginal rate of substitution of money for a good with the price of the good because of certain limitations. An important limitation arises from the fact that in the actual world some of the goods have to be bought in indivisible quantities. This is particularly true of durable goods, e.g. washing machine, television set, etc. The indivisibilities of the goods make it impossible to adjust the quantities of good bought and thereby prevents the equality of the marginal rate of substitution of money for a commodity with its price.

The indifference curves analysis is applicable only to an individual consumer and not to a group of individuals or the community as a whole. It deals only with the choices of an individual and not with choices of a group. We can draw an indifference curve indicating choices of an individual consumer. But we cannot draw indifference curves indicating the choices of a group of individuals or those of the community as a whole.

The indifference curves analysis is based on the unrealistic assumption of perfect competition and homogeneity of goods.

In the real world the consumer is confronted with differential products and monopolistic competition.

The indifference curves analysis fails to explain consumer behaviour when the individual is confronted with choices involving 'risk' or 'uncertainty of expectation'. Let us consider a situation in which the individual is confronted with three alternatives A, B and C, such that he prefers A to B and C to A. Let us suppose, A is certain to occur, but the chances of occurrence of B and C are 50:50. In this situation the individual choice will be determined by comparative ratios of preference intensity. If the ratio of individual's preference intensity for A relative to that for B is much higher than the similar ratio between C and A, the individual will prefer A (certain) to 50:50 chance of B or C. The comparative ratios of preference intensities can be varied to show that in some situations the individual will choose 50:0 prospect of B or C to A (certain). This shows that unless the consumer can say how large his preference for A over B and for C over A is, it is not possible to tell which alternative he is likely to choose. It is obvious that ordinal utility system cannot be applied to such a situation. The choice in such a situation can be determined only if the consumer knows the differences in the amounts of utility or satisfaction which he obtains from various alternatives. Thus, the ordinal utility system cannot analyse the consumer behaviour when the consumer is confronted with choices involving risk or uncertainty of expectation. In contrast, the cardinal utility system is capable of analysing consumer behaviour in situations involving uncertainty of expectation because it permits quantitative estimates of utilities.

The indifference curves analysis is based upon the weak ordering hypothesis. According to this hypothesis, the consumer can be indifferent between certain combinations. Though the possibility of relation of indifference is not denied, it has been pointed out that the indifference curves analysis exaggerates the role of indifference in demand theory. The assumption of innumerable positions of indifference does not appear to be realistic. Professor Hicks himself realises this drawback of the indifference curves analysis in his book *Revision of Demand Theory* when he says, "The older theory may have exaggerated the omnipresence of indifference; but to deny its possibility is purely to run to the other extreme".

Professor Samuelson has criticised the indifference curves analysis for its predominantly introspective nature. He tries to formulate his demand theory from observed consumer behaviour. He considers the behaviouristic approach to be scientific. His theory is based upon the strong ordering hypothesis, i.e. 'choice reveals preference'.

In spite of the criticisms of the indifference curves analysis mentioned above, the indifference curves technique is considered superior to the Marshallian utility analysis.

NOTES

1. Tapas Majumdar, *Measurement of Utility*, p. 70.
2. *Ibid.*, p. 76.
3. *Ibid.*, p. 75.
4. *Ibid.*, p. 76.
5. J.R. Hicks, *A Revision of Demand Theory* (Oxford, 1956), p. 20.

Theory of Production

11

Having analysed the demand side of the pricing problem in the last five chapters, let us now turn to the supply side. The supply of a product depends upon its cost of production, which in turn depends upon (i) the physical relationship between inputs and output and (ii) the prices of inputs. The physical relationship between inputs and output plays an important role in determining the cost of production. The theory of production is concerned with the physical relationship between inputs and output.

It is an economic process that uses resources to create a commodity that is suitable for exchange. This can include manufacturing, storing, shipping, and packaging. Some economists define production broadly as all economic activity other than consumption. They see every commercial activity other than the final purchase as some form of production. Production is a process, and as such it occurs through time and space. Because it is a flow concept, production is measured as a "rate of output per period of time". There are three aspects to production processes:

(i) the quantity of the commodity produced,

(ii) the form of the good created, and

(iii) the temporal and spatial distribution of the commodity produced.

A production process can be defined as any activity that increases the similarity between the pattern of demand for goods, and the quantity, form, and distribution of these goods available to the market place.

The inputs or resources used in the production process are called factors of production and these are usually grouped into six categories: (a) Labour, (b) Capital, (c) Land, (d) Raw materials, (e) Machinery, and (f) Entrepreneur.

Most studies of production use either one of two alternative approaches, i.e. they have either descriptive or normative purpose. The two resulting theories differ quite much from each other even when the object of study is the same.

Descriptive theory contains knowledge about past or present production but does not much help for modifying it to correspond better to latest requirements. Academic or historical studies are often of this type. They are sometimes categorized into two types: extensive studies of a large number of cases, and intensive studies of one or a few cases.

Normative theory of production contains generally applicable knowledge and tools that can be used in the management of production, especially for optimizing existing production and planning new production. Research for creating normative theory is usually extensive because it needs a large number of cases for its material.

Moreover, a third type of research can take place in connection of the "commission". It means simply studying and planning the execution of individual tasks, e.g. preparing for a new type of service, or removing problems in existing service.

The goal of manufacture is another possibility of categorising theory of manufacture. There are only a few important types of goals of production that have attracted the interest of researchers, which means that by studying them it will be easier to get a good total view on the present theory of production. These often used points of view in the current theory of production include:

(a) Technology of production
(b) Economy of production
(c) Quality of products
(d) Timing of production

(e) Logistics
(f) Ecology of production
(g) Occupational health and safety engineering
(h) Motivation and psychology of work
(i) Theory of autonomous groups.

The physical relationship between inputs and output of a firm is known as *Production Function*. The production function shows for a given state of technology and managerial ability, the maximum rates of output which can be obtained from different combinations of the productive factors. The production function of a firm can be studied by keeping the amounts of some factors fixed and varying the quantities of other factors. This is done for deriving the law of variable proportions. The production function of a firm can also be studied by varying the amounts of all factors. This is done for deriving the laws of returns to scale. Thus, in the theory of production, we study three things, viz. (i) the law of variable proportions, (ii) the laws of returns to scale, and (iii) the combination of inputs which a firm will choose in order to minimise its cost of production or to maximise its rate of output.

Before we take up a discussion of the theory of production, it would be useful to explain the concept of "Equal Product Curve", which is an important tool of analysis in the theory of production.

Equal Product Curves

The equal products curves are also known as production indifference curves or iso-product curves or isoquants. An equal product curve is a convenient device for compressing the three-dimensional picture of a production function, two input axes and output surface, into two dimensions. Each equal product curve represents the various input combinations which can be used to produce a given output. Each point on the various isoquants is a maximum output which can be obtained with that input combination.

Depending on the degree of substitutability of the factors of production, isoquant can take various shapes:

(a) **Linear isoquant:** This type of isoquant has perfect substitutability of factors of production.

(b) **Input-output isoquant:** This type of isoquant has strict complementary of the factors of production. It takes the shape of a right angle and is called 'Leontief isoquant' after Leontief, who invented the input-output analysis.

(c) **Kinked isoquant:** This assumes limited substantiality of factors of production. Here substitutability of factors is possible only at the kinks and there are only a few processes for producing any one commodity.

(d) **Convex isoquant:** Continuous substitutability of factors over a certain range is allowed in this kind of production. Here beyond a certain limit factors cannot substitute each other.

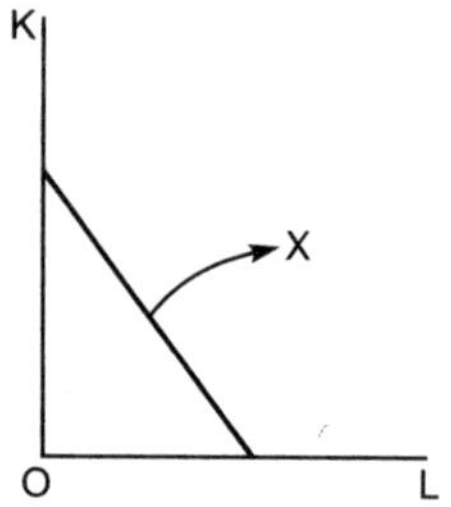

Fig. 11.1 Linear isoquant

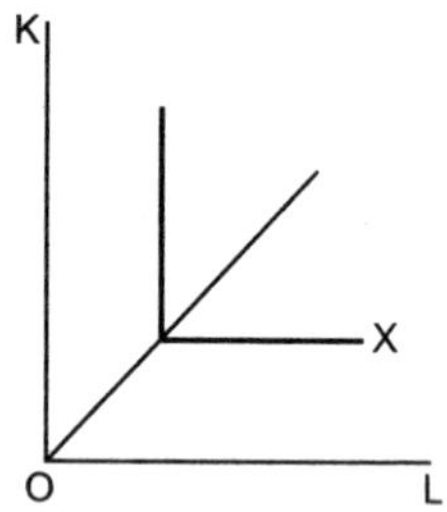

Fig. 11.2 Input-output isoquant

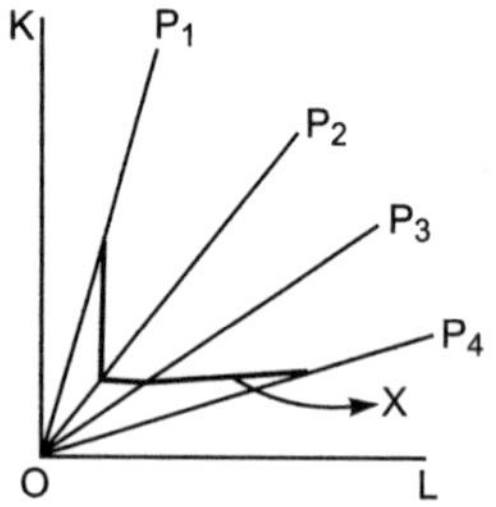

Fig. 11.3 Kinked isoquant

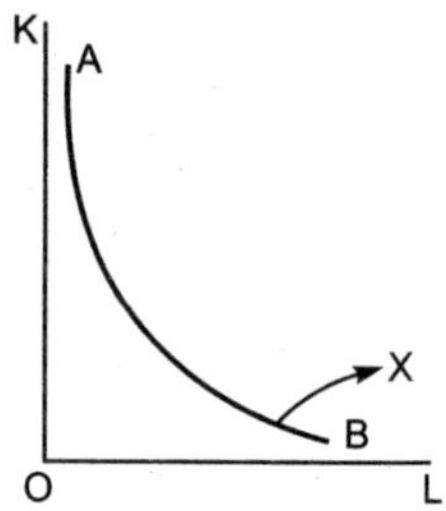

Fig. 11.4 Convex isoquant

Kinked isoquants are more practical and realistic but for economic theory we mostly consider the continuous isoquants, because they are mathematically easy to handle by the simple rules of calculus. Continuous isoquants can be considered as an approximation to the kinked isoquant because as we increase the number of processes the kinks come closer and closer, until at the limit the isoquant becomes a smooth curve.

Let us explain the concept of an isoquant with the help of a numerical example. Suppose that a firm can produce a given output (say 40 units) of a commodity by using anyone of the following alternative combinations of the two factors X and Y.

Combination	Units of Factor X	Units of Factor Y
A	2	28
B	3	22
C	4	17
D	5	13
E	6	10
F	7	8

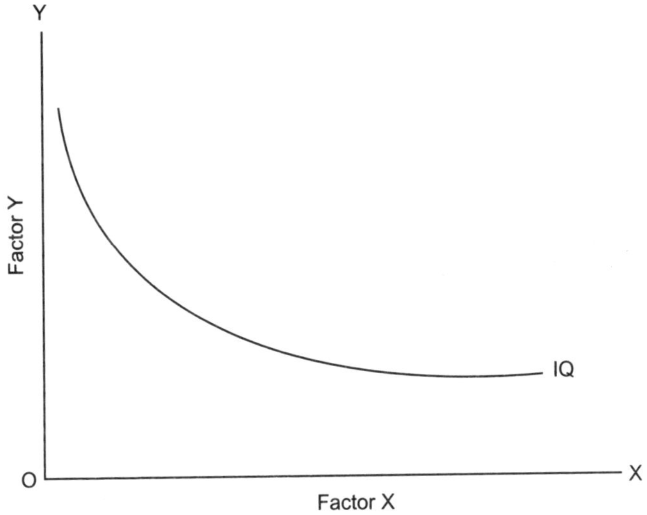

Fig. 11.5

If all the above combinations are plotted and joined, we get an isoquant I as shown in Fig. 11.5 indicating that every combination represented on it can produce 40 units of the commodity. The further the isoquant from the origin, larger is the output represented. By representing the isoquants as continuous curves, it is implied that the inputs are perfectly divisible. In other words, it is implied that they come in any size units or fractions of a unit. This makes more sense if we talk in terms of tons of cotton or hours of work than in terms of numbers of locomotives. Even in the latter case, however, the problem of indivisibility can be overcome by changing the measure and form of the input unit from numbers of locomotives to units of diesel power. There may, of course, sometimes be limitations on the available size of a given input.

There is considerable similarity between production indifference curves and the consumption indifference curves. A production indifference curve indicates all those combinations of the two factors which yield a certain given output in the same manner as a consumer's indifference curve indicates all those combinations of the two goods which yield a certain level of satisfaction. There are, however, two important differences between equal product curves and indifference curves. First, while it is possible to label equal product curves in terms of quantities of output produced, there are no units available in terms of which the indifference curves can be designated. Production of goods being a physical phenomenon is easily amenable to absolute measurement in physical units like quintals, metres, litres, etc. In contrast, it is not possible to measure satisfaction or utility. That is why indifference curves are designated by ordinal numbers as I, II, III, etc. indicating that a higher indifference curve represents a higher level of satisfaction than a lower one. Secondly, since each equal product curve indicates a specified amount of production, it is possible to say by how much one equal product curve represents greater or smaller production than another. The same, however, is not true in case of consumer indifference curves. Since satisfaction cannot be measured, it is not possible to say by how much one indifference curve represents greater or smaller production than another. To this extent, the tool of equal product curves is more useful than the tool of indifference curves.

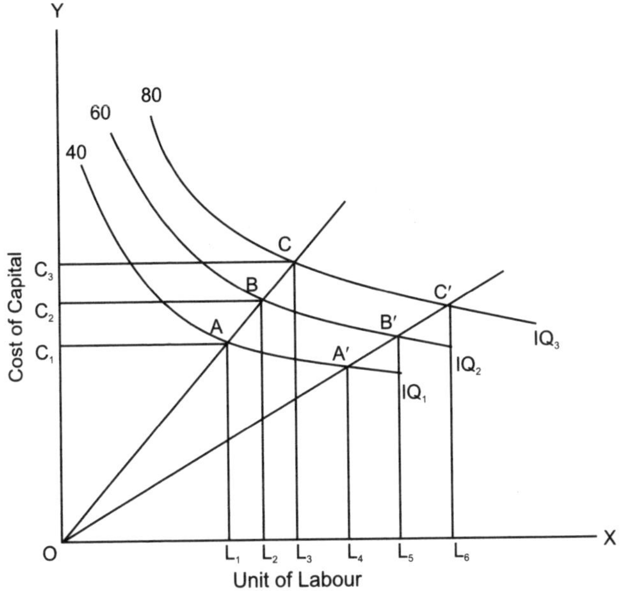

Fig. 11.6 Isoquant map

Not one but many isoquants may be possible for a consumer. It may be open to him to produce 40 units, 60 units, 80 units and so on. Each isoquant indicates different combinations of two variable inputs which can produce a given amount of output. An isoquant map is shown in Fig. 11.6.

A straight line from the origin, like OABC, represents a constant capital-labour input ratio. For instance, at points A, B and C, 40, 60 and 80 units are produced at the capital-labour input ratio $OC_1/OL_1 = OC_2/OL_2 = OC_3/OL_3$. Similarly, the line OA′B′C′ also shows a constant capital-labour input ratio L_4A'/OL_4, $L_5B'/OL_5 = L_6C'/OL_6$. The capital-labour ratio is the slope of the line from the origin to the isoquant. On the same isoquant, the level of output remains unchanged but capital-labour input ratio declines continuously as we move from left to the right. In contrast, along the line OABC or OA′B′C′, level of output changes but the capital-labour input ratio remains unchanged.

Marginal Rate of Technical Substitution

Marginal rate of technical substitution refers to the rate at which one input must be substituted for another at the margin so as to keep the level of output unchanged. To be more concrete, the marginal rate of technical substitution of factor X for factor Y may be defined as the amount of factor X which must be substituted to replace one unit of Y, the volume of production remaining unchanged. It is the negative of the slope of an isoquant. Mathematically,

Rate of technical substitution (of X for Y)

= RTS (of X for Y) = – (Slope of isoquant)

= – Change in input Y/Change in input X

Where all of these changes refer to a situation in which output is held constant. The particular value of this trade off rate will depend not only on the level of output but also on the quantities of X and Y being used. Its value depends on the point on isoquant map at which the slope is to be measured. The marginal rate of technical substitution of X for Y, denoted by $MRTS_{X,Y}$, measure how steep an isoquant is. The $MRTS_{L,K}$ tells us the following:

(a) The rate at which the quantity of Y can be decreased for every one unit increase in the quantity of X, holding the quantity of output constant, or

(b) the rate at which the quantity of Y must be increased for every one unit decrease in the quantity of X, holding the quantity of output constant.

The concept of marginal rate of technical substitution in production is thus similar to the concept of marginal rate of substitution in the theory of demand. The concept is illustrated with the help of the table given below:

Combination	Units of Factor X	Units of Factor Y	MRTS of X for Y
A	2	28	–
B	3	22	6
C	4	17	5
D	5	13	4
E	6	10	3
F	7	8	2

Each of the combinations A, B, C, D, E, and F yields the same volume of output. As we move down the table from combination A to combination B, 6 units of Y are replaced by 1 unit of X, level of production remaining unchanged. The marginal rate of technical substitution here is 6. If we move further from combination B to combination C, 5 units of Y are replaced by 1 unit of X, the volume of production remaining unchanged. The marginal rate of technical substitution at this stage is 5. Similarly movement from combination C to D involves MRTS of 4 and so on.

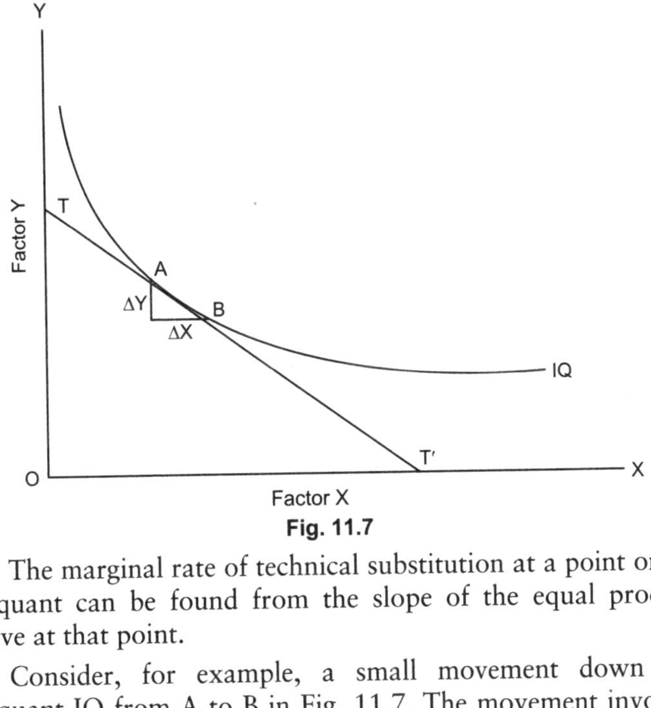

Fig. 11.7

The marginal rate of technical substitution at a point on an isoquant can be found from the slope of the equal product curve at that point.

Consider, for example, a small movement down the isoquant IQ from A to B in Fig. 11.7. The movement involves replacement of a small amount of factor Y (i.e. ΔY) by a small amount of factor X (i.e. ΔX), the volume of production remaining unchanged. The slope of the isoquant at point A, therefore, is $\frac{\Delta Y}{\Delta X}$. As the distance from A to B diminishes the slope of the curvilinear segment AB approaches the slope of the tangent TT′ at point A. In the limit, for a very small movement in the neighborhood of A the slope of the tangent at A measures the rate of substitution. Thus, the slope of the equal product curve at any point gives the marginal rate of technical substitution at that point.

The marginal rate of technical substitution of X for Y can also be defined as the ratio of the marginal physical products of two factors. As, by definition, the volume of output remains unchanged along the equal product curve, the loss in physical output involved in a small reduction in factor Y would be equal to the gain in physical output resulting from a small increase in factor X. The loss in output is equal to the marginal physical product of factor Y (MP_Y) multiplied by the amount of reduction in Y. Similarly, the gain in output is equal to the marginal physical product of factor X (MP_X) multiplied by the increase in X.

Thus,

$$\text{Loss of output} = \text{Gain in output}$$

$$\Delta Y \times MP_Y = \Delta X \times MP_X$$

$$\frac{\Delta Y}{\Delta X} = \frac{MP_X}{MP_Y}$$

Since $\frac{\Delta Y}{\Delta X}$, by definition, is the marginal rate of technical substitution of factor X for factor Y,

$$MRTS_{XY} = \frac{MP_X}{MP_Y}$$

Marginal Rate of Technical Substitution and the Marginal Product of the Factors

Let us first define the ridge line. It is defined as the locus of points of isoquants where the marginal products of the factors are zero. Let us assume that there are two factors of production, capital (depicted by the Y-axis) and the labour (depicted by the X-axis). The upper ridge line implies that the MP of capital is zero and the lower ridge line implies that the MP of labour is zero. Production techniques are efficient only inside the ridge lines and at all other points outside the ridge lines the marginal products of factors are negative and methods of production are inefficient. The range of isoquants over which they are convex to the origin defines the range of efficient production and here the marginal products of factors are positive but declining. The ridge line and the efficient range of production can be shown in Fig. 11.8.

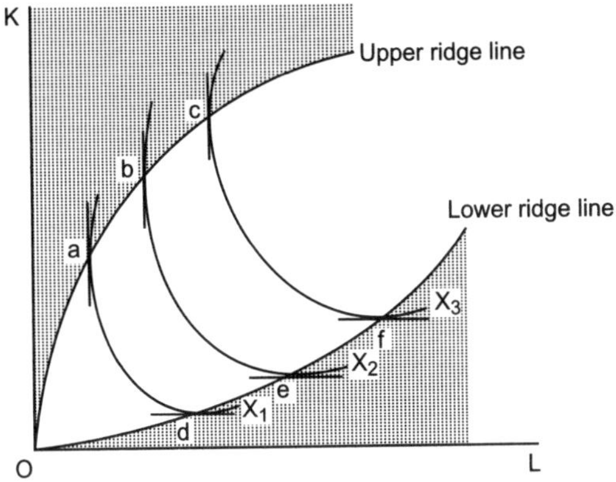

Fig. 11.8

We can prove that the MRTS is equal to the ratio of the marginal products of the factors:

$$\text{i.e.} \qquad MRTS_{L,K} = -\frac{\partial K}{\partial L} = \frac{\partial X/dL}{\partial X/dK} = \frac{MP_L}{MP_K}$$

where,
X = Output
L = Labour
K = Capital

Proof:

Due to change in capital (K) by ∂K, the output X will change by $(\partial K)\left(\frac{\partial X}{\partial K}\right)$.

Similarly, if labour (L) is changed by an infinitesimal amount ∂L, the output X will change by $(\partial L)\left(\frac{\partial X}{\partial L}\right)$.

As we know that output X is constant along an isoquant, so that the total change in X must be equal to zero. Thus, we have

$$dX = (\partial K)\left(\frac{\partial X}{\partial K}\right) + (\partial L)\left(\frac{\partial X}{\partial L}\right) = 0$$

i.e.
$$-\frac{\partial K}{\partial L} = \frac{\partial X/\partial L}{\partial X/\partial K} = \frac{MP_L}{MP_K}$$

Along the ridge lines the MRTS = 0.

In particular along the upper ridge line we have

$$MRTS_{K,L} = \frac{\partial X/\partial K}{\partial X/\partial L} = \frac{0}{dX/dL} = 0$$

And along the lower ridge line we get

$$MRTS_{K,L} = \frac{\partial X/\partial L}{\partial X/\partial K} = \frac{0}{\partial X/\partial K} = 0$$

MRTS as a measure of the degree of substitutability of factors has defect due to its dependence on the units of measurement of the factors. To come out of this problem elasticity of substitution is used. The elasticity of substitution is defined as the percentage change in the capital-labour ratio, divided by the percentage change in the MRTS.

Symbolically, we can write,

$$\sigma = \frac{\text{Percentage change in } K/L}{\text{Percentage change in MRTS}}$$

Or,
$$\sigma = \frac{d(K/L)/(K/L)}{d(MRS)/MRS}$$

It is a pure number independent of the units of measurement of K and L, since both the numerator and the denominator are measured in the same units.

The slope of the line through the origin representing a particular process can be used as a measure of the factor intensity. Let us see the following figure.

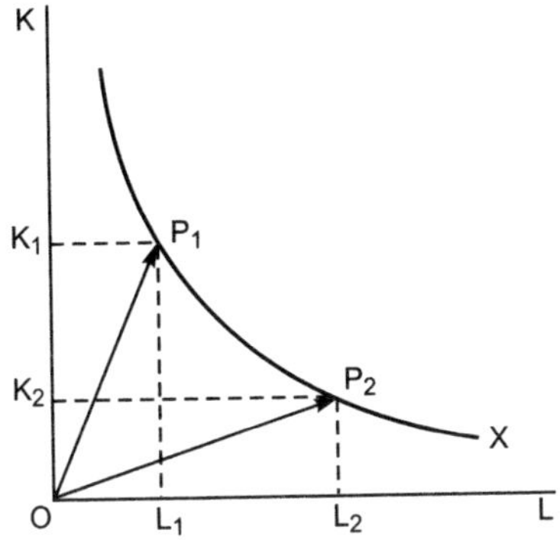

Fig. 11.9

Here we see that the factor intensity is the capital-labour ratio and process P_1 is more capital intensive than process P_2. i.e.

$$\frac{K_1}{L_1} > \frac{K_2}{L_2}$$

The upper part of the isoquant represents more capital intensive processes and the lower part of the isoquant represents more labour intensive techniques.

Diminishing Marginal Rate of Technical Substitution

The marginal rate of technical substitution of a factor (say capital) for another factor (say labour) diminishes as more and more labour is substituted for capital. This proposition sounds plausible and is not difficult to explain. As additional units of labour are added to a fixed amount of capital, the marginal product of labour diminishes. This is a shift along the marginal product curve. Further, as the amount of capital is decreased, the labour would have a smaller quantity of capital to work with, and as a result the marginal product of labour will further decline. This is a downward shift of the marginal product of labour curve. Thus, as more and more labour is substituted for capital, the marginal product of labour must decline.

For similar reasons, as more and more labour is substituted for capital, the marginal product of capital rises. With the quantity of labour fixed, as less and less capital is used, the marginal product of capital rises. At the same time there is an increase in labour input which shifts the marginal product of capital curve upwards. The same two forces are operating in this case: (i) a movement along a marginal product curve and (ii) a shift in the position of the curve. In this case, however, both forces operate to increase the marginal product of capital. Thus, as labour is substituted for capital the marginal product of capital increases.

Marginal rate of technical substitution, as defined earlier, is the ratio of the marginal product of labour to the marginal product of capital. As labour is substituted for capital, the marginal product of labour declines and that of capital rises. Hence, the marginal rate of technical substitution of capital for labour declines as labour is substituted for capital so as to maintain the volume of output unchanged.

There are, however, two exceptions to this general proposition. One is the case of factors which are perfect substitutes for each other. When the two factors are perfect substitutes for each other, for all practical purposes, they can be considered to be the same factor. Hence, the marginal rate of technical substitution remains constant throughout. The isoquant for perfect substitutes would take the shape of a straight line, as shown in Fig. 11.10, instead of being convex to the origin.

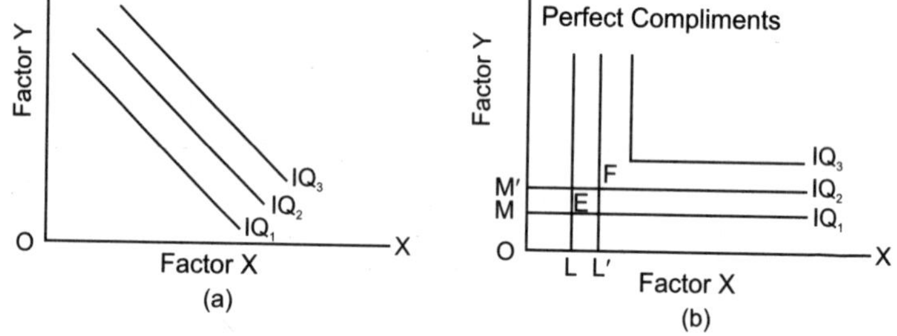

Fig. 11.10

The second exceptional case relates to factors which are perfect complements. In this case isoquants take a right-angled shape as shown in Fig. 11.10. Perfect complementary factors are those which are employed for production in a fixed proportion. In Fig. 11.10(b), OL of factor X and OM of factor Y are employed obtain a level of output indicated by isoquant IQ_1. An increase in one factor without being accompanied by a proportional increase in the other factor will not lead to any increase in output. The isoquant, therefore, is right-angled (one arm being a vertical straight line and the other a horizontal straight line) at the combination containing two factors in a fixed proportion. In Fig. 11.10(b), if the input of factor X is increased from OL to OL′ without any increase in the input of factor Y, there would be no increase in output and hence the lower portion of the isoquant IQ is a horizontal straight line. Similarly, if the input of factor Y is increased from OM to OM′ without any increase in the input of factor X, there would be no increase in the output at all and as such the equal product curve is a vertical straight line. In case of perfect complementary factors, the output can be increased only by a simultaneous increase in both the factors in the required ratio. In Fig. 11.10(b), when the input of factor X is increased from OL to OL′ and that of factor Y from OM to OM′ so that we have a factor combination F, the output would increase and we would obtain a new isoquant IQ_2. It may be pointed out that no substitution is possible in case of factors which are perfect complements of each other.

One point should be noted here that we cannot derive diminishing MRTS from the assumption of diminishing marginal productivity of factors. We can prove it as the following:

Let us consider the production function $Y = f(K, L)$

The MRTS at any point is given by $\frac{f_K}{f_L}$. In order to have diminishing MRTS, it must be that $dMRTS/dK < 0$. But as $dMRTS/dK = d(f_K/f_L)/dK$ and f_K and f_L vary with K and L, then we must take total derivatives. Thus, we have

$$dMRTS/dK = d(f_K/f_L)/dK$$
$$= [(f_{KK} + f_{KL} \cdot dL/dK)\, f_L - (f_{LK} + f_{LL} \cdot dL/dK)\, f_K]/f_L^2$$

as $dL/dK = -f_K/f_L$ along any isoquant and given that $f_{KL} = f_{LK}$ by Young's Theorem, then:

$$dMRTS/dK = [f_{KK}\, f_L - 2f_{LK}\, f_K + f_{LL} \cdot f_K^2/f_L]/\, f_L^2$$

or simply:

$$dMRTS/dK = [f_{KK}\, f_L^2 - 2f_{LK}\, f_K f_L + f_{LL} \cdot f_K^2]/\, f_L^3$$

Now, by assumption, f_K, $f_L > 0$ and, by diminishing marginal productivity, $f_{KK} < 0$ and $f_{LL} < 0$. This is obviously not sufficient to determine the sign of dMRTS/dK. Specifically, the numerator will only be negative if, in addition, we assume that $f_{LK} > 0$, and the theory of diminishing marginal productivity implies no such thing. Thus, a diminishing MRTS is, in itself, a separate assumption and cannot be derived from the diminishing marginal productivity of factors.

Properties of Equal Product Curves

The general characteristics of equal product curves are basically the same as those of indifference curves and can be proved in the same manner as in case of indifference curves. The important properties of equal product curves are mentioned below:

1. Equal product curves, like indifference curves, slope downward to the right. In other words, the curves have a negative slope. This is so because if the amount of factor X is increased, in order to keep production unchanged, the amount of factor Y must be reduced.
2. Equal product curves do not intersect each other. If they did, it would mean that a firm can produce two different quantities of output with the same combination of resources. This cannot happen if the firm is always using the most efficient techniques of production.
3. Equal product curves, like the indifference curves, are convex to the origin. The convex shape of the equal product curve means that as we move down the curve, a smaller and smaller quantity of factor Y is required to be substituted for a given increment of factor X so as to keep the volume of production unchanged. The

convexity of the equal product curves is owing to the operation of the principle of the diminishing marginal rate of technical substitution. The principle of diminishing marginal rate of technical substitution works because the factors of production are not perfect substitute for each other. If, for example, X is labour and Y is capital and production problem is to dig a canal, the more of Y that is given up, the more difficult it becomes to substitute X for Y. Ultimately a point is reached at which a large number of units of labour must be substituted for a unit of capital. The degree of convexity of equal product curves depends on the rate at which marginal rate of technical substitution diminishes. The higher the rate at which the MRTS declines, the more convex would be the equal product curves and vice versa.

4. Just as an indifference curve lying to the right indicates larger satisfaction, in the same manner an equal product curve lying to the right represents a larger volume of output. If any two combinations are taken on the two indifference curves in such a way that represent an equal amount of one of the factor, say Y, the curve lying to the right would naturally represent a larger amount of the other factor, say X. Since the combination on the curve lying to the right contains the same quantity of factor X and a larger quantity of factor Y as compared with the combination on the curve lying towards the left, it would naturally yield a larger volume of production.

Production Function

Production function refers to the physical relation between a firm's inputs of resources and its output of goods or services per unit of time, leaving prices aside. It involves concepts which are useful tools in all fields of economics. The main concepts are:

(a) the marginal productivity of the factors of production,

(b) the marginal rate of substitution and the elasticity of substitution,

(c) factor intensity,

(d) the efficiency of production and

(e) the returns to scale.

It can be expressed algebraically as

$$P = f(a, b, c, \ldots, n)$$

where P is the rate of output of a given commodity per unit of time and a, b, c,..., n the quantities of factors A, B, C,..., N employed per unit of time. To be more concrete, the production function states the maximum amount of output that can be produced from any chosen amounts of various inputs or, in other words, it states the minimum quantities of various inputs which are needed to yield a specified amount of output. Production function is a technological or engineering concept and is found for the firm by its engineers or production managers.

The production function of a firm depends upon the state of technology. With the improvements in technology, the production function changes and the new production function gives a larger flow of output from given inputs, or requires smaller quantities of inputs for producing a given amount of output.

The product output which a firm can produce depends upon the quantities of productive resources employed. The firm can increase or decrease output by increasing or decreasing the quantities of all the productive resources employed. Alternatively, as the productive resources can normally be combined in varying proportions to produce a commodity, the output can also be increased up to a certain maximum level by increasing the quantity of one productive resource while keeping the quantities of other resources unchanged. In other words, there can be two important types of production functions. One is the relation between inputs and outputs when the quantities of all inputs are varied. The other is the production function when the quantities of some inputs are kept constant and the quantity of one input (or quantities of some other inputs) is varied. The first type of production function forms the subject matter of the law of returns to scale while the second one forms the subject matter of the law of variable proportions.

Production Function of a Multiproduct Firm

Let us consider that a firm produces two goods X and Y using two factors, labour (L) and capital (K). Then for each product production function can be given as

$$X = f_1(L, K)$$

$$Y = f_2(L, K)$$

Here we shall use the device of the Edgeworth box to obtain the production-possibility curve of the firm. Let us assume that the firm has OL amount of labour and OK amount of capital measured along X-axis and Y-axis respectively of Fig. 11.11.

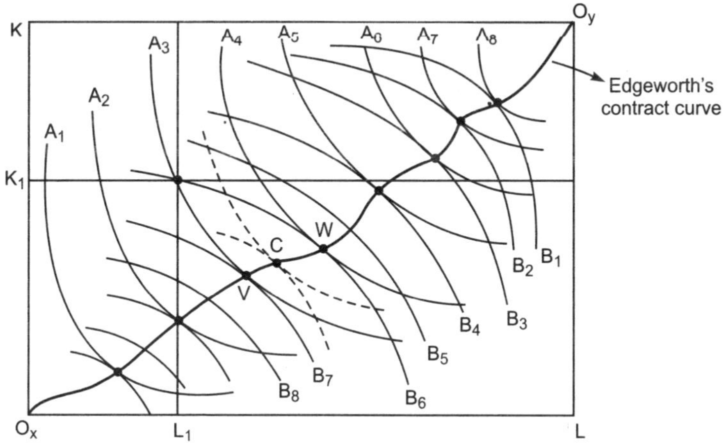

Fig. 11.11

Any point of the Edgeworth box shows a certain combination of goods X and Y that can be produced by the available factors of production. The set of isoquants denoted by A which are convex to the origin O_x represent the production function for the good X and the production function for good Y is represented by the set of isoquants denoted by B which are convex to the origin O_y. The point of tangency of the two sets of isoquants gives the contract curve. Only points lying on the contract curve are efficient. The choice of actual point on the contract curve depends on the ratio of the prices of the two goods. Production-possibility curve of the firm shows the required levels of X and Y for the firm. This shows the locus of points of levels of X and Y which use up all the available resources of the firm. We derive the production possibility curve from the contract curve. Any point on the contract curve defines a combination of X and Y levels of output which lies on the production-possibility curve. Production-possibility curve of the firm can be shown in Fig. 11.12.

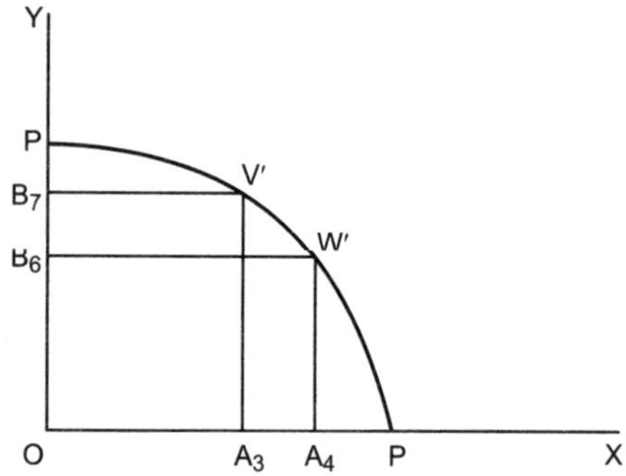

Fig. 11.12

Mathematical Derivation of the Production-possibility Curve

The slope of isoquants A and B are given by

$$-\frac{\partial K}{\partial L} = \frac{MP_{L,X}}{MP_{K,X}} = MRTS^{X}_{L,K}$$

and $$-\frac{\partial K}{\partial L} = \frac{MP_{L,Y}}{MP_{K,y}} = MRTS^{Y}_{L,K}$$

where, $MRTS^{X}_{L,K}$ = Marginal rate of technical substitution of factors K and L in the production of X.

$MRTS^{Y}_{L,K}$ = Marginal rate of technical substitution of factors K and L in the production of Y.

At the point of tangency of the two isoquants on the contract curve we have

$$-\frac{\partial K}{\partial L} = \frac{MP_{L,X}}{MP_{K,X}} = \frac{MP_{L,Y}}{MP_{K,Y}}$$

The slope of the production-possibility curve is given by

$$-\frac{\partial Y}{\partial X} = MRPT_{X,Y}$$

where, $MRPT_{X,Y}$ = Marginal rate of product transformation.

A reduction in the level of Y releases factors of production

$$\partial L_Y(MP_{L,Y}) + \partial K_Y(MP_{K,Y})$$

An increase in the level of x requires additional factors

$$\partial L_X(MP_{L,X}) + \partial K_X(MP_{K,X})$$

If the factors are to be fully employed, then the quantities released from the decrease in Y must be equal to the quantities used in increasing X. Thus, we have

$$-\partial L_Y = +\partial L_X$$

$$-\partial K_Y = +\partial K_X$$

Now the slope of production possibility curve is written as

$$-\frac{\partial Y}{\partial X} = \frac{\partial L_Y(MP_{L,Y}) + \partial K_Y(MP_{K,Y})}{\partial L_X(MP_{L,X}) + \partial K_X(MP_{K,X})} \qquad \text{(i)}$$

For efficient production the firm must stay on the curve, not inside it. Thus, we have

$$[\text{Slope of isoquant A}] = \frac{MP_{L,X}}{MP_{K,X}} = \frac{MP_{L,Y}}{MP_{K,Y}}$$

$$= [\text{Slope of isoquant B}] \qquad \text{(ii)}$$

$$MP_{L,X} = MP_{K,X}\left(\frac{MP_{L,Y}}{MP_{K,Y}}\right) \qquad \text{(iii)}$$

and

$$MP_{L,Y} = MP_{K,Y}\left(\frac{MP_{L,X}}{MP_{K,X}}\right) \qquad \text{(iv)}$$

Dividing the equation (i) by ∂L_Y $(= - \partial L_X)$ we get

$$- \frac{\partial Y}{\partial X} = \frac{MP_{L,Y} + MP_{K,Y}\left(\frac{\partial K_Y}{\partial L_Y}\right)}{-MP_{L,X} - MP_{K,X}\left(\frac{\partial K_X}{\partial L_Y}\right)} \qquad \text{(v)}$$

Substituting equations (iii) and (iv) in equation (v) we get

$$- \frac{\partial Y}{\partial X} = \frac{MP_{K,Y}\left(\frac{MP_{L,X}}{MP_{K,X}} + \frac{\partial K_Y}{\partial L_Y}\right)}{-MP_{K,X}\left(\frac{MP_{L,Y}}{MP_{K,Y}} + \frac{\partial K_X}{\partial L_Y}\right)}$$

Or, $- \frac{\partial Y}{\partial X} = \frac{MP_{K,Y}}{MP_{K,X}}$ = Slope of the production-possibility curve.

Similarly, we have

$$- \frac{\partial Y}{\partial X} = \frac{MP_{L,Y}}{MP_{L,X}}$$

Thus, the slope of the production-possibility curve or the product transformation curve is given by

$$- \frac{\partial Y}{\partial X} = \frac{MP_{L,Y}}{MP_{L,X}} = \frac{MP_{K,Y}}{MP_{K,X}}$$

Law of Variable Proportions

Law of variable proportions plays a very important role in economic theory. There are situations in which it may not be possible or feasible to expand all inputs in the same proportion—according to scale. A special case arises when one or several of the inputs remain fixed, while one or several others (the combination may be taken as a unit) are varied with respect to fixed factor(s), which may be land, plant, equipment, managerial capacity, etc. Which factors are fixed and which are variable, in fact, depends on the problem under study. The Marshallian concept of time period is of great use in this concept. In one case (long-run) it is possible to increase all inputs according to scale. This situation, where all factors are variables, mostly applies to the problem of planning the optimal size of the enterprise. In the other case (short-run), some inputs are fixed and some (or one) are variable. In the short-run, major attention is paid to the effect of changing factor proportions. The long-run situation involves considerable planning and capital investment, which often can not be quickly reversed or modified. The short-run situation arises mostly in day-to-day operations. It normally requires some investment in working capital (inventory, manpower, materials, etc.) to be used with pre-existing fixed inputs.

Yield in Quintals of Rice on a 50-Acre Farm with Varying Labour Inputs

No. of workers	Total Physical Products	Marginal Physical Product of Labour	Average Physical Product per Worker
1	2	3	4
0	0		0
1	8	8	8
2	20	12	10
3	36	16	12
4	56	20	14
5	75	19	15
6	90	15	15
7	98	14	14
	END OF FIRST STAGE		
8	104	14	13
9	108	4	12
10	110	2	11
	END OF SECOND STAGE		
11	110	0	10
12	108	–2	9
13	104	–4	8

Let us explain the law with the help of a hypothetical example. Consider the production of rice on a 50-acre piece of land. Keeping the acreage of land fixed, the number of workers employed are steadily increased from one upwards. Land and labour are the only factor inputs. The table shows the effect of employing every additional worker to this piece of land on total physical product, marginal physical product and average physical product. Consider first the total physical product shown in column 2. It reaches a maximum when 10 workers are employed and the 11th worker does not add anything at all to it. Thereafter it starts declining. A closer examination would show that upto the 4th worker it rises at an increasing rate and from 5th upto the 10th at a decreasing rate. Column 3 of the table shows these results directly. It may be pointed out that the law of diminishing marginal returns starts operating when the marginal product tends to decline and not when the total product does so. Column 4 shows the average product of labour, which is simply the total product of a given number of workers divided by the same number. Like the total and marginal products, the average products also first rises and then declines, but does so more slowly. A point worth noting is that the three products do not start declining at the same time. Marginal product is the first to reach its maximum. The other two keep rising. When a few more workers are employed, the average product also starts declining. At this point the average product is equal to the marginal product. The total product continues to rise further. It reaches its maximum when the marginal product declines to zero. With the marginal product becoming negative, the total also starts declining.

The behaviour of the three products when the varying quantity of one factor (labour) is combined with a fixed quantity of the other (land) is shown in Fig. 11.13. Number of workers employed is measured along the X-axis and Y-axis represents the total product, average product and the marginal product. The total product curves TP goes on increasing upto a point and after that it starts declining. It rises first at an increasing rate and latter at a diminishing rate. It reaches its maximum at point H and starts declining thereafter. The AP and MP curves have been derived from the TP curve. The MP curve represents the slope of TP curve at each point. When the slope of the TP curve is zero at the point H, the MP is also zero. Average and marginal product curves also first rise and then fall; the marginal product curve starts declining earlier than the average product curve. The behaviour of the total, average and marginal products as a result of the increase in the variable factor is generally divided into three stages which are explained below.

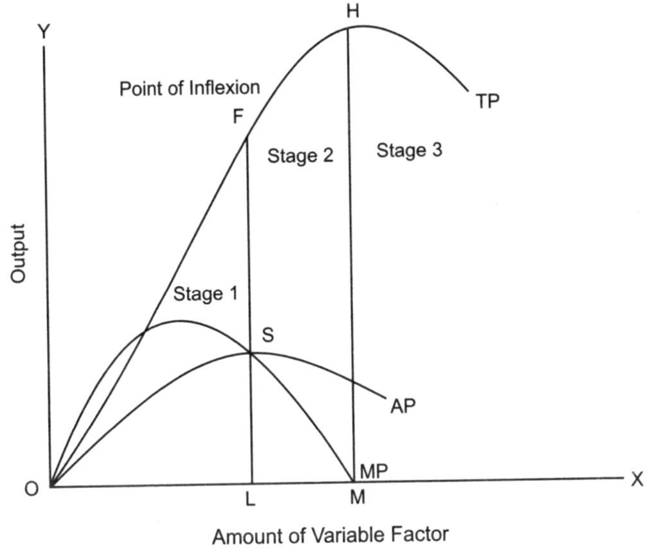

Fig. 11.13

Stage 1. In this stage, the total product rises upto a point at an increasing rate. In Fig. 11.13, the slope of the total product curve TP is increasing from origin to the point F, i.e. upto the point F, the total product increases, which means that the marginal product MP rises. From point F onwards, the total product curve goes on rising but its slope starts declining which means, from point F onwards the total product increasing at a diminishing rate, which means that the marginal product declines but is positive. The point F where the total product ceases to increase at an increasing rate and starts increasing at a diminishing rate is known as the *point of inflexion.* Corresponding vertically to this point of inflexion, marginal product is the maximum, after which it starts sloping downward. During stage 1, the marginal as well average physical products are rising but the marginal physical product rises faster than the average physical product. Since the marginal physical product is larger than the average physical product, the former pulls up the latter. When the marginal physical product starts declining, it is still larger than the average physical product and tends to pull up the latter. Thus, during the stage 1, while the marginal physical product first rises and then declines, the average physical product curve rises throughout this stage. When both the marginal physical product and the average physical product are equal, the marginal physical product neither pulls up nor pushes down the average physical product. This marks the end of stage 1 and the start of stage 2.

Stage 2. In this stage, the total physical product continues to increase, though at a diminishing rate until it reaches its maximum at point H, where the second stage comes to an end. In this stage both the marginal physical product and the average physical product are diminishing but the decline is larger in the marginal physical product than that in the average physical product. Since the marginal physical product is lower than the average physical product, the former pulls the latter down. Stage 2 is very important because the firms try to produce in this range. This stage is called the stage of diminishing returns.

Stage 3. This stage starts when the MP curve touches the X-axis and the TP curve reaches its highest point. In this stage the total physical product diminishes and, therefore, the total physical product curve (TP) slopes downward. Consequently, the marginal physical product becomes negative and the curve MP goes below the X-axis. This stage is known as the stage of negative returns. Since the marginal physical product is negative, no firm would intentionally like to operate in this stage. This stage, therefore, is not of much practical importance.

Stage of Operation. In which stage a rational producer would choose to produce? It is evident that no producer would like to operate either in the first or in the third stage. Since in the third stage total physical product is declining and the marginal physical product is negative, no firm would choose to operate in this stage. In this stage too much labour is employed in the absolute sense. Even if the labour is available free of any cost, a rational producer would not go beyond the second stage where its marginal product is zero. Similarly the firm will not choose to stop in the stage 1 because in this stage the total physical product is increasing at an increasing rate and the marginal as well as the average physical products are also increasing. It is profitable to expand production. A firm operating in stage 1 means that it is not making the best use of the fixed factor and is not fully utilising the opportunities for increasing production by increasing the amount of labour employed whose average physical product is rising throughout this stage. It is, therefore, evident that a rational producer will always choose to produce in stage 2 where the marginal physical product as well as the average physical product of labour is diminishing. The particular point in this stage at which the producer would choose to produce depends upon the prices of the factors. The stage 2 represents the range of rational production decisions. This is, therefore, the only relevant stage for the competitive firm.

Laws of Returns to Scale

Laws of returns to scale can be used for the long-run analysis of production function. In the long-run all factors are variable therefore output can be increased by changing all factors by the same proportion, or by different proportions. When change in output takes place due to change in all factors by same proportion, it is termed as the 'return to scale'.

Let us suppose we start with initial level of production

$$X_0 = f(L, K)$$

and we increase all the factors by the same proportion λ. We obtain a new level of output X^*, higher than the original level X_0,

$$X^* = f(\lambda L, \lambda K)$$

If X^* increases by the same proportion λ as the inputs, there is constant returns to scale.

If X^* increases less than proportionally with the increase in the factors, we have decreasing returns to scale.

If X^* increases more than proportionally with the increase in the factors, we have increasing returns to scale.

If we factor out λ, then the new level of output X^* can be expressed as a function of λ (to any power ν) and the initial level of output.

$$X^* = \lambda^{\nu} f(L, K)$$

Or

$$X^* = \lambda^{\nu} X_0$$

And this type of production function is called homogeneous. If λ cannot be factored out, the production function is non-homogeneous.

Thus, we can define a homogenous function as a function such that if each of the inputs is multiplied by λ, then λ can be completely factored out of the function. The power ν of λ is called the degree of homogeneity of the function and is a measure of the returns to scale.

If $\nu = 1$, returns to scale is constant and the production function is called linear homogeneous.

If $\nu < 1$, returns to scale is decreasing.

If $\nu > 1$, returns to scale is increasing.

Economies of scale has two parts: one is returns to scale and the other is monetary economics. Returns to scale are technical part of the economics of scale.

Product line

The concept of product line is used to describe the expansion of output. It shows the movement from one isoquant to another as we change both factors or a single factor. It describes the technically possible alternative paths of expanding output. What path will actually be chosen by the firm will depend on the prices of factors. The product curve passes through the origin if all factors are variable and if only one factor is variable the product line is a straight line parallel to the axis of the variable factor. An isocline is the locus of points of different isoquants at which the MRS of factors is constant. In case of homogeneous production function, the isoclines are straight lines through the origin. K/L ratio is constant along any one isocline and different for different isoclines.

Explanation of Various Stages

Having explained the stages through which the output moves when the varying quantity of one factor is combined with a fixed quantity of the other, let us now examine the causes of increasing returns in stage 1, diminishing returns in stage 2 and negative returns in stage 3.

Increasing Returns

The law of increasing returns is a matter of empirical fact. Marshall stated the law as follows: "An increase of labour and capital leads generally to improved organization, which increases the efficiency of the work of labour and capital. Therefore, in those industries which are not engaged in raising raw produce, an increase of labour and capital generally gives a return increased more than in proportion, and further this improved organization tends to diminish or even override an increased resistance which nature may offer to raising increased amounts of raw produce".[1] Marshall's definition contains two important points. First, increasing returns arise out of improved organisation of business enterprise. Secondly, the law operates only in those industries which are not engaged in primary production. Marshall believed that the law of increasing returns operates in manufacturing and the law of diminishing returns applies to agriculture. This view is not accepted by the modern economists. According to them, there is no basic difference between agriculture and industry and both can lie subject to diminishing or increasing returns. Marshall's first point, i.e. increasing returns arise out of improved organisation of business enterprise, however, as we shall see shortly, is quite valid.

Mrs. Joan Robinson gives a broader and more acceptable definition of the law of increasing returns. She states the law as follows: "When an increased amount of any factor of production is devoted to a certain use it is often the case that improvement in organisation can be introduced which will make the natural units of the factor (men, acres, or money capital) more efficient, so that an increase in output does not require a proportionate increase in the physical amount of the factor. This law or rather tendency, like the Law of Diminishing Returns, may apply equally to all the factors of production, but unlike the Law of Diminishing Returns, it does not apply in every case. Sometimes, an increase of the factors will lead to improvements in efficiency, and sometimes it will not".[2] This definition has three important points. In the first place, as pointed out by Marshall also, increasing returns result from improvements in organisation. Secondly, increasing returns are not confined to industry only and can operate in any field of productive activity including primary production. Thirdly, the law of increasing returns is not inevitable like the law of diminishing returns. In other words, while it is certain that ultimately every productive activity will be subject to the law of diminishing returns, the law of increasing returns may or may not operate in a particular field of economic activity.

What are the causes of the tendency towards increasing returns? The three major reasons for increasing returns are: (i) existence of indivisible factors, (ii) internal economies, and (iii) external economies.

Indivisibility of Factors: There is an optimum combination of the two inputs which leads to the maximum output. Given the state of technology, there is an optimum ratio between the quantities of variable and invariable inputs which lead to the maximum output or the minimum costs. But because of the indivisibility of certain inputs, it is not possible to always maintain this optimum ratio between the fixed and variable inputs. Indivisibility of an input means that owing to technological requirements a minimum quantity of that must be employed irrespective of the level of output. Very often, in the beginning, the amount of fixed input is excessive in relation to the amount of variable input. As such, if more and more units of the variable input are associated with a constant amount of the fixed input, the fixed input is utilised more intensively which leads to a rapid increase in production. In the beginning when the variable input is relatively small in quantity, the fixed input remains underutilised and, therefore, when the variable input is increased, the fixed input is used more fully which results in increasing returns.

Internal Economics: Expansion of production leads to several internal economies which cause increasing returns. Specialisation or division of labour leads to improved efficiency. Expansion of a firm makes possible a better utilisation of its by-products. A large firm can easily afford the latest and up-to-date machinery, services of highly paid specialists and experts. It can borrow funds from the money market at very favourable rates of interest. It can buy raw materials required by it at comparatively cheaper prices. It can afford to spend large amount on advertisement and publicity. It makes possible linking of various processes. A diary, for instance, can have its own fodder farm. All such internal economies lead to a reduction in costs and increasing returns.

External Economies: While internal economies arise as a result of the expansion of a particular firm and are available only to that firm, external economies arise as a result of the expansion of an industry and are available to all the firms in that industry. With the expansion of an industry, workers start moving to areas where the plants are situated which facilitates recruitment of labour. Several subsidiary industries spring up and provide intermediate products to the main industry. Expansion of textile industry, for instance, stimulates growth of chemicals and textile machinery industries. Research institutions grow and each firm need not incur expenditure on research. Institutes for technical training appear. Trade journals which provide scientific and commercial information spring up. Specialised transport and banking facilities grow.

Increasing Returns and Perfect Competition

There has been a lot of controversy as to whether or not increasing returns are compatible with perfect competition. Without going into this entire controversy, it may be mentioned that increasing returns and perfect competition are not compatible with each other. Increasing returns occur only so long as the size of the firm is below the optimum. In a state of perfect competition, each firm in equilibrium is of optimum size, i.e. it is producing at the minimum cost of production. In other words, the firm is already availing of all the possible economies of large scale production. The concept of perfect competition necessarily involves the concept of perfect market which implies that the industry has developed the maximum possible extent of specialisation. As such there is no further scope for increasing returns through increased specialisation. Under perfect competition the size of the firm becomes stable and there is no inducement for expansion in its size. If there were any scope for gaining through increasing returns by expansion in size, the firm would certainly have expanded. The fact that under perfect competition the size of the firm has become stable shows that the forces responsible for increasing returns have been exhausted. Thus, perfect competition is not compatible with increasing returns.

Can Increasing Returns Continue Indefinitely?

Obviously not. There is a limit to the operation of the law of increasing returns. If the size of the production unit exceeds this limit, the law of increasing returns will be replaced by the law of diminishing returns. If there were no limit to the operation of the law of increasing returns, it would have been possible for a single firm to meet the entire world demand for the product by continuous expansion in its size. It would have been possible, for instance, for a small piece of land to meet the entire world demand for food. The world would have been highly prosperous and the problems of rent and population would not have haunted us. But the fact is that the law of increasing returns operates only upto a certain limit. The advantages of specialisation, internal and external economies are available only within certain limits. If the size of the production unit goes beyond these limits, the advantages of specialisation, internal and external economies give place to diseconomies of large scale production and the cost of production starts rising. Thus, the law of increasing returns does not work indefinitely and beyond a certain stage is replaced by the law of diminishing returns.

Law of Diminishing Returns

The law of diminishing returns is of basic importance in economic theory. It has formed the basis of number of economic doctrines formulated by the classical economists. It was represented as an inexorable law of nature. It was responsible for a lot of pessimistic thinking in Economics and earned for it the title of a 'dismal science'. It provided basis for the Malthusian theory of population and the Ricardian theory of rent. The marginal productivity theory, which determines the price of a factor of production, is also based on the working of this important law.

The classical economists associated the law of diminishing returns with agriculture. Marshall defined the law thus: "An increase in capital and labour applied in the cultivation of land causes *in general* a less than proportionate increase in the amount of produce raised unless it happens to coincide with an improvement in the arts of agriculture".[3] The modern economists, in contrast, believe that the law of diminishing returns is not confined to agriculture alone and applies to all those fields of production, including manufacturing, where some inputs are fixed while others are variable.

As seen above, increasing returns arise in the first stage from a fuller utilisation of the fixed factor as more and more units of the variable factor are associated with it. Once the stage is reached at which the variable factor is enough to ensure an efficient utilisation of the fixed factor, further increase in the variable factor will lead to diminishing returns because then the quantity of fixed factor becomes inadequate in relation to the quantity of the variable factor.

The diminishing returns, like the increasing returns, arise from the indivisibility of the fixed factor. In stage 1 when the indivisible fixed factor is not being fully utilised, increase in the quantity of the variable factor leads to a fuller and more effective use of the fixed factor which results in increasing returns. As the doses of variable factor are added, a stage is reached where the ratio between the fixed and the variable factors becomes ideal or optimum and yields the maximum returns. This is the point of optimum proportions. Additional doses of the variable factor beyond this stage will disturb the optimum proportions and result in a decline in the returns per unit of the variable factor. Just as increasing returns arise in the first stage from a fuller utilisation of the fixed indivisible factor, diminishing returns occur in the second stage from an excessive use of the fixed indivisible factor. If the fixed factor were perfectly divisible, it would be possible to combine different factors in the optimum proportion and, therefore, there would arise neither increasing returns nor diminishing returns.

According to Mrs. Joan Robinson, the diminishing returns arise because different factors of production are imperfect substitutes for each other. She says, "What the Law of Diminishing Returns really states is that there is a limit to the extent to which one factor of production can be substituted for another, or, in other words, that the elasticity of substitution between factors is not infinite. If this were not true it would be possible, when one factor of production is fixed in amount and the rest are in perfectly elastic supply, to produce part of the output with the aid of the fixed factor, and then, when optimum proportion between this factor and other factors was attained to substitute some other factor for it and to increase output at constant cost. Thus the Law of Diminishing Returns entails that the various elements required for the production of any commodity should be divided into groups, each group being a factor of production, in such a way that the elasticity of substitution between one factor and another is less than infinite".[4] If the different factors were perfect substitutes for each other, the law of diminishing returns would not operate. As seen above, diminishing returns arise because the fixed factor is inadequate in relation to the variable factor. But if the variable factor were a good substitute for the fixed factor, the inadequacy of the fixed factor could be easily removed by substituting the variable factor for the fixed factor and the law of diminishing returns held in abeyance.

Law in Terms of Physical Quantities: The law as stated above refers to the physical quantities of the factors of production and the physical quantities of output. Neither the factors of production nor the output are conceived in money terms. The output which diminishes is in terms of physical quantities and not in terms of money.

Some economists have expressed the law in terms of money units. In their formulation the term 'diminishing returns' refers to the diminishing revenue which results from successive doses of money-outlays. The revenue resulting from successive doses of money-outlays diminishes because of two reasons. In the first place, as the firm increases its purchases of productive factors, it has to pay higher and higher prices for them which means an increase in the cost of production. In other words, successive doses of money-outlay purchase smaller and smaller quantities of the factors of production. The additional output is less than in proportionate to the increase in cost. Secondly, the increased output can be sold only at a lower price. The marginal revenue, therefore, progressively diminishes with the increase in output.

These diminishing returns cannot be considered as an example of the working of the law of diminishing returns. They are not owing to indivisibility of a factor of production or owing to a mal-combination of the factors of production. They arise on account of a change in the prices of the factors of production and the output.

Negative Returns (stage 3): As a larger and larger quantity of the variable factor continues to be associated with the fixed factor, a stage is reached when the total product diminishes and the marginal product becomes negative. The negative returns arise because the quantity of the variable factor becomes so excessive in relation to the fixed factor as hinders the smooth functioning of the production process and the total output, instead of rising, starts declining. Too much quantity of the variable factor also impairs the efficiency of the fixed factor. The proverb "too many cooks spoil the broth" aptly applies to this situation. In this situation, a reduction in the quantity of the variable factor would result in an increase in the total output.

Law of Constant Returns

The law of constant returns represents a transition between the stages of the law of increasing returns and the law of diminishing returns. The law of increasing returns cannot give place to the law of diminishing returns without first yielding place to the law of constant returns, for howsoever short period it may be.

The law of constant returns operates when all the factors of production are increased in a given proportion. It represents an optimum combination of the various factors of production. When with the increase in production, increasing returns give place to constant returns, the situation serves a warning to the producer that if he further increases his production, the law of diminishing returns would start operating.

Assumptions of Law of Diminishing Returns

The law of diminishing returns, as state above, is subject to the following assumptions:

In the first place, it is assumed that the techniques of production are given and remain unchanged. If there occurs an improvement in the techniques of production, the marginal and average product may size instead of diminishing. But this should not be taken to mean that an improvement in the techniques of production will make the law invalid. It only means that the operation of the law is postponed for the time being.

Secondly, there must be some inputs whose quantity is kept fixed. It is only then that we would be able to change factor proportions and trace their effects on factor proportions. The law would not apply if all the factors are varied in the same proportion.

Thirdly, the law assumes that the different factors of production can be used in varying proportions to produce a product. The law would not apply in those cases where the factors must be used in fixed proportions to produce a product. When different factors of production are required to be employed in a rigidly fixed ratio, the increase in the employment of one factor would not result in any increase in production, or in other words, the marginal product would be zero and not diminishing. But such cases are rare in actual practice and generally the law of diminishing returns does hold true.

Fourthly, it is assumed that the different units of the variable factor are exactly similar to each other. If the successive units are larger in size or better in quality, increments in production resulting from them may be larger than before. The law of diminishing returns would thus operate only if the successive units of the variable factor are uniform.

Returns to Scale and the Elasticity of Substitution for a Cobb-Douglas Production Function

We consider the Cobb-Douglas production function,

$$Q = AL^{\alpha}K^{\beta}$$

Initial output is given by

$$Q_1 = AL_1^{\alpha}K_1^{\beta}$$

where L_1 and K_1 denote the initial quantities of labour and capital, and Q_1 denotes the initial output. Now let us increase all input quantities by the same proportional amount λ, where $\lambda > 1$, and let Q_2 denotes the resulting volume of output. Therefore, the final output is given by

$$\begin{aligned} Q_2 &= A(\lambda L_1)^{\alpha}(\lambda K_1)^{\beta} \\ &= \lambda^{\alpha+\beta} A L_1^{\alpha} K_1^{\beta} \\ &= \lambda^{\alpha+\beta} Q_1 \end{aligned}$$

From this we can see that if,

(a) $\alpha+\beta > 1$, then $\lambda^{\alpha+\beta} > \lambda$, and so $Q_2 > \lambda Q_1$ and hence increasing returns to scale.

(b) $\alpha+\beta = 1$, then $\lambda^{\alpha+\beta} = \lambda$, and so $Q_2 = \lambda Q_1$ and hence constant returns to scale.

(c) $\alpha+\beta < 1$, then $\lambda^{\alpha+\beta} < \lambda$, and so $Q_2 < \lambda Q_1$ and hence decreasing returns to scale.

Now let us derive the elasticity of substitution for Cobb-Douglas production function. The marginal product of labour and capital are found by taking the partial derivatives of the production function with respect to labour and capital, respectively.

$$MP_L = \frac{\partial Q}{\partial L} = \alpha A L^{\alpha-1} K^{\beta} \qquad \text{(i)}$$

$$MP_K = \frac{\partial Q}{\partial K} = \beta A L^{\alpha} K^{\beta-1} \qquad \text{(ii)}$$

As we know that

$$MRTS_{L,K} = \frac{MP_L}{MP_K}$$

Thus, for this Cobb-Douglas production function, we have

$$MRTS_{L,K} = \frac{\alpha A L^{\alpha-1} K^{\beta}}{\beta A L^{\alpha} K^{\beta-1}} = \frac{\alpha K}{\beta L} \qquad \text{(iii)}$$

Rearranging the terms we get,

$$\frac{K}{L} = \frac{\beta}{\alpha} MRTS_{L,K} \qquad \text{(iv)}$$

Therefore, $\Delta(K/L) = (\beta/\alpha)\Delta MRTS_{L,K}$

Or, $$\frac{\Delta(K/L)}{\Delta MRTS_{L,K}} = \frac{\beta}{\alpha} \qquad \text{(v)}$$

Also we have from equation (iv) $$\frac{MRTS_{L,K}}{K/L} = \frac{\alpha}{\beta} \qquad \text{(vi)}$$

Now using the definition of the elasticity of substitution we have

$$\sigma = \frac{\%\Delta\left(\frac{K}{L}\right)}{\%\Delta MRTS_{L,K}} = \frac{\Delta\left(\frac{K}{L}\right) \Big/ \frac{K}{L}}{\left(\frac{\Delta MRTS_{L,K}}{MRTS_{L,K}}\right)}$$

$$= \left(\frac{\Delta\left(\frac{K}{L}\right)}{\Delta MRTS_{L,K}}\right)\left(\frac{MRTS_{L,K}}{\frac{K}{L}}\right) \qquad \text{(vii)}$$

Substituting equations (v) and (vi) in equation (vii) we get,

$$\sigma = \frac{\beta}{\alpha} \cdot \frac{\alpha}{\beta} = 1$$

Thus, elasticity of substitution along a Cobb-Douglas production function is equal to 1 for all values of K and L.

NOTES

1. Marshall, *Principles of Economics*, p. 265.
2. Joan Robinson, *The Economics of Imperfect Competition*, p. 339.
3. Marshall, *Principles of Economics* (8th Ed.), p. 125.
4. Joan Robinson, *op. cit.*, p. 330.

12 Cost of Production

The price of a product is determined by the demand for and supply of it. The major force behind the supply of a product is its cost of production. In deciding whether to produce or not, how much to produce and sell, and whether to expand or contract output, the producer is influenced by the cost of production in relation to the price of the product. To understand the determination of price, therefore, it is very necessary to understand the nature of costs. The term 'cost' has several meanings. We briefly discuss below important of these.

Money Costs

The most widely used concept of cost is the 'money cost' of production, which refers to the total amount of money spent by a firm on the production of a commodity. The money cost includes expenses like wages and salaries paid to workers and managerial staff, payment for raw materials purchased, expenditure on machines and equipment, rent on buildings, interest on capital invested and borrowed, expenditure on power, light, fuel, transportation and advertisement, insurance charges and taxes of all types. A private producer is interested only in the money cost of production.

The total money cost of production may be classified under two heads, viz. (i) explicit cost and (ii) implicit cost. Explicit cost includes those payments which are made by the entrepreneur for obtaining goods and services which do not belong to the entrepreneur himself, e.g. wages and salaries paid to workers, rent paid on land, interest paid on borrowed capital, payments for raw materials, power, fuel, etc. The implicit or imputed cost, in contrast, refers to the estimated cost of the factors of production which are owned and supplied by the entrepreneur himself, e.g. interest on capital invested by the entrepreneur himself at the prevailing rate of interest, estimated rent of the land and buildings used which belong to the employer, salary for the work which the entrepreneur may do himself for the firm.

Real Costs

The concept of real cost was given by Marshall who defined it as follows: "The exertions of all the different kinds of labour that are directly or indirectly involved in making it, together with the abstinences or rather the waitings required for saving the capital used in making it, all the efforts and sacrifices together will be called the real costs of production of that commodity".[1] Thus, according to Marshall, the real cost of production is the efforts and sacrifices undergone by the different members of society in producing a commodity. The sacrifice of the capitalist, for instance, consists of foregoing the use of his money for immediate consumption. Similarly, when engaged in work, the labourer deprives himself of enjoying leisure. While a private producer is interested mainly in money costs of production, the real cost of production is more important from the point of view of society. But real cost normally does not correspond to monetary expenses of production. To cite Marshall, "If the purchasing power of money in terms of effort has remained about constant, and if the rate of remuneration for waiting has remained about constant, then the money measure of costs corresponds to real costs; but such a correspondence is never to be assumed lightly". Many times, a highly unpleasant and disagreeable work may not carry high wages (e.g. sweeper's job). Similarly, a very pleasant and light job may not carry low wage (e.g. job of a university professor).

Opportunity Cost (or Social Cost)

Economists are interested mainly in the cost which a society incurs when its productive resources are used for producing a certain commodity. At any point of time, a society possesses a certain amount of productive resources either individually or collectively owned. From the point of view of the society, the object of economic activity is to obtain the maximum possible from the given productive resources. What is 'possible', of course, depends not only upon the efficient and full utilisation of productive resources but also on the specific list of commodities produced. With the same amount of productive resources, a society can build a larger number of small and simple houses than the number of palatial houses. In their private valuation schemes, some members of society, however, may attach much greater significance to living in a palatial building than to living in a small and simple house. Balancing the relative resource a cost of a commodity with its relative social desirability requires a knowledge of both social valuations and social cost. Since this broad problem has been discussed in detail in later chapter, here we confine ourselves to only social cost.

The social cost of using a certain amount of resources to produce a unit of commodity X is the number of units of commodity Y which must be foregone in the process. This is also known as the *alternative* or opportunity cost of production. In other words, the opportunity cost is the most attractive alternative foregone or the next best choice sacrificed.

Significance of Opportunity Cost

The concept of opportunity cost is basic to economic theory. Robbin's famous definition of economics is based on the fact that the resources are limited and can be put to alternative uses. It is the concept of opportunity cost which explains the emergence of price. Since the goods and productive resources are limited and capable of being put to alternative uses, they command a price. If they were available in plenty, no alternatives would be foregone, and hence they would command no price. The concept of opportunity cost has a wide application in economic theory. It applies to the determination of values not only internally but also internationally. It also applies to the determination of factor prices. The factors of production have alternative uses and, therefore, they must be paid at least the price which they can obtain in the alternative uses.

Limitations of Opportunity Cost

In the first place, the concept of opportunity cost cannot be applied to productive services which are fixed or specific. A specific factor has no alternative use and hence its opportunity cost is zero. But the cost of such a factor does enter into the price of the product which it assists to produce.

Secondly, if the factors are prevented from moving or are themselves unwilling to move to alternative occupations, their prices do not reflect their opportunity cost.

Thirdly, there may be difference between individual and social costs. The smoke of a factory may involve large sacrifice of alternatives in the form of harmful effects on the health of the people which cannot be measured in terms of money.

Fourthly, it is very difficult to determine the alternatives foregone. If a factor is lumpy as in the modern complex productive system, for instance, it has no alternative use once it is installed. But its cost does enter into the price of the product which it assists to produce.

Lastly, the concept assumes the existence of perfect competitions which is not true in the real world.

In spite of the limitations and complications mentioned above, the concept of opportunity cost is the most widely accepted one.

Economic versus Accounting Costs

Economic costs are synonymous with opportunity cost and are the sum of all decision—relevant explicit and implicit costs. Whereas the accounting costs are the costs that would appear on accounting statements and are explicit costs that have been incurred in the past. The purpose of accounting statements is to serve an audience outside the firm like general public, investors, governments, so accounting costs must be objectively verifiable.

Sunk versus Non-sunk Costs

Sunk costs are the costs that have already been incurred and cannot be recovered while non-sunk cost is a cost that will be incurred only if a particular decision is made and are thus avoidable if the decision is not made, that is why it is also called avoidable cost. When evaluating alternative decisions, the decision maker should ignore sunk costs and consider only non-sunk costs. For example, in deciding whether to build a factory, which cost 100 crore rupees, is a non-sunk cost. It is a cost the firm incurs only if it builds the factory. After the factory is built, the 100 crore rupees becomes a sunk cost. It is a cost the firm incurs no matter what it later choose to do with the factory, so this cost is unavoidable. To identify what costs are sunk and what costs are non-sunk in a particular decision, one should keep in mind which costs would change as a result of making one choice as opposed to another.

Derivation of Cost Curves from a Production Function

Let us consider a Cobb-Douglas type production function and the cost equation as

$$X = b_0 L^{\alpha_1} K^{\alpha_2} \quad \text{(i)}$$

$$C = wL + rK \quad \text{(ii)}$$

Our task is to derive the cost function, i.e. the total cost as a function of output, i.e.

$$C = f(X) \quad \text{(iii)}$$

This problem can be solved as the constrained output maximisation problem:

Maximise $\quad X = b_0 L^{\alpha_1} K^{\alpha_2} \quad$ (iv)

Subject to $\quad \bar{C} = wL + rK \quad$ (v)

$\bar{C}$ denotes that the firm has a given amount of money to spend on both factors of production, i.e. $\bar{C}$ is a constraint.

Our composite function becomes

$$\phi = X + \lambda(\bar{C} - wL - rK) \quad \text{(vi)}$$

where, λ = Lagrangian multiplier

First Order Condition of Maximisation: The first order condition for maximisation is that the first derivatives of the function with respect to L, K and λ shall be equal to zero.

$$\frac{\partial \phi}{\partial L} = \alpha_1 \frac{X}{L} - \lambda w = 0 \quad \text{(vii)}$$

$$\frac{\partial \phi}{\partial K} = \alpha_2 \frac{X}{K} - \lambda r = 0 \qquad \text{(viii)}$$

$$\frac{\partial \phi}{\partial \lambda} = (C - wL - rK) = 0 \qquad \text{(ix)}$$

From equations (vii) and (viii) we get

$$\alpha_1 \frac{X}{L} = \lambda w \quad \text{and} \quad \alpha_2 \frac{X}{K} = \lambda r$$

Dividing these two expression we get

$$\frac{\alpha_1}{\alpha_2} \cdot \frac{K}{L} = \frac{w}{r}$$

Therefore, $$K = \frac{w}{r} \cdot \frac{\alpha_2}{\alpha_1} L \qquad \text{(x)}$$

Substituting the value of K in the production function equation (i) we get

$$X = b_0 L^{\alpha_1} \left[\frac{w}{r} \frac{\alpha_2}{\alpha_1} L \right]^{\alpha_2}$$

$$X = b_0 \left[\left(\frac{w}{r} \right) \left(\frac{\alpha_2}{\alpha_1} \right) \right]^{\alpha_2} L^{(\alpha_1 + \alpha_2)} \qquad \text{(xi)}$$

In equation (xi) the terms in brackets is the constant term of the function. It includes the three coefficients of the production function, b_0, α_1, and α_2 and the prices of the factors of production. Solving equation (xi) we get

$$\frac{1}{b_0 \left(\frac{w}{r} \frac{\alpha_2}{\alpha_1} \right)^{\alpha_2}} X = L^{(\alpha_1 + \alpha_2)}$$

Or $$\left[\frac{1}{b_0 \left(\frac{w}{r} \frac{\alpha_2}{\alpha_1} \right)^{\alpha_2}} \cdot X \right]^{\frac{1}{(\alpha_1 + \alpha_2)}} = L$$

Or $$L = \left(\frac{r\alpha_1}{w\alpha_2}\right)^{\alpha_2/(\alpha_1+\alpha_2)} \cdot \left(\frac{X}{b_0}\right)^{1/(\alpha_1+\alpha_2)} \quad \text{(xii)}$$

Substituting the value of L from equation (xii) into equation (x) we get

$$K = \frac{w}{r}\frac{\alpha_2}{\alpha_1}\left(\frac{r\alpha_1}{w\alpha_2}\right)^{\alpha_2/(\alpha_1+\alpha_2)} \left(\frac{X}{b_0}\right)^{1/(\alpha_1+\alpha_2)}$$

$$K = \left(\frac{w\alpha_2}{r\alpha_1}\right)^{\alpha_1/(\alpha_1+\alpha_2)} \left(\frac{X}{b_0}\right)^{1/(\alpha_1+\alpha_2)} \quad \text{(xiii)}$$

Substituting equations (xii) and (xiii) into equation (ii) we get

$$C = \left(\frac{1}{b_0}\right)^{1/(\alpha_1+\alpha_2)} \cdot \left[w\left(\frac{r\alpha_1}{w\alpha_2}\right)^{\alpha_2/(\alpha_1+\alpha_2)} + r\left(\frac{wb_2}{rb_1}\right)^{\alpha_1/(\alpha_1+\alpha_2)} \right] \cdot X^{1/(\alpha_1+\alpha_2)}$$

Rearranging the above expression we get

$$C = \left\{ \left(\frac{1}{b_0}\right) \left[\left(\frac{\alpha_1}{\alpha_2}\right)^{\alpha_2} + \left(\frac{\alpha_2}{\alpha_1}\right)^{\alpha_1} \right] \right\}^{1/(\alpha_1+\alpha_2)} \cdot \left\{ w^{\alpha_1/(\alpha_1+\alpha_2)} . r^{\alpha_2/(\alpha_1+\alpha_2)} \right\} . X^{1/(\alpha_1+\alpha_2)}$$

This is the required cost function depending on the output (X), the production function coefficients, b_0, α_1, α_2 and the price of factors, w and r.

If the prices of factors are given, cost depends only on output X, and we can draw the diagram of cost curves with cost function

$$C = f(X)$$

Here we consider other determinants of costs, like production technology and the prices of factors, as constant.

Equilibrium of the Firm

Here we shall consider two ways to find out the equilibrium of the firm.

(a) maximisation of output subject to a cost constraint, and

(b) minimisation of cost for a given level of output.

Maximisation of Output Subject to a Cost Constraint

The problem of the firm can be stated as follows:

Maximise $X = f(L, K)$

Subject to $\bar{C} = wL + rK$

Composite function can be written as

$$\phi = X + \lambda(\bar{C} - wL - rK) \quad \text{(i)}$$

where λ = Lagrangian multiplier

First Order Condition of Maximisation: The first order condition for the maximisation of a function is that its partial derivatives shall be equal to zero. The partial derivatives of the above function can be written as

$$\frac{\partial \phi}{\partial L} = \frac{\partial X}{\partial L} + \lambda(-w) = 0 \quad \text{(ii)}$$

$$\frac{\partial \phi}{\partial K} = \frac{\partial X}{\partial K} + \lambda(-r) = 0 \quad \text{(iii)}$$

$$\frac{\partial \phi}{\partial \lambda} = \bar{C} - wL - rK = 0 \quad \text{(iv)}$$

From equations (ii) and (iii) we get

$$\frac{\partial X}{\partial L} = \lambda w \quad \text{or} \quad \lambda = \frac{\partial X/\partial L}{w} = \frac{MP_L}{w} \quad \text{(v)}$$

$$\frac{\partial X}{\partial K} = \lambda r \quad \text{or} \quad \lambda = \frac{\partial X/\partial K}{r} = \frac{MP_K}{r} \quad \text{(vi)}$$

Thus, from equations (v) and (vi) we get

$$\frac{\partial X/\partial L}{w} = \frac{\partial X/\partial K}{r}$$

Or

$$\frac{MP_L}{MP_K} = \frac{\partial X/\partial L}{\partial X/\partial K} = \frac{w}{r} \quad \text{(vii)}$$

Thus, the firm is in equilibrium when it equates the ratio of the marginal productivities of factors to the ratio of their prices.

Second Order Condition for Equilibrium: To fulfill this condition, the marginal product curves of the two factors of production of the firm should have a negative slope.

The slope of the marginal product curve of labour is the second derivative of the production function:

$$\text{Slope of } MP_L \text{ curve} = \frac{\partial^2 X}{\partial L^2} \qquad \text{(viii)}$$

Similarly for capital,

$$\text{Slope of } MP_K \text{ curve} = \frac{\partial^2 X}{\partial K^2} \qquad \text{(ix)}$$

The second order conditions are

$$\frac{\partial^2 X}{\partial L^2} < 0 \quad \text{and} \quad \frac{\partial^2 X}{\partial K^2} < 0 \qquad \text{(x)}$$

And
$$\left(\frac{\partial^2 X}{\partial L^2}\right)\left(\frac{\partial^2 X}{\partial K^2}\right) > \left(\frac{\partial^2 X}{\partial L \partial K}\right)^2 \qquad \text{(xi)}$$

These conditions are sufficient to establish the convexity of the isoquants.

Minimisation of Cost for a Given Level of Output

This problem can be stated as follows:

Minimise $C = f(X) = wL + rK$

Subject to $\bar{X} = f(L, K)$

Composite function of the problem can be written as

$$\phi = C - \lambda\,[\bar{X} - f(L, K)]$$

Or
$$\phi = (wL + rK) - \lambda\,[\bar{X} - f(L, K)] \qquad \text{(xii)}$$

First Order Condition: The partial derivative of ϕ with respect to L, K, and λ shall be equal to zero.

$$\frac{\partial \phi}{\partial L} = w - \lambda \frac{\partial f(L,K)}{\partial L} = 0 = w - \lambda \frac{\partial X}{\partial L} \qquad \text{(xiii)}$$

$$\frac{\partial \phi}{\partial K} = r - \lambda \frac{\partial f(L,K)}{\partial K} = 0 = r - \lambda \frac{\partial X}{\partial K} \qquad \text{(xiv)}$$

$$\frac{\partial \phi}{\partial \lambda} = -[\bar{X} - f(L, K)] = 0 \quad \text{(xv)}$$

From equations (xiii) and (xiv) we get

$$w = \lambda \frac{\partial X}{\partial L} \quad \text{and} \quad r = \lambda \frac{\partial X}{\partial K} \quad \text{(xvi)}$$

And $$\frac{w}{r} = \frac{\partial X/\partial L}{\partial X/\partial K} = MRS_{L,K} \quad \text{(xvii)}$$

Second Order Condition:

$$\frac{\partial^2 X}{\partial L^2} < 0 \quad \text{and} \quad \frac{\partial^2 X}{\partial K^2} < 0$$

And $$\left(\frac{\partial^2 X}{\partial L^2}\right)\left(\frac{\partial^2 X}{\partial K^2}\right) > \left(\frac{\partial^2 X}{\partial L \partial K}\right)^2$$

Thus, the sufficient condition is fulfilled by the assumption of negative slope of the marginal product of factors.

Cost Curves in Short-run and Long-run

The money cost of production of a commodity depends upon three variables, viz. (i) prices paid for the various factors of production, (ii) the scale of output of the firm, and (iii) the period of production under consideration, i.e. whether the period at the disposal of the firm is short or long enough to make necessary adjustments in all the factors of production. When we talk of average cost of production for a unit of commodity, for instance, we always have in view a certain factor cost, a given output and a given period of time. In what follows, we will assume that factor costs or prices are given, and study the behaviour of second and third variables together.

The element of time exerts an important influence on the cost of production. There are some inputs or factors which can be immediately increased or decreased with the changes in the level of output. If a firm desires to expand its production, for instance, it can immediately employ more workers and also buy and use more raw materials. The factors whose volume of employment can be readily adjusted to the changes in the scale of production are known as variable factors. In contrast, there are factors which cannot be quickly adjusted to changes in the scale of factors, e.g. capital equipment, building, top management personnel, etc. It takes a long time to acquire and install equipment with a larger production capacity. Similarly, it takes time to enlarge the building of the factory. Such factors are known as fixed factors.

Corresponding to the distinction between variable and fixed factors, a distinction has been made between the short-run and the long-run. The short-run is a period of time in which output can be adjusted only by changing the amount of variable factors like labour, raw materials, etc. In the short period, the quantities of fixed factors cannot be adjusted to the changes in production. In other words, in the short period, the firm cannot install a new plant or abandon an old one. In contrast, long period is defined as the period in which the quantities of all factors can be adjusted to the changes in production. As all the factors are variable in the long-run, the distinction between variable and fixed factors relates only to the short period.

Corresponding to the distinction between fixed factors and the variable factors, the total cost of production has been divided into fixed costs and variable costs. Variable costs are those costs which vary more or less proportionately with the changes in output, e.g. cost of raw materials or of casual or daily labour employed. If a firm wants to increase production, it has to spend more on raw materials, wages, fuel, power, transport, etc. Marshall calls variable costs as prime costs or direct costs or special costs. Prime costs are direct costs because the quantity produced by a firm depends directly on them.

In contrast, fixed costs are those costs which do not change with the changes in the volume of output, e.g. cost of machinery, rent of building, insurance premium, etc. An increase in production does not lead to an increase in the rent of the factory or the cost of equipment. Marshall calls fixed costs as supplementary costs or overhead costs. They are called supplementary or general or indirect costs because the quantity produced by a firm does not depend directly on them. They are called overhead costs because they are common to all units of the commodity produced and not special to any one of them.

The distinction between variable and fixed costs holds true only in the short period. In the long-run, no input is fixed. In the long-run, the size of the equipment or building can be changed. The classification between fixed and variable costs depends on the duration of period under consideration. As Marshall points out, prime costs relatively to long periods become supplementary costs relatively to short periods.[2] The inputs which are fixed in the short-run become variable over a long period of time. In fact, as Marshall has pointed out, the distinction between fixed and variable costs is only of degree and not of kind. It is difficult, for instance, to say whether the wages of a clerk constitute fixed costs or variable costs. They would be variable costs if the services of the clerk can be terminated when the production ceases and fixed costs if the services cannot be so terminated.

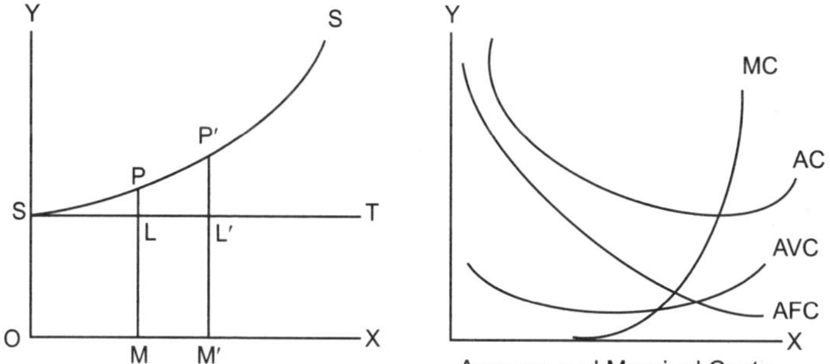

Total Cost: Fixed and Variable
(a)

Average and Marginal Costs
(b)

Fig. 12.1

Total cost of a given output consists of total fixed cost and total variable cost. The total fixed cost remains constant for all units of output but the variable cost increases with the increase in output. Total variable cost is zero when there is no output and increases with an increase in output, though the rate of increase is not constant. In the beginning it increases rapidly, but subsequently, owing to the economics of large scale production, it does not increase as rapidly as before though it rises very fast at a later stage owing to diseconomies that set in.

In Fig. 12.1(a), SS is the total cost curve and it includes the total fixed cost (indicated by the distance between the curve ST and X-axis) and the total variable cost (shown by the distance between the curve SS and ST).

Average cost per unit is the total cost divided by the number of units produced $\left(\text{ATC}=\dfrac{\text{TC}}{\text{O}}\right)$. It consists of average fixed cost and average variable cost. Average fixed cost is the total fixed cost divided by output $\left(\text{AFC}=\dfrac{\text{TFC}}{\text{O}}\right)$. The AFC curve is negatively sloped throughout because as output increases, the ratio of fixed cost to total output must decline. The AFC curve takes the form of a rectangular hyperbola. Average variable cost is the total variable cost divided by output $\left(\text{AVC}=\dfrac{\text{TVC}}{\text{O}}\right)$. Average variable cost at first declines because of economies of production and then rises as the diseconomies of large scale production set in.

By adding the two costs, we can obtain the average cost per unit of output $\left(\text{ATC}=\dfrac{\text{TC}}{\text{O}}=\dfrac{\text{TFC}}{\text{O}}+\dfrac{\text{TVC}}{\text{O}}=\text{AFC}+\text{AVC}\right)$. Over the range of values for which both AFC and AVC decline, ATC, which is the sum of two costs, must obviously decline. But even after AVC turns up, the marked decline in AFC causes the ATC to continue declining. But as output increases further, there is a short rise in AVC which more than offsets the decline in AFC. ATC, therefore, reaches its minimum and rises thereafter. Thus, the average total cost curve (ATC), like the AVC curve, first declines, then reaches its minimum value, and finally starts rising. It is thus almost of a 'U' shape.

Average Variable Cost

The shape of AVC curve can also be explained in terms of the law of variable proportions. Upto a certain point the average variable cost declines because of the working of the law of increasing returns. At this point (the point of minimum

AVC), the AVC remains stable for some time because of the working of the law of constant returns. Thereafter the AVC starts rising because of the working of the law of diminishing returns.

The AVC normally takes a 'U' shape. But the curve can take several different shapes which will generally lie between two extreme shapes shown in Fig. 12.2.

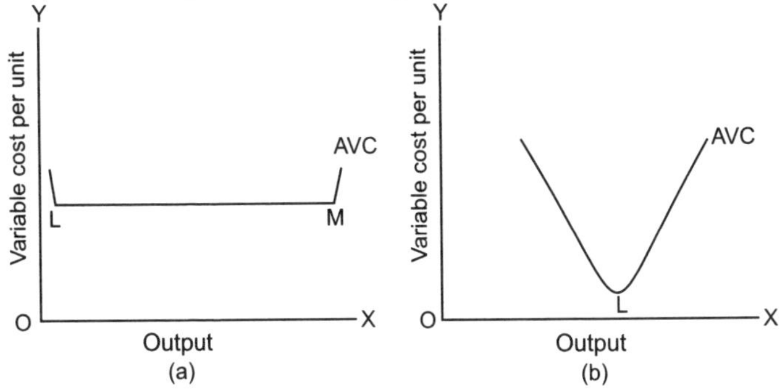

Fig. 12.2

At one extreme the average variable cost curve may be very wide and flat bottomed U, showing constant costs over a wide range of output, as shown in Fig. 12.2(a). The stability of average variable cost over a wide range may be because the plant in the firm possesses a high degree of divisibility and flexibility in its operation. In other words, the plant may have a number of units in it. If the output to be produced is small, only a few units in the plant may be set into operation. As the output to be produced increases, more and more units may be commissioned. The flexibility and divisibility of the plant has the advantage that the cost of operating the entire plant is not spread over a small output, and as such the average variable cost remains low.

At the other extreme, the average variable cost curve may be practically V-shaped, as shown in Fig. 12.2(b). This indicates that the firm is able to make the most efficient utilisation of the plant only at one critical point.

Marginal Cost

Marginal cost is defined as the change in total cost resulting from an additional unit of production. In other words, marginal cost is the addition to the total cost of producing n units instead of n – 1 units where n is a certain given number. Algebraically speaking,

$$MC_n = TC_n - TC_{n-1}$$

It may be pointed out that the marginal cost is independent of the fixed cost. As fixed costs do not vary with the change in output, there are no *marginal fixed costs* when the output is increased in the short-run. Thus, marginal costs flow from changes only in variable costs, irrespective of the amount of fixed costs. The independence of marginal cost from the fixed cost can be shown algebraically as below:

$$\begin{aligned} MC_n &= TC_n - TC_{n-1} \\ &= (TVC_n + TFC) - (TVC_{n-1} - TFC) \\ &= TVC_n + TFC - TVC_{n-1} - TFC \\ &= TVC_n - TVC_{n-1} \end{aligned}$$

Thus, marginal cost is the addition to the total variable costs when the output is increased by one unit and is independent of the amount of fixed costs.

Relation Between Average Cost and Marginal Cost Curves

If we know only the total cost curve, we can derive from it the other two cost curves, i.e. the average cost curve and the marginal cost curve. From any total cost curve, average cost at any level of output is indicated by the slope of a straight line from the origin through the point in question. Similarly, the marginal cost is indicated by the slope of a tangent to the total cost curve at any given output. The method is the same as explained in the earlier chapter in regard to revenue curves.

The marginal cost curve bears a unique relation to the average cost curve which is derived from the same total cost curve. When AC is declining with an increase in output, MC is less than AC. When AC is increasing with an increase in output, MC is greater than AC. It follows that at the output at which AC is minimum, MC is equal to AC. This relationship is shown in Fig. 12.3.

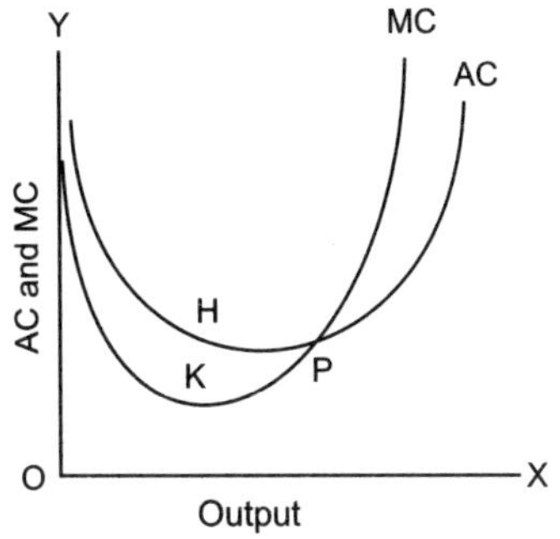

Fig. 12.3

So long as average cost curve is falling, the marginal cost curve is below it. When the average cost curve starts rising, the marginal cost curve is above it. In other words, during the declining phase, the marginal cost curve declines more rapidly than the average cost curve. Likewise, during the rising phase, the marginal cost curve rises faster than the average cost curve. At the point of intersection P where MC is equal to AC, AC is neither rising nor declining. In other words, at point P, AC has just ceased declining but has not yet started rising. It follows that the point P, where the MC curve crosses the AC curve to go above it, is the minimum point on the AC curve. In other words, the marginal cost curve intersects the average cost curve at the lowest point on the latter curve.

It may be pointed out that it is not possible to generalise about the direction in which marginal cost would move from the way average cost is moving. In other words, when the average cost is declining, it cannot be said that the marginal cost would also be declining. When the average cost is declining, what can be said with certainty is only that the marginal cost will be below the average cost but the marginal cost may be rising or declining. Similarly, when the average cost is rising, it does not follow from it that the marginal cost will also be rising. When average cost is rising, the marginal cost must lie above it but the marginal cost itself may be either rising or declining. In Fig. 12.3, upto point K, the marginal cost is declining as well as lies below the average cost. As a consequence, the average cost is declining. But beyond point K and upto point P, marginal cost curve lies below the average cost curve and as a consequence the average cost is declining. But in the range KP while marginal cost is rising, the average cost is declining. This is because though MC is rising between K and P, it lies below AC. Thus, when average cost is declining, the marginal cost may be declining or rising.

Why Short-run Average Cost Curve U-shaped?

We have seen above that the short-run average cost curve is normally U-shaped. How can we explain this shape of the average cost curve? We can explain it in two ways. Let us first take the simpler of the two explanations. The average total unit cost consists of the average fixed cost and the average variable cost. With the increase in output, the average fixed cost declines rapidly because the total fixed cost is spread over a larger output. In the initial stages, the average variable cost would also fall, though not to the same extent, because the production of the firm was below its normal capacity. Both these tendencies would make the average total unit cost to fall in the initial stages of output. But after sometime, with the increase in production, the average variable cost will start rising fast. This happens when the firm produces beyond its normal capacity. Every firm has a certain normal capacity and the cost of production would be the lowest when the actual production corresponds to this capacity. In case the actual production is extended beyond the normal capacity, the average variable cost would rise because of the excessive strain on the capacity of the firm. After a certain stage, the continued decline in the average fixed cost may become inadequate to offset the rise in the average variable cost. The net result would be that the average total unit cost will start rising. Thus, the average total unit cost will first decline and then rise and the average total unit cost curve will take a U-shape. The greater the preponderance of fixed costs in the total costs of a firm before its normal capacity is reached and the sharper the rise in its variable costs after the production goes beyond the normal capacity, the more pronounced will be the U-shape of its short-run average total unit cost curve.

Let us now turn to the second explanation of the U-shape of the short-run average total unit cost curve. In the initial stages, with the increase in the volume of output, the average cost of production falls because of the internal economies which become available to the firm as it expands its output. The internal economies which become available to a firm with the expansion of its output are of four main types, viz. (i) labour economies, (ii) managerial economies, (iii) technical economies, and (iv) marketing economies. Labour economies refer to the economies which flow from the introduction of division of labour into the operations of the firm. The larger is the scale of output, the greater is the scope for division of labour. Division of labour increases the efficiency of labour and thus lowers the cost of production. Managerial economies refer to economies in the cost per unit of management of the firm. With the expansion of output, the total cost of the management of the firm is spread over a larger output which leads to a reduction in the cost of management per unit of production. The salary of the General Manager of the firm, for instance, will not double with the doubling of the output of the firm. Technical economies refer to the economies in expenditure which flow from techniques of production. If, for instance, a die is being cast to mould the body of a new model of a sewing machine, the cost of the die per sewing machine would decline with the expansion in the output of sewing machines. Marketing economies refer to economies in the cost of marketing the product of the firm with expansion in its scale of output. The cost of advertisement, for instance, will not double with the doubling of the output of the firm.

Thus, in the initial stages of output, the average cost of production of the firm would fall with an expansion in output on account of economies of labour, management, techniques of production, and marketing. The same idea can be expressed by saying that some of the factors of production are indivisible and would be used more fully at a larger output than at a smaller output. In other words, the cost of these factors per unit of output would be lower for a larger output than for a smaller output. But as production is expanded, a point is reached beyond which expansion in output would not result in a decline in the average cost of production. At this point all the factors of production are being used by the firm in the most efficient manner and as a result the average cost of production is at the lowest level. This level of output is known as the optimum output because at this level of output, the firm is making an optimum use of all the factors of production.

But once the output of the firm exceeds the optimum level, the average cost will start rising because of the excessive strain on the individual factors and the consequent impairment of their efficiency. When the output exceeds the optimum level, the management becomes unwieldy and supervision becomes ineffective which lead to unnecessary delays, wastage of raw materials, loss of labour power, corruption, etc. All this results in a rise in the cost of production. Thus, we have explained why the short-run average cost curve will assume a U-shape.

The Break-even Point and the Shutdown Point

Break-even point is the point at which price equals the minimum of average total cost, i.e. P = ATC, and economic profit is zero. In this case, the market price line intersects the marginal cost curve exactly where it crosses the average total cost curve. The firm earns positive profits if the price is greater than the break-even point and has negative profits if the price is lower than the break-even point as shown in Fig. 12.4.

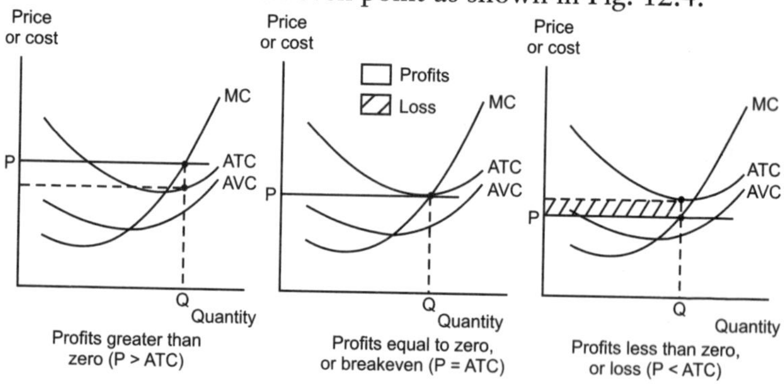

Fig. 12.4

Even if a firm has negative profit it does not shutdown because, if the firm shutdown, losses would be even larger. In the short-run, the firm has to pay fixed cost and thus by continuing operations, it can minimise its losses.

Shutdown point is the point at which price equals the minimum of average variable cost, i.e. P = minimum AVC. If the price falls below the minimum point of the average variable cost curve and is not expected to rise again then in this situation the firm should shutdown its production. In this case, the market price equals marginal cost at a quantity where total revenue is smaller than the variable costs of the production and it is better to shutdown the production. This is shown in Fig. 12.5.

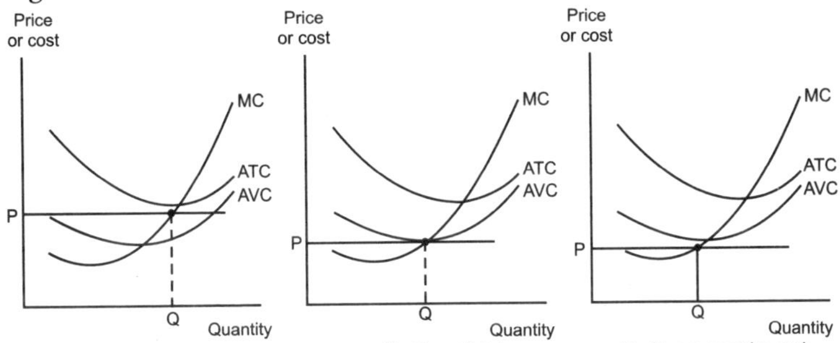

Profits are negative but price is greater than average variable cost: do not shutdown. (P > AVC)

Shutdown Point (P = AVC)

Profits are negative and price is less than average variable cost: shutdown. (P < AVC)

Fig. 12.5

If the price is above average variable cost, i.e. P > AVC, the firm should not shutdown, even if the price is below average total cost and the profits are negative because total revenue is greater than variable costs, shutting down would eliminate this extra revenue. Therefore, it is better to keep producing in the short-run.

Long-run Cost Curves

In the long-run, as we have already seen, all the inputs are variable and the firm can have any desired scale of plant. In other words, the firm can vary the quantities used per unit of time of land, buildings, machinery, management, and all other productive resources. There will be no average fixed cost curve.

We shall be concerned only with the long-run average cost curve, the long-run total cost curve, and the long-run marginal cost curve.

Long-run Average Cost Curve

Long-run average cost curve indicates the least possible average cost of producing different quantities of output. In order to understand how a long-run average cost curve is derived, it would be helpful to imagine the long-run as a series of alternative short-run situations into any of which the firm can move. Suppose it is possible for the firm to build only three alternative scales of plant. These are represented by SAC_1, SAC_2 and SAC_3 in Fig. 12.6.

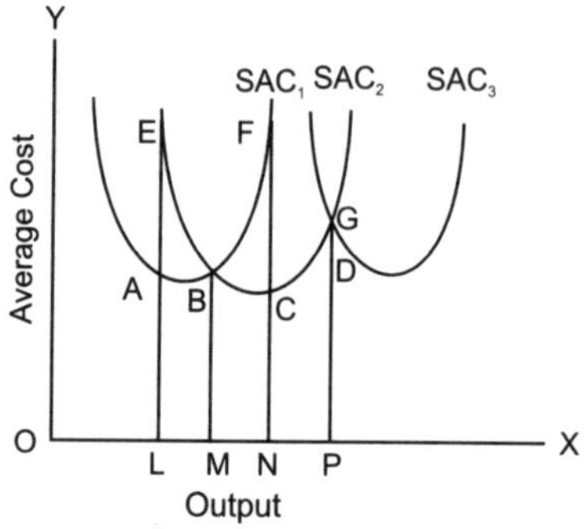

Fig. 12.6

Each SAC curve is a short-run average cost curve for a given scale of plant. These short-run average cost curves are also known as plant curves because in the short-run plant is fixed and each short-run average cost curve corresponds to a particular plan. In the long-run, the firm can build any one of the possible scales of plant, or it can shift from one plant to another.

Which scale of plant should the firm build? The reply would depend on the long-run output per unit of time to be produced. Whatever the desired output, the firm would like to produce that output at the minimum possible average cost. Suppose the desired output is OL. The firm should build the scale of plant represented by SAC_1 because it will produce the output OL at an average cost which is lower than the average cost at which this output can be produced by another plant. The average cost of producing OL output is LA on SAC_1 curve while the same is LE on the SAC_2 curve. It would be seen from the figure that the average cost LA is lower than LE. Similarly, all other outputs upto OM can be produced at a lower cost with the smaller plant SAC_1 than with the larger plant SAC_2. Thus, in the long-run, the firm would produce any output upto OM on plant SAC_1. For output OM, the firm would be indifferent between plants SAC_1 and SAC_2 because the average cost on both the plants is uniform, i.e. MB. In case the firm plans to produce an output which is larger than OM but less than OP, it will not be economical to produce on plan SAC_1. Outputs larger than OM but smaller than OP can be produced at a lower average cost on plant SAC_2 than on plant SAC_1. The average cost of producing an output ON on plant SAC_2 is NC while it is NF on plant SAC_1. It would seen from the figure that the average cost NC is much lower than the average cost NF. Thus, for outputs between OM and OP, it would economical for the firm to use the plant SAC_2. If the firm desires an output larger than OP, the average cost would be lower on plant SAC_3 than on plant SAC_2.

We are now in a position to define the long-run average cost curve. It shows the least possible average cost of producing various outputs when the firm has enough time at its disposal to build any desired scale of plant. In the figure, the solid portions of the SAC curves form the long-run average cost curve. The broken line portions of the SAC curves do not have any relevance so far as the long-run average cost is concerned.

The possible scales of plant which a firm can build in the long-run are infinite in number. For every conceivable size of plant there would be another plant infinitesimally larger or infinitesimally in size. There would be a short-run average cost (SAC) curve corresponding to each size of the plant. As a consequence there would be a series of SAC curves as shown in Fig. 12.7.

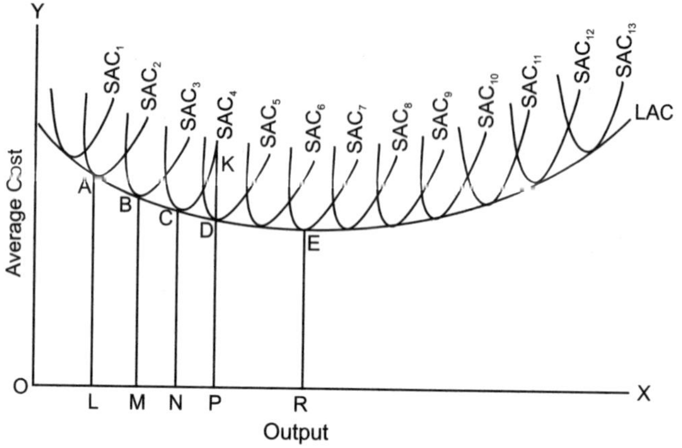

Fig. 12.7

In fact, even here any number of additional SAC curves can be drawn between any two of those shown in the figure. The outer portions of the SAC curves form a solid line which is the long-run average cost curve (i.e. LAC). As the LAC consists of very small segments of the innumerable SAC curves, it can be considered just tangent to all possible SAC curves representing different scales of plant which the firm can conceivably build. In fact, long-run average cost curve is nothing but the locus of all these tangency points. For any output that the firm may desire to produce in the long-run, it will pick up a point on the long-run average cost curve corresponding to that output and then build a relevant plant and operate on the corresponding short-run average cost curve. In the figure, if the desired output is OL, the firm will construct a plant corresponding to SAC_2 and operate on this curve at point A. Similar would be the case for all other outputs. The long-run average cost curve is also known as *envelope curve* because it envelops or supports a family of short-run average cost curves form below. The LAC curve is also called the *planning curve* because it represents the cost-output data which are useful to a firm when it is formulating its policy in regard to its scale of operations over a long period of time.

We now turn to the relationship between the LAC curve and the various SAC curves enveloped by it. First, long-run average cost curve will not be above the short-run average cost curve for any level of output. This is because adjustments to reduce costs are more possible in the long-run than in the short-run. The average cost of production may be higher in the short period than in the long period because of the existence of certain indivisible factors. Since there are no indivisible factors in the long-run, the long-run average cost will be lower than the short-run average cost. Thus, the long-run average cost curve will never cut a short-run average cost curve though the long-run average cost curve is tangential to the short-run average cost curves.

Secondly, the long-run cost curve can lie below any single short-run cost curve for some levels of outputs. But for any particular level of output, the long-run average cost curve has to be tangent to one of the short-run average cost curves. For instance, if the desired output is ON in the foregoing figure, the cost of production would be the lowest on the SAC_4 which is tangential to LAC for the output ON. If the firm desires to increase its output to OP, in the short-run, it can produce this output on SAC_4 at an average cost of PK. But in the long-run since there is enough time to change the size of the plant, it can produce the same output on a new plant SAC_5 at an average cost of PD which is lower than PK. Thus, in the long-run the firm can produce a given output on more than one short-run cost curves but it will produce on that short-curve on which the average cost of production is the lowest and the long-run cost curve will be tangential to that short-run average cost curve.

Shape of Long-run Average Cost Curve

It will be seen from the foregoing figure that the long-run average cost curve first declines and then after a certain point it rises. In other words, the long-run average cost curve takes a U-shape, which is, of course, less pronounced than the U-shape of the short-run average cost curve. It may, however, be pointed out that the LAC is not tangent to the minimum points of the short-run average cost curves. When the long-run average cost curve is declining, LAC is tangent to the falling portions of the short-run average cost curves. This means that for any output smaller than OP, it will not be economical to operate a plant at its minimum unit cost. Similarly, when the long-run average cost curve is rising, it will be tangent to the rising portions of the short-run average cost curves. This means that for any output larger than OP, it would be economical to build a plant with a given optimal capacity and to operate it to produce larger than its capacity, i.e. it should be operated at a point which is beyond the point of minimum average cost of production.

Thus, on a continuous long-run average cost curve, both for outputs less than OP and more than OP, no plant is operated at its point of minimum cost. Only that plant would be operated at the point of its minimum average cost of production the minimum point of whose short-run average cost curve coincides with the minimum point of the long-run average cost curve. In the figure for producing an output OP, the plant SAC_5 is operated at its minimum cost of production, i.e. PD. In other words, the plant SAC_5 is being operated at its optimum output.

The plant SAC_5 is called the optimum plant because it is the most efficient of all scales of plant that the firm can build. The optimum scale of plant can also be thought of as that scale of plant with a short-run average cost curve tangent to the long-run average cost curve at the minimum points of both. If the size of the plant is either larger or smaller than SAC_5, the average cost of production would be higher. The optimum output or the least-cost output of the plant SAC_5 is OP. Thus, an optimum firm is that firm which is producing optimum output (i.e. least-cost output) with the optimum plant. In the foregoing figure, the firm would be of the optimum size if it is using SAC_5 plant and produces output OP on this plant. Firms will not always build optimum scales of plant and operate them at optimum levels of output. As we shall see later on, they will do so in the long-run under conditions of pure competition. They are, however, not likely to do so under pure monopoly, oligopoly, and monopolistic competitions.

The optimum size of the firm widely differs from industry to industry. In some fields like agriculture, extractive industries, wholesale and retail trading, the optimum size is relatively small. In other words, in such industries, the minimum point of the long-run average cost curve is reached at a relatively small volume of output. Figure 12.8 shows a firm whose optimum size is relatively small.

In contrast, the optimum size of the plant is comparatively very large in some industries, e.g. steel industry, machine building industry and public utilities. Figure 12.9 shows a firm whose optimum size is comparatively large.

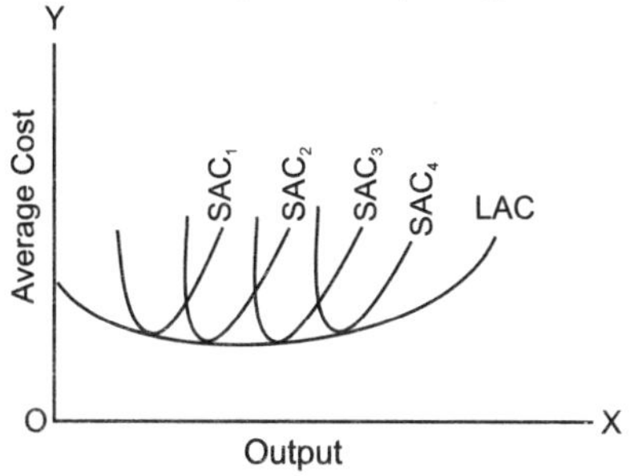

Fig. 12.8

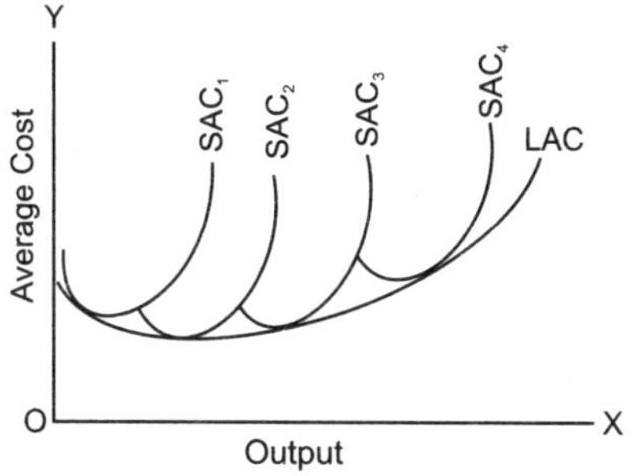

Fig. 12.9

In industries in which the optimum size of the firm is comparatively large, there are normally a smaller number of firms, each of which is quite large in size.

Constant Costs

The long-run average cost will remain constant at all levels of output if the production function is homogeneous of the first degree (or linear and homogeneous) and also the prices of inputs remain constant. As seen earlier, linear homogeneous production function means constant returns to scale. When production is subject to the law of constant returns and the prices of inputs remain unchanged, the cost per unit of output remains unchanged. In this case, the long run average cost curve will take the shape of a horizontal straight line as shown in Fig. 12.10.

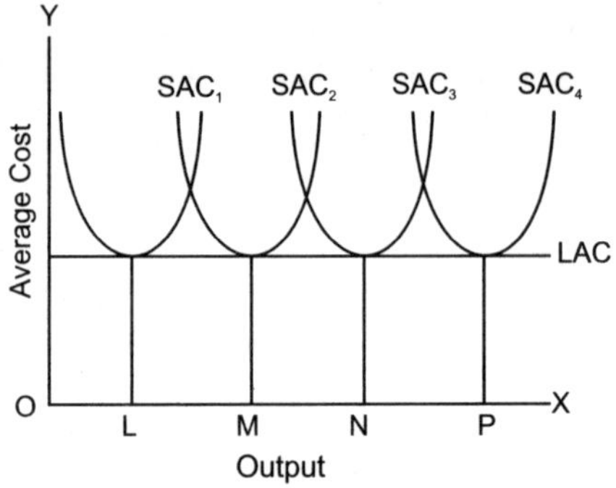

Fig. 12.10

It would be seen that all the short-run average cost curves (viz. SAC_1, SAC_2, SAC_3, SAC_4) have the same minimum average cost of production. In other words, the firm may build any size of plant, the minimum average cost of production would be the same. It may, however, be pointed out that though all levels of output would be produced at the same minimum average cost of production, the different sizes of plants will be built for producing different volumes of output. Plant SAC_1, for instance, would be used if the amount to be produced is OL. Similarly plant SAC_2 would be used producing OM output, SAC_3 plant for producing ON output and SAC_4 plant for producing OP output. This is because the average cost of production is lowest for output OL on plant SAC_1, for output OM on plant SAC_2, for output ON on plant SAC_3 and for output OP on plant SAC_4.

It is held by some economists (e.g. Kaldor, Mrs. Joan Robinson, Stigler) that there would be no internal economies or diseconomies of scale when all the factors of production are completely divisible. In this case, according to them, therefore, the long-run average cost curve will take the shape of a horizontal straight line indicating that the long-run average cost is constant for all the levels of output. They hold that internal economies arise because of the existence of certain indivisible factors. But Prof. Chamberlin is of the opinion that even if all the factors of production are perfectly divisible, the economies of scale would arise because of the use of more specialised machinery and the scope for a greater degree of division of labour at higher levels of output.

U-shape of Long-run Average Cost Curve

We have said earlier that the long-run average cost curve normally takes a U-shape, i.e. with the expansion of output, first it declines and then after sometime it starts rising. What is the explanation for this shape of the long-run average cost curve?

The U-shape of the short-run average cost curve, as seen earlier, is explained with the help of law of variable proportions. In other words, SAC curve is U-shaped because initially the average cost declines on account of the decline in the fixed cost but after sometime it starts rising on account of the decline in fixed cost being more than offset by the rise in the average variable cost—the latter happens because average product reaches a maximum and then declines. But this has nothing to do with the U-shape of the LAC. The U-shape of the LAC is explained by increasing or decreasing returns to scale in the production function and certain financial economies and diseconomies of scale.

With the increase in the size of the plant and the scale of operation considering expansion from the smallest possible plant, certain economies of scale become available. In other words, after adjusting all inputs optimally, the average cost of production can be reduced by increasing the size of the plant. Adam Smith gave the most important reason for this, i.e. specialisation and division of labour. Substantial gains can be realised by division of jobs and specialisation of workers in one or the other job. Proficiency can be gained by concentrating on a single job. If a plant is of a small size and employs only a small number of workers, each worker will normally have to perform several jobs in the production process. In this case not only the workers are deprived of an opportunity to specialise but also a part of their work time is wasted in moving around and changing tools. In contrast, a large plant employing a large number of workers provides opportunities for workers to specialise in a single job, gaining proficiency and saving time consumed in changing location and tools. This would obviously lead to a reduction in the average cost of production.

Technological factors are the second force which contribute to economies of scale. If the production process requires several different machines, each with a different rate of output, the scale of production may have to be quite large to permit full utilisation of the varying production capacities of different machines. Suppose, for instance, that only two types of machines are required by the cotton textile industry, one for making cloth and the other for giving a finish to it. Further, suppose the first machine can produce 3,000 yards of cloth per day and the second machine can finish 20,000 yards of cloth per day. In this case, if the production capacity of both the machines is to be fully utilised, the output would have to be 60,000 yards of cloth per day.

Another form of technological economies is that the cost of purchasing and installing larger machines is normally proportionately less than the cost of smaller machines. A machine which can produce 60,000 yards of cloth per day, for instance, will not cost twenty times as much as a machine which can produce only 3,000 yards of cloth per day—nor does it require twenty times as much building space, twenty times as money men to work it and so on.

Still another form of technological economies is the qualitative and quantitative change in equipment which becomes possible with the increase in the scale of output. Take the case of digging a canal. The smallest scale of operation is one man and one shovel. But when the scale of operation expands beyond a certain point, one does simply continue adding men and shovels. A stage comes when it becomes profitable to replace unskilled workers and shovels by a modern digging machine and a few skilled workers. Thus, expansion in the scale of production makes possible introduction of modern automatic equipments which reduce the average cost of production.

Marketing economies are the third force which contribute to economies of scale. Large scale purchasing of raw and semi-processed materials enables a producer to obtain materials at more favourable prices. Cost of advertising per unit of production declines with the expansion of scale of production.

Financial economies are the fourth force which contribute to economies of scale. Financial of large scale business is comparatively easier and cheaper. Banks are normally willing to give loans at lower rates of interest to large and well-known firms then to small firms. A large and well-known company can also place its bonds and stocks on organised security markets at more favourable terms.

Thus, specialisation (or division of labour), technological factors, marketing and financial economies enable a producer to reduce his average cost of production by expanding the scale of production. These forces provide an explanation of the negatively sloped portion of the LAC curve.

The rising or positively sloped portion of the LAC curve is explained by diseconomies of scale which set in after the scale of the firm has reached a certain point, which implies limitations to efficient management.

With the expansion of the firm beyond a certain stage, top management has to delegate responsibility and authority to the lower management. Supervision tends to become ineffective. It becomes difficult to attain a proper co-ordination between different activities. Red tape and paper work increases. All this leads to a decline in the efficiency of management and hence to an increase in the average cost of production.

While both the SAC and LAC are U-shaped, the U-shape of the LAC is less pronounced than the U-shape of SAC. What is the explanation for this? We can explain this in two ways. The first and the simpler explanation lies in the behaviour of the fixed and variable costs. As already explained, there are no fixed factors in the long-run. If output is to be curtailed, therefore, the fixed costs can be reduced in the long-run which is not possible in the short-run. Similarly, if an increase in output is desired, in the long-run, the firm can expand output not only by increasing variable factors but also by increasing fixed factors. Thus, the fixed factors can be better adjusted to the needs of the firm in the long-run than in the short-run. As such, when the output is curtailed, the average fixed cost will rise less sharply in the long-run than in the short-run. For the same reason, when the output is expanded, the average fixed cost will decline less sharply in the long-run than in the short-run. This constitutes an important reason for the falling portion of the average total unit cost curve being less sharp in the long period than in the short period.

We have already seen earlier that in the short period, the average variable cost rises rapidly when the output exceeds the normal capacity of the firm. Since in the long-run, there is enough time to expand the normal capacity of the firm, the rise in the average variable cost is much less than that in the short-run. Thus, we have explained as to why the U-shape of the average cost curve is less pronounced in the long period than in the short period.

Let us now turn to the second explanation for the U-shape of the average cost curve being less pronounced in the long period than in the short period. We have already seen that some of the factors of production are indivisible in the short period while they are completely divisible in the long period. Since all the factors of production can be used in varying proportions in the long-run, the scale of operations can be better adjusted to the needs of output. The same is not possible in the short period because of the existence of certain indivisible factors. Since in the long-run, the firm is in a position to adjust its plant and the scale of operations to the demand for its product, the average cost of production would be lower in the long-run than in the short-run.

Long-run Marginal Cost Curve

We have explained earlier what the marginal cost is, how the short-run marginal cost curve can be derived and what relation it bears to the short-run average cost curve. Now we shall see what the long-run marginal cost is, how the long-run marginal cost curve can be derived and what relation it bears to the long-run average cost curve. The long-run marginal cost curve shows the change in the long-run total cost per unit change in the firm's output when the firm has adequate time to change the output by making proper adjustments in the quantities of all inputs used, including those which constitute its plant. The long-run marginal cost curve can be directly derived from the long-run total cost curve because the long-run marginal cost at any level of output is shown by the slope of the total cost curve at the point corresponding to that level of output. The LMC curve can also be derived from the LAC curve because the LMC curve is related to the LAC curve in the same manner as SMC curve is related to the SAC curve.

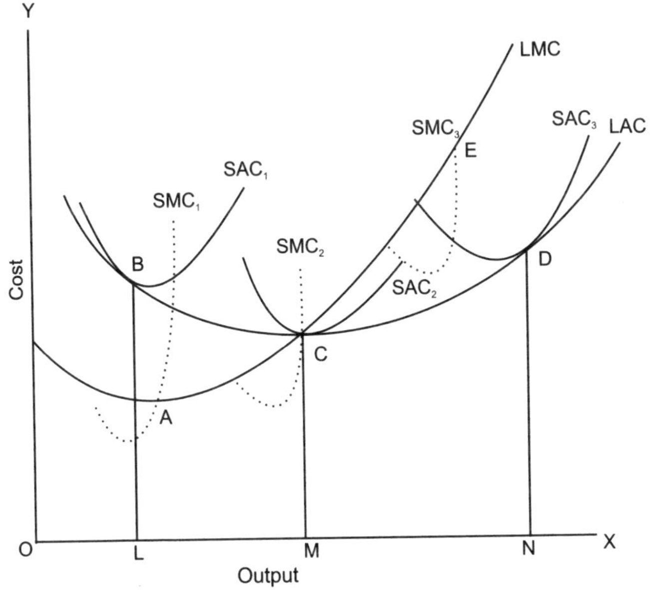

Fig. 12.11

Figure 12.11 shows how LMC is derived from LAC enveloping a family of short-run average and marginal cost curves. If the output to be produced in the long-run is OL, it would be produced on the LAC curve at point B which is the point of tangency with the short-run average cost curve SAC_1. Thus, in the long-run, output OL will be produced with the plant corresponding to the short-run average cost curve SAC_1 and the short-run marginal cost curve SMC_1. Corresponding to the tangency point B between the short-run average cost curve SAC_1 and the long-run average cost curve LAC, there is a point A on the short-run marginal cost curve SMC_1. This means that the marginal cost of producing output OL in the long-run would be LA. Point A, therefore, must lie on the long-run marginal cost curve corresponding to output OL. If the output is to be increased to OM, in the long-run it will be produced at point C which is point of tangency between LAC and SAC_2. C is also a point on the short-run marginal cost curve SMC_2 corresponding to output OM. Point C must, therefore, lie on the long-run marginal cost curve corresponding to output OM. Similarly, it can be shown that point E must lie on the marginal cost curve corresponding to output ON. If we join points BCE, we get the long-run marginal cost curve LMC.

LAC and SAC curves bear an important relation with the SMC and LMC curves. This relationship shows, as would be seen in Fig. 12.11, that at the level of output at which a particular SAC curve is tangent to the LAC curve, the corresponding SMC curve intersects the LMC curve. In other words, at the level of output at which the short-run average cost is equal to the long-run average cost, the corresponding short-run marginal cost is equal to the long-run marginal cost. This proposition can also be proved with the help of short-run total cost curve and the long-run total cost curve.

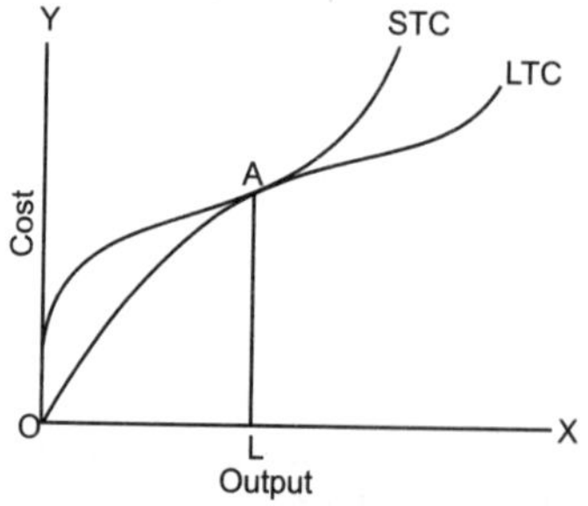

Fig. 12.12

It will be noticed in Fig. 12.12 that the long-run total cost curve (LTC) lies below the short-run total cost curve (STC) at all levels of output excepting output OL at which the LTC and STC curves are tangent to each other. This means that LAC is lower than SAC at all levels of output excepting output OL. LAC would be equal to SAC at point OL at which LTC curve is tangent to the STC curve. But the long-run marginal cost (LMC) must also be equal to the short-run marginal cost (SMC) at output OL or the point of tangency A. This is so because the marginal cost is shown by the slope of the total cost curve at any point and the LTC and STC curves have the same slope at the point of tangency A. Thus, at output OL, where SAC is equal to the LAC, SMC is equal to the LMC.

As would be seen from Fig. 12.12, the long-run marginal cost (LMC) curve, like the long-run average cost (LAC) curve, takes a U-shape. LMC curve, however, is flatter than the short-run marginal cost curve. This would naturally be so because LAC curve is flatter than the short-run cost curves. It may also be pointed out that the relationship between the LMC curve and the LAC curve is the same as between the SMC curve and the SAC curve. When the LMC curve lies below the LAC curve, the latter would be declining and when the LMC curve lies above the LAC curve, the latter would be rising. When the LMC curve is equal to LAC, the latter would neither be rising nor declining. In other words, LMC curve cuts the LAC curve at the latter's minimum point.

Comparative Statics Analysis of Changes in Input Prices

Let us consider the Fig. 12.13.

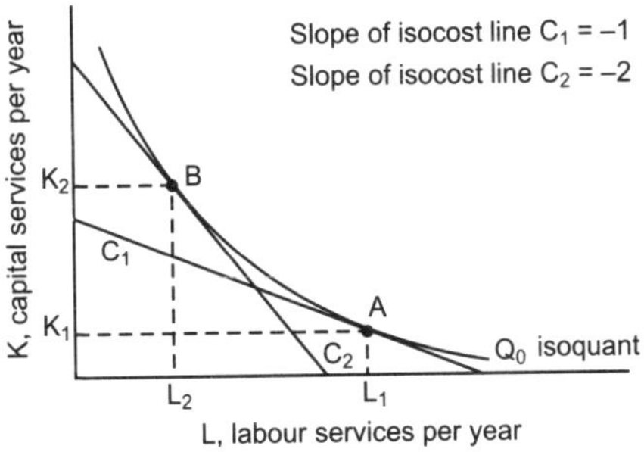

Fig. 12.13

Here we have considered that the price of labour w changes, the price of capital r held constant at 1 and the quantity of output held constant at Q_0. As w increases from 1 to 2, the cost-minimising quantity of labour goes down from L_1 to L_2 while the cost-minimising quantity of capital goes up from K_1 to K_2. Thus, the increase in the price of labour causes the firm to substitute capital for labour.

In Fig. 12.13 we see that the increase in w makes the isocost lines steeper, which changes the position of the tangency point between the isocost line and the isoquant. Thus, the tangency between the isocost line and the isoquant occurs farther up the isoquant with diminishing $MRTS_{L,K}$. Since the labour has become more expensive relative to capital, the firm uses more capital and less labour to produce the required level of output. Now, when w/r decreases, the firm uses more labour and less capital and hence the tangency moves farther down the isoquant.

Two important assumptions have been made for the above mentioned relationship. First, at the initial input prices, the firm must be using a positive quantity of both inputs. That is corner point solution is ruled out. Second, the isoquants must be smooth, i.e. without kinks.

Now let us consider Fig. 12.14.

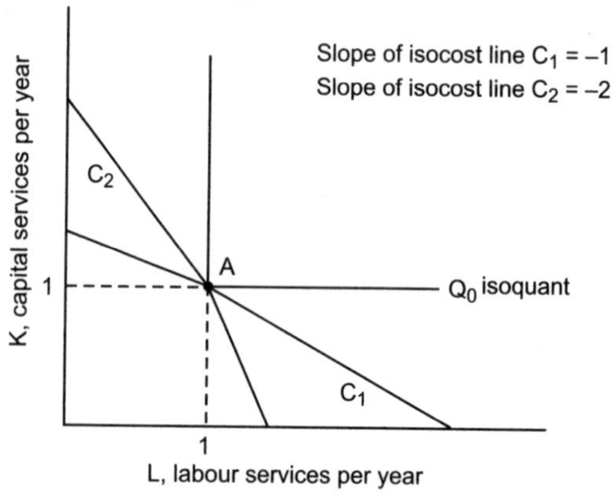

Fig. 12.14

This figure shows the condition when a firm has a fixed proportions production function and has a kink in the isquants. Here we see that like a corner point situation, an increase in the price of the labour leaves the cost-minimising quantity of labour unchanged.

Comparative Statics Analysis of Changes in Output

Consider the following figure (Fig. 12.15).

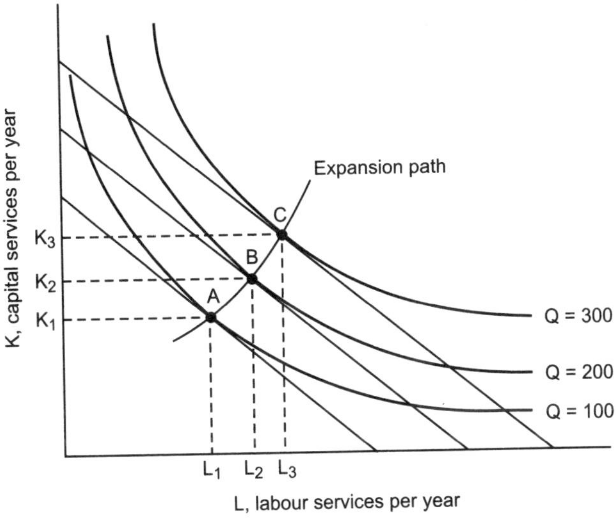

Fig. 12.15

Here we shall make a comparative statics analysis of the cost-minimisation problem for changes in output quantity Q, with the price of inputs, capital and labour, held constant. The cost-minimising combination of inputs moves from point A to point B to point C, along the expansion path as the Q increases. As the quantity of output increases, the quantity of each input also increases, which confirm that in this case, both labour and capital are normal inputs. An input is said to be normal if for producing more output more of it, is required. In the case of normal inputs, the expansion path will be upward sloping.

On the other hand, if one of the inputs is inferior, i.e. the firm uses less of it as output increases, the expansion path can be represented by Fig. 12.16.

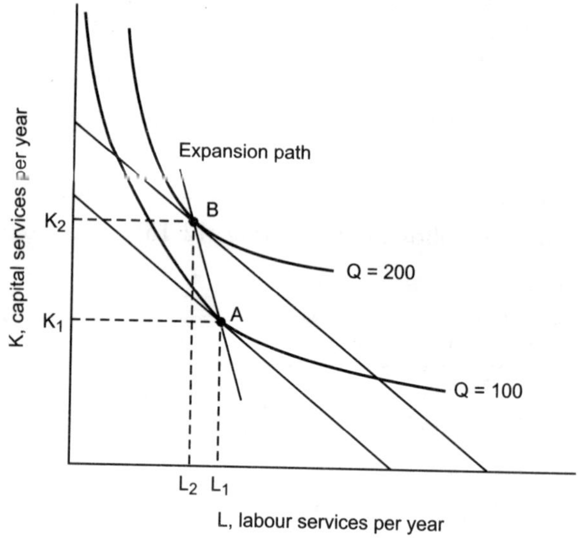

Fig. 12.16

In the figure, we have considered the labour as an inferior input. In this condition, the expansion path is downward sloping as shown in Fig. 12.16.

If both the inputs are inferior then they would decrease as the output increases. But if the firm is minimising cost, it must be technically efficient, and if it is technologically efficient, a decrease in both inputs would decrease output. Thus, both inputs cannot be inferior.

Shephard's Lemma

It states that the rate of change of the long-run total cost function with respect to an input price is equal to the corresponding input demand function. Mathematically,

$$\frac{\partial TC(Q, w, r)}{\partial w} = L^*(Q, w, r) \quad \text{(i)}$$

$$\frac{\partial TC(Q, w, r)}{\partial r} = K^*(Q, w, r) \quad \text{(ii)}$$

Shephard's Lemma provides a key link between the production function and the cost function. This is called duality. It works like this:

According to Shephard's Lemma we can derive the input demand functions if we know the total cost function. In turn, if we know the input demand function, we can infer properties of the production function from which it was derived and can derive the equation of the production function. Thus, the cost function is dual to the production function and for any production function; there is a unique total cost function that can be derived from it using the cost-minimisation problem.

Proof:

Let us assume that for a fixed Q, L_0 and K_0 are the cost-minimising input combination and their prices are w_0 and r_0 respectively. Thus, we have

$$L_0 = L^*(Q, w_0, r_0) \tag{iii}$$

$$K_0 = K^*(Q, w_0, r_0) \tag{iv}$$

Let us define a function for w and r as

$$g(w, r) = TC(Q, w, r) - wL_0 - rK_0 \tag{v}$$

Since L_0, K_0 is the cost-minimising input combination when $w = w_0$ and $r = r_0$ then

$$g(w_0, r_0) = 0 \tag{vi}$$

Since (L_0, K_0) is a feasible input combination to produce output Q at other input prices (w, r) besides (w_0, r_0), then

$$g(w, r) \leq 0 \quad \text{for} \quad (w, r) \neq (w_0, r_0) \tag{vii}$$

From equations (vi) and (vii) we find that the function g(w, r) attains its maximum when $w = w_0$ and $r = r_0$. Hence, at these points, its partial derivatives with respect to w and r must be zero.

$$\frac{\partial g(w_0, r_0)}{\partial w} = 0 \Rightarrow \frac{\partial TC(Q, w_0, r_0)}{\partial w} = L_0 \tag{viii}$$

$$\frac{\partial g(w_0, r_0)}{\partial r} = 0 \Rightarrow \frac{\partial TC(Q, w_0, r_0)}{\partial r} = K_0 \tag{ix}$$

But since $L_0 = L^*(Q, w_0, r_0)$ and $K_0 = K^*(Q, w_0, r_0)$ we have

$$\frac{\partial TC(Q, w_0, r_0)}{\partial w} = L^*(Q, w_0, r_0) \tag{x}$$

$$\frac{\partial TC(Q, w_0, r_0)}{\partial r} = K^*(Q, w_0, r_0) \quad \text{(xi)}$$

Since (w_0, r_0) is an arbitrary combination of input prices, conditions (x) and (xi) hold for any pair of input prices. Hence, Shephard's Lemma is proved.

NOTES

1. Alfred Marshall, *Principles of Economics*, p. 339.
2. *Ibid.*, pp. 420-21.

Returns to Scale

13

In the last chapter, we studied the behaviour of output when the quantity of one of the factors is kept fixed while that of the other is varied, or in other words, when the proportion in which the factors of production are employed is altered. In this chapter we shall study the behaviour of output when there is a simultaneous increase or decrease in different factors of production in such a way that the ratio in which they are combined is kept constant, or in other words, when the scale of output is altered. An increase (or decrease) in the scale of output means that all the factors of productions are increased (or decreased) in the same proportion.

Before we study returns to scale, it would be useful to be clear about the distinction between variations in scale and variations in factor proportions. The distinction is explained with the help of Fig. 13.1.

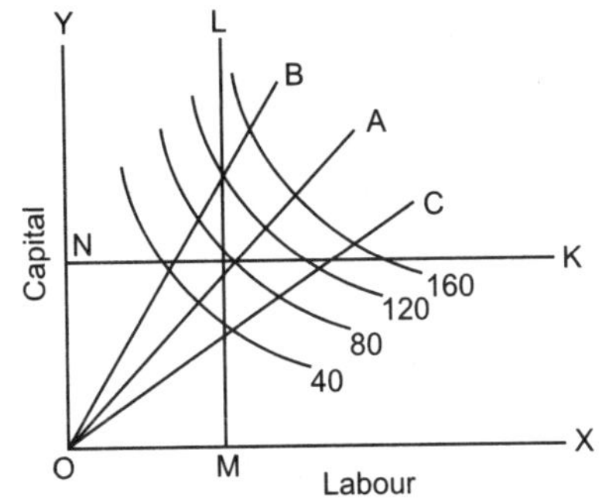

Fig. 13.1

In the figure, the two factors—labour and capital are measured along X-axis and Y-axis respectively. It is assumed that labour and capital are the only two factors required for producing a product. An equal-product map has been drawn. Let us take any point N on Y-axis and draw a horizontal line NK parallel to X-axis. ON represents the quantity of capital which remains fixed along the line NK. As we move towards right on the line NK, the quantity of capital remains unchanged at ON while the amount of labour varies. In other words, as we move towards right on the NK, the proportion in which the two factors are combined changes, i.e. there is a rise in the ratio in which the variable factor (labour) is combined with the fixed factor (capital). Thus, a movement along the line NK represents a variation in factor proportions. Similarly, a vertical line ML parallel to Y-axis represents a variation in factor proportions, i.e. the quantity of capital varies while the amount of labour remains fixed.

Let us now draw a straight line OA passing through the origin. It would be seen that along the line OA both the quantities of labour and capital vary. Further, since the line OA is a straight line passing through the origin, the ratio between the two factors along the line OA remains the same throughout. The upward movement along the line OA shows an increase in the absolute quantities of the two factors with their ratio remaining unchanged, or in other words, it shows the increase in scale. Similarly, if any other straight line passing through the origin like OB or OC is drawn, it will indicate, like the line OA, change in scale but would represent a *different given* proportion of factors which remains unchanged along the line. Thus, the various straight lines passing through the origin show different proportions between the two factors but along each line the proportion between two factors remains the same throughout.

Validity of Concept of Returns to Scale

Some economists have questioned the concept of returns to scale on the ground that all factors cannot be increased and as such the proportion between them cannot be kept constant. It has been pointed out, for instance, that in a single firm, it is not possible to vary entrepreneurship along with a change in other factors. The entrepreneurship and his decision-making are indivisible and cannot be varied. In other words, the entrepreneur is a fixed factor in all production functions. Thus, indivisibility of entrepreneurship has presented a serious problem in any meaningful discussion of the returns to scale. The problem, however, can be solved by assuming entrepreneurship to be variable in the sense that the larger the amount of other factors employed, the more the entrepreneur exerts himself. This assumption has considerable validity because it is natural that with the expansion of business the entrepreneur puts in a larger amount of work. Thus, when labour and capital are increased in a proportion, it can be assumed that the entrepreneurship increases automatically in the same proportion. In this sense, it is possible to conceive returns to scale.

In what follows, however, for the sake of simplifying the analysis, it is assumed that only two factors (viz. labour and capital) are required for producing a product. This assumption enables us to proceed our analysis in terms of equal-products curves.

Constant, Increasing and Decreasing Returns to Scale

Returns to scale may be constant, increasing or decreasing. If all the factors are increased in a given proportion and as a result the output increases in the same proportion, the returns to scale are said to be constant. Increasing returns to scale prevail when a certain percentage increase in all the factors of production results in a higher percentage increase in the total output. Thus, if a fifty per cent increase in all factors of production results in more that fifty per cent increase in output, the returns to scale would be increasing. On the other hand, decreasing returns to scale are said to prevail when a certain percentage increase in all the factors of production results in a lower percentage increase in the total output.

Constant Returns to Scale

The constant returns to scale, as seen above, mean that a certain percentage increase in all the factors of production leads to the same percentage increase in the total output. In mathematical terminology, constant returns to scale are described as linear homogeneous production function or homogeneous production function of the first degree. Linear and homogeneous production function is of great importance in economics. Empirical data shows that production function for the economy as a whole is not much different from the homogeneous function of the first degree. Empirical data also indicates that the production function of an individual firm also takes the shape of a homogeneous function of the first degree over a considerable range of production.

Figure 13.2 shows the constant returns to scale with the aid of equal-product curves.

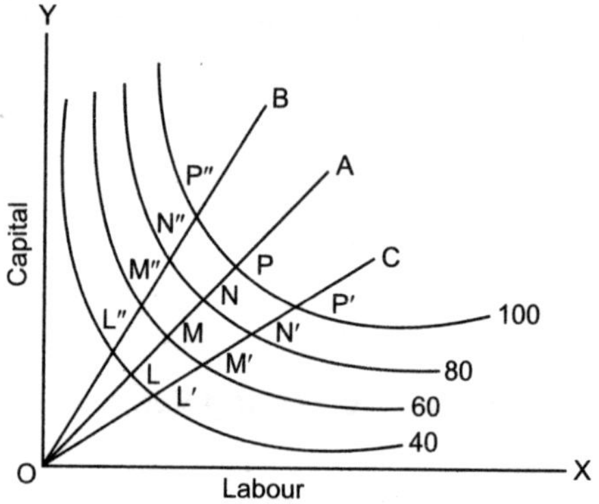

Fig. 13.2

It is assumed that production requires only two factors of production, viz. labour and capital. We draw some straight lines passing through the origin which indicate the increase in scale as we move upwards. It would be seen that the successive equal-product curves are equi-distant from each other along each straight line drawn from the origin. Thus, along the line OA, LM=MN=NP, along the line OC, L′M′=M′N′=N′P′ and along the line OB, L″M″=M″N″=N″P″. This shows that if both labour and capital are increased in a given proportion, production increases by the same proportion. Thus, the above figure exhibits constant returns to scale.

Some economists are of the opinion that production function must display constant returns to scale. They argue that if all the factors of production are doubled, there is no reason why production should also not double. If two exactly similar plants are built and fed with raw materials, labour, etc. in equal quantity and of uniform quality, there is no reason why the production should be more or less than just the double. They argue that if constant returns do not arise, it is because all factors of production cannot be increased in the same proportion. They put forward two reasons why all factors of production cannot be increased in the same proportion. In the first place, the quantities of some inputs cannot be increased in proportion because their available supplies are limited. Secondly, the quantities of some inputs cannot be varied in the required proportion because they are available only in certain indivisible quantities.

This view has invited a lot of criticism. Professor Chamberlin and some other economists hold the view that constant returns to scale cannot always prevail. They are of the opinion that increasing returns to scale can arise even if all the factors were completely divisible and could be varied in required quantities. With an increase in all factors of production, increasing returns to scale can arise because (i) greater specialisation becomes possible and (ii) introduction of specialised machinery or other inputs of a superior quality become possible owing to a wider range of technical possibilities opened up by a larger amount of resources.

Some other economists have pointed out that we cannot meaningfully talk of multiplying all the factors in a given situation. Two factories existing side by side, for instance, cannot be the same things as doubling of one factory in isolation. The existence of a second factory at a close distance affects labour discipline, air pollution, cost of labour training, etc. The change in the quantities of the various factors in a certain proportion may, therefore, not result in change in production in the same proportion. If a single large factory is more efficient than two small factories having an aggregate capacity equal to the large one, the entrepreneur would have no incentive to duplicate the inputs in the sense of establishing another factory close to the previous one.

Cobb-Douglas Function

Many economists have studied actual production functions and employed statistical techniques to find out relations between changes in physical inputs and physical outputs. A famous statistical production function is the Cobb-Douglas production function formulated by the American economists Paul H. Douglas and C.W. Cobb. The function originally applied not to an individual firm but the entire manufacturing of the United States. Senator Douglas published his production function in the *American Economic Review*, March 1948. He took labour and capital as the only inputs and reached the conclusion that capital and labour roughly contributed ¾ and ¼ respectively to the total manufacturing production. In mathematical terminology, the function is

$$Q = kL^a C^{1-a}$$

where Q stands for the manufacturing output, L represents the quantity of labour employed, C is the quantity of capital employed and k and a are positive constants (and $a<1$).

This is a linear and homogeneous production function. It signifies that constant returns to scale apply to the total of manufacturing industries. This can be proved mathematically. Let us assume that the labour and capital increase 'g' times and see its effect on output.

$$\begin{aligned} \therefore \quad Q &= k(gL)^a \cdot (gC)^{1-a} \\ &= k(g^a L^a) \cdot (g^{1-a} C^{1-a}) \\ &= kg(L)^a \cdot (C^{1-a}) \\ &= g \cdot k\,L^a C^{1-a} \\ &= g \cdot Q \end{aligned}$$

This shows that if the inputs are doubled, the output will also double. In other words, we may say that production is subject to constant returns to scale.

Increasing Returns to Scale

Increasing returns to scale mean, as stated above, that a certain percentage increase in all the inputs leads to a higher percentage increase in the total output. Professor Chamberlin is of the view that returns to scale increase because of greater opportunities for specialisation of labour and machinery.[1] Another important cause of increasing returns lies in dimensional relations. The output from an enlarged capital good increases in a greater proportion than the increase in cost. If a one-foot cube wooden box is enlarged into a three-feet cube wooden box, the wood required would increase by nine times but the increase in capacity would be twenty-seven times. Similarly if the diameter of a tube is doubled, its flow would be more than doubled.

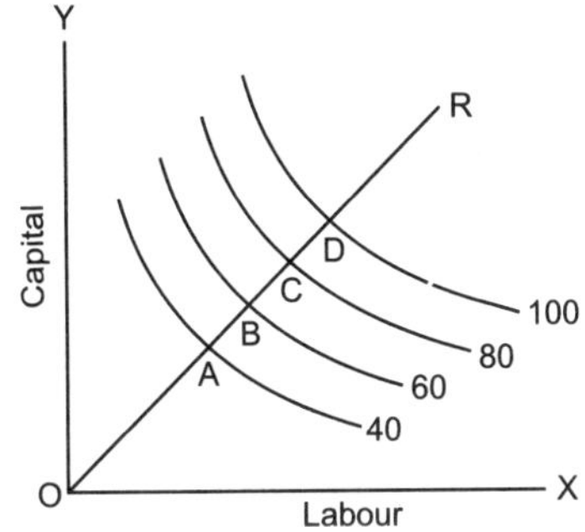

Fig. 13.3

Figure 13.3 shows increasing returns to scale. As the returns to scale increase, the successive equal-product curves lie at diminishing smaller distances along the straight line passing through origin. This means equal increases in output are obtained by smaller and smaller increases in inputs.

Decreasing Returns to Scale

When a firm goes on expanding beyond a certain point, the returns to scale starts declining. After the firm crosses the optimum size, the economies of large scale production are replaced by diseconomies of production. There arise difficulties of management, control and co-ordination. With the expansion of the firm, it becomes more and more difficult to co-ordinate the various activities of the firm. Supervision becomes difficult. More and more men are required on the administrative side. The men who manage the firm and take final decisions get far removed from the actual level of operations. They have, therefore, to take decisions on the basis of second hand information. Red-tapism increases and it becomes difficult to take quick decisions. Their initiative, particularly at the lower level, starts declining. The personal contacts management and workers diminish; this leads to a decline in the morale of the labour and to the emergence of labour troubles. Thus, the difficulties and complexities of large-scale management are an important factor explaining diminishing returns to scale.

Another factor responsible for diminishing returns to scale is the technical diseconomies which result when the production is enlarged beyond the optimum point. Every plant has an optimum size which is the most efficient and economical. If the plant of a size larger than this is employed, it will result in technical diseconomies and consequently to diminishing returns to scale.

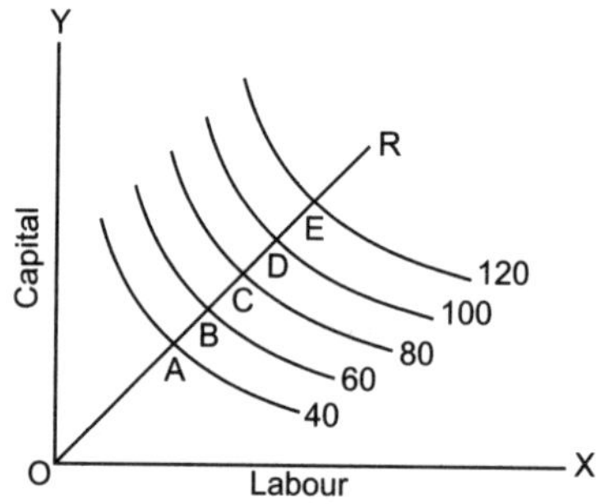

Fig. 13.4

Figure 13.4 shows diminishing returns to scale. As the returns to scale diminish, successive equal-product curves lie at progressively larger and larger distances on a straight line passing through the origin. This means equal increases in output are obtained by a larger and larger increase in output.

Least Cost Factor Combinations

An important decision which every producer has to make relates to the particular combination of factors which he should employ for producing a product. He has to make a choice out of the various combinations of factors which can produce a given level of output. Various combinations of factors which yield a given level of output, as explained earlier, are indicated by a equal-product curve. An equal-product map consists of a family of equal-product curves which indicate various technical possibilities of producing different levels of output.

It is assumed that the operations of the producer are guided by the motive of maximising profits. In order to maximise profits, the producer would try to minimise his cost for producing a given output, or in other words, he would seek to maximise output for a given outlay. The choice of a particular combination of factors by an entrepreneur is governed by (i) technical possibilities of production, and (ii) the prices of factors employed for the production of a particular product. Technical possibilities of production are indicated by the equal-product map, which we have already explained. We explain below how the prices of factors can be introduced into the study.

Iso-cost Line

An iso-cost curve shows the different combinations of factors of production which a firm can purchase, given the cost outlay to be made by the firm and the price per unit of each resource. All points on an iso-cost represent an equal or the same cost. An iso-cost enables the entrepreneur to know different combinations of inputs which cost him the same. Let us assume that there are only two inputs, namely X and Y, and their respective prices are P_x and P_y. We further assume that the total cost outlay of the firm is T. In Fig. 13.5 units of input X are measured along the horizontal axis and those of Y along the vertical axis.

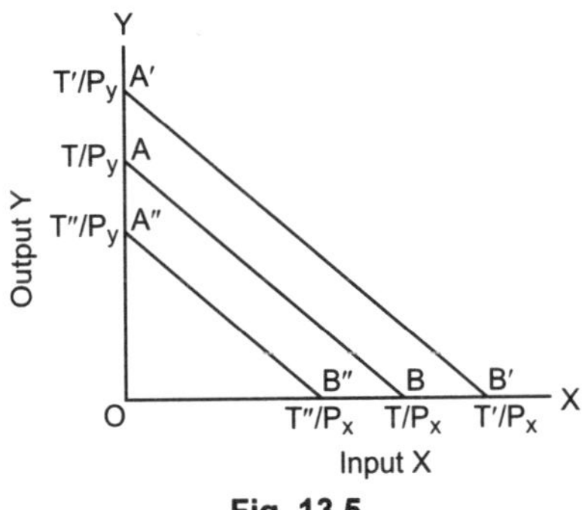

Fig. 13.5

If the firm uses input X only, it can purchase T/P_x units of X. In case it uses input Y only, it can purchase T/P_y units of Y. A straight line joining the two points A and B on Y-axis and X-axis respectively shows all combinations of X and Y which the firm can purchase with its given cost outlay and is known as an iso-cost curve. An iso-cost line is defined as the locus of factor combinations that can be purchased for a given total cost. It is also known as the *price line* or the *outlay line*.

If the total cost outlay of the firm is increased to T′, the iso-cost line will shift upwards to A′B′ which is parallel to the original iso-cost line AB. Similarly, if the total cost outlay is decreased to T″, the iso-cost will shift downward to A″B″ which is parallel to the original iso-cost line AB. Thus, a family of iso-cost lines can be drawn parallel to each other, each indicating the various factor-combinations which can buy for a particular outlay. The larger the outlay, the higher is the corresponding iso-cost line and conversely.

The iso-cost line will also shift if there is a change in the prices of factors, outlay cost remaining unchanged.

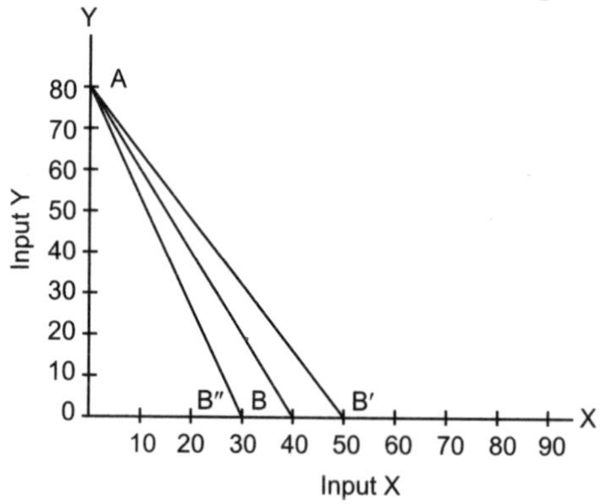

Fig. 13.6

Suppose the outlay cost of the firm is Rs. 400 and the prices of a unit of inputs X and Y are Rs. 10 and Rs. 5 respectively. With this data in regard to the total outlay cost and prices of inputs X and Y, the iso-cost line will be AB. If now the price of input X declines from Rs. 10 to Rs. 8 per unit, the firm would be able to buy 50 (or OB′) instead of 40 (or OB) units of X if it spends the entire outlay on input X. Thus, the decline in the price of input X shifts the price line from AB to AB′. Similarly, if the price of input X rises to the Rs. 12 per unit, the price line would shift to the position AB″. In the same manner shifts in the price line can be shown if the change is in the price of input Y.

The slope of the iso-cost line, like that of the price line in indifference curves analysis of demand, is equal to the ratio of the prices of two inputs. The slope of the iso-cost line is given by

$$AB = \frac{\text{Price of Factor X}}{\text{Price of Factor Y}}$$

Least Cost Factor Combination

By 'maximum economic efficiency' is meant the least cost combination of inputs for producing a given output. Identification of economically efficient resource combinations requires knowledge of both production possibilities and input prices. In general, the cost of producing a given output is minimum at the point where the equal-product curve touches the price line representing the smallest possible outlay. In other words, the least cost of producing a given output is at the point where the equal-product curve (which is likely to be convex to the origin) is tangent to the linear price line. At any point other than the point of tangency, the equal-product curve intersects the higher price line and as such involves a greater cost for producing a given output (Fig. 13.7).

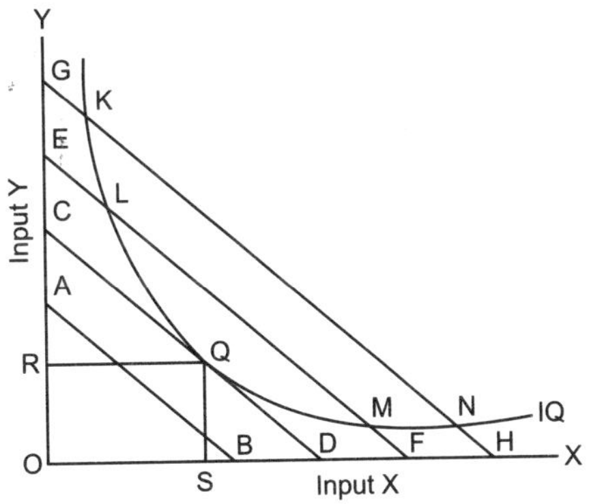

Fig. 13.7

Let us assume that the entrepreneur wants to produce 200 units of output which is represented by the equal-product curve IQ. The 200 units can be produced by a number of input combinations like K, L, Q, M, N, etc. lying on the equal-product curve IQ. But it is evident from the figure that the cost of producing 200 units will be the minimum at point Q at which the iso-cost line CD is tangent to the given equal-product curve IQ. Since all other points on curve IQ (viz. K, L, M, N) lie on iso-cost lines, higher than CD, the total cost of producing this output would be larger. Thus, the tangency point of the given equal-product curve with the iso-cost line indicates the least cost combination of factors for producing a given output.

At the point of tangency between the equal-product curve and the price line, the slope of the price line is equal to the slope of the product curve, i.e. $\frac{P_x}{P_y} = \frac{MP_x}{MP_y}$. In other words, the total cost of producing a given output will be least if the inputs are employed in a manner that the ratio of the marginal products of the factors are proportional to the ratio of their prices. This result can be easily generalised to include any number of factors. The above equation can alternatively be written as $\frac{MP_x}{P_x} = \frac{MP_y}{P_y}$. In other words, the condition for a least cost factor combination is that the ratio of marginal product of X to its price must be equal to the ratio of the marginal product of Y divided to its price. Let us see what happens if $\frac{MP_x}{P_x} > \frac{MP_y}{P_y}$. Such a situation would provide an incentive to the producer to substitute input X for input Y. The inequality means that the additional output (or marginal product) per rupee of X is larger than the additional output per rupee of Y. If by mistake the producer is too much of Y (or too little of X), he can reduce his cost by reallocating his rupee outlay (assuming that the law of diminishing returns operates so that the marginal product of Y increases and that of X diminishes as more rupees are spent on X and fewer rupees on Y) until ultimately the contribution of each input per rupee is in balance, i.e. $\frac{MP_x}{P_x} = \frac{MP_y}{P_y}$.

It may be pointed out that the least cost factor combination for a firm is not permanently fixed. It changes with variations in the relative prices of factors. With a change in relative prices, relatively larger quantities will be employed of those factors which become comparatively cheaper.

It may also be emphasised that what is required is that the marginal physical product of each factor should be proportional to its price, and not necessarily equal to it. Similarly, marginal physical products of different factors need not necessarily be equal unless all the factor-prices happen to be equal. It would be ridiculous to equate the product of a worker with that of an acre of land but the product of an additional rupee spent on each of the factors must be the same, or in other words, the marginal physical product per rupee must be the same for all factors of production. This is similar to the condition that in order to maximise his satisfaction, the consumer must spend money on different commodities in such a manner that the marginal utility of a rupee is the same in every use.

NOTE

1. It may, however, be pointed out that a greater degree of specialisation of labour and machinery almost invariably involves some change in factor propositions.

Concept of Revenue

14

The term 'revenue' means the receipts obtained by a firm from the sale of certain quantities of a commodity at different prices. The concept of revenue may refer to total revenue, average revenue, or marginal revenue. Total revenue is the total sale proceeds of a firm from the sale of a commodity at a given price. It can be obtained by multiplying the total number of units of the commodity sold with the price per unit of the commodity. Thus, TR = PQ where TR stands for total revenue, P for price per unit and Q for the quantity sold. Average revenue (AR) is the average receipts from the sale of certain units of the commodity. It can be obtained by dividing the total revenue by the number of units sold. Thus, $AR = \frac{TR}{Q}$.

Marginal revenue (MR), at any level of firm's output, is the revenue added to the total revenue by the sale of an additional (or marginal) unit of the firm's product. Algebraically speaking, MR = Difference between TR from sale of n units and TR from sale of n + 1 units.

For the first unit of the commodity sold, total, average and marginal revenues are identical because each is equal to the price of the commodity. If the sales are to be expanded to the rate of two units per period of time, the price would have to be lowered. The marginal revenue of the second unit is equal to the total revenue from the sale of two units minus the total revenue from the sale of one unit. Since MR = TR for one unit, it follows that TR for two units = MR for one unit + MR for two units. Generalising this, we can say total revenue is the sum of all marginal revenue figures.

If we know the total revenue curve, we can easily derive the average revenue and marginal revenue curves from it. The process is shown in Fig. 14.1.

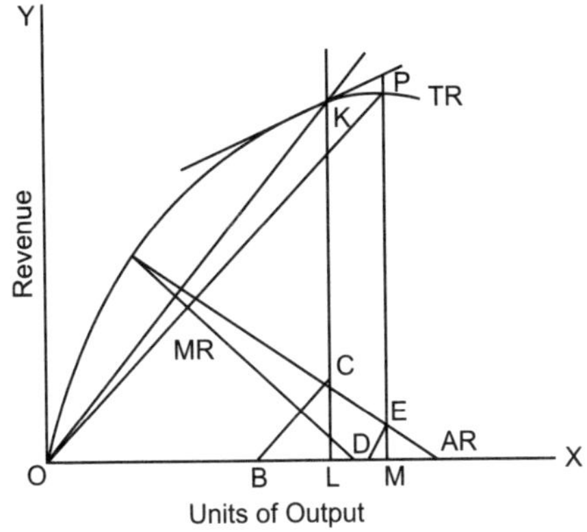

Fig. 14.1

Any line drawn from origin to any point on the curve TR will indicate the average revenue or the price per unit for that level of output. The line OK, for instance, shows the price per unit of the commodity when the level of output is OL. If we take one unit to the left of OL on the X-axis and draw a line BC parallel to OK, we get one point C on the average revenue curve. Since the slope of OK indicates the price per unit and BC is parallel to OK, the slope of the line BC also shows the price unit. As BL represents one unit, CL represents the price per unit when the output sold is OL. C is, therefore, a point on the average revenue curve indicating the average revenue or price per unit corresponding to an output OL. Similarly, we can obtain other points on the average revenue curve. Similarly, when output is OM and DM represents one unit of the commodity, the average revenue or price is EM. DE is drawn parallel to OP. As the slope of the line OP shows the price per unit corresponding to output sold OM and DE is parallel to OP, the slope of the line DE also shows the price per unit. E is, therefore, another point on the average revenue curve.

Similarly, marginal revenue curve can also be derived from the total revenue curve. The method is shown in Fig. 14.2.

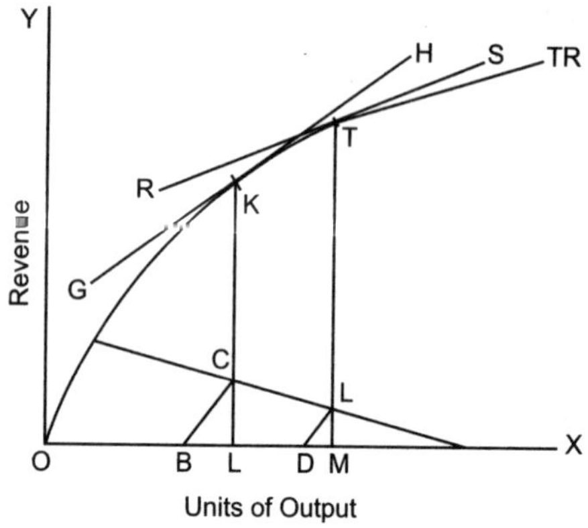

Fig. 14.2

Take any point on the total revenue curve and join it with the X-axis (or output axis). Then draw a tangent to that point on the total revenue curve. Taking one unit to the left of the level of output (appropriate to that point on the total revenue curve), draw a line parallel to the tangent. This will give us one point on the marginal revenue curve. In the above figure we have taken the point K on the total revenue curve and joined with X-axis at L. Then we have drawn a tangent GH to the point K on the total revenue curve. Taking one unit BL to the left of L, we have drawn a line BC parallel to the tangent GH. Since GH shows the rate at which the total revenue is changing (or the marginal revenue) at output OL and BC is parallel to GH, the slope of line BC also shows the marginal revenue. It indicates the revenue attributable to unit BL. CL is, therefore, the marginal revenue corresponding to the output sold OM. C is thus a point on the marginal revenue curve. Similarly, we can obtain another point E on the marginal revenue curve corresponding to the level of output OM. By continuing this process, we can obtain all the points on the marginal revenue curve which means the marginal revenue curve itself.

Relationship Between Average and Marginal Revenues

The concept of total revenue is not of much importance in the determination of price. It is the concepts of marginal revenue and average revenue which are important in price analysis. There exists a precise and definite relationship between the marginal revenue and the average revenue. So long as the average revenue curve is declining, the marginal revenue will be lower than average revenue. The marginal revenue curve may be rising, declining or horizontal but generally it is a declining one. When average and marginal revenue curves take the shape of straight lines, the marginal revenue curve will cut any perpendicular to the Y-axis half-way to the average revenue curve (Fig. 14.3).

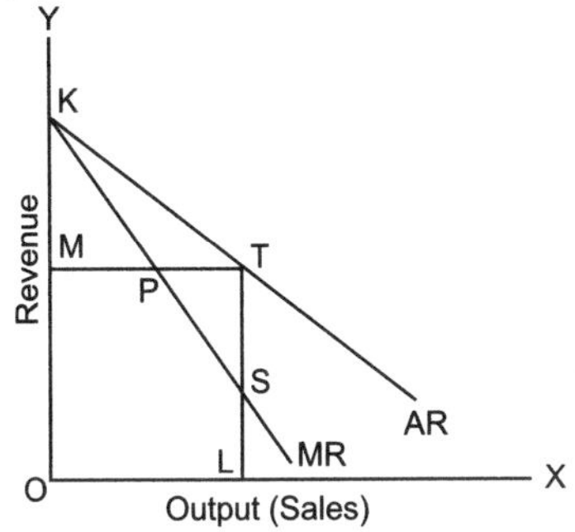

Fig. 14.3

AR and MR show the average and marginal revenue curves respectively. Let us suppose that the firm is selling OL units of output. The total revenue of the firm from the sale of this output can be shown in two ways, viz. (i) by multiplying average revenue by the number of units sold or (ii) by summing up the marginal revenues of all units. The area of OLTM = OKSL because both the areas indicate total revenue. But the area OMPSL is common in both the areas. Hence, area ΔMPK = area ΔPST. $\angle$KMP = $\angle$PTS because both are right angles. $\angle$MPK = $\angle$SPT because of being vertically opposite angles. Therefore, ΔMPK and ΔPST are equal in all respects. MP, therefore, is equal to PT or P is the middle point of MT. Thus, MR curve lies half-way between the average revenue curve and the Y-axis. This also implies that the slope of the straight line marginal revenue curve, KM/MP is twice the slope of the straight line average revenue curve, KM/MT.

The case studied above is the simplest one in which average and marginal revenue curves are straight lines. The above relation between the marginal revenue curve and the average revenue curve will not hold true if the average revenue curve is either convex to the origin or concave to the origin. When the AR curve is convex to the origin, the MR curve crosses any line perpendicular to the Y-axis at a point less than half-way from the AR curve. In contrast, if the AR curve is concave to the origin, the MR curve crosses any line perpendicular to the Y-axis at a point more than half-way from the AR curve. These two cases are shown in Fig. 14.4.

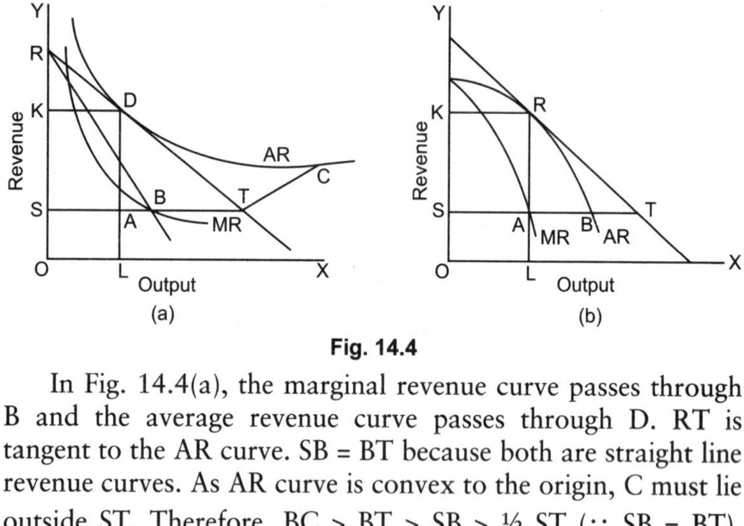

Fig. 14.4

In Fig. 14.4(a), the marginal revenue curve passes through B and the average revenue curve passes through D. RT is tangent to the AR curve. SB = BT because both are straight line revenue curves. As AR curve is convex to the origin, C must lie outside ST. Therefore, BC > BT > SB > ½ ST (∵ SB = BT). Similarly, it can be proved from Fig. 14.4(b) that when AR curve is concave to the origin, the MR curve crosses any line perpendicular to the Y-axis at a point more than half-way from the AR curve.

The fundamental relationships formulated above provide us with an extremely simple method of deriving marginal revenue curve from the average revenue curve. When the average revenue curve takes the shape of a straight line, we know that the perpendicular drawn from any point on the average revenue curve to the Y-axis is bisected by the marginal revenue curve. If the average revenue curve is known, the corresponding marginal revenue curve can be easily drawn. The case is more difficult when the average revenue curve takes the shape not of a straight line but a curve. In this case, the method of deriving the marginal revenue curve from it depends upon the fact that the marginal value corresponding to any point on the average revenue curve is the same as the marginal value corresponding to the tangent at that point. This must be the position because the rate of change of cost is the same at this point as on the tangent and on the curve, and when we are calculating the increase in total cost resulting from a small increase of output at this point it is a matter of indifference whether we calculate the increase from the curve or from the tangent. Figure 14.5 illustrates the derivation of the marginal revenue curve from the average revenue curve.

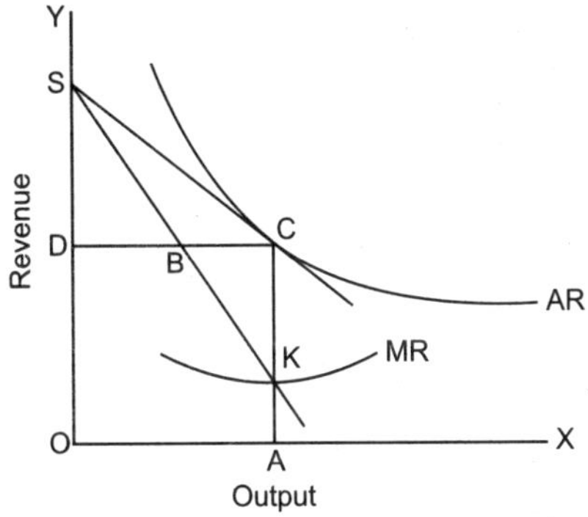

Fig. 14.5

Let SC be the tangent to the average revenue curve AR at point C. We draw CD and CA perpendicular to Y-axis and X-axis respectively. The marginal cost corresponding to output OA is the same for the curve to which SC is tangent at C and for the tangent itself. Let SK bisect DC at B and cut CA at K. Then, taking the tangent SC as the average revenue curve, SK is marginal to it. The marginal curve, therefore, passes through point K. By the same process, we can obtain other points on the marginal revenue curve or, in other words, the MR curve in itself. Mrs. Joan Robinson calls SK as the correspondent to the tangent at point C.

We have seen above that marginal revenue corresponding to any point on an average revenue curve is the same for the curve and for its tangent at that point. From this it follows that if a number of average curves are tangential to each other at a certain point, the corresponding marginal values must be the same for all the curves. In other worlds, the level of output at which the average curves are tangential, the marginal curves must cut.

Average and Marginal Revenue Curves Under Perfect Competition

The most important characteristic of perfect competition is the existence of a very large number of firms, each of which produces only a small portion of the total output of the commodity. As such no single firm can influence the market price of the commodity by changing the volume of its output. Under perfect competition, therefore, the price for an individual firm is given and can sell as much as it like at the given price. In other words, under perfect competition, the demand for the product of an individual firm is perfectly elastic. Thus, under perfect competition, the price for an individual firm remains unchanged whatever the quantity it may choose to sell. The average revenue curve will, therefore, take the shape of a straight line parallel to X-axis as shown in Fig. 14.6.

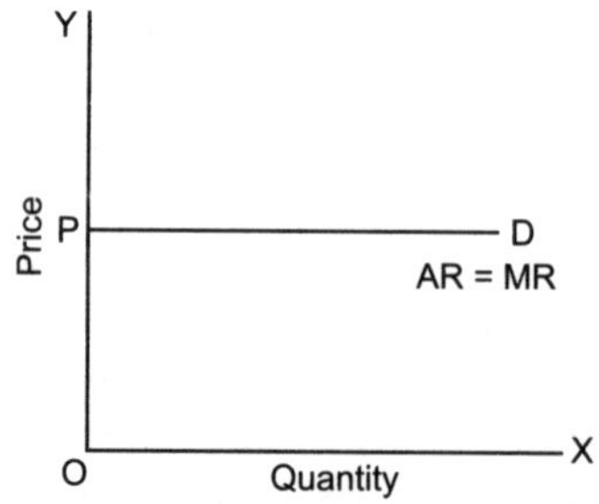

Fig. 14.6

The figure shows that the firm can sell any quantity at the ruling price OP. We have already seen that when the demand curve is perfectly elastic, the average revenue curve coincides with the marginal revenue curve.

Revenue Curves Under Monopoly and Imperfect Competitions

Under monopoly as well as under imperfect competition, both the average revenue curve and the marginal revenue curve slope downwards from the left to the right and the marginal curve is below the average curve. The reason for this shape of the curves is that, under monopoly as well as under imperfect competition, the demand curve of an individual firm is less than perfectly elastic, the precise degree of elasticity depending on the number of sellers in the market, the extent of mutual interdependence and the nature of the commodity itself. In other words, a firm under monopoly or under imperfect competition can sell a larger output only by reducing its price. Since the price has to be reduced not only for the additional (or the marginal) unit but for all the units sold (or also for the previous or supramarginal units), the marginal revenue will be less than the average revenue. In other words, the revenue brought in by the marginal unit is equal to its price minus the loss incurred on the sale of earlier units at a lower price. The marginal revenue curve, therefore, lies below the average revenue curve as is shown in Fig. 14.7.

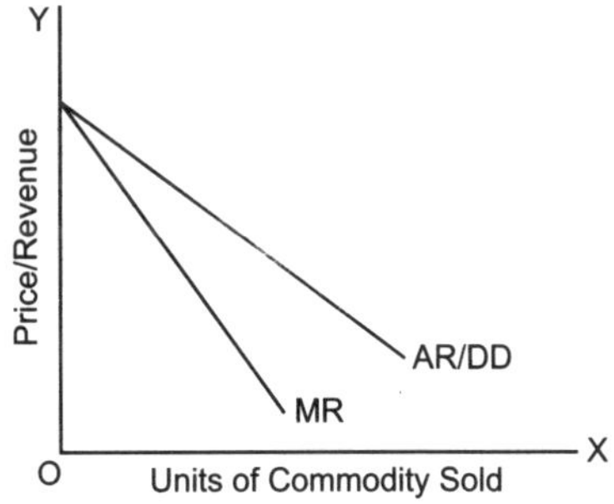

Fig. 14.7

Special Cases of Revenue Curves

We consider below the relationship between average and marginal revenue curves in certain special cases. These cases are of importance, both because they contribute to our understanding of the general relationships and because we will be concerned with these cases in our subsequent analysis. The first case is when the demand curve or the average revenue curve takes the shape of a rectangular hyperbola, i.e. has unitary elasticity throughout its length. When the elasticity of demand is unity, the marginal revenue will be zero. If the elasticity of the AR curve is unitary throughout its length, the marginal revenue will be zero throughout or, in other words, the marginal revenue curve will coincide with the X-axis (Fig. 14.8).

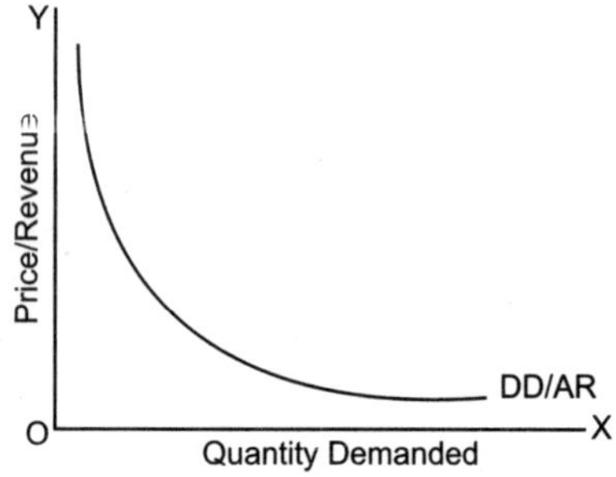

Fig. 14.8

The figure given below shows the second case.

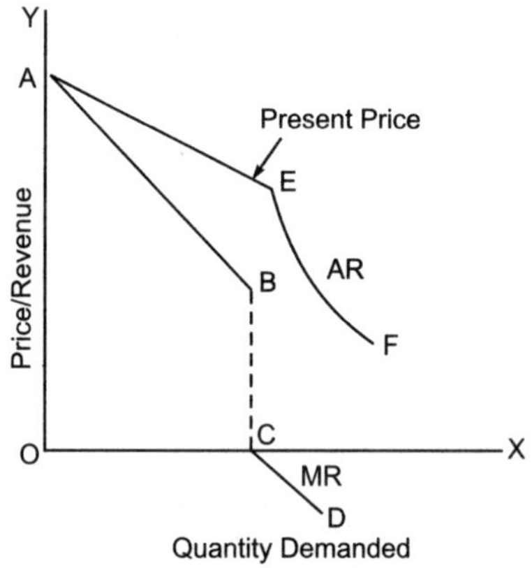

Fig. 14.9

When a firm expects its competitors to follow price decreases but not price increases, the demand curve takes the shape of curve AF with a kink at E. This type of situation is faced by a firm under oligopoly. When the firm in question reduces the price of its product, the competing firms follow suit. But when it increases the price of its product, the competing firms do not follow it. This leads to a kinked average revenue curve, the kink occurring at the existing price level. If the firm concerned raises its price above the existing level indicated by point E in Fig. 14.9, its sales decline quickly because other firms do not increase their prices. In contrast, if it lowers the price below the present level, it obtains only its proportionate share of the increased sales by the industry concerned as other competing firms also reduce their prices. When the average revenue curve is kinked, the marginal revenue curve will be discontinuous at the point of the kink as shown in the figure. AB is the MR curve corresponding to the portion of the AR curve between A and E. CD is the MR curve at a lower level with a steeper slope corresponding to the portion of AR curve between E and F. CB shows the discontinuous portion of the MR curve.

The figure given below shows the third case.

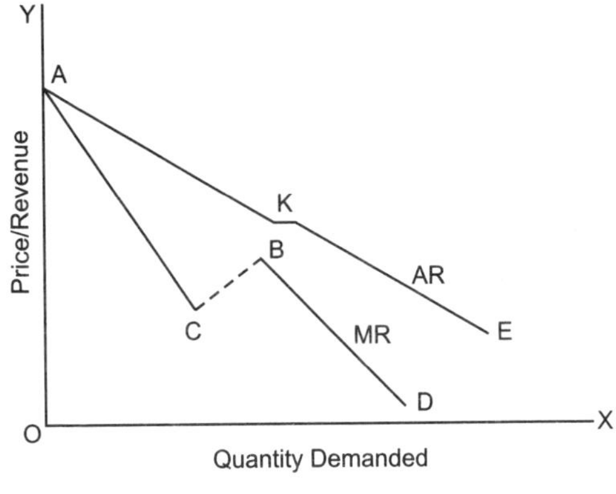

Fig. 14.10

Sometimes a kinked demand curve may show a high elasticity in the lower portion of the AR curve beyond the kink and a low elasticity in the higher portion of the AR curve above the kink. This type of kinked average revenue curve arises in case of a firm under oligopoly where a reduction in price below the present price by the firm concerned brings in large additional customers from competing firms while an increase in price above the kink by the firm does not lead to loss of too many customers to the competing firms. AC is the marginal revenue curve corresponding to AK portion of the average revenue curve and BD portion of the marginal revenue curve corresponds to KE portion of the average revenue curve. BC represents the discontinuous portion or the gap of the marginal revenue curve. This discontinuous portion, however, instead of occurring at the lower level, occurs at a higher level. This is because the KE portion of the average revenue curve is more elastic than the AK portion and as a consequence the marginal revenue curve corresponding to the former portion starts at a higher level.

Principle of Profit Maximisation

15

The entire analysis of the firm equilibrium is based on the assumption that the entrepreneur aims at maximising his profits. Such a behaviour on the part the entrepreneur has been considered to be quite rational. In recent years, however, doubts have been expressed as to whether the maximisation of profits is the only motive which governs the behaviour of a rational entrepreneur and whether this is the best policy for him. It has also been questioned as to whether in actual practice the entrepreneur tries to maximise his profits.

According to Mas-Colell, Whinston and Green, business firms maximise profits as a means to maximise the utility of their owners. In other words, businessmen maximise profit as a means to maximise utility, so profit maximisation follows from utility maximisation. And according to Scitovsky, a fundamental fact from which any theory of profit must start is that profit is maximised for its own sake, independently of the utility that businessmen may derive therefrom. If we logically coherent with the premise that profit is the primary aim of the firm, the utility function of businessmen cannot be well behaved. In other words, profit is not maximised as a means to utility maximisation and the two principles, rather than complementary, are at odds. The very notion of profit maximisation implies that the pursuit of profit is not conditioned by the utility or sacrifice that businessmen may derive from profit maximisation. Scitovsky, as well as Mas-Colell, Whinston and Green deserve special credit for taking up explicitly the question as to the theoretical foundation of the principal of profit maximisation.

The strategy of Mas-Colell, Whinston and Green to justify the position of profit maximisation as the basic principle for the study of the firm is to show that profit maximisation, and not employment or market share maximisation, is the logical outcome of utility maximisation. According to them, profit maximisation is the only goal on which all the owners of a firm would always agree independently of their utility functions. For the firm, money and profit is a tool, a means towards the true end, which is the improvement of the utility of its owners. Profit is a necessary intermediate step in so far the goods produced by the firm do not happen to enter in the utility function of the producers. In the hypothetical case that the utility of the owners of the firm depended on goods produced by the firm, the owners would consume these goods straight away, and there would be no need for any monetary exchange or for any profit. Profit making consists basically in the production of goods for exchange for other goods that happen to fit better the preferences of the owners of the firm. The money derived from the sale of the products of the firm may be a very valuable tool to facilitate the barter of goods, but it is not a necessary element in the process, because the activity of a business firms starts and ends in goods. The point that Mas-Colell, Whinston and Green intend to make is that since profit is just a means to utility maximisation, profit maximisation is but utility maximisation looked at from the standpoint of the producer who produces goods that happen to be useless for him. If the goods produced by the firm happened to enter in the utility functions of its owners, they would consume their whole profit within their firm and it would be very easy to see that the productive activity of the firm is just a means to the maximisation of the utility of its owners. As Mas-Colell, Whinston and Green put it, the fact that the owners of the firm have to go through the intermediation of monetary profit to obtain the goods that maximise their utility should no obscure this basic fact. Profit as such is not the end-goal of the firm, but a means to its true end-goal, which is utility maximisation. The flows of money to and from the firm are intermediate steps in the activity of the firm, which ultimately consists in a barter of goods.

According to Scitovsky, profit maximisation is totally unrelated to the income and welfare of the owners of the firm, which he refers to as "businessmen". For him the characteristic feature of profit maximisation is that it does not depend on income or utility; exactly the contrary to the thesis of Mas-Colell, Whinston and Green. Profit maximisation as described by Scitovsky is that it implies zero income elasticity of supply of entrepreneurship means that the ultimate goal of profit maximisation is the very activity of profit maximisation, not of any of its possible results. Thus, profit maximisation by the business firms will go ahead independently of the utility or sacrifice that this may involve for the businessmen concerned. This means that firms do not maximise profit in order to improve the utility level of any of its owners. The primary goal of the owners of the firm, the reason why they undertook the investment, is to make profit for its own sake. In other words, the principle of profit maximisation implies that the growth of the capital of the firm is not subordinated to the welfare of the owners, but the welfare of the owners to the growth of the firm. This is the logical consequence of posing profit as the primary goal of business activity. The monetary result of profit maximisation would affect the "ardour and energy" if the primary goal of the firm was the utility of its owners. But the entrepreneur maximises profit independently of the utility that he might obtain by exchanging his profit for consumable goods. In this sense, profit maximisation is, in Scitovskyan terms, "unnatural", because it implies a paradoxical separation of money from consumption and makes of money, which Mas-Colell, Whinston and Green were mistakenly modeled as a pure intermediary, the primary goal of the firm, to which the production of utility is subordinated. According to Scitovsky, thus, profit maximisation is an unconditional principle, i.e. the pursuit of profit is not a function of utility, but if anything, utility a result of profit maximisation. The profit maximising producer does not seek profit as a means to anything else or for the sake of something else than profit. On this score, Scitovsky, unlike Mas-Colell, Whinston and Green, takes account of the fact that the actual behaviour of business firms is regulated by their profits and that this implies that all the other variables of business activity, including the welfare of the shareholders, are conditioned by profit and that profit is not conditioned by anything (except, of course, by natural accidents).

Profit maximisation is not a generalisable norm for a successful capitalist society. Indeed, it is not an ethical principle at all, for it violates Kant's categorical imperative—that one should "act only according to that maxim whereby you can at the same time will that it should become a universal law". Profit maximisation is a situational ethic, applicable only to economic activity, i.e. activity carried out under competitive conditions. Monopoly providers of public goods—security, justice and so forth—must not act under profit maximisation.

In many countries, bribe-paying foreign enterprises, deposit-receiving foreign banks, arms-selling foreign enterprises are all complicit—heavily complicit—in creating and sustaining those confiscatory states. So, too, of course, are domestic businesses. But what is wrong with what they are doing? They are profit maximising, after all.

So the big problem with competitive capitalism is not that it is uncreative. It is certainly highly creative. The problem is that it is unnatural. There have to be rules, ethical norms and institutional constraints governing profit maximising behaviour, to ensure that the maximisation operates for the social good.

Profit Maximisation vs. Security

It has been pointed out that the price and output policy followed by an entrepreneur may be influenced not only by his desire to maximise his profits at a particular time or during a particular period of time but also by the motive of having a steady flow of profits for a long time. In other words, the behaviour of the entrepreneur is also influenced by the desire for secure profits. To cite K.W. Rothschild:[1]

> Profit maximisation has up till now served as the wonderful master key that opened all the doors leading to an understanding of the entrepreneur's behaviour. True, it was always realised that family pride, moral and ethical considerations, poor intelligence and similar factors may modify the results built on the maximum profits assumption; but it was rightly assumed that these 'disturbing' phenomena are sufficiently exceptional to justify their exclusion from the main body of price theory.
>
> But there is another motive which cannot be so lightly dismissed, and which is probably of a similar order of magnitude as the desire for *secure* profits. This motive has, of course, not completely escaped the attention of economists. But they usually thought they could subordinate this aspect of entrepreneurial behaviour to that of profit maximisation by simply postulating that it is *long-run* profits he is trying to maximise. Since, however, uncertainty is an essential feature in this changing world, it is clear that the vague knowledge a firm possesses of its demand and cost schedules cannot extend far into the future. Any theory, therefore, which tries to explain price behaviour in terms of marginal curves derived from *long-term* demand and cost curves really by-passes the problem of uncertainty, and thus the very factor which gives rise to that desire for security which the theory tries to explain. (Italics in original)

According to Prof. Rothschild, the major reason for the neglect of security motive is the preoccupation of price theory with the cases where the number of competitors is large—perfectly or monopolistically competitive market—or where a complete monopoly exists; for in these cases the problem of security does not arise. The absolute monopolist enjoys security against competitors by virtue of his monopoly power. The small competitor, for whom the security is very important, operates under such market conditions that he alone cannot do anything to safeguard his position. All that a small competitor can do is to take full advantage of every opportunity as it comes up. Maximisation of short-term profits is, therefore, quite a reasonable assumption about the behaviour of an entrepreneur operating under competitive conditions.

But when we enter the field of duopoly and oligopoly, this assumption does not appear to be quite valid. "For here we find neither the safety of the single monopolist nor the impotence *vis-a-vis* his environment of the small competitor. Here is both the desire for achieving a secure position as well as the power to act on this desire".[2] The main reason why, in spite of the growth of oligopolistic elements, the security motive has been neglected is that some of the most conspicuous actions motivated by the desire for maximum security are identical with actions aiming at maximum profits. The outstanding trend towards monopolistic agreements, for instance, serves both ends. "But there are other cases where the two motives lead to conflicting patterns of behaviour. Where profit maximisation demands prices fluctuating with every change in revenue and cost conditions, security maximisation may demand rigid prices; while profit maximisation should tend to create firms of optimum size, security considerations will favour the oversized firm; again, where we should expect reserve funds to be invested in response to expected returns, we may find their practically unconditional reinvestment in their own firm".[3]

Sales Maximisation Hypothesis

Prof. Baumol believes that the ultimate objective of a firm is to maximise sales rather than maximising profits. According to him, the firm tries to increase sales not simply as a means to further other objectives like operational efficiency and profits but because for a businessman "sales have become an end in and of themselves". He therefore considers sales maximisation to be the most valid assumption about the behaviour of the firm. He believes that there exists strong empirical evidence in support of his hypothesis that oligopolist is concerned more with sales than with profits. To cite Baumol:[4]

> Surely it is common experience that when one asks an executive, 'How's business?' he will answer that his sales have been increasing (or decreasing), and talk about

> profits only as an after-thought, if at all. And I am told the requirement for acceptance to membership in Young Presidents' Organization (an honorific society) are that the applicant be under 40 years of age and president of a company whose annual sales volume is over a million dollars. Presumably it makes no difference if this firm in imminent danger of bankruptcy.... Almost every time I come across a case of conflict between profits and sales the businessmen with whom I worked left little doubt as to where their hearts lay. It is not unusual to find a profitable firm, in which some segment of its sales can be shown to be highly unprofitable.... When such a case is pointed out to management, it is usually quite reluctant to abandon its unprofitable markets. Businessman may consider seriously proposals which promise to put these sales on a profitable basis.... But a programme which explicitly proposes any cut in sales volume, whatever the profit considerations, is likely to meet a cold reception.

Professor Baumol, however, concedes that while attempting to promote sales, the businessmen do not completely ignore the costs incurred on output and the profits to be made. He also accepts that sometimes there may be a conflict between a firm's sales objective and profit objective. He states that in the real world, businessmen normally promote sales subject to the limitation that costs incurred are covered plus a usual rate of return on investment is obtained. The management does not bother to earn profits higher than this. Once the minimum profit level is attained, sales rather than profits become the overriding goal. Baumol emphasises that "the typical oligopolist's objective can usefully be characterised, approximately, as sales maximisation subject to minimum profit constraint. Doubtless this premise over-specifies a rather vague set of attitudes but I believe it is not too far from truth. So long as profits are high enough to keep stockholders satisfied and contribute adequately to the financing of company growth, management will bend its efforts to the augmentation of sales revenues rather than to further increase in profits".[5]

It might be objected that an attempt to maximise sales rather than profits indicates irrational behaviour on the part of an entrepreneur. Prof. Baumol, however, points out that it might not be so. He puts forward an entirely different concept of rationality. According to him, rationality does not consist in choosing between different ends. On the other hand, it implies pursuing the ends *efficiently and consistently*. He states "People's objectives are whatever they are. Irrationality surely must be defined to consist in decision patterns which make it more difficult to attain one's own ends that are for some reason considered to be right. Unless we are prepared to determine other people's values, or unless they pursue incompatible objectives, we must class behaviour as rational if it efficiently pursues whatever goals happen to have been chosen".[6]

Baumol's Static Models of Sales Maximisation

The basic assumptions of Baumol's static models of sales revenue maximisation are as follows:

(a) We consider a single period time.

(b) The goal of the firm is to maximise its total sales revenue, not the physical volume of output.

(c) The decision taken in the current period does not influence the decision of the firm in the subsequent periods.

(d) The demands and expectations of the shareholders, the bank and other financial institutions set the condition of minimum profit constraint.

(e) The U-shaped of the cost curve and the downward sloping of the demand curve are accepted by Baumol in his analysis of sales revenue maximisation hypothesis.

(f) The firm is able to pursue an independent price policy.

We shall analyse the model based on the above assumption under four conditions.

(a) *We consider the hypothesis with a single-product and without advertising*:

Let us consider the following figure which shows the total cost and total revenue curves of the firm.

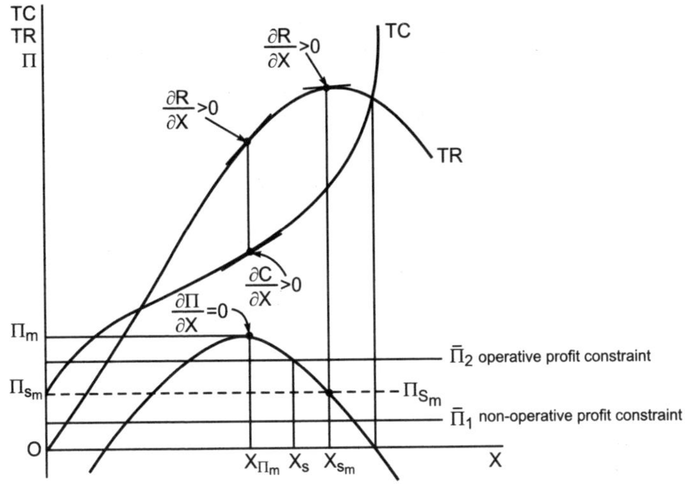

Fig. 15.1

In Fig. 15.1, we see that the sales revenue is maximised at the highest point of total revenue curve. Here we have zero price elasticity and also the slope of the total revenue curve is equal to zero.

Here one point should be noted that if the firm's objective is to maximise profit then it will produce at the level of output X_{Π_m}. But in the Baumol's hypothesis, the objective of the firm is to maximise sales keeping in mind a minimum level of profit which will be acceptable to shareholders and the financer of the operation. Here two types of equilibrium are possible: (1) the profit constraint provides no effective barrier to sales maximisation and (2) the profit constraint provides effective barrier to sales maximisation.

Let us consider the profit level $\bar{\Pi}_1$. Here firm will produce X_{S_m} which maximise its sales revenue and the profit of the firm is Π_{S_m}. At this point the minimum profit constraint is not operative. Again if the minimum profit acceptable to firm is $\bar{\Pi}_2$ then in this case the firm will produce $X_S (< X_{S_m})$ unit of output and it will not able to attain the maximum sales revenue.

In case the profit constraint is operative, then Baumol's hypothesis states that the sales maximiser will produce a higher level of output as compared to a profit maximiser. We can prove this statement as follows.

For a profit maximiser the optimum output is produced at the point where MR = MC. In Fig. 15.1, the optimum output produced by a profit maximiser firm is X_{Π_m}. As the marginal cost is always positive then at level X_{Π_m}, the marginal revenue is also positive. It implies that TR is still increasing at X_{Π_m}. In other words, the maximum of the TR curve occurs to the right of the level of output at which profit is maximised. Hence, we find that $X_{S_m} > X_{\Pi_m}$ that is sales maximiser produces higher output than the profit maxiomiser.

(b) *We consider the hypothesis with a single-product and with advertising*:

In this case also the goal of the firm is sales maximisation subject to an exogenously determined minimum profit constraint. In this case Baumol introduced advertising as a major instrument of the firm and assumed that sales revenue increases with advertising expenditure. It implies that advertising will always shift the demand curve of the firm to the right and the firm will sell a larger quantity and earn larger revenue. This case can be analysed mathematically as follows.

We have given:

$$\text{Total revenue function} = R = f_1(X, a)$$

$$\text{Total production cost function} = C = f_2(X)$$

$$\text{Minimum acceptable profit} = \bar{\Pi}$$

$$\text{Total cost of advertising function} = A(a)$$

The problem of the firm is to maximise

$$R = f_1(X, a)$$

Subject to the minimum profit constraint

$$\Pi = R - C - A \geq \bar{\Pi}$$

Given that

$$\frac{\partial R}{\partial a} > 0, \qquad \frac{\partial C}{\partial X} > 0, \qquad X > 0$$

In this analysis, Baumol had also assumed that $\frac{\partial R}{\partial a} > 0$ which implies that the constraint is operative.

Using Lagrangian multiplier the maximising problem can be written as

$$\phi = R + \lambda(R - C - A - \bar{\Pi}) \tag{i}$$

where λ is the Lagrangian multiplier and it must be positive. The necessary conditions for maximisation are

$$\frac{\partial \phi}{\partial X} \leq 0, \qquad \frac{\partial \phi}{\partial a} \leq 0, \qquad \frac{\partial \phi}{\partial \lambda} \geq 0 \tag{ii}$$

Differentiating equation (i) with respect to X we have

$$\frac{\partial \phi}{\partial X} = \frac{\partial R}{\partial X} + \lambda\left(\frac{\partial R}{\partial X} - \frac{\partial C}{\partial X}\right) \leq 0 \tag{iii}$$

Since X > 0, the equation (iii) holds as an equality. Solving equation (iii) we get

$$\frac{\partial C}{\partial X} = \frac{\lambda + 1}{\lambda} \cdot \frac{\partial R}{\partial X} = \left(1 + \frac{1}{\lambda}\right)\frac{\partial R}{\partial X} \tag{iv}$$

Since $\lambda > 0$ therefore we have

$$\frac{\partial C}{\partial X} > \frac{\partial R}{\partial X}$$

i.e.

$$MC > MR \tag{v}$$

But for the profit maximiser MC = MR therefore the output of a sales maximiser will be larger than the output of a profit maximiser.

Now differentiating equation (i) with respect to advertising we get

$$\frac{\partial \phi}{\partial a} = \frac{\partial R}{\partial a} + \lambda\left(\frac{\partial R}{\partial a} - \frac{\partial A}{\partial a}\right) \leq 0 \qquad \text{(vi)}$$

Since a > 0, therefore equation (vi) holds as an equality. Solving equation (vi) we get

$$\frac{\partial A}{\partial a} = \left(1 + \frac{1}{\lambda}\right)\frac{\partial R}{\partial a}$$

Or

$$\left(\frac{\partial A}{\partial a} \Big/ \frac{\partial R}{\partial a}\right) = \left(1 + \frac{1}{\lambda}\right) \qquad \text{(vii)}$$

But for a profit maximiser $\left(\frac{\partial A}{\partial a} \Big/ \frac{\partial R}{\partial a}\right) = 1$ (viii)

Thus, from, (vii) and (viii) we see that for $\lambda > 0$, advertising expenditure will be higher for a sales maximiser.

This model allows for excessive production expenditure and lower price as well as for the case of excessive advertising and higher price. Baumol's model is even compatible with strong price competition, which may result in a price lower than the MC.

Substituting $MR = P\left(1 - \frac{1}{e}\right)$ in the inequality MC > MR we get

$$MC > P\left(1 - \frac{1}{e}\right)$$

Thus, with appropriate values of $|e|$ we can get

$$MC > P > MR$$

(c) *We consider the hypothesis with a multi-product firm and without advertising*:

With given resources and costs the equilibrium condition of the multi-product firm is given by

$$\frac{\partial R/\partial X_i}{\partial R/\partial X_j} = \frac{\partial C/\partial X_i}{\partial C/\partial X_j} \qquad \text{(ix)}$$

This states that the firm is in equilibrium when the ratio of the marginal revenue from any two commodities (i and j) is equal to the ratio of their marginal cost. Here one point should be noted that the firm wants to allocate the given resources among the various commodities it produces so as to maximise sales revenue. The firm will produce the same quantities of the various products as if it were a profit maximiser and hence will reach the same equilibrium situation.

On the other hand, if the resources and costs are not given then a different combination will be reached by the multi-product firm which depends on whether it is a profit maximiser or a sales maximiser. Then the equilibrium condition of the firm is given by

$$\frac{\partial R/\partial X_i}{\partial R/\partial X_j} = \frac{\partial \Pi/\partial X_i}{\partial \Pi/\partial X_j} \qquad \text{(x)}$$

This states that the ratio of marginal revenues of commodities i and j must be equal to the ratio of their marginal profitabilities which is the equilibrium condition of the sales maximising firm.

(d) *We consider the hypothesis with a multi-product firm and with advertising*:

As usual the objective of the firm is to maximise sales subject to a minimum profit constraint. The problem of the firm can be stated as

Maximise $R = f_1 (X_i, a_i)$

Subject to $\Pi = R - C - A = \overline{\Pi}$

where

Advertising expenditure on commodity i = a_i

Total revenue function = $R = \sum P_i X_i$

Total production cost function = $C = f_2(X_i)$

Minimum acceptable profit = $\overline{\Pi}$

Total cost of advertising function = $A = \sum a_i$

The above stated problem of the firm can be written using Lagrangian form as follows:

$$\phi = R + \lambda(R - C - A - \bar{\Pi}) \tag{xi}$$

Differentiating equation (xi) with respect X_i and X_j we get

$$\frac{\partial \phi}{\partial X_i} = \frac{\partial R}{\partial X_i} + \lambda\left(\frac{\partial R}{\partial X_i} - \frac{\partial C}{\partial X_i}\right) = 0 \tag{xii}$$

$$\frac{\partial \phi}{\partial X_j} = \frac{\partial R}{\partial X_j} + \lambda\left(\frac{\partial R}{\partial X_j} - \frac{\partial C}{\partial X_j}\right) = 0 \tag{xiii}$$

From equations (xii) and (xiii) we get

$$\frac{\partial R/\partial X_i}{\partial R/\partial X_j} = \frac{\partial C/\partial X_i}{\partial C/\partial X_j} \tag{xiv}$$

Thus, the equation (xiv) is the same as the equation (ix) because of the assumption that advertising is not a function of output.

Differentiating equation (xi) with respect to a_i we get n equations which can be solved for the levels of advertising expenses on each product.

Thus, we have

$$\frac{\partial \phi}{\partial a_i} = \frac{\partial R}{\partial a_i} + \lambda\left(\frac{\partial R}{\partial a_i} - 1\right) = 0 \tag{xv}$$

$$\frac{\partial \phi}{\partial a_j} = \frac{\partial R}{\partial a_j} + \lambda\left(\frac{\partial R}{\partial a_j} - 1\right) = 0 \tag{xvi}$$

Solving equations (xv) and (xvi) we get the additional equilibrium condition as

$$\frac{\partial R/\partial a_i}{\partial R/\partial a_j} = 1$$

Or

$$\frac{\partial R}{\partial a_i} = \frac{\partial R}{\partial a_j} \tag{xvii}$$

This implies, marginal revenue of advertising commodity i = marginal revenue of advertising commodity j.

If the condition is opposite, i.e. there is no equality between the marginal revenue of advertising of two commodities then the firm can increase R by reallocating the total advertising expenditure among the different products having higher marginal revenue.

Thus, we need to solve 2n + 1 equations for the n outputs, the n advertising expenditure and for the Lagrangian multiplier.

Hence, we have

$$\frac{\partial R}{\partial X_i} = \frac{\lambda}{1+\lambda} \cdot \frac{\partial C}{\partial X_i} \qquad (i = 1, 2, 3, \ldots, n) \quad \text{(xviii)}$$

$$\frac{\partial R}{\partial a_i} = \frac{\lambda}{1+\lambda} \qquad (i = 1, 2, 3, \ldots, n) \quad \text{(xix)}$$

$$R - C - A = \overline{\Pi} \qquad \text{(xx)}$$

Since the marginal cost is always positive $\left(\frac{\partial C}{\partial X_i} > 0\right)$ and also the marginal revenue of advertising is positive $\left(\frac{\partial R}{\partial a_i} > 0\right)$ therefore $\lambda/(\lambda+1) > 0$.

Hence, we have

$$\frac{\partial R}{\partial X_i} > 0$$

This implies that the firm will not be in equilibrium if $\Pi > \overline{\Pi}$, because by increasing its advertising expenditure it will attain a higher sales. In other words, the profit constraint is always operative.

From equation (xviii) we have

$$\frac{\partial R}{\partial X_i} = \left(\frac{\lambda}{\lambda+1}\right)\left(\frac{\partial C}{\partial X_i}\right)$$

Or $$\frac{\partial C}{\partial X_i} = \left(\frac{\lambda + 1}{\lambda}\right)\left(\frac{\partial R}{\partial X_i}\right) = \left(1 + \frac{1}{\lambda}\right)\frac{\partial R}{\partial X_i}$$

For $\lambda > 0$ we have

$$\frac{\partial C}{\partial X_i} > \frac{\partial R}{\partial X_i}$$

This implies that the marginal cost for any one commodity is greater than its marginal revenue.

Satisfaction or Utility Maximisation

Since the ultimate objective of an individual is to attain satisfaction or utility, some economists like Prof. Benjamin Higgins, Melvin Reder and Tibor Scitovsky have replaced profit maximisation by the more general concept of *utility maximisation* or what is known as *preference function maximisation*. They have pointed out that profit maximisation need not necessarily mean utility or satisfaction maximisation. An entrepreneur obtains satisfaction not only from the material goods which he buys with money profits obtained by putting in entrepreneurial activity or work but also from the leisure available to him. Leisure or what Hicks calls "quiet life" is an important part of a person's welfare. The preference for leisure should also, therefore, be incorporated into the analysis of an entrepreneur who is assumed to maximise his satisfaction or utility.

So long as we do not make a special assumption about the entrepreneur's psychology or behaviour in regard to work and leisure, maximisation of profits will not ensure maximisation of satisfaction or utility. We draw below the entrepreneur's indifference map between net or pure money profits and leisure.

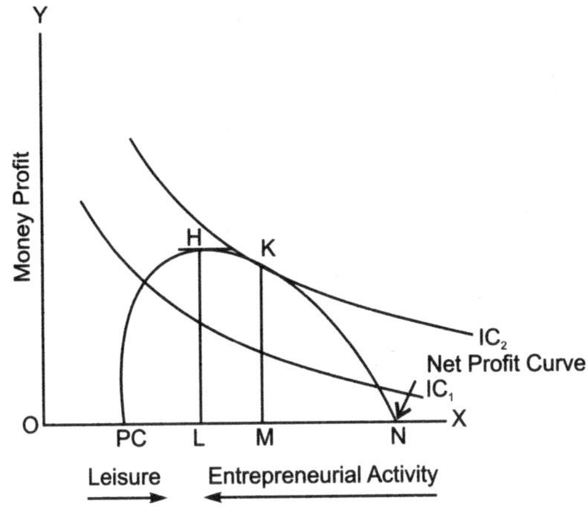

Fig. 15.2

In Fig. 15.2, money profits are measured along the Y-axis and leisure (from left to right) along X-axis. An indifference curve in the figure indicates the various combinations of money profits and leisure which provide the same amount of satisfaction to the consumer. The higher is the level of the indifference curve, the larger is the amount of satisfaction which the entrepreneur obtains. It is further assumed that the entrepreneurial activity is a variable factor and its quantity per unit of output is fixed. This enables us to measure entrepreneurial activity in terms of output. The larger the amount of output to be produced, the greater would be the amount of entrepreneurial activity to earn net money profits and as such the smaller the amount of leisure available. The curve PC is the net profit curve which indicates the net profits earned by the entrepreneur by producing different volumes of output or, in other words, by putting in different amounts of entrepreneurial activity.

The point at which the net income curve is tangential to an indifference curve is the entrepreneur's point of maximum satisfaction and determines his optimum rate of output. In the figure, K is the point at which the entrepreneur obtains the maximum satisfaction. The point of maximum satisfaction may or may not be the point of maximum net profits. In the figure, the net profits are maximum at point H. Thus, the satisfaction-maximising output (NM) is smaller than the profit-maximising output (NL). This shows that when leisure enters into the preference function of the entrepreneur, he is likely to produce an output which is smaller than the profit-maximising output.

An indifference curve can be tangential to the income curve at the point of maximum net profits (i.e. H) only if it is horizontal or even upward-sloping over a part of its range. This is, however, very unlikely and conflicts with our common notion of the shape of indifference curves. Horizontal indifference curves between net money profits and leisure mean that the entrepreneur's choice between more or less activity—or in other words, between more income and more leisure—is independent of his income. This is tantamount to saying that leisure does not enter into an entrepreneur's preference function. Horizontal indifference curves are equivalent to Marshall's famous assumption of constant marginal utility of money, or in modern terminology, to a zero income elasticity of supply of entrepreneurship. In order, therefore, that maximum profits should maximise his satisfaction, the entrepreneur's psychology must be such that the amount of work and energy put in by him remains independent of the income he earns.

Apparently it may appear strange and unrealistic to attribute such a psychology to an entrepreneur because if his objective is to earn money, it is somewhat natural that the amount he is already earning should affect the ardour and energy with which he tries to earn more money. Scitovsky, however, points out, "the assumption that the entrepreneur's willingness to work is independent of his income need not imply that he is not interested in the material rewards of his work. It may also mean that he is so keen on making money that his ambition cannot be damped by a rising income. The latter interpretation seems to be the more realistic one. Businessmen regard the income they earn as an index of their success and efficiency; and their ambition of excelling in their profession manifests itself in the desire to make more money. We claim that a businessman's entrepreneurial activity will remain unaffected by a rise in his income if he makes money, not in order to have more to spend, but for its own sake, because it is an index and token of his success in life.... This is likely to be the case, partly because the desire for success is more insatiable than the demand for material goods, and partly because it is not a high but a rising income that is a sign of business success".[7] Thus, Scitovsky believes that the classical economists were completely justified in assuming that the entrepreneur aims at maximising his profits because they were concerned with the type of entrepreneurs whose psychology happened to be such that for them maximising profits was identical with maximising satisfaction.

Higgins on Profit and Satisfaction Maximisation

Professor Benjamin Higgins also holds the view that the entrepreneur aims at maximising his satisfaction, or what he calls utility index, rather than profits. He, however, does not attribute to the entrepreneur a special type of psychology as Scitovsky does. According to Higgins, profit maximisation is a survival condition under perfect competition. But, under conditions of imperfect competition, the force of profit maximisation is much weaker because such conditions permit the entrepreneur margins with which they can satisfy desires other than the desire of profit. Higgins classifies the desires or forces which lead to non-profit maximisation into three categories. In the first place, there are desires and forces which lead the entrepreneur to produce below the level of profit maximising output, e.g. desire for leisure. Secondly, there are forces that lead the entrepreneur to produce beyond the level of profit maximising output, e.g. desire to own a large farm, to weild larger power, to enjoy greater prestige, etc. Thirdly, there are forces that make the entrepreneur stay where he is, i.e. whether he is producing above or below the level of profit maximising output. Such cases arise owing to ideas of "just price" or owing to reluctance on the part of the entrepreneur to experiment.

Empirical Study on Profit Maximisation

The Oxford economists, Hall and Hitch, interviewed some thirty-eight entrepreneurs on price policy and found that the businessmen did not try to maximise their profits by equating marginal cost with marginal revenue. In fact, they were not familiar with the concepts of marginal cost and marginal revenue. The study revealed that they fixed the prices of their products on the basis of "full-cost principle". According to this principle, the businessmen do not try to earn abnormal profits and charge prices which cover their average cost including normal or conventional profits.

According to Hall and Hitch, firms do not set their price and output at the levels determined by the intersection of the MC and MR curves, but they set a price to cover the average variable cost, the average fixed cost and a normal profit margin.

That is

$$P = AVC + AFC + \text{Profit margin}$$

The following reasons have been given by Hall and Hitch in support of the breakdown of marginalism:

(a) The application of the condition MC = MR is not possible because firms do not know their demand curve and the marginal costs.

(b) Full-cost principle is assumed to be right pricing strategy because it allows a fair profit and covered the costs of production when the plant is normally utilised.

Thus, according to them, firm's main preoccupation is price, and not the output and therefore it will set its prices on the basis of the above average-cost principal and sell at that price whatever the market would take.

NOTES

1. K.W. Rothschild, "Price Theory and Oligopoly", *The Economic Journal*, Vol. LVII (1947). Reprinted in American Economic Association, *Readings in Price Theory* (London, 1953), pp. 450-51.
2. *Ibid.*, p. 451.
3. *Ibid.*, p. 452.
4. W.J. Baumol, *Business Behaviour, Value and Growth*, pp. 47-48.
5. *Ibid.*, pp. 49-50.
6. *Ibid.*, p. 47.

7. T. Scitovsky, "A Note on Profit Maximisation and Its Implications", *The Review of Economic Studies*, Vol. XI (1943). Reprinted in American Economic Association, *Readings in Price Theory* (London, 1953), pp. 356-57.

16 Equilibrium of Firm and the Industry Under Perfect Competition

A firm is the smallest unit of production or sale in the economy. It may have different organisational forms such as an individual enterprise, a partnership, a joint stock company, a corporate body, a cooperative enterprise or a public utility agency. Again it may be a producer, seller, trader, exporter or a financer. In any one of these capacities, firms have similar basic tendencies of profit maximisation which is the difference between cost of production and revenue or returns. To maximise profit firm has to keep its cost of production as low as possible and charge a high price and sell as much quantity of products as possible. This motive of profit maximisation of the firm is related to the behaviour of the consumer.

Perfect competition is an idealised structure of an industry in which price competition is dominant in fact the only form of competition possible. It is also sometimes known as pure or price competition. In neo-classical economics and microeconomics, perfect competition describes a market in which no buyer or seller has market power. Such markets are usually allocatively and productively efficient. The notion of perfect competition derives from the earlier classical notion of free competition. According to Adam Smith, freely competitive markets is one in which there is no impediment to free contracting and free entry and exist of productive resources. The implication was that all units of the same type of productive resource would tend to earn the same reward as in other freely competitive markets, and as result product price would tend toward their natural levels, i.e. toward the levels allowing paying labour, land and capital their naturals rates determined by the classical theory of income distribution. This is a long-run theory of product price, in which what is essential is free mobility of productive resource, in particular free entry of firms, and competition is viewed as a dynamical process akin to a competition in a race. In such a conception, competition in a product market is the stronger, the closer the price of the product gets to its natural level. A perfect competitive market may have several distinguishing characteristics, including:

(a) *Fragmented industry*: The industry is fragmented. It implies that it consists of many buyers and sellers. The contribution of each buyers and sellers in the market is so small that it has an imperceptible impact on the market price. Also each seller's input purchases are so small that they have an imperceptible impact on input prices.

(b) *Undifferentiated products*: The industry is defined as a group of firms producing a homogeneous product, i.e. consumers perceive the products to be identical no matter who produces them. The technical characteristics of the product as well as the services associated with its sale and delivery are identical.

(c) *Perfect knowledge*: Consumers have perfect information about prices all sellers in the market charge, i.e. all sellers and buyers have complete knowledge of the conditions of the market. Information is free and costless.

(d) *Equal access to resources*: All firms, current as well as prospective entrants, have access to the same technology and inputs. Firms can hire inputs, such as labour, capital and materials, as they need them, and they can release them from their employment when they do not need them, i.e. the factors of production are free to move from one firm to another throughout the economy. Also, raw materials and others factors are not monopolised and labour is not unionised.

(e) *No government regulation*: Governments have no control on the market that means tariffs, subsidies, rationing of production or demand and so on are ruled out.

(f) *Profit maximisation*: All the firms in the industry have similar goal of profit maximisation.

The above mentioned characteristics have three implications for how perfectly competitive markets work:

(a) The characteristic of market fragmentation implies that sellers and buyers act as price takers. It means while making an output decision, a firm takes the market price of the product as given and a buyer takes the market price as given when making purchase decisions. Also, while making inputs decision, a firm takes input prices as fixed.

(b) The law of one price, i.e. transactions between buyers and sellers occur at a single market price, is implied by the characteristics of product homogeneity and perfect knowledge.

(c) The characteristic of equal access to resources implies that the industry is characterised by free entry, i.e. there is no barrier to entry or exit from the industry. Entry or exit may take time, but firms have freedom of movement in and out of the industry. Here one point should be noted that free entry does not mean that a new firm incurs no cost when it enters the industry but that it has access to the same technology and inputs that existing firms have.

In this chapter, we shall develop a theory of perfect competition that takes into consideration each of these three implications: price-taking behaviour by firms, a common market price charged by each in the industry and free entry.

Principle of Profit Maximisation

An important assumption made in the analysis of firm equilibrium is that the entrepreneur aims at maximising his profits. This assumption about the behaviour of the entrepreneur forms the corner stone of the entire economic theory. An attempt on the part an entrepreneur to maximise profits is considered to be quite of a rational behaviour. It would be assumed in what follows that the entrepreneur tries to maximise profits.

In making this assumption, it is, however, very essential to be clear about the nature of the profits which the entrepreneur tries to maximise. Economic profit is a pure surplus or excess of total receipts over all costs of production incurred by the firm. The costs of the firm also include the *opportunity costs* of all resources used by the firm which belong to the entrepreneur. The entrepreneur may employ in his firm, for instance, some capital and land owned by him. The remuneration which he gets for this capital and land would not constitute his profit because he would have received this remuneration by lending his capital and renting his land to some other entrepreneur. Similarly he obtains remuneration for the routine management and supervision which he does for the firm. This remuneration also would not constitute his profit because he would have very well received this had he offered his services as manager to some other firm. Thus, pure profits are the surplus of total revenue over total costs (including the costs of resources belonging to the entrepreneur). This residual income is the profits of entrepreneurship proper. It is profit in this sense which the entrepreneur tries to maximise.

Marshall called entrepreneur's remuneration for management and supervision as normal profits and the residual income as super-normal profits. This dichotomy of entrepreneur's income is very important for an analysis of the firm's behaviour. Normal profits are the minimum amount which the entrepreneur must get in order to stay in business. Normal profits, as stated above, are an integral part of the costs of the firm and, therefore, have no concern with the maximisation problem. It is the super-normal profits which the entrepreneur aims at maximising. They are of the nature of economic rent for they are over and above the normal profits which the entrepreneur must get to stay in business.

Here we should also make a distinction between economic profit and accounting profit. As we know that economic cost measures the opportunity cost of the resources that the firm uses to produce and sell its products, whereas accounting cost measures the historical expenses the firm incurred to produce and sell its output. Similarly, economic profit is the difference between a firm's sales revenue and the totality of its economic costs, including all relevant opportunity costs. In determining economic profit, explicit as well as implicit costs are deducted from total revenue. Thus, we have

Economic profit = Sales revenue – Economic costs

or, Economic profit = Total revenue – (Explicit + Implicit costs)

Accounting profit is the difference between total revenue and total explicit costs of a firm. Only such costs are deducted from the revenue which has been fully paid out. Thus, we have

Accounting profit = Sales revenue – Accounting costs

or, Accounting profits = Total revenue – Explicit costs

Economic profit is smaller in value than accounting profit. Whenever we discuss profit maximisation, we are talking about economic profit maximisation. Economic profit is the appropriate objective for a firm that is acting on its owners' behalf.

Second Order Condition for Equilibrium of Firm

The first order condition for equilibrium output of the firm is that at this level of output, its marginal revenue should be equal to its marginal cost. In addition to this, there is a second order condition which must be satisfied if the firm is to be in a position of stable equilibrium. The equality between marginal revenue and marginal cost is a necessary but not a sufficient condition of firm's equilibrium. The second order condition for a firm to be in equilibrium requires that the marginal cost curve must intersect the marginal revenue curve from below, and not from above, at the point of equilibrium. In other words, the marginal cost must be greater than the marginal revenue beyond the equilibrium output. If this condition is not satisfied, the firm will not be maximising its profits and hence will not be in equilibrium.

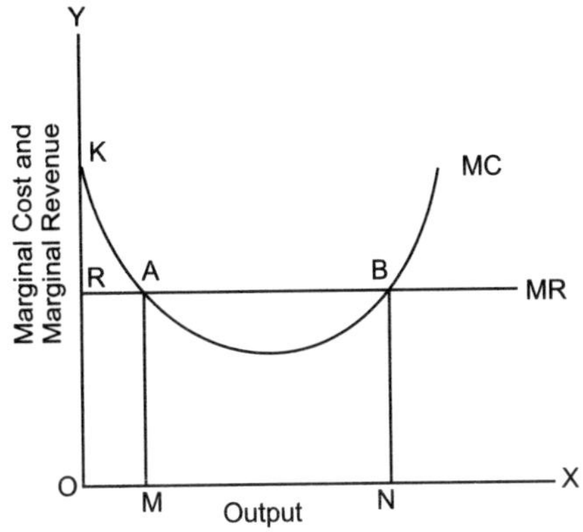

Fig. 16.1

In Fig. 16.1, marginal revenue curve is a horizontal straight line and the marginal cost curve is U-shaped. The MC curve is cutting MR curve at two points, A and B. The firm is not in equilibrium at point A at which output is OM. At this point, though marginal cost equals marginal revenue, since marginal cost curve is cutting marginal revenue curve from above, marginal cost is less than marginal revenue for output beyond OM. The firm can, therefore, increase its profits by expanding output. In fact, at output OM, the firm is not making any profits; on the contrary, it is incurring a loss equal to the area KRA. As the firm can increase its profits by expanding output beyond OM, A cannot be a point of equilibrium. At point B, the marginal cost curve is cutting the marginal revenue curve from below and beyond this point marginal cost is greater than marginal revenue and as such expansion of output beyond ON would add more to cost than to revenue. Thus, the firm's profits are maximised at output ON and the firm is in equilibrium at point B.

The above leads to the conclusion that a firm would be in equilibrium only when (i) MC = MR and (ii) MC curve intersects the MR curve from below at the point of equilibrium.

The above two conditions of equilibrium hold true both in the short-run and in the long-run. Whether the period under consideration is short or long, the firm aims at maximising its profits and the profits are maximised only when these two conditions are satisfied. The only difference is that in the short period it is the short-run marginal cost curve and in the long period it is the long-run cost curve which is relevant for comparing with the marginal revenue curve. Again, these two conditions of equilibrium hold good whether the firm is operating under perfect competition, monopoly, or imperfect competition. The only difference lies in the shape of marginal revenue and marginal cost curves.

Short-run Equilibrium of a Firm

The firm is said to be in equilibrium when it maximises its profit which is the difference between the total cost and total revenue. Thus, we have

$$\Pi = TR - TC$$

where

$$\Pi = \text{profit}$$
$$TR = \text{total revenue}$$
$$TC = \text{total cost}$$

Here Π is the profit above the normal rate of return on capital and the remuneration for the risk bearing function of the entrepreneur. The equilibrium of the firm can be shown graphically by using the TR and TC curves or the MR and MC curves.

We have TR = $f_1(X)$ and TC = $f_2(X)$, given the price P, where X is the output.

First Order Condition of Profit Maximisation

The first order condition for the profit maximisation requires that the first derivative of the function with respect to X should be equal to zero. Thus, differentiating the total-profit function and equating to zero we get

$$\frac{\partial \Pi}{\partial X} = \frac{\partial TR}{\partial X} - \frac{\partial TC}{\partial X} = 0$$

$$\frac{\partial TR}{\partial X} = \frac{\partial TC}{\partial X}$$

The term $\frac{\partial TR}{\partial X}$ is the slope of the total revenue curve which is the marginal revenue and $\frac{\partial TC}{\partial X}$ is the slope of the total cost curve which is the marginal cost. Thus, we get the first order condition for profit maximisation as

$$MR = MC$$

Given that MC > 0, MR must also be positive at equilibrium. Since MR = P the first order condition can be written as

$$MC = P$$

Second Order Condition of Profit Maximisation

The second order condition of profit maximisation requires that the second derivatives of the function should be negative. That is

$$\frac{\partial^2 \Pi}{\partial X^2} = \frac{\partial^2 TR}{\partial X^2} - \frac{\partial^2 TC}{\partial X^2} < 0$$

Or, $$\frac{\partial^2 TR}{\partial X^2} < \frac{\partial^2 TC}{\partial X^2}$$

Since $\frac{\partial^2 TR}{\partial X^2}$ is the slope of the MR curve and $\frac{\partial^2 TC}{\partial X^2}$ is the slope of the MC curve therefore the second order condition can be written as

Slope of MR < Slope of MC

Thus, we see that MC has a steeper slope than the MR and MC must cut the MR from below. As we know that in pure competition the slope of the MR curve is zero, hence the second order condition can be written as

$$0 < \frac{\partial^2 TC}{\partial X^2}$$

This implies that the MC curve must have a positive slope, or the MC must be rising.

Now we shall show the equilibrium of the firm diagrammatically. Figure 16.2 shows the total revenue and the total cost curves of a firm in a perfectly competitive market.

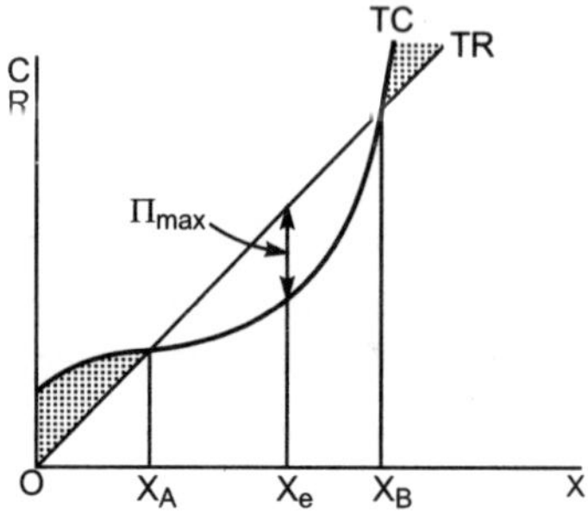

Fig. 16.2

In the figure we see that the total revenue curve is a straight line through the origin showing that the price is constant at all levels of output. In the perfect competition, a firm is a price taker and can sell any amount of output that it wants at the market price. Here the TR of the firm increases proportionally with its sales. Since all units are sold at the same price therefore we have

$$MR = AR = P$$

In Fig. 16.2, we see that the firm maximises its profit at the output X_e where the distance between the TR and TC curves is the maximum. If we consider the point below X_A or the above X_B, we see that the firm has losses.

Now we shall derive the above result using marginal cost and marginal revenue. This alternative approach uses price as an explicit variable and shows the behavioural rules that leads to profit maximisation of the firm (Fig. 16.3).

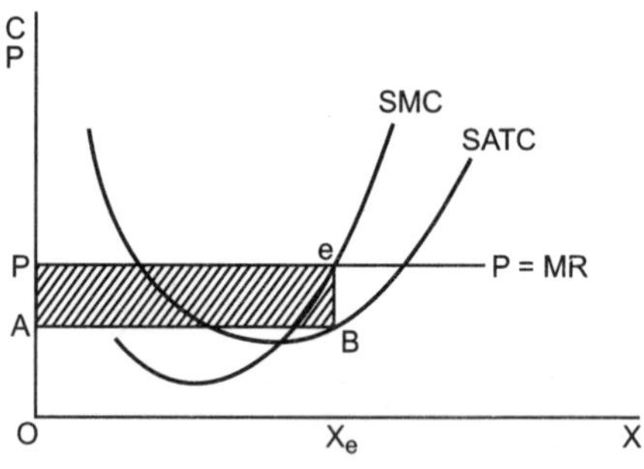

Fig. 16.3

As we know that the demand curve is also the average revenue curve and the marginal revenue curve of the firm in a perfectly competitive market. In the figure, the marginal cost curve cuts the average total cost curve at its minimum point. The law of variable proportions is followed therefore both the curves are U-shaped. The firm is at equilibrium where MC curve cuts the MR curve. In Fig. 16.3, it is the point e where output is X_e. If MC < MR the firm does not maximise its total profit since it pays the firm to expand its output. On the other hand, if MC > MR the firm is at low level position and it is better for the firm to cut its production. Finally if MC = MR the firm gains the maximum profit. Thus, it is the profit maximising condition in the short period. However, this is not the sufficient condition for profit maximisation since it may be fulfilled without reaching the equilibrium point. Therefore, we introduce the second condition for profit maximisation. This condition requires that the MC should be rising at the point of its intersection with the MR curve which implies that the MC must cut the MR curve from below, i.e. the slope of the MC must be steeper than the slope of the MR curve. Figure 16.4 represents both the conditions of the profit maximization.

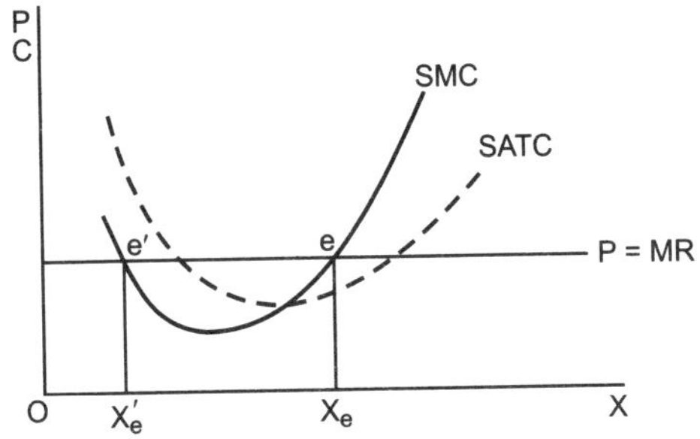

Fig. 16.4

In the figure we see that at point e both the conditions of profit maximisation are satisfied. One point should be noted that the MC is always positive because the firm has to spend some resources in order to produce an additional unit of output. Thus, at equilibrium MR is also positive. Equilibrium of the firm does not guarantee the excess profit. Excess profits or losses depend on the level of the average total cost curve at the short-run equilibrium. To earn excess profit, ATC of the firm should be below the price at equilibrium. However, if ATC is above the price the firm makes a loss. When a firm is making a loss, it will have to decide whether to continue production or not. This decision will, in fact, depend on then different total costs levels. If the firm is in the short-run and is making a loss whereby

(a) Total cost (TC) is greater than total revenue (TR)

(b) And whereby total revenue is equal to total variable cost (TVC).

It is advisable for the firm to continue production. If it fails to achieve these conditions, it is advised to close down so that the only costs the firm will have to pay will be the fixed cost. Even if the firm stops producing, it will have to continue to meet the level of fixed costs. Since whether the firm produces or not, it will have to pay fixed costs, it is better for it to continue production in an attempt to decrease total costs and increase total revenue, thus making profits. This can be done by (a) increasing productivity and (b) adopting new methods of production.

Short-run Supply Curve When All Fixed Costs are Sunk

We are going to derive the supply curve for a price taking firm when all fixed costs are sunk. Since non-sunk fixed costs = 0 therefore we have total fixed cost = sunk fixed cost. Let us consider Fig. 16.5.

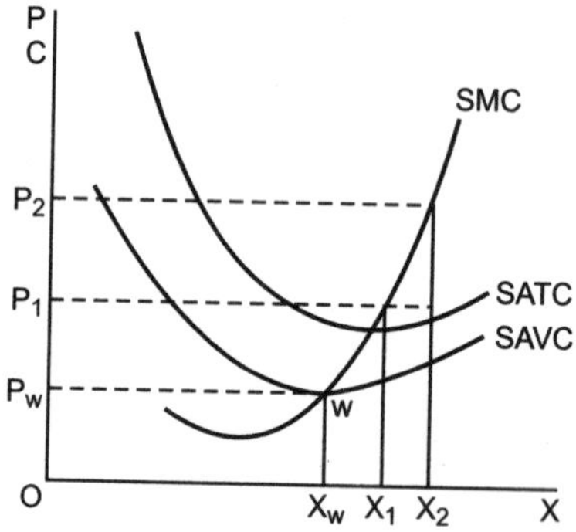

Fig. 16.5

The figure shows the short-run marginal cost curve (SMC), short-run average cost curve (SAC) and average variable cost curve (AVC) of a firm. Consider the three possible market prices for the product X: P_w, P_1 and P_2 per unit of X. If we apply the P = MC profit maximising condition, the firm's profit maximising output level when the prices are P_w, P_1 and P_2 would be X_w, X_1 and X_2 respectively. Each of these quantities represents a point at which the firm's short-run marginal cost SMC equals the relevant market price P, or P = MC.

The short-run supply curve of the firm shows how the firm's profit maximising output decision changes as the market price changes, assuming that the firm cannot adjust all of its inputs such as quantity of capital or land. Graphically, for the prices P_w, P_1 and P_2, the firm's short-run supply curve coincides with the short-run marginal cost curve SMC (Fig. 16.6).

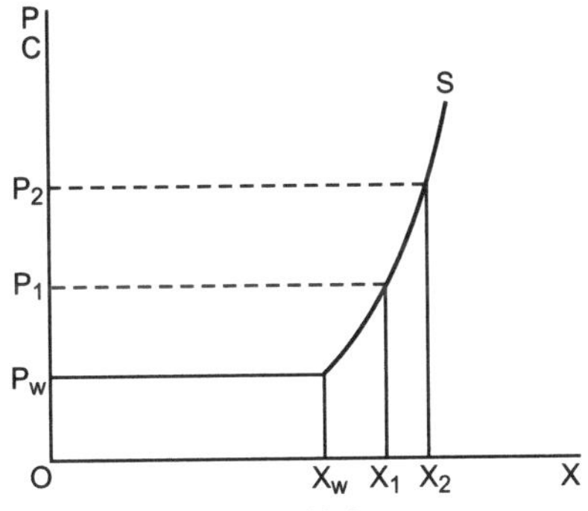

Fig. 16.6

However, the firm's short-run marginal cost curve and the firm's short-run supply curve do not necessarily coincide at all possible prices. More generally, the firm is better off cutting its losses by temporarily shutting down if the market price P is less than the average variable cost AVC at the output X at which P equals short-run marginal cost, or P < AVC. We can now draw the short-run supply curve. We know that

(a) A profit maximising price-taking firm, if it produces positive output, produces where P = SMC and SMC slopes upward.

(b) A profit maximising price-taking firm never produces where P < AVC.

Thus, the firm would never produce on the portion of the SMC curve where SMC < AVC. This is the portion below the minimum level of AVC curve. It implies, the firm will not produce any thing if price is below the minimum level of AVC. Thus, supply curve of the firm has two parts.

(a) If the market price is less than the minimum level of AVC, the firm will supply zero output. At this point the firm's supply curve is a vertical and coincides with the vertical axis. This price of the firm is called the shutdown price, the price below which it produces nothing in the short-run.

(b) If the market price is greater than the minimum level of price, the firm will produce a positive amount of output, and its short-run supply curve will coincide with its short-run marginal cost curve.

The industry supply curve is the horizontal summation of the supply curves of the individual firms. It is assumed that the factor prices and the technology are given and that the number of firms is very large. Under these conditions the total quantity supplied in the market at each price is the sum of the quantities supplied by all firms at that price.

Short-run Supply Curve of a Firm When Some Fixed Cost are Sunk and Some are Non-sunk

Now we are considering the case when the firm has some non-sunk fixed cost. Here we have TFC = SFC + NSFC and NSFC > 0.

where TFC = total fixed cost

SFC = sunk fixed cost and

NSFC = non-sunk fixed cost

Here also the profit maximising condition is the same as in the above section which states that firm maximises its profit by equating price to marginal cost. However, the rule that defines when the firm produces zero output, as opposed to positive, is different from the case discussed in the previous section. As we know that the firm's average non-sunk cost is equal to the sum of its average variable cost and its average non-sunk fixed cost.

That is, $$\text{ANSC} = \text{AVC} + \text{NSFC/Q}$$

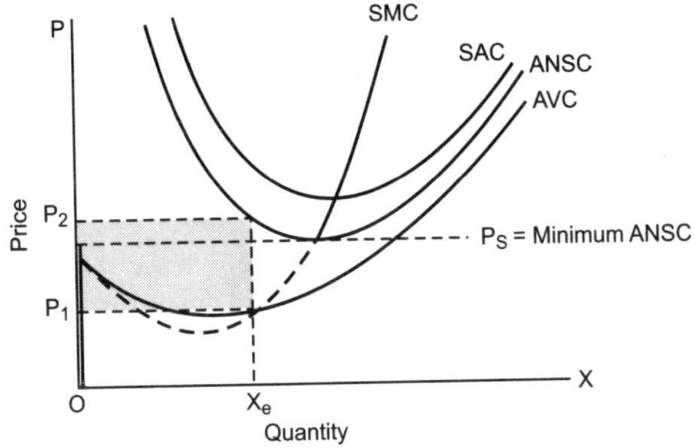

Fig. 16.7

In Fig. 16.7, we see that the average non-sunk cost curve is U-shaped and lies between the SAC and the AVC. At the minimum point, SMC = ANSC. Thus, the ANSC curve behaves much like the SAC curve. Let us consider the price P_1. If the firm maximises its profit at this price, it would produce at the point at which price equals marginal cost. Thus, it will produce at X_e. But at this price firm has to incur a loss. For every unit of X it produced, it would lose the difference between the price of P_1 and its average non-sunk cost P_2. If the firm does not produce, its loss would only be its sunk fixed costs SFC, i.e. by temporarily shutting down, the firm would avoid both its variable costs and its non-sunk fixed costs. Thus, at the price P_1, the firm cuts its loss by not producing. By doing so it avoids an additional loss of $X_e (P_2 - P_1)$.

Hence, we see that the firm is better off cutting its short-run losses by not producing if the market price is less than the average non-sunk cost at the output at which market price equals short-run marginal cost. Now we are in the position of drawing the firm's short-run supply curve. In the above discussion we have seen that

(a) A profit maximising price-taking firm, if it produces positive output, produces where P = SMC and SMC is rising.

(b) A firm with non-sunk fixed costs would never produce where P < ANSC.

The above mentioned points imply that the firm would never produce on the portion of the SMC curve where SMC < ANSC. This portion is below the minimum level of ANSC curve. Thus, we find that if price is below the minimum level of ANSC which has been denoted by P_S in Fig. 16.7, the firm will produce nothing. In the figure, we see that the short-run supply curve for the firm is a vertical spike for prices below the minimum level of average non-sunk cost, and it coincides with the short-run marginal cost curve for prices above this level.

Long-run Equilibrium of a Firm

In the long-run, a firm can adjust both its plant size and its rate of output to maximise its profit. Therefore, equilibrium is achieved when the firm adjusts its plant so as to produce at the minimum point of its long-run AC curve, which is tangent to the demand curve defined by the market price. In the long-run, the firm earns just the normal profit. If the profit is more than the normal then new firms will be attracted in the industry which will leads to a fall in price, i.e. a downward shift in the individual demand curves and an upward shift in the cost curves due to the increase of the prices of factors as the industry expands. This process will continue until the LAC is tangent to the demand curve defined by the market price. On the other hand, if the firm makes a loss then it will leave the industry which will force the price to rise and the costs may fall as the industry contracts. Figure 16.8 shows the equilibrium adjustment process of a firm in the long-run.

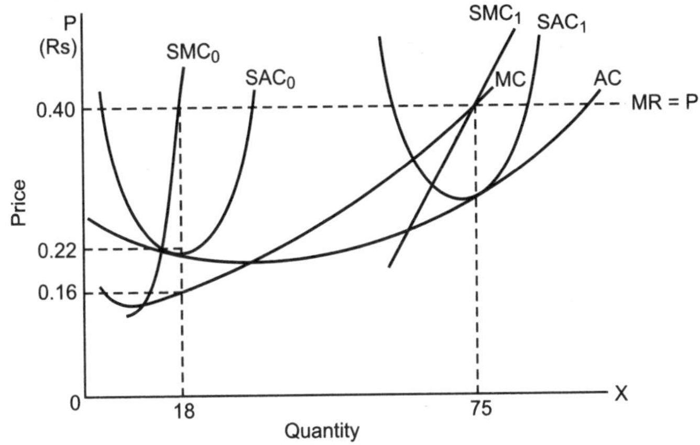

Fig. 16.8

As the firm looks out over the long-run horizon and contemplates the possible output levels it might produce, it should evaluate the cost of those outputs using its long-run cost functions. The long-run equilibrium condition is given by the following expression

$$LMC = LAC = P$$

That means the marginal cost is equal to the price and to the long-run average cost.

Given the technology and the prices of factors of production, the firm adjusts its plant size so as to produce that level of output at which the LAC is the minimum possible. Therefore, we have the condition

$$SMC = LMC = LAC = LMC = P = MR$$

That is at the equilibrium the short-run marginal cost is equal to the long-run marginal cost and the short-run average cost is equal to the long-run average cost.

Thus, we see that at the minimum point of the LAC the corresponding plant is worked at its optimal capacity where LAC and SAC coincide. And we also find that the LMC cuts the LAC at its minimum point and the SMC cuts the SAC at its minimum point. Thus, at the minimum point of the LAC the above equality between short-run and long-run costs is satisfied. The profit maximising quantity is the point at which long-run marginal cost equals the market price as shown in Fig. 16.8. To produce this quantity, the firm utilizes a plant size that is cost minimising for this output level.

Long-run Supply Curve of a Firm

From the above analysis we find that a firm's long-run supply curve is its long-run marginal cost curve. The long-run supply curve of a firm coincides with its long-run marginal cost curve at the point where price is above the minimum level of long-run average cost. For prices below the minimum long-run average cost, a firm would produce no output. The reason for this is that at market price below the minimum long-run average cost, the firm would earn negative economic profit, even after making all available adjustments in its input mix to minimise total costs. The long-run supply curve can be shown by the following figure.

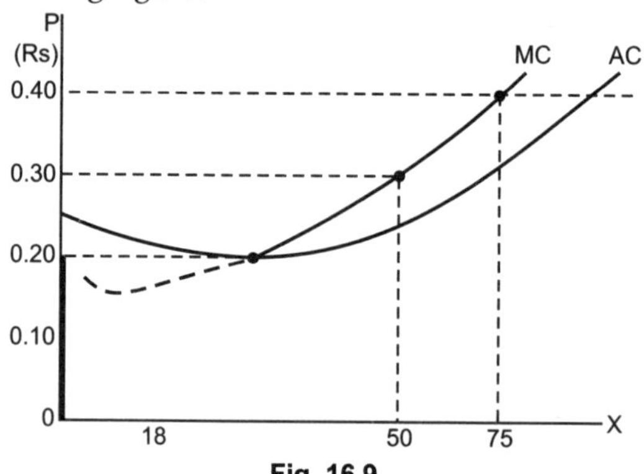

Fig. 16.9

If the firm anticipates that the market price will remain below the minimum long-run average cost for the foreseeable future, its best course of action would be to leave the industry. The logic underlying the construction of the firm's long-run supply curve and the short-run supply curve is the same. In both the cases, if firm produces positive output we consider the relationship between price and marginal cost to determine the optimal level of output. The difference between the short-run and the long-run is that in the long-run, all costs are avoidable, whereas in the short-run, some costs might not be avoidable if the firm produces nothing.

Equilibrium of Industry

An industry is said to be in equilibrium when it has no tendency either to expand or contract its output. The output of the industry can be varied in two ways: (i) by a change in the plant capacities of the existing firms and (ii) by entry of new firms or exist of some of the old firms. Thus, an industry would be in equilibrium when the existing firms have no incentive to vary their plant capacities, nor is there any incentive for new firms to enter the industry or for existing firms to leave the industry. For an industry to be in equilibrium, two conditions must be satisfied. In the first place, each firm must be in equilibrium. We have already seen that this condition would be fulfilled when the marginal cost is equal to marginal revenue and the marginal cost curve intersects the marginal revenue curve from below at the point of equilibrium. Secondly, there should be no inducement for new firms to enter the industry and for existing firms to leave the industry. This condition would be fulfilled when the entrepreneurs are earning just *normal profits*, i.e. profits which are just sufficient to induce them to continue in the industry, and when no entrepreneur outside the industry thinks that he could earn even normal profits if were to enter it. If all the firms in the industry are earning normal profits, there will be no inducement for any firm to leave the industry. Nor will there be an inducement for any new firm to enter the industry because, under the prevailing conditions, it cannot expect to earn normal profits if it enters the industry in question. In case, some firms in the industry are earning super-normal profits, the new firms will be attracted to enter the industry because, under the prevailing conditions, they can expect to earn at least the normal profits if they enter the industry. In contrast, if some firms are earning sub-normal profits, they would leave the industry and go elsewhere in search of normal profits. Thus, the industry would be in equilibrium when all the firms in it are earning just normal profits.

In economics average cost includes not only the average cost of production but also normal profits. In other words, normal profits form an integral part of the average cost.

Normal profits represent a fixed amount of money which the firm must earn whatever be its level of output. If the firm cannot earn normal profits, it will not stay in the industry. The larger the volume of output, the smaller would be the normal profits per unit of output because the fixed amount of normal profits would be spread over larger output. This provides us an additional reason for the average cost curve to slope downward over the low ranges of output.

Short-run Supply Curve of an Industry

In the above section we have derived the short-run supply curve for an individual price-taking firm. Now we are going to find out the supply curve of an industry which consists of large number of firms.

Since the number of firms in an industry is fixed in the short-run, market supply at any price is given by the summation of the quantities that each established firm supplies at the market price. To show the industry supply curve, let us consider two types of firms: 100 firms of type 1 and 100 firms of type 2. The short-run supply curve of type 1 is given by SS_1 and that of type 2 is given by SS_2 (Fig. 16.10).

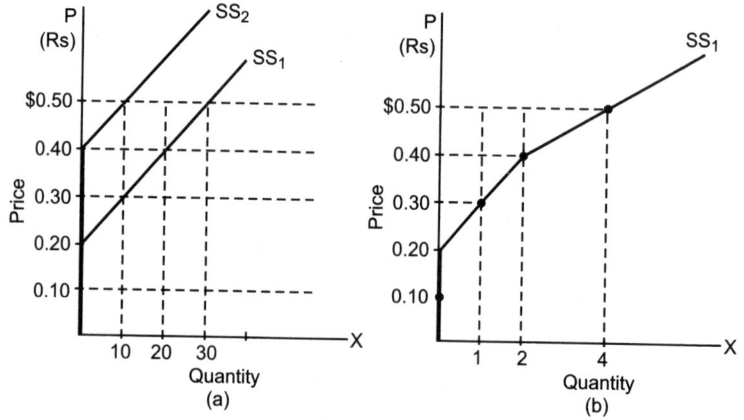

Fig. 16.10

Since the short-run supply curve is derived by horizontal summation of the supply curve of the individual firms therefore the second part of the figure shows the short-run market supply curve SS which tells us the quantity supplied in the aggregate by all firms in the market. The market supply curve tells us the marginal cost of producing the last unit supplied in the market. This is because over the range of prices for which the firm is willing to produce positive output, each firm's supply curve coincides with its marginal cost curve. In the above mentioned method of deriving the industry supply curve, one assumption is made that the prices that firms pay for their inputs are constant as the market output varies.

Long-run Equilibrium of an Industry

One of the properties of the long-run is that a firm can enter the industry if it can earn positive economic profits and thereby create wealth for its owners at the prevailing market price. The industry is said to be in the long-run equilibrium when a price is reached at which all firms are in equilibrium producing at the minimum point of their LAC curve making just normal profit. At this point supply equals demand and firms have no incentive to enter or exit the industry. A long-run perfectly competitive equilibrium is characterised by a market price, a number of identical firms and quantity of output per firm that satisfies following three conditions:

(a) Each firm maximises its long-run profit with respect to output and plant size which implies that a firm's long-run marginal cost equals the market price.

(b) Each firm's economic profit is zero which implies that a firm's long-run average cost equals the market price.

(c) Market demand equals market supply that is at the given market price, market demand equals market supply, given the number of firms and individual firm supply decision.

Figure 16.11 shows the long-run equilibrium of the industry.

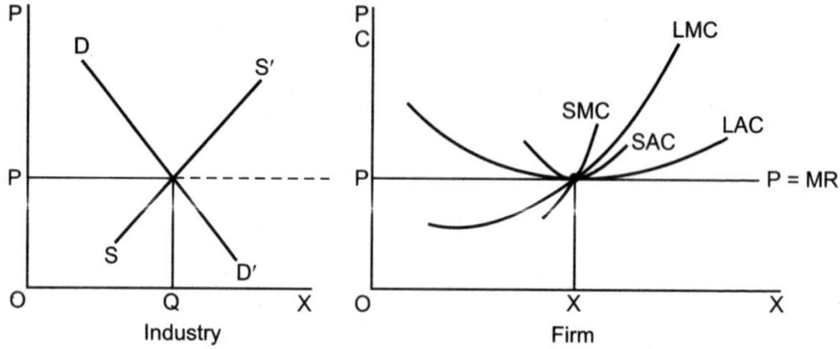

Fig. 16.11

At the market price, P, the firms produce at their minimum cost, earning just normal profits. The firm is in equilibrium because at the level of output X we have following identity which ensures that the firm maximises its profit.

$$LMC = SMC = P = MR$$

At the price P the firms earn just normal profit and all costs are covered so that there is no incentive for entry or exit. Hence, the industry is in equilibrium at price P and the condition of equilibrium is given by the identity

$$LAC = SAC = P$$

Due to uniqueness of price, all firms in the industry have the same minimum long-run average cost. This condition does not imply that all firms are of the same size or have the same efficiency, despite the fact that their LAC is the same in equilibrium. If a firm is more efficient then it will employ more productive factors of production. These more efficient factors must be remunerated for their higher productivity; otherwise they will be bid off by the new entrants in the industry. The rent paid to the more efficient factors becomes the cost of the individual firm. This will shift the LAC of the more efficient firms upwards as the market price rises, even if the factor prices for the industry as a whole remain constant as the industry expands. In this situation LAC of the efficient firm will be tangent at the higher market price. There will be no change in the LMC of the efficient firm. Thus, the more efficient firms will be in equilibrium, producing that output at which the new LAC of the efficient firm will be at its minimum. Thus, at this situation when more productive resources properly remunerated, all firms have the same unit cost in their long-run equilibrium. Figure 16.12 shows the whole situation.

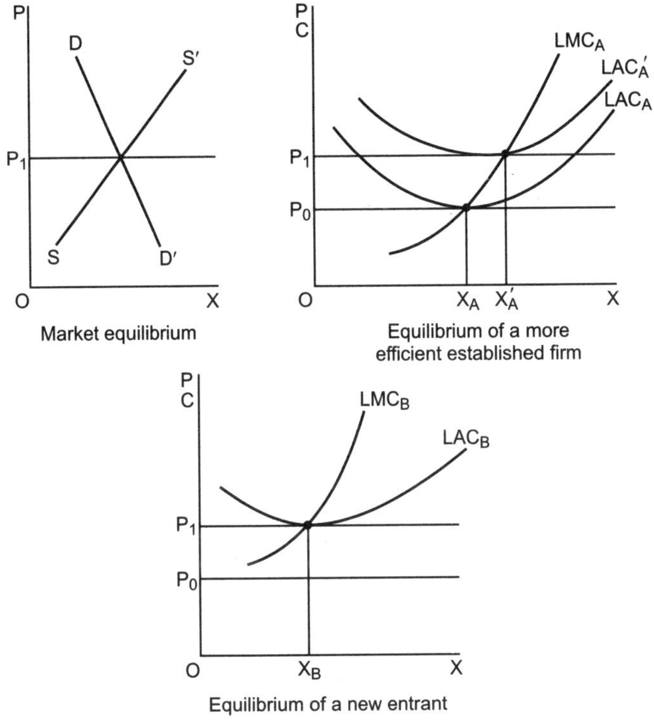

Fig. 16.12

Long-run Supply Curve of an Industry

The long-run supply curve of an industry shows the total quantity of output that will be supplied in the market at various prices, assuming that all long-run adjustments, such as adjustments in plant size and new firms entering the market, take place. Here one point should be noted that we cannot obtain the long-run industry supply curve in the same way as we have obtained in the short-run. This is due the fact that in the long-run industry supply can vary as firms enter or exit the market which implies that there is no fixed set of individual firm supply curves which can be added together. Figure 16.13 illustrates the long-run supply curve of an industry.

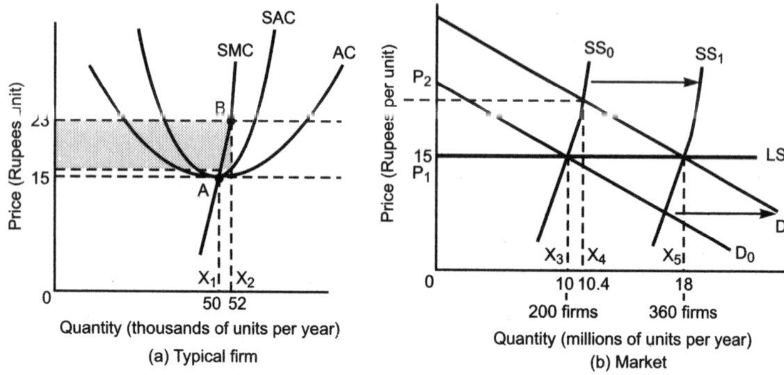

Fig. 16.13

Initially, the market is in long-run equilibrium at a price of P_1. At this price, each of the 100 (say) identical firms produces at its minimum efficient level of X_1 unit per year, so market supply is 100 X_1 units per year. Point A in the first part of the figure shows the long-run equilibrium position of a typical firm.

Let us suppose that the market demand shifts from D_0 to D_1 which has been shown in the second part of the figure. We also consider that the shift in demand is expected to persist, so the market will reach a new long-run equilibrium. In the short-run, with 100 firms in the market, equilibrium occurs at a price of P_2, with each firm maximising profit by producing X_2 units per year and with total market supply and demand at 100 X_2 units per year. This situation is depicted by point B in the first part of the figure and for the industry it is represented by the intersection of the short-run supply curve SS_0 and the new demand curve D_1 which has been shown in the second part of the figure. At price P_2, each of the 100 firms in the market earns a positive economic profit equal to the shaded area of the rectangle in the first part of the figure. The prospect of an economic profit attracts new firms into the market, shifting the short-run supply curve rightward. This process continues until the short-run supply curve shifts to SS_1 and the price has fallen back to P_1 per unit as shown by the intersection of SS_1 and D_1 in the second part of the figure.

At this point, let us suppose 100 new firms have entered the industry, and each firm maximises its profit by producing at its minimum efficient level of X_1 unit per year. Once price falls to P_1, there is no incentive for additional entry or exit because each firm earns zero economic profit.

Thus, we see that in a perfectly competitive industry which is initially in long-run equilibrium at a price P, additional market demand will be satisfied in the long-run by the entry of new firms. We can expect an increase in the equilibrium price in the short-run but in the long-run this process of new entry will drive the equilibrium price back down to its original level. Hence, the long-run market supply curve will be a horizontal line corresponding to the long-run equilibrium price P. In Fig. 16.3, the line LS represents the long-run market supply curve corresponding to the long-run equilibrium price of P_1. At this point of equilibrium, the market mechanism leads to an optimal allocation of resources which can be shown by the following prevailing conditions.

(a) The minimum feasible cost of production is maintained.

(b) The price paid by the consumers is the minimum possible price which just covers the marginal cost of the product, i.e. price = opportunity cost.

(c) There are no wastes of resources because plants are used at full capacity in the long-run.

(d) Only normal profits are possible.

Given the production possibility curve and consumers' preferences, perfect competition will lead to the optimal allocation of resources under the following three conditions.

(a) If the consumers' sovereignty, expressed by the price system, reflects the correct ranking of preferences of the community.

(b) If there are no unexhausted economies of scale in any one industry.

(c) If resources and technology are given, there is no growth in the economy and no technical progress.

If the above three conditions are fulfilled, perfect competition leads to the optimal resource allocation which can be shown by the point of tangency of the given production possibility curve with the highest possible indifference curve.

Industry Equilibrium under Dynamic Changes

In this section we are going to find out the effects on industry equilibrium due to various dynamic changes in the economy. We shall consider the situations like a shift in the market demand, a shift in the costs due to changes in factor prices and imposition of tax by the government. Let us explain all these case one by one.

(a) ***A Shift in the Market Demand*:**

Let us consider the following figures.

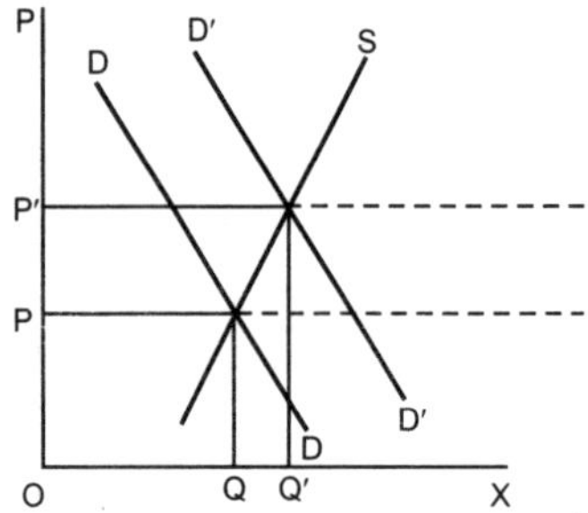

Fig. 16.14

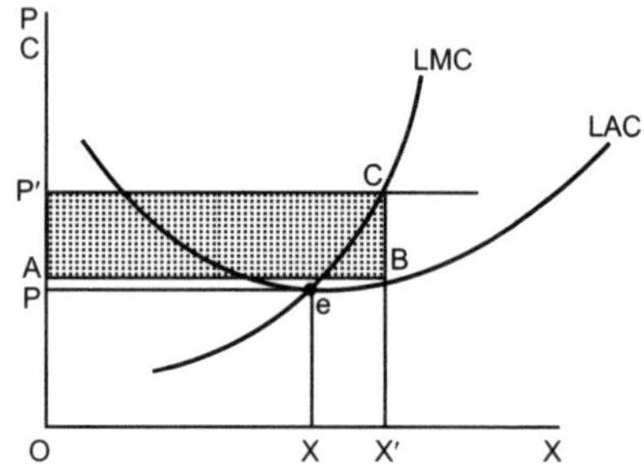

Fig. 16.15

We suppose that the market demand shifts to the right due to change in the determinants of the market demand. In the short-run the supply curve is given. Due to shift in market demand, price will rise and the quantity supplied will increase by an expansion of the production of the existing firms which will be realising excess profits at the higher market price. In the long-run new firms will join the industry which will shift the market supply to the right and will cause price to fall below the short-run equilibrium level. The new equilibrium price will be determined by the cost condition of the industry. Thus, here we have three costs conditions: (a) constant-cost, (b) increasing-cost, and (c) decreasing-cost industry.

Constant-cost industry: When changes in industry output have no effects on input prices, we have a constant-cost industry. The following figure shows the case of long-run equilibrium of an industry which grows with constant-costs.

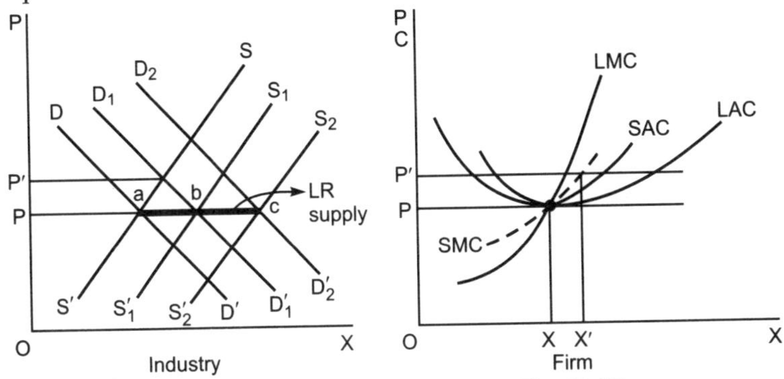

Fig. 16.16 **Fig. 16.17**

The expansion of industry output that occurs as a result of new entry does not affect the prices of inputs used by firms in the industry. As a result, when the new firms enter the industry, cost curves of incumbent producers do not shift. This assumption holds when an industry's demand for an input is a small part of the total demand for that input. In this case, increases or decreases in the industry's use of that input would not affect its market price. Let us start with the initial level of long-run equilibrium situation where the demand-curve price line of the firm is tangent to the long-run and the short-run average total cost curves at their minimum points. Suppose that market demand shifts from DD' to D_1D_1'. This will result in the increase in the short-run price to P' and the existing firms increase their output, operating their plant above full capacity. In Fig. 16.16, the increased quantity is shown by a movement along the market supply SS'. However, this situation will not continue in the long-run because the excess profits shall attract new entry. Therefore, LAC curve does not shift upwards. The new firms will produce under the same LAC conditions as the already established firms. Entry will continue until the new supply curve S_1S_1' intersects the shifted demand curve at the initial price P. This process will continue. New firms will enter in the industry and the supply curve will shift to the right until it cuts the new demand curve at the initial price. Hence, the long-run industry supply is given by a straight line parallel to the quantity-axis at the initial price level. In Fig. 16.16, the long-run industry supply curve is represented by the straight line abc. Here one point should be noted that constant cost is not the same as constant returns to scale. Firms in an industry can have constant returns to scale, but the industry need not be constant-cost.

Increasing-cost Industry

When an expansion of industry output increases the price of an input, we have an increasing-cost industry. An industry is likely to be increasing cost if firms use industry-specific inputs-scarce inputs that only firms in that industry use. In this case long-run supply curve has a positive slope, indicating that the prices of factors increase as the industry output expands. Now consider the following figure (Fig. 16.18) which shows the adjustment of the industry supply to the growing market demand under condition of increasing costs.

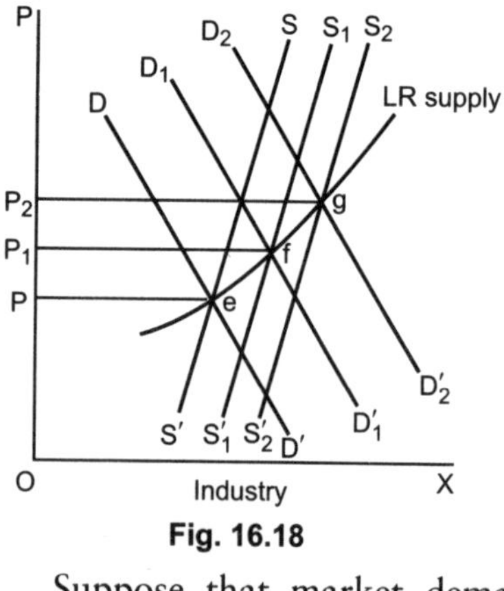

Fig. 16.18

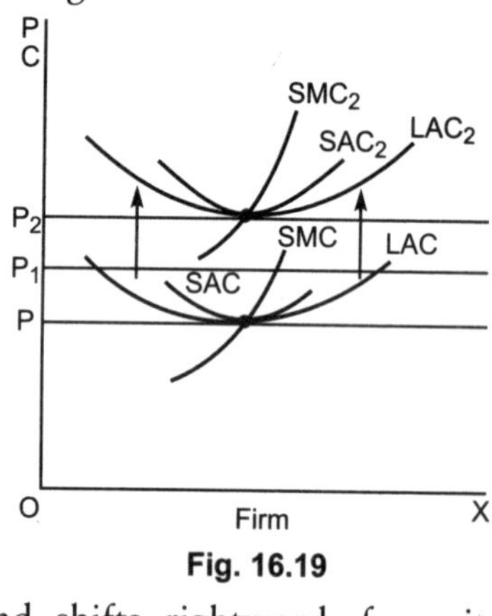

Fig. 16.19

Suppose that market demand shifts rightward, from its initial equilibrium DD′ to the new level D_1D_1'. It will result in the increase in price in short-run to P_1. The quantity supplied will increase because the existing firms will work beyond its optimal capacity. This excess profit will attract new firms in the industry. Since the output of the industry increases through new entry, the prices of industry-specific inputs begin to rise. The increase in input prices causes each firm's long-run and short-run cost functions to shift upward as shown in Fig. 16.18. We see that the LAC of all firms shifts upwards, while the LMC shifts to the left with the increasing factor prices. This will result in leftward shift in the industry supply. At the same time, the quantity supplied increases as new firms enter the industry and thus the market supply will tend to shift to the right.

The adjustment process stops when price falls to a point at which firms earn zero profits. The shift of the supply curve will lead to a fall in price as compared with the short-run level P_1 if the increase in factor prices permits it. If the increase in factor costs is substantial the new equilibrium price might stay at the short-run level despite the shift in supply. The new market price will be higher than the original level. The long-run market supply curve in an increasing-cost industry is upward sloping. The upward sloping market supply curve tells us that increases in price are needed to elicit additional industry output in the long-run. The increase in price compensates for the increase in the minimum level of long-run average cost that are driven by the increase in industry output and resulting increase in input prices. In an increasing-cost industry output can expand in the long-run only at an increasing supply price.

Decreasing-cost Industry

An industry is said to be decreasing-cost industry if an increase in industry outputs decrease the prices of some or all inputs. In a decreasing-cost industry, each firm's average and marginal cost curves may fall, not because the firms produce with economies of scale, but because input prices fall when the industry produces more. Consider Figs. 16.20 and 16.21 which describe the process of adjustment of the industry supply to the expanding market demand.

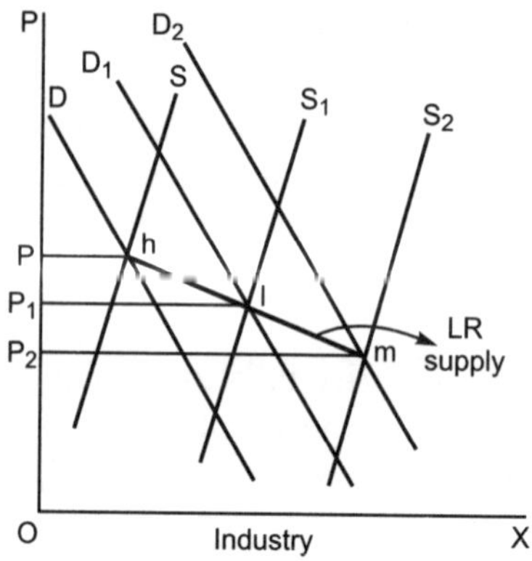

Fig. 16.20

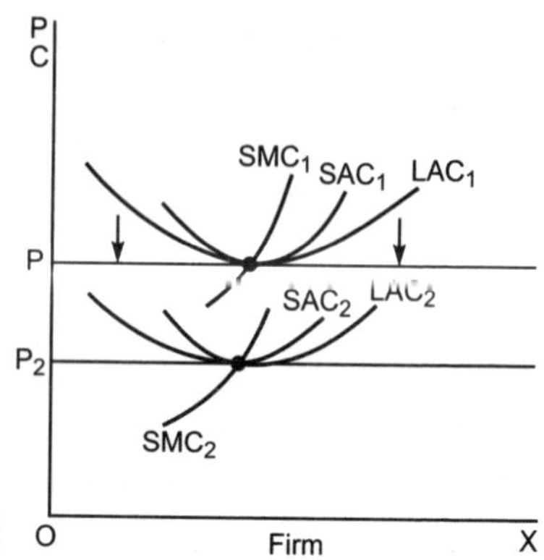

Fig. 16.21

In the figure we see that as the market demand shifts to the right from D to D_1, price increases in the short-run and the new firms will enter the industry. As industry output increases through new entry, the prices of industry-specific inputs begin to fall, causing each firm's long-run and short-run cost curves to shift downward as shown in the figure. The industry supply shifts so far to the right that price in the long-run falls below the initial level. The long-run supply curve can be given by the line hlm in the figure which has a negative slope. The above discussion implies that if there are strong external economies the industry supply can expand in the long-run at a decreasing price. The long-run supply curve in the figure has been drawn taking into account both entry by new firms and changes in input prices; it is downward sloping because producer faces lower input prices when the market produces larger quantities.

(b) *A Shift in the Costs due to Changes in Factor Prices*:

In this case we shall consider two situations: (a) an increase in the fixed cost and (b) an increase in the variable cost.

Let us consider the first situation, i.e. an increase in the fixed cost. This will leads to an upward shift in both the AFC and the ATC curves but the AVC and the MC curves are not affected. Now consider the Figs. 16.22 and 16.23.

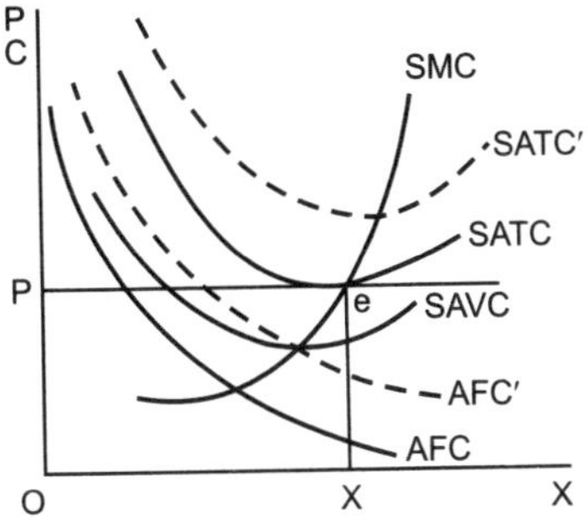

Firm

Fig. 16.22

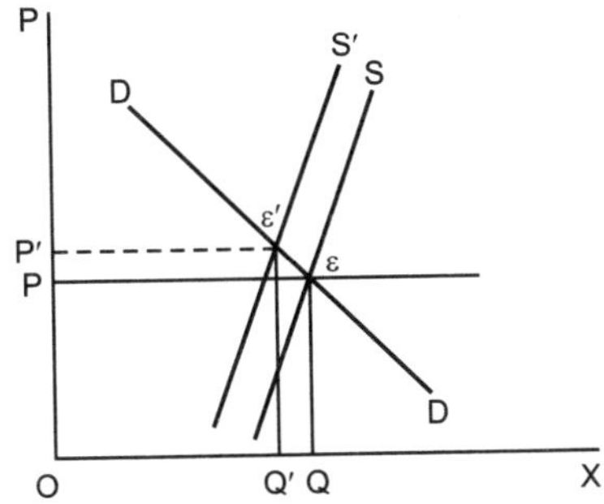

Industry

Fig. 16.23

Since MC curve is the supply curve of the firm, the equilibrium position of the firm is not affected in the short-run. However, in the long-run, the firm earns just normal profits, it will not now cover its higher total average costs and will go out of business. Thus, in, the long-run industry-supply curve will shift upwards to the left. This will result in lower output, higher price and fewer firms in the industry.

Now we shall consider the situation of an increase in the variable costs. This will result in an upward shift of AVC, ATC and the MC curves of the firm to the left. Since MC is the supply curve of the firm, the increase in the variable costs will results in a decrease in the quantity supplied by the firm at the going market price. This can be shown by Figs. 16.24 and 16.25.

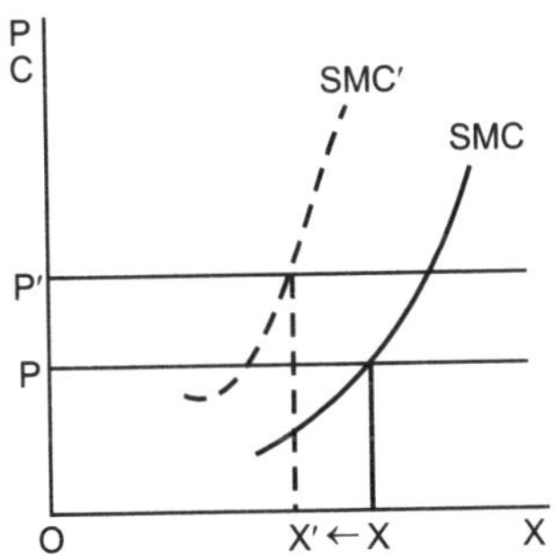

Firm

Fig. 16.24

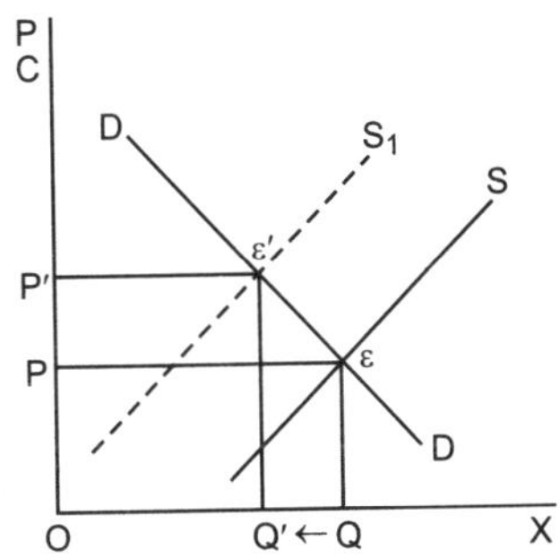

Industry

Fig. 16.25

From the above figure we see that even in the short-run, the market supply curve will shift upwards to the left and, given the market demand, price will rise. Also the number of firms will be same in the new market equilibrium situation but the quantity will be lower and the price higher than the initial equilibrium situation.

(c) ***Imposition of a Tax:***

In this section we shall consider the effect of the imposition by the government of a lump-sum tax, a profit tax and a specific tax.

Let us start with the imposition of a lump-sum tax. Since the lump-sum tax is like a fixed cost to the firm therefore its effect will be similar to the fixed cost. Thus, in the short-run the MC curve will not be affected and the firm will continue to produce the same output as before the imposition of the tax. In the long-run if the firm was earning just normal profits prior to the tax, it will not be able to cover its ATC at given market price and hence will close down. This will result in leftward shift of the market supply curve which in turns will result in lower output and higher price.

Now if the government imposes a profit tax then this will also put similar effect as a lump-sum tax. It will reduce the profits of a firm but will not affect its MC which implies that the short-run equilibrium of the firm and the industry will not change. In the long-run equilibrium will be reached with a higher price, lower output and a smaller number of firms in the industry.

Now we shall consider the case of imposition of a specific sales tax by the government. Since a given amount of money per unit of output produced is taken away therefore it will affect the MC of the firm by shifting it upwards to the left, and the amount produced at the going price will be reduced which will shift the price up.

The burden of the specific tax that will be borne by the consumer depends on the price elasticity of supply, given the market demand. In general, the most elastic the market supply the higher the proportion of the tax that the consumer will bear and the less the burden of the firm from the specific tax. If the market supply has a positive slope, the specific tax will be paid partly by the buyer and partly by the firm. On the other hand, if the market supply is elastic, the firms will be able to pass on to the consumer more of the specific tax. This situation can be shown in Fig. 16.26.

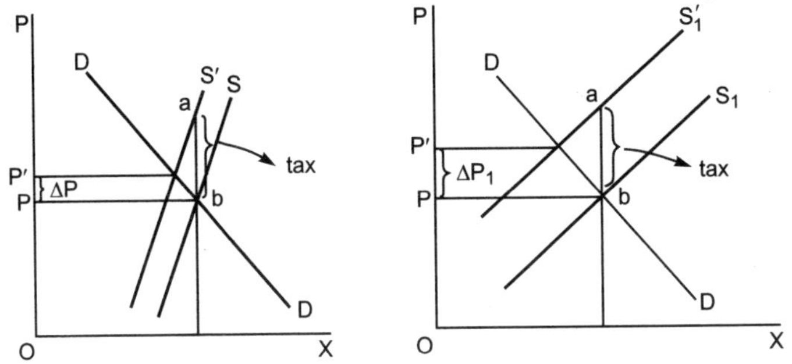

Fig. 16.26

In the figure we see that the demand curves are identical and the initial price is the same but the supply in the second figure is more elastic. Let there be a specific tax equal to ab. It will raise the price by ΔP in the first figure and by ΔP_1 in the second figure. Clearly we see that $\Delta P_1 > \Delta P$, i.e. the tax burden to the consumer is greater in the case of a more elastic supply curve.

In case of an infinitely elastic market supply curve, the increase in price is equal to the specific tax and the whole tax burden is borne by the consumer. If the supply curve has a negative slope the imposition of a specific tax results in an increase in the price which is greater than the tax.

Economic Rent, Consumer Surplus and Producer Surplus

Economic rent measures the economic surplus that is attributable to an extraordinarily productive input whose supply is limited. Specifically, economic rent is equal to the difference between the maximum amount a firm is willing to pay for the services of the input and the input's reservation value—the return that the owner of an input could get by deploying the input in its best alternative use outside the industry. We thus have

Economic rent = maximum amount firm is willing to pay for services of input – return that input owner gets by deploying the input in its best alternative use outside the industry.

In perfect competition, there are no economic rents, as new firms enter a market and compete until prices fall and all rent is eliminated. Reducing rent does not change production decision, so economic rent can be taxed without any adverse impact on the real economy, assuming that it is really rent.

Producer surplus is the benefit on the production side from participating in the market. The concepts of consumer surplus and producer surplus are widely used for evaluating policy changes. Cost-Benefit Analysis recognises that benefits accrue as surplus and so are not always measured in market transactions. Producer surplus consists of gross profits accruing to firms and economic rents accruing to input owners. It is often depicted as the area to the left of the supply curve and below the horizontal line representing price.

The producers' and consumers' surpluses are shown with supply and demand curves in Fig. 16.27.

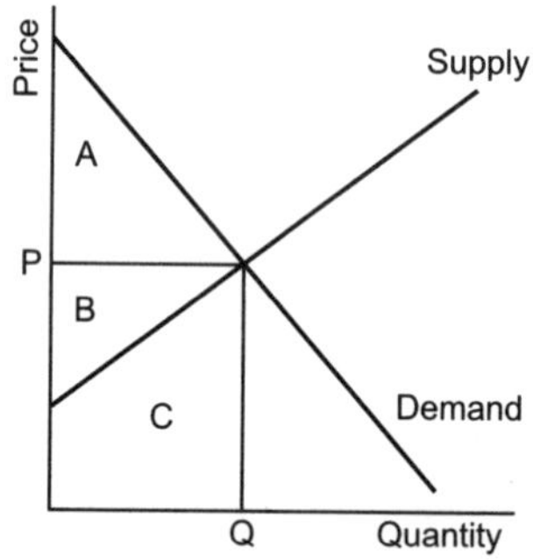

Fig. 16.27

The total value to consumers of quantity Q is represented by areas A + B + C. Because the consumers must pay B + C, only the area A is surplus for them. Producers get revenue of B + C. B is their surplus because only payments of C are needed to attract the resources necessary to produce quantity Q. One point should be noted that producer's surplus flows through to the owners of the factors of production, unlike economic profit which is zero under perfect competition. If the market for factors are perfectly competitive as well, producer's surplus ultimately ends up as economic rent to the owners of scarce inputs.

Limitations and Justification of Perfect Competition

Free markets are moral because they allocate resources and distribute commodities in ways that maximise utility and respect the liberty of buyers and sellers. Since markets having these benefits depend crucially on their competitiveness, anti-competitive conditions and practices are morally dubious. Monopoly and oligopoly practices are two principal types of anti-competitive practices and conditions that free market economies spawn. Under monopoly conditions, a market segment is controlled by a single seller and under oligopoly conditions a market segment is controlled by just a few sellers.

Though real markets are all imperfect, perfect competition serves as a useful idealisation not only for economic purposes of explaining and predicting the behaviour of actual markets but also for ethical purposes, i.e. for understanding and assessing the moral case for keeping markets as perfectly competitive as possible. Under this idealisation, a perfectly competitive market is defined in terms of seven conditions which are as follows:

(a) *Distribution*: Numerous buyers and sellers, none of whom has a substantial market share.

(b) *Openness*: Buyers and sellers are free to enter or leave the market.

(c) *Full and perfect knowledge*: Each buyer and seller has full and perfect knowledge of each others' doings.

(d) *Equivalent goods:* Goods being sold are similar enough that buyers don't care whose they buy.

(e) *Non-subsidisation*: Costs of producing or using goods are borne entirely by the buyers and sellers.

(f) *Rational economic agency*: All buyers and sellers act as egoistic utility maximisers, i.e. try to buy or produce as low as possible and sell as high as possible.

(g) *Non-regulation*: No external parties such as governments regulate the price, quantity, or quality of goods.

Freely competitive markets, in addition, presuppose

(a) *An underlying system of production*: So there is goods to exchange.

(b) *An enforceable private property system*: So buyers and sellers have ownership rights to transfer.

(c) *A system of contracts*: To administer such transfers.

Perfect competition gets its ethical importance from the fact that it is the self-regulative abilities of free markets—in response to supply and demand—that provides the principle arguments for the moral superiority for free markets. Where supply exceeds demand, prices, profits, and production decrease; where demand exceeds supply, prices, profits, and production increase: thus under conditions of perfect competition production naturally tends toward the equilibrium point (where supply equals demand) and goods find their "natural price" (= ordinary costs of production + normal rates of profit). The principle of *diminishing marginal utility* affects demand and states that each additional item consumed is less valuable than each earlier item and the principle of *increasing marginal costs* affects supply and states that each additional item produced beyond a certain point costs more to produce than each earlier item.

There are three principles moral benefits alleged for free markets.

(a) Serving demands of capitalist (contribution-based) justice.

(b) Maximising economic utility.

(c) Safeguarding negative rights of economic liberty.

Even so, this would-be moral justification of them is limited by additional considerations of positive rights, of care and of character and it is challenged by competing egalitarian, needs-based and socialist-contribution-based conceptions of distributive justice. Finally, to the extent that actual "free-market" policies fail to be perfectly competitive, their claim to actually having the alleged benefits (and with it their claim to morality) is diminished. Monopoly and oligopoly conditions are morally problematic due to their violation, especially, of the two "basic conditions" for the existence of perfect competition, distribution, and openness.

In the standard economic model, all markets are assumed to be "perfectly competitive", such that no one buyer or seller has the power to influence the prices or other market conditions buyer or seller faces. Since perfect competition is central to the conception of perfect markets, it has been extensively analysed. There are a number of conditions that are required in order for perfect competition to exist.

(a) Each market must involve trading in one homogeneous good, so that price, rather than other considerations, is the overwhelming influence on consumer choice, i.e. any one unit of the good must be virtually identical to any other. But practically it is not true because the product of a firm may be slightly different from that of another firm.

(b) Each market must have no significant barriers to entry, including no brand-name loyalties, and no need for high levels of advertising, as well as no technological and financial barriers to entry. We assume that there is no government intervention in the market. But government can intervene in the market on special cases.

(c) There must be no increasing returns to scale, because increasing returns create barriers to entry. If the technology of production allows vastly lower costs to larger producers than to smaller ones, then the industry will come to be dominated by a few large firms, creating an oligopoly (or even monopoly) rather than perfect competition.

(d) All factors of production must be mobile, i.e. labour, capital, and raw materials must be able to be moved from one location to another, rather than being at the mercy of a single local firm or industry. But in real case the factor of production may or may not be free to move from one firm to another firm.

(e) There must be numerous, small buyers and sellers, all of whom are compelled to be price takers since they cannot acquire significant market power.

(f) Information about the market must be freely and equally available to all actual and potential market participants, i.e. everyone needs to know about prices, quantities, and qualities of goods and services for sale must be public, or readily accessible.

These assumptions imply additional features of perfect competition, e.g. consider the assumption that a perfectly competitive industry is made up of numerous small firms and consumers, all of them price takers. This implies that the market plans of each buyer and seller are independent, and that collusion between firms or consumers to influence prices is impossible (since there are so many other participants in the market).

Perfect competition is also justified on the ground that it provides a simple and a logical starting base for economic analysis of the market and gives a very useful knowledge about the structure of the market. Many complicated economic phenomena of the market can be explained with this concept of the market.

Pricing Under Perfect Competition

17

Perfect competition is a very exacting concept. It provides a basis for the most important model of business behaviour. The essence of perfect competition is that the market is completely *impersonal*. There is no rivalry among various suppliers of a commodity in the market. Similarly, the various buyers of a commodity do not recognise their competitiveness with each other. In other words, perfect competition refers to a situation in which there is no direct competition either among various suppliers of a commodity or among various buyers of a commodity. Thus, the concept of perfect competition in economic theory is diametrically opposite of the businessman's concept of competition.

Conditions of Perfect Competition

A market, to be perfectly competitive, must satisfy a number of conditions, which are briefly mentioned below.

Large Number of Buyers and Sellers: The number of buyers and sellers must be so large that none of them individually is in a position to influence the price and output of the industry as a whole. In other words, the demand of an individual buyer and the supply of an individual seller in relation to the total demand for and the total supply of the commodity concerned should be so small that neither the individual buyer nor the individual supplier can influence the price. Every buyer as well as the seller has to accept the price of the product as given. Each seller adjusts his supply and each buyer adjusts his purchases to the given market price. If a large number of sellers or buyers act in the same way at the same time, changes in the quantity supplied or demanded would certainly affect the market price. But if perfect competition prevails, the change in price resulting from the actions of individual buyers and sellers would go unnoticed.

Homogeneous Product: In a perfectly competitive market, the product of any one seller must be identical to the product of any other seller so as to ensure that the buyers are indifferent as to the firm from which they buy. When the product of different sellers is identical or homogeneous, no seller can charge a price even slightly above the ruling market price; if he does so, his customers will at once turn to the other sellers who are offering the product at the ruling market price.

Absence of Artificial Restrictions: There is complete freedom in buying and selling of goods. The buyers are free to buy from any sellers they like and the sellers are free to sell to any buyers they choose. There is no discrimination on the part of either buyers or sellers. The prices are free to change in response to changes in the demand and supply conditions. No efforts are made by the government, the producers or any other agency to control or influence the supply, demand or price of the products.

Free Entry or Exit for Firms: The firms are free to enter or leave the industry. It implies that whenever abnormal profits arise, new firms are attracted into the industry. Similarly, when the industry is suffering losses, some firms leave it.

Perfect Mobility of Goods and Factors: There exists perfect mobility of goods as well as of factors between industries. The goods are free to move to those places where they can fetch the highest price. Similarly, factors of production are free to move into any use or industry which they consider to be more profitable for them. They are also free to leave any industry if they consider their remuneration there to be inadequate.

Perfect Knowledge of Market Conditions: Consumers, producers, and owners of productive resources must possess perfect knowledge if the market is to be perfectly competitive. If the consumers do not possess complete knowledge about prices, they might make purchases at prices higher than the ruling prices. In such a situation, there will not be a uniform price in the market. Similarly, if the workers do not possess complete knowledge about wage rates, they might not sell their services to the highest bidder. The producers must also possess complete knowledge about their costs as well as prices so as to produce the most profitable volume of output. Even this is not sufficient. Perfect knowledge includes not only complete knowledge of the present but also of the future. Perfect competition cannot prevail without complete knowledge of present as well as of future.

Absence of Transport Costs: A perfectly competitive market also assumes that no transport costs are involved in moving goods from one place to another. Existence of perfect competition assumes that a single price prevails everywhere in the market at any particular point of time. This assumption would not hold true when there exist transport costs because the price of the same product would differ at different places owing to different amounts of transport costs involved for different destinations from the place of supply. In fact, two similar products would not be considered homogeneous if they do not happen to be at the same place.

Pure Competition

Sometimes a distinction is made between perfect competition and pure competition. The former term is particularly popular with the British economists while the American economists are found of using the latter term. In fact, the term pure competition is used in a rather restricted sense. The pure competition requires the fulfillment of only the first four conditions while perfect competition also requires the fulfillment of the last three conditions. According to Prof. Chamberlin, pure competition means "competition unalloyed with monopoly elements" while perfect competition requires "perfection in many other respects than in the absence of monopoly".

Does Perfect Competition Exist?

The concept of perfect competition is only of theoretical importance. It does not exist anywhere in the real world. Even basic agricultural markets do not fulfill the seven conditions mentioned above. This, however, should not be taken to mean that the concept of perfect competition is useless. Prof. Ferguson makes two strong points in support of the study of perfect competition in spite of the fact that it does not exist anywhere in the real world.[1]

> .... First, generality can be achieved only by means of abstraction. Hence no theory can be perfectly descriptive of real world phenomena. Further, the more accurately a theory describes one specific real world case the less accurately it describes all others. In any area of thought a theoretician does not select his assumptions on the basis of their realism; the conclusions, not the assumptions, are tested against reality.
>
> This leads to a second point of great, if pragmatic, importance. The conclusions derived from the model of perfect competition have, by and large, permitted accurate explanation and prediction of real world phenomena. That is, perfect competition frequently works as a theoretical model of economic processes. The most persuasive evidence supporting this assertion is the fact that despite the proliferation of more "sophisticated" models of economic behaviour, economists today probably use the model of perfect competition in their research more than ever before.

Perfect competition helps us in understanding the working of an economy, where competitive behaviour leads to an optimum allocation of resources and the most efficient organisation of production. It provides us a hypothetical model against which we can appraise the actual working of economic institutions and organisations in any economy.

Analysis of determination of price and output under perfect competition is comparatively simple and uncomplicated. As such, it serves a useful introduction to the analysis of pricing under more realistic, but at the same time more complicated organisations of market. It also provides an opportunity to study some fundamentals common to all types of markets.

Further, though there exists no perfectly competitive markets, there do exist some markets (e.g. markets for agricultural products) which are not very far from perfect markets.

Time Element in Theory of Price

The element of time has an important bearing in the determination of price. Marshall was the first economist to formally recognise the role of time element in the determination of price. He made the price analysis more realistic by introducing the element of time. The importance of time element arises from the fact that one of the two determinants of price, namely supply, depends on the time allowed to it for adjustment. If the demand for a commodity increases, for instance, its supply would also increase. This, however, does not mean that the supply would increase immediately corresponding to the increase in demand. The reason for this is that it always takes some time to increase supply in response to an increase in demand. The cost conditions of a firm, as we have already seen in an earlier chapter, also vary according to the time permitted for an increase in supply.

It may be pointed out that Marshall's distinction between short and long periods was not based on clock or calendar time but on *operational* time in terms of economic forces at work. Time was considered to be short or long according to the extent of adjustment in the forces of supply. The greater the adjustability of supply forces the greater was the length of time irrespective of clock or calendar time.

Marshall studied equilibrium between the forces of demand and supply in four periods of time, viz. (i) Market Period, (ii) Short Period, (iii) Long Period, and (iv) Secular Period.

Market Period: The market period is a very short period in which supply is limited by the existing stock of goods. The period is too short to make any adjustment in supply in response to a change in demand. The maximum that can be supplied in the market period is the stock of the goods that has already been produced. The market period may be a day, a few days, or even a few weeks depending upon the nature of the commodity involved. The market period for a perishable item like milk may be just a single. In contrast, the market period for wheat may spread over several weeks. In the market period while the supply is fixed, the demand remains a variable factor. Thus, in this period, a temporary equilibrium is reached between fixed supply and variable demand. This market equilibrium price would be temporary and give place to a different equilibrium price with every change in demand.

Short Period: In this period, the supply can be adjusted to the change in demand only to a limited extent and not to the full extent. The changes in supply can be brought out only by changing the quantity of variable factors employed or by working the existing capital equipment more or less intensively. The time is too short to permit any change in the capital equipment or the organisational set-up of the firm. It is also not possible for new firms to enter the industry during this period. Equilibrium between demand and supply during this period is called short period equilibrium. Changes in market price tend to cluster around the short period equilibrium price.

Long Period: In this period, the firms have enough time to adjust supply of a commodity to the change in demand for it. There is enough time to make changes in the capital equipment and the organisation set-up of the firms. New plants can be built and the old ones abandoned. The new firms can enter the industry and the some of the existing firms can leave the industry if the changes in demand require so. The size of the firms as well as that of the whole industry expands or contracts according to the variations in demand. Since the quantity employed of all factors can be varied in the long-run, there are no fixed factors. In short, this period is long enough for supply to completely adjust to a change in demand through changes in the size of the capital equipment and the organisational set-up of the firms. Equilibrium between demand and supply during this period is known as long period equilibrium. Variations in short period price tend to cluster around the long period equilibrium price.

Secular Period: In this period, a very long period of time is available for supply to fully adjust to any change in demand. The duration of this period may extend to a decade or even more. In addition to changes that can take place in the long period, the secular period provides adequate time for certain other fundamental changes like changes in the techniques of production and management, changes in the supply of capital and raw materials, size of population, economic organisation, etc. Equilibrium between demand and supply in this period is referred to as secular equilibrium. The period involved in secular equilibrium is so long that a study of this equilibrium is not of much theoretical interest.

Relative Importance of Demand and Supply: By introducing time element in price determination, Marshall was able to resolve the controversy that existed among economists before him as to whether the price is determined by demand or supply. Marshall explained that price was determined by both the forces of demand supply. But, "As a general rule", said Marshall, "the shorter the period which one considers the greater must be the share of our attention which is given to the influence of demand on value; and the longer the period the more important will be the influence of cost of production on value. Actual value at any time—the market value as it is often called—is often influenced by passing events and causes whose action is fitful and short-lived than by those which work persistently. But in the long-run these fitful and irregular causes in a large measure efface one another's influence, so that in the long-run persistent causes dominate values completely."[2]

In the determination of price, while demand plays a dominant role in the short period, it is the supply which plays that role in the long-run. Roughly speaking, it can be said that in the very short-run price is determined by demand and in the long-run it is determined by supply. Thus, both those who believed that the price was determined by demand as well as those who believed that it was determined by supply, were correct. The difference in the two views arose because the former economists were stressing price determination in the market period in which demand plays the dominant role while the latter economists were emphasizing price determination in the long period in which the dominant role is played by the supply force. Though roughly speaking both the categories of economists were correct, scientifically speaking, both were wrong. In fact, price is determined by the interaction of forces of demand and supply. In price determination, fixity of supply in the market period plays as much important role as the variability of demand. To cite Marshall's famous analogy of scissors, "We might as reasonably dispute whether it is the upper or the under blade of a pair of scissors that cuts a piece of paper, as whether value is governed by utility or cost of production. It is true that when one blade is held still and the cutting is effected by moving the other, we may say with careless brevity that the cutting is done by the second, but the statement is not strictly accurate and is to be executed only so long as it claims to be merely a popular and not a strictly scientific account of what happens". Thus, neither the upper blade nor the lower blade alone can do the cutting and both are needed for the work of cutting.

Marshall and, following him, modern economists study the effect on price of varying response of supply during different time periods to a sudden and once-for-all change in demand. In contrast, they do not study the effect on price of the adjustment in demand in response to a change in supply conditions. The reason for this has been very well explained by Stonier and Hague in the following words: "There is no reason why, if supply conditions change, demand condition should change as well, or if they do, why they should change differently in the short-run and the long-run. Changes in consumer's tastes are not dependent on technology in the way that supply conditions are. Admittedly, consumer's tastes may, and probably will, change as time goes on. But this will be a change of data and not a change induced by changed supply conditions. There is no necessary reason why the long-run demand curve should differ from the short-run demand curve, however add the behaviour of supply has been..... We must expect that the longer is the period during which demand and supply are coming into equilibrium, the more changes will have time to take place. If we were to study the changes in demand and supply which would take place in respect to any change of data during many successive very short periods of time, we should find that we had introduced unnecessary and intolerable detail into the analsyis."[3]

We study below equilibrium between demand and supply in (i) market period, (ii) short period, and (iii) long period.

Equilibrium in Market Period

We have already seen that market period is one in which a certain fixed amount of the commodity is already in existence. The period is too short to permit any increase in production. In some cases the quantity available can be increased almost instantaneously but the cost of quick production is so high as to preclude rapid increases in production. The duration of the market period depends on the nature of the commodity and its production process. It is very short in case of industries in which production goes on continuously. In such industries output can be increased without much delay. In contrast, there are some industries which operate only during certain seasons but whose products are consumed throughout the year. In agriculture, for instance, crops are harvested only once in a year. After the crop has been harvested, the quantity of the commodity cannot be increased till the next harvest. In such cases market period is quite long.

What would be the nature of the supply curve in the market period? We would study supply curve in the market period separately for perishable goods and non-perishable durable goods. The supply of perishable goods is limited by the available quantity in a day. It cannot be held back for the next period and must be sold on the same day whatever the price they may fetch. In economics those goods are considered to be perishable which cannot be utilised in the next period. This may be owing to physical deterioration of the goods concerned, e.g. fresh vegetables and fruits. The deterioration may be in the economic sense and not physical in case of some goods, e.g. calendars and greeting cards. All services, like those of doctors, lawyers, skilled and unskilled workers, are extremely perishable in the sense that they cannot be stored. The service not rendered for a particular day is lost forever.

In case of perishable goods, price is determined, so far as present actions are concerned, by demand alone. Since supply cannot be varied, the cost of production does not come into the picture at all. Supply curve takes the shape of a vertical line as shown in Fig. 17.1.

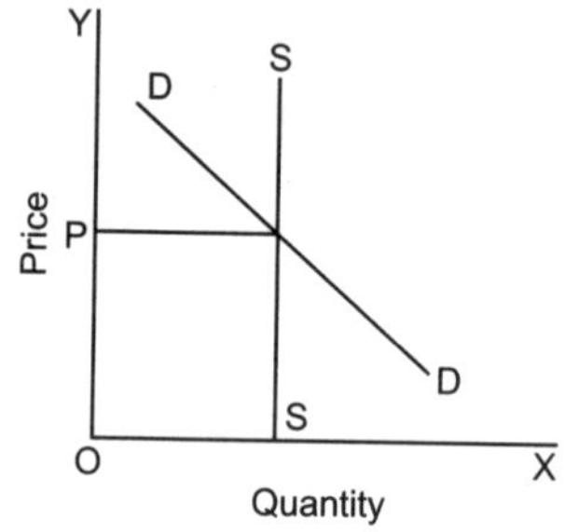

Fig. 17.1

DD is the market demand curve. With perfect competition between buyers and sellers an equilibrium price OP is determined at which quantity demanded is equal to the available supply. The equilibrium price is established at the point where the downward sloping demand curve DD intersects the vertical supply curve SS. At a price lower than this, demand would exceed supply and the buyers would bid the price up. At a price higher than this, a part of the supply would be left unsold and competition between sellers would bring the price down.

In case of non-perishable goods, the supply curve will not take the shape of a vertical straight line throughout its length because some of the goods can be held back, and carried over to the next market period. The sellers of such goods have a reservation price below which they would not sell at all and would hold back the goods in expectation of better prices after some time. The reserve price of a seller is determined by a number of factors, important of which are mentioned below: (i) The reserve price depends upon the seller's expectations in regard to the future price. If they expect the price to rise in future, their reserve price will be higher and conversely. (ii) The second factor that determines the reserve price is the sellers' preference for liquidity. If they need cash very urgently, they would be anxious to sell their goods and as such their reserve price will be low. The reverse would be the case if their need for cash is not very urgent. Thirdly, the reserve price depends upon the costs involved in storing the goods. The duration of period for which goods have to be stored, therefore, is important. The longer the period and the higher the costs of storage, the lower would be the reserve price and conversely. Fourthly, the reserve price depends upon the future cost of production of the goods concerned. If the costs are expected to rise in future, the reserve price would be higher and conversely. Fifthly, the reserve price depends on the durability of the goods. The greater the durability, the higher would be the reserve price and vice versa. Finally, some obstinate dealers have a tendency to attach too much importance to the costs incurred in the past and decide the reserve price on the basis of costs incurred in the past even if it might involve them in great loss.

Given the two price levels, one at which the suppliers are prepared to supply the entire stocks of goods, and the other at which the sellers will hold back the entire stock, the quantity of goods which will be offered in the market will differ with price. Within these two extreme prices, the sellers will supply a larger quantity at a higher price than at a lower price. Thus, at or below the reserve price, the quantity offered for sale would be zero and the quantity offered will increase with the rise in price till the price reaches the extreme level at which the suppliers are ready to supply the entire quantity. The supply curve for such goods, therefore, would slope upwards upto a certain point and thereafter take the shape of a vertical straight line. Figure 17.2 shows such a supply curve.

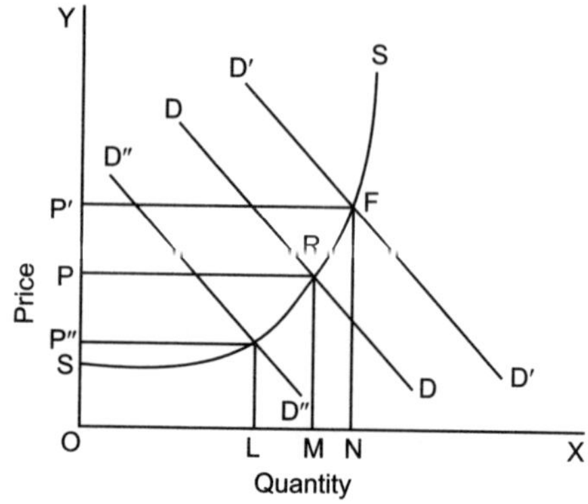

Fig. 17.2

In the figure, SFRS is the market period supply curve, ON being the total stock of goods. Upto price OP′, the quantity offered for sale varies with the price. At price OS, the suppliers hold back their stocks and offer nothing for sale. SF portion of the supply curve, therefore, slops upwards from left to the right. At price OP′, the entire available stock is offered for sale. Beyond OP′, the amount offered for sale remains unchanged whatever the price.

The demand for the commodity is represented by the curve DD. The market supply curve SS and the demand curve DD intersect at point R and OP is the price determined by them. At price OP, the quantity sold is OM. The total stock of the commodity being ON, the quantity held back at this price is ON – OM = MN. If the demand declines from DD to D″D″, the new equilibrium price would decline to OP″. At this price, the quantity sold would be OL and the quantity held back would be ON – OL = LN. Thus, at a lower price, the quantity held back would increase. Now, if the demand rises from DD to D′D′, the new equilibrium price would rise to OP′. At this price, the entire available stock ON is sold and no quantity is held back. If the demand curve rises beyond D′D′, the amount sold would remain unchanged at ON and as such only the price would rise above OP′.

In a perfectly competitive market, as already seen earlier, there prevails a single uniform price. Once the market price is determined, an individual seller has to take it as given. Thus, the demand curve which is downward sloping for all sellers taken together is a horizontal straight line at the level of ruling market price for an individual seller. An individual entrepreneur under perfect competition can thus dispose of his entire output at the ruling market price. He need not lower his price even if his reserve price is lower than the ruling market price. In case his reserve price is above the ruling market price, he would not be able to sell anything at all.

An important conclusion that emerges from the above analysis of price determination in the market period is that the cost of production does not enter into the calculations of the sellers and as such does not influence the market price. If the market price 'today', for instance, is below the cost of production but the seller expects a further decline 'tomorrow', he would dispose of his stock to-day. In contrast, he may not sell his stock even if the ruling price 'today' is above his cost if he expects a better price 'tomorrow'. Cost of production thus does not influence the amount to be offered for sale.

Another noteworthy point in regard to price determination in the market period under perfectly competitive conditions is that the equilibrium market price is highly fluctuating because the market demand and market supply remain changing constantly. Industry's market supply, which consists of supply schedules of individual firms, depends by and large on the expectations of sellers in regard to future prices. Market demand also depends on similar considerations. As such, market supply and demand tend to shift constantly which results in frequent changes in the market equilibrium price.

Equilibrium in Short-run

In the short-run, a firm can vary its output but does not have enough time to change its scale of plant. The number of firms in the industry is fixed since the time is not enough for new firms to enter or for the existing firms to leave the industry. Any change in the output of the industry can come only from the given plant capacity of existing firms. Since each individual firm is too small to influence the ruling price, the only problem confronting it is to decide the output which it would like to produce and sell.

Equilibrium of Firm

It is assumed that the firm's primary objective is to maximise its profits or to minimise its losses if it cannot make profits. In fact, this may not be the sole objective of a firm. But still this assumption is made because it provides a convenient starting point for the theory of the firm. The term 'profit' refers to the difference between the firms' total receipts and its total costs.

Profit Maximisation: Total Curve. Since each firm aims at maximising its profits, it compares total costs with total receipts at various possible levels of output and chooses that level of output at which its total receipts exceed total costs by the greatest amount.

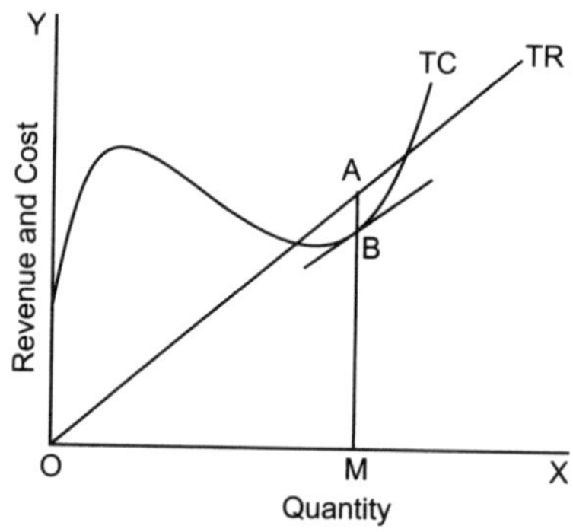

Fig. 17.3

Figure 17.3 shows total revenue at different levels of output against short-run total costs at various outputs. The total cost curve is the short-run total cost curve whose shape we have already discussed in detail in an earlier chapter. We explain below the shape of the total revenue curve.

Since the firm can sell any amount of output at the same price per unit, its total revenue curve will be a linear upward sloping curve starting from origin. If the sales of the firm are zero, its total receipts will also be zero. If the sales are one unit of output per unit of time, the total receipts of the firm will be equal to the price per unit of the output. If the sales are two units, the total revenue will be twice the unit price of output. Sale of each additional unit of output would increase the total receipts of the firm by a constant amount—the price per unit of product—and as such the total revenue curve would be upward sloping and linear.

The profits of the firm are maximum at output OM where the vertical distance between the total revenue curve and the total cost curve is the greatest. The vertical distance BA indicates the amount of profit. At output OM the slopes of the two curves are equal. At outputs less than OM, the slope of the total revenue curve is greater than that of the total cost curve. As such the distance between the two curves goes on increasing with an increase in output. At outputs larger than OM, the slope of the total cost curve is greater than that of the total revenue curve. As such the distance between the two curves goes on narrowing with an increase in output.

While total revenue-total cost approach is useful from certain viewpoints, it lacks analytical interpretation of business behaviour. For this purpose, marginal approach is more useful.

Profit Maximisation: Marginal Curves. The necessary condition for profit maximisation can be restated in terms of marginal revenue and marginal cost. Since marginal cost is equal to the slope of the total cost curve and marginal revenue is equal to the slope of the total revenue curve, the profits would be maximised at the output at which marginal cost is equal to marginal revenue.

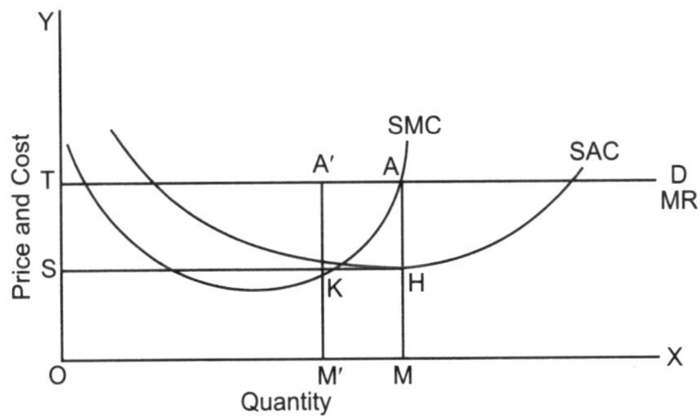

Fig. 17.4

In Fig. 17.4, the marginal cost and marginal revenue are equal at the output OM and hence the profits are maximised at this output. At outputs less than OM (say at output OM′), the marginal cost (M′K) is less than marginal revenue (M′A′) and as such an increase in output would add more to the firm's receipts than to its costs, or in other words, would lead to net contributions to profits. Similarly, at outputs beyond OM, marginal cost exceeds marginal revenue and as such an increase in output beyond OM adds more to the firm's costs than to its receipts, or in other words, would lead to a decline in total profits.

At output OM, the total profits of the firms are represented by the rectangle SHAT. Price per unit is MA and the cost per unit is MH. Profit per unit, therefore, is MA – MH = HA. The output being OM or SH, total profits would be SH × HA = SHAT. It may be pointed out that the profit per unit is not maximum at output OM. This is so because while deciding the level of output, the firm is guided by the total profits and not by profit per unit of output.

Loss Minimisation: In case the ruling market price is below the short-run average cost of production at all possible outputs, the firm would suffer losses instead of making profits. We have already seen that in the short-run the time at the disposal of the firm is not enough to change its scale of plant. The firm has, therefore, to choose between (i) producing at a loss and (ii) discontinuing production. In case the firm decides to adopt the latter alternative, it would still have to bear fixed costs.

In actual practice, the firm's choice between producing at a loss and discontinuing production would depend on whether or not the price covers the average variable costs.

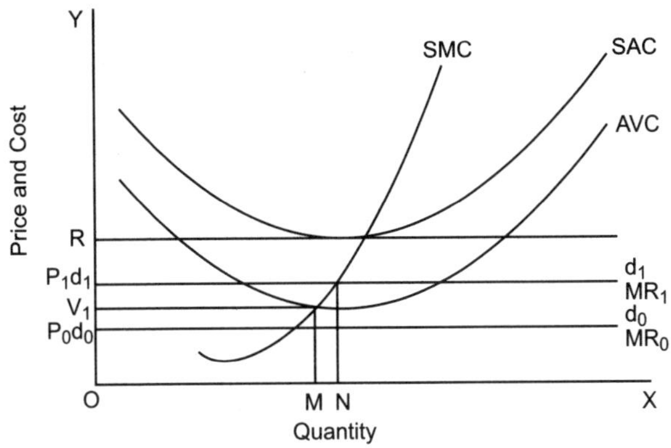

Fig. 17.5

Suppose the market price of the product is OP_0 in Fig. 17.5. If the firm produces an output OM at which SMC is equal to MR_0, total receipts of the firm would be $OP_0 \times OM$. For this output, total variable cost is also equal to $OP_0 \times OM$. Total receipts of the firm, therefore, just cover its total variable costs. Total costs of the firm include total variable costs as well as total fixed costs. If the total receipts of the firm just cover its total costs, the firm's loss would be equal to its total fixed costs. In this case, it will make no difference for the firm whether it continues production or not. Whether it continues production or not, its loss would be equal to its total fixed costs.

If the market price is below the minimum average variable costs, the firm would minimise losses by discontinuing production. When the production is discontinued, the loss would be equal to total fixed costs. If the firm continues production at a price below OP_0, the total variable costs would exceed the total receipts because the average variable cost is greater than the price. In such a situation, the loss would be equal to total fixed costs plus that part of total variable costs which are not covered by total receipts.

If the market price is above the minimum average variable costs but below the short-run average cost, it would be in the interest of the firm to continue production. At a price OP_1, for instance, an output of ON would result in a loss less than the total fixed costs. Total receipts would equal to $OP_1 \times ON$ while total variable costs would be $OV_1 \times ON$. Total receipts exceed total variable costs by an amount equal to $V_1P_1 \times ON$. This excess of total receipts over total variable costs can be used to meet a part of the fixed costs and thus the losses can be reduced to an amount less than total fixed costs. Loss in this case would equal to $P_1R \times ON$.

At output ON when market price is OP_1, equality between short-run marginal cost and marginal revenue shows that the losses are minimum. At an output smaller than ON, marginal revenue is greater than short-run marginal cost and as such an increase in output will lead to a greater increase in total receipts than in total costs; or in other words, it will lead to a reduction in losses. Beyond output ON, the short-run marginal cost exceeds marginal revenue and, therefore, an increase in output will lead to a greater increase in total costs than in total receipts; or in other words, it will lead to an increase in losses. The losses thus are minimum at the output where short-run marginal cost is equal to marginal revenue.

To summarise the above analysis, a firm would maximise its profits or minimise its losses when it produces an output at which the short-run marginal cost equals marginal revenue or price. Minimisation of losses would, however, require the firm to stop production altogether if the ruling market price is below the firm's average variable costs.

Short-run Supply Curve of the Firm

That part of a firm's short-term marginal cost curve which lies above the average variable cost curve is the firm's short-run supply curve for the product. The short-run marginal cost curve indicates the different quantities which the firm would be ready to supply in the market at different possible prices. At each possible price, the firm would produce the quantity for which its short-run marginal cost equals price (or marginal revenue) so as to maximise its profits or minimise its losses. Supply becomes zero at any price below the average variable cost.

Industry

So far we had taken the market or industry price to be given. Now we possess the necessary tools to see how it is determined. Industry price is the result of interactions between demanders and suppliers of a good. We have already discussed in an earlier chapter the forces underlying an industry demand curve. Now we turn to industry supply curve.

Short-run Supply Curve of Industry: The short-run marginal cost curve of a firm is derived from its marginal product curve under the assumption that the unit price of the variable input is fixed. This assumption is not unrealistic in case of most of firms and inputs because an individual firm is normally so small, in relation to all users of the input taken together, that changes in the quantity purchased by it will not influence the market price of the input. In other words, most of the markets for inputs are more or less perfectly competitive, at least from the demand side. Thus, an individual firm can increase its production by using more inputs without influencing the market price of inputs.

But if all producers in an industry simultaneously increase production by employing more inputs, a marked influence would be felt by the market for inputs. A single textile mill, for instance, can double its output by purchasing double the amount of cotton without exerting any visible influence on the price of cotton, but if all mills double their output, there would occur a substantial rise in the prices of cotton. As such, the industry supply curve cannot be obtained simply by horizontally summing the marginal cost curves of individual firms. An increase in the industry output would normally raise the prices of inputs and thus shift upward the marginal cost curve of each firm. When the output increases, the industry supply curve, therefore, would normally be more steeply sloped and less elastic. Similarly, when the output declines, the prices of input would fall which would make the industry supply curve less steeply sloped and more elastic. The concept of a competitive industry supply curve, therefore, is less accurate. Nevertheless, this does not invalidate the basic fact in the short-run the amount supplied varies directly with price. This is all we need to draw a positively sloped market supply curve.

As a first approximation the industry short-run supply curve may be visualised as the horizontal summation of the short-run supply curves of all firms in the industry. It indicates the various quantities of the commodity which all the firms together would offer for sale in the market at different possible prices. Such an industry short-run supply curve would be valid only if the supplies of inputs to the industry as a whole are perfectly elastic, or in other words, an increase in the production of the industry through larger purchases of inputs by all firms does not lead to a rise in the prices of the inputs.

The assumption of input prices remaining constant with changes in the volume of production of the industry as a whole is not entirely invalid. The variations in input prices as a result of changes in the volume of output of the industry are not likely to be substantial in view of the following considerations:

(i) In the short period under consideration, it is assumed that the new firms cannot enter the industry and the existing firms cannot enlarge the scale of their plant and equipment. The scope for expansion in output by the existing firms with the help of their existing plant is, therefore, limited. The limited changes in the volume of output of the industry are not likely to cause large variations in the prices of inputs.

(ii) The industry in question may be only one of the several industries using the same inputs. As such, a change in the volume of output of this industry may not much affect the prices of these inputs.

(iii) The entire micro-analysis is based on the assumption of full employment. Under conditions of full employment, an increase in the consumer demand for the product of one industry can occur only if simultaneously the demand for the product of some other industry declines.

Thus, when a particular industry expands its output, some other industry will contract its output. As such, when the former industry employs more inputs, the latter would release some of its inputs. Expansion of output in the former industry would not result in a rise in the prices of any of its inputs if it employs them in the same ratio in which the latter industry releases them. But the greater likelihood is that the two industries employ the inputs in different ratios. In such a situation, there would occur a rise in the prices of inputs peculiar to the expanding industry and a decline in the prices of inputs peculiar to the contracting industry. The net rise in the prices of inputs used by the expanding industry may not be substantial.

Short-run Equilibrium: Figure 17.6 shows determination of market price, industry output and the output of one representative firm of the industry.

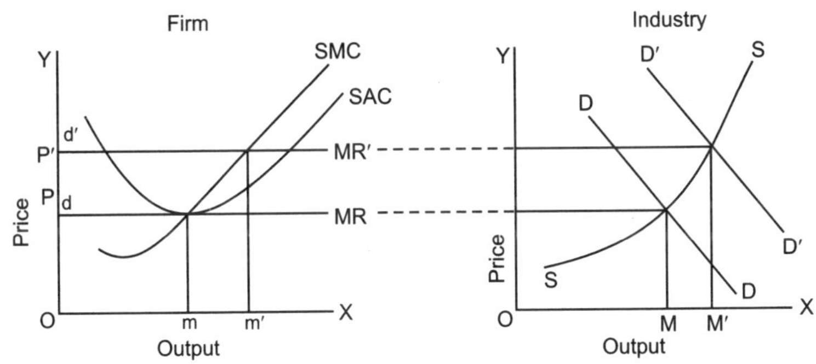

Fig. 17.6

The output axis of the industry figure is on a much smaller scale than that of the firm. The price axes of the two figures are identical. Curve DD in the industry figure shows the industry demand curve for the product. SAC and SMC curves in the firm figure are the short-run average cost and short-run marginal cost curves respectively of the representative firm. The industry short-run supply curve SS is obtained by a horizontal summation of all individual supply curves. The short-run equilibrium price is OP at which the quantity demanded is equal to the quantity supplied, i.e. OM. The demand curve and the marginal revenue curve faced by the firm will be horizontal at this price. In order to maximise profits, the representative firm, and each firm in the industry would produce that level of output at which SMC = MR = P. In the firm figure such an output is Om. The output of all firms taken together would be OM. The industry as a whole and each individual firm in the industry are in short-run equilibrium.

Let us now suppose that the industry demand for the product increases to D′D′. What would be the effect of this on the short-run equilibrium price and output? The increase in demand would result in a shortage of the commodity at the old price P. Competition among the buyers would drive up the price to P′. The demand curve and marginal revenue curve faced by the firm would shift upto the level of the new market price. In order to maximise its profits, each firm in the industry would expand its output upto the level at which its short-run marginal cost equals its higher marginal revenue and higher market price. The new short-run equilibrium output of the firm will be Om′ and that of the industry OM′.

Modified Supply Curve: If a simultaneous change in the use of inputs by all firms leads to a change in the prices of inputs, it would not be valid to obtain the industry short-run supply curve simply by a horizontal summation of individual firm supply curves. Though changes in the quantities bought by an individual firm may not affect the prices of inputs, a simultaneous action by all firms may result in a change in input prices. If an increase in industry output through increase in the use of inputs raises input prices, the individual firm cost curves will shift upwards. Similarly, if a decline in industry output through a decrease in the use of inputs lowers input prices, the individual firm cost curves will shift downwards. It is also possible that some input prices rise while others decline. Such a change would change the shape of the cost curves slightly and cause some shift up or down depending upon whether it is the input price increases or input price decreases which play a more dominant role.

The net effect of rise in input prices as a result of expansion of output would be to make the industry short-run supply curve less elastic. In Fig. 17.6, an increase in demand leads to a rise in price and marginal revenue which induces firms to expand output. If the expansion in output leads to a rise in input prices, the SAC and SMC curves will shift upward and to the left. The new SMC curve will intersect the MR curve at a smaller output than would be the case had the SMC curve not shifted. The industry supply curve in this case is obtained by summing individual firm profit maximising outputs at each possible level of industry price.

Long-run Equilibrium

In the long-run period, there is enough time for the existing firms to change the scale of their plant, for new firms to enter the industry, and for old firms to leave the industry if they so choose. If, for instance, a decline in demand is expected to last for a long time, some of the old firms will let their plant and equipment to wear out without replacement with the ultimate objective of either reducing the size of their plant or learning the industry altogether. Similarly, if an increase in demand is expected to continue for a long time, old firms would be induced to enlarge the size of their plant and the potential firms would be attracted to enter the industry.

Firm Equilibrium

We have already seen that in the long-run there are no fixed cost and all costs are variable. When all costs are variable and avoidable, a firm would continue production only if the price is adequate to cover its minimum average cost. While in the short-run a firm temporarily suspends production if the price is below its minimum average variable cost, in the long-run, it leaves the industry altogether if the price is inadequate to cover its minimum average cost.

In case the firm decides to continue production in the long-run, it would produce a volume of output at which its long-run marginal cost is equal to the ruling price or the marginal revenue. For, it is only at this level of output that the firm's profits are maximised. We have already explained this basic condition of equilibrium in regard to the firm's short-run operations. But what distinguishes long-run from short-run is that the former allows the existing firms to change their size of plant, the new firms to enter the industry and the old firms to leave the industry. If the price, which must be equal to the long-run marginal cost, is higher than the average cost at that level of output, the firm would be making excess profits. This would induce the existing firms to expand the size of their plant and the new firms to enter the industry. The resulting expansion in output would push the price down till the excess profits are wiped off. In the long-run, therefore, the price should not only be equal to the marginal cost but also must not be above or below the average cost. The two conditions are satisfied when price is equal to the minimum average cost. In other words, at the point of equilibrium, the firm's horizontal MR curve is tangent to its U-shaped LAC curve, which can only be at the latter's minimum point. Also it is at this point that marginal cost is equal to the average cost. This position is shown in Fig. 17.7. The firm is in long period equilibrium at price OP.

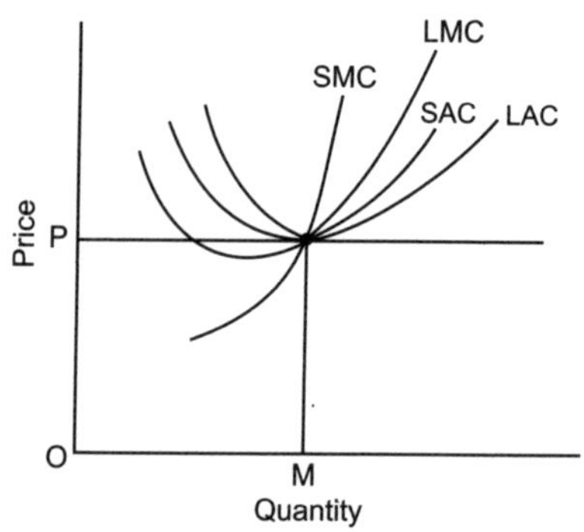

Fig. 17.7

Since the firm is in long-run equilibrium, it must also be in short-run equilibrium. The reverse, of course, may not always be true. In order to be able to produce the quantity OM at the lowest unit cost, the firm builds a plant associated with the short-run average cost curve SAC, whose lowest point is the same as that of LAC curve. But SMC curve must also intersect SAC curve at its lowest point. Thus, when a firm is in long-term equilibrium, P = LMC = LAC = SAC = SMC.

Industry Equilibrium: The above condition of equilibrium holds in case of all firms in the industry. In a state of long-term equilibrium, therefore, price must be equal to the minimum average cost of each firm. Under perfect competition, as we have already seen, each firm has to accept the same given price. It may be argued that all firms may not be equally efficient in producing a commodity. Some firms may have the advantage of superior managements; some firms may employ more efficient factors of production while others may have the benefit of a more favourable location. In the absence of homogeneous factors of production, the minimum long-run average cost of production of all firms may not be uniform. Since in the long-run no firm operates at a loss, the more efficient firms may earn excessive or super-normal profits. But it may be pointed out that the superior or more efficient factors of production, whether management, skill, or location have to be bought and paid for by the firm. The remuneration of more efficient factors would naturally be higher than that of the less factors. The firm which employs superior factors of production would, therefore, have to bear added costs of production and as a result the minimum long-run average cost would tend to be identical for all firms. Mrs. Joan Robinson calls the super-normal profits as the rent of the superior factors.

It is also possible that with given cash outlays, a certain firm—say firm A—is able to produce a larger output per unit of time than another firm—say firm B—because the owner-manager of the former firm is more efficient than that of the latter one. Apparently, this means that A's average cost of production is lower than that of B. But, in fact, the difference in costs of the two firms disappears if we take into account the fact the implicit cost to firm A of its owner-manager is higher. What it actually means is that the firms A and B have the same minimum average cost but the optimum point of A is reached at a higher rate of output than that of B. In other words, having the benefit of a superior-manager, firm A enjoys certain internal economies which enable it to lower its long-run average cost even after that of firm B has started rising. But if the competitive nature of the industry is to be maintained, A's long-run average cost must also start rising after an output which forms only a very small part of the total industry output. In case A's long-run average cost continues declining long after those of other firms have started rising, it would start producing a significant portion of the total industry output and thus one of the fundamental rules of perfect competition would be violated. This means that any special advantage available to an individual firm should be of a minor order. Thus, the long run competitive equilibrium requires that there are a large number of firms, each producing a level of output at which P = LMC = LAC = SAC = SMC. In a condition of long period industry equilibrium, there is no inducement for new firms to enter the industry, nor any of the existing firms want to leave the industry.

Long-run Industry Supply

Given an industry in long-run equilibrium, we now proceed to analyse the effect of a change in demand on the long-run costs of production and price. Suppose there takes place an increase in demand for the product concerned. It is assumed that the increase in demand is once-for-all and no further change in it occurs during the process of adjustment. The new long-run price may be higher than, equal to, or lower than the old price, depending upon whether the production in industry is subject to the law of increasing, constant or decreasing costs.

Increasing Costs: Let us first consider an industry which operates under increasing costs. It is assumed that the industry is initially in long-run equilibrium. Then suppose that there occurs an increase in the demand for the product. We analyse below the short-run effects and long-run effects of this increase in demand and then establish the long-run industry supply curve for the product.

Figure 17.8 shows the long-run equilibrium of the firm as well as that of the industry. DD represents the industry demand curve and SS the industry short-run supply curve. LAC and SAC represent the firm's long-run average cost curve and short-run average cost curves respectively. SMC

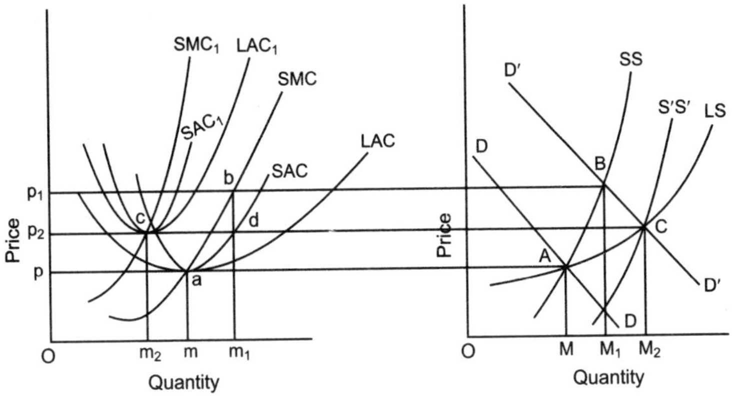

Fig. 17.8

represents the firm's short-run marginal cost curve for scale of plant SAC. The long-run marginal cost curve is not shown because it is not essential for the analysis and unnecessarily complicates the figure. Since the industry as well as the firm are in long-run equilibrium, they are necessarily in short-run equilibrium also. We can, therefore, consider the market demand curve and the market short-run supply curve as establishing the industry price p. The demand curve and the marginal revenue curve for the firm are horizontal and equal to price p at levels of output of the firm. The firm produces an output Om at which its SMC (and LMC) equals marginal revenue or price. The industry output is OM which is the sum total of the outputs of individual firms at price p. The number of firms in the industry is just adequate to make price equal to the minimum short-run and long-run average costs of the firm at output Om. The firm is using the optimum scale of plant at the optimum rate of output. Neither any profits nor any losses are being incurred.

Now suppose the industry demand curve shifts to D′D′. This raises the price to Op_1 as the new demand curve and the old short-run supply curve intersect each other at B. In order to maximise profits, the firm increases its output to Om_1, the output at which SMC equals the new marginal revenue. As a result of similar action on the part of all firms, the industry output increases to OM_1. In this position the firm is making a pure profit equal to output OM_1 multiplied by lid which is the difference between price p_1 and the short-run average cost at output OM_1. Thus, the short-run effects of an increase in demand for the product concerned are (i) a rise in price and (ii) some expansion in output by working the plant more intensively.

Now let us analyse the long-run effects. The existence of profits induces the existing firms to expand their plant capacities and the new firms to enter the industry. This shifts the industry short-run supply curve to the right. The increase in supply brings the price down. Simultaneously, the increase in industry output causes the cost curves of all firms to shift upwards because the industry is operating under increasing costs. This happens in an industry which uses an appreciable proportion of the total supplies available of the resources required for producing the commodity concerned.

Any given set of cost curves assumes that an individual firm can obtain any quantity of resources at a constant price per unit. No individual firm's purchases of resources are so large as to influence their prices. The rise in the prices of resources results from the combined increase in the demand for resources coming from the new firms entering the industry and the existing firms expounding their scale of output. The forces leading to an increase in the prices of resources are completely beyond the control of an individual firm. The rise in the prices of resources and the resultant upward shifts of the cost curves are, therefore, the consequence not of *internal diseconomies* but of *external diseconomies* of expanding production in the industry.

Thus, as the industry expands, on the one hand, the price of the products declines and, on the other hand, prices of resources rise. This process continues till the entire pure profit is eliminated. The expansion of the industry comes to an end and the industry is again in long-run equilibrium. The new equilibrium price is p_2 and the new cost curves are LAC_1, SAC_1, and SMC_1. The new long-run industry price p_2 lies between the original long-run price p and the short-run high price p_1. The new output of the firm is Om_2 at which SMC_1 equals the new long-run marginal revenue and price. The output of the industry increases to OM_2 because the expansion of capacity in the industry shifts the short-run supply curve to SS_1.

Would the new long-run firm output be equal to, larger than, or smaller than the old long-run output Om? The answer depends on the manner in which the cost curves shift upward. Whether the cost curves shift straight up, slightly to the left, or slightly to the right depend upon the relative increases in the prices of different types of resources. The new equilibrium firm output in the figure is smaller than the original firm output. This is because the prices of inputs fixed in the short-run have increased more than those of other inputs. In order to economise use of inputs whose prices have risen more, the firm builds a smaller plant. But if the prices of all inputs rise proportionally, the same combinations of outputs will be the least-cost combinations. The cost curves will shift straight up and the new firm equilibrium output would be the same as before. In this case, the entire increase in the industry output would come from new firms. Finally, if the prices of fixed inputs rise more than those of other inputs, it would be cheaper to operate on a larger scale. In this case, part of the increase in industry output would come from an expansion in the size of existing firms and the remaining from new firms.

The long-run industry supply curve LS in the figure is obtained by joining all points of long-run equilibrium for the industry. It can also be conceived of as the horizontal summation of the minimum points of all individual firm LAC curves as the expansion of industry output shifts firm cost curves upward. It shows the various industry outputs which will be forthcoming at different possible prices when there is enough time for the existing firms to suitably adjust their plant capacities, for new firms to enter the industry and for old firms to leave the industry if they choose so.

Constant Costs: The process of analysis in case of an industry operating under constant costs is fundamentally similar that for an industry operating under increasing costs.

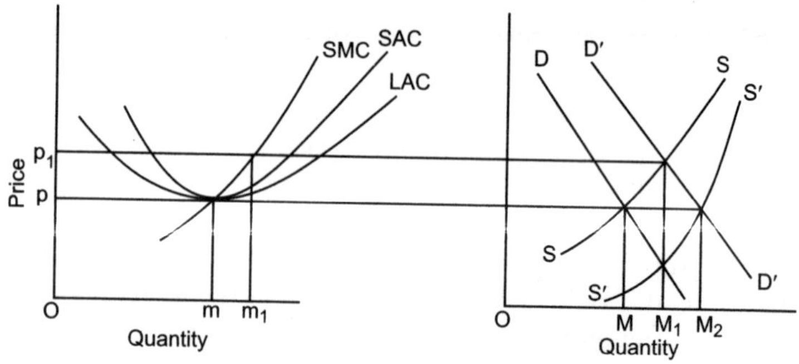

Fig. 17.9

Starting from the position of long-run equilibrium shown in Fig. 17.9, suppose the demand increases from DD to D′D′. The short-run effects are the same as in case of industry operating under increasing costs. The price rises from Op to Op_1. The firm output increases from Om to Om_1 and the industry output expands from OM to OM_1. The individual firms enjoy pure profits. This, in the long-run, attracts new firms in the industry which shifts the industry short-run supply curve to the right, resulting in a decline in price. If the industry in question uses only a small portion of the total supplies of various inputs, a change in its output will not affect the input prices. As such, the cost curves of individual firms will not undergo any change at all. The entry of new firms will wipe out the profits and push the price back down to p. Price would become equal to the minimum long-run average cost and the long-run equilibrium will be established again. The new short-run supply curve will be S′S′. Individual firm output would be at a level at which short-run marginal cost equals marginal revenue and price p. The industry supply would expand to OM_2. The long-run industry supply curve will be LS. It will be horizontal at the level of minimum long-run average costs.

Decreasing Costs: Though possible, decreasing costs are not very common. The process of analysis for an industry operating under decreasing costs is the same as before. Starting from the position of long-run equilibrium, we assume that the industry demand curve shifts from DD to D′D′ as shown in Fig. 17.10.

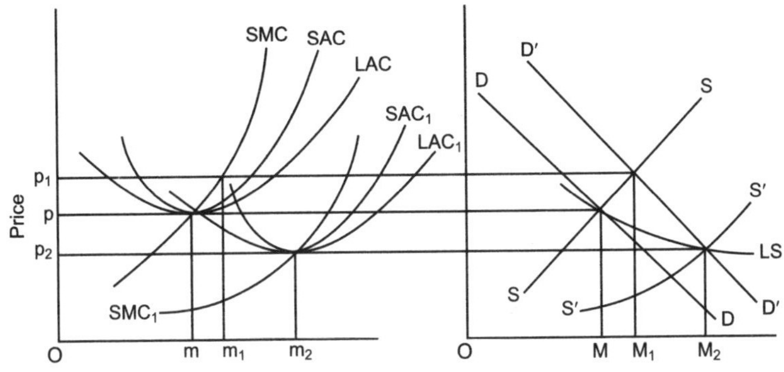

Fig. 17.10

The short-run effects are the same as before. The increase in demand raises the industry price from Op to Op_1. The firm output expands to Om_1 and the industry output to OM_1. The representative firm makes a pure profit equal to Om_1 multiplied by the difference between p_1 and SAC at output Om_1. The existence of pure profits attracts new firms in the industry in the long-run. This shifts the industry short-run supply curve to the right. The entry of new firms pushes the prices down.

Since the industry operates under decreasing costs, the expansion of output in the industry leads to a decline in the prices of inputs, which shifts cost curves downward. Thus, both the price of the product and the costs of production are declining. Ultimately, the declining product price overtakes the declining costs and the pure profits are wiped out. The new long-run equilibrium price is p_2 which is lower than the original price p. The individual firm output is Om_2, at which both short-run and long-run marginal costs are equal to marginal revenue or price. The new industry output is OM_2. The long-run supply curve slopes downward to the right.

In the real world, the increasing cost industries are likely to be the most common of the three types of cases analysed above. The most unlikely is the case of decreasing cost industries. Constant cost and decreasing cost industries are likely to become increasing cost industries as they grow older. In decreasing cost industries, once the scope for external economies is exhausted, the industry would become subject to constant costs and subsequently to increasing costs.

The disturbing force leading to a chain of adjustments explained above was the increase in demand for the product in question. It can as well be a decline in demand, in which case the individual firms would incur losses. The emergence of losses would lead certain firms to leave the industry and some other to decrease their plant capacities till the equilibrium is established again. Or the disequilibrium might be caused by a major technological development which induces new firms to enter the industry till the long-run equilibrium is established again.

NOTES

1. C.E. Ferguson, *Microeconomic Theory* (Illinois, 1969), p. 225.
2. Marshall, *Principles of Economics*, pp. 349-50.
3. Stonier and Hague, *A Text Book of Economic Theory*, 2nd Edition, p. 152.

Monopoly

18

Pure Monopoly

Pure monopoly is a market situation in which there is only one seller of a product for which there are no close substitutes. The entire market for the product is available to the firm alone. There are no similar products whose price and output would perceptibly influence the price and output of the monopolist. In other words, the cross elasticity of demand between the monopolist's product and other products is zero or low enough to be ignored by all firms in the economy. The monopolist does not believe that his actions will evoke any retaliation from firms in other industries. Nor does he believe that the actions of firms in other industries are of sufficient importance for him to be taken into consideration. The monopolist is the industry from the producing point of view.

Since single firm control the total supply in a pure monopoly, it can able to exert a significant degree of control over the price by changing the quantity of product supplied. A monopoly has full control over a product and there is no real alternative to its product. A monopolist does not undergo price pressure from competitors but it may face pricing pressure from potential competition. For example, if a firm raises the price of its product too high, then others may enter the market seeing huge profit. The monopoly profit theorem does not hold true if there exist:

(a) stranded customers in the monopoly good,
(b) poorly informed customers,
(c) high fixed cost in the tied good,
(d) economies of scale in the tied good,
(e) price regulation for the monopoly product.

There are several reasons due to which monopoly occurs:

(a) When a businessman acquires resources for a product which other fellow people cannot get.

(b) When one gets skilled enough such that others cannot touch his level of skill for that service.

(c) The product gives excellent utilities and is most user friendly.

(d) May be the product or service is newly invented and hence the technoiogy available reserved with that supplier.

(e) A violation to above definition of monopoly can be when there are enough competitors but the service provided by this monopolist is unique in every sense to satisfy customers need.

There are certain areas of productions which are exclusively reserved for the government sector and government puts lots of restriction on production of these goods by the private firms. Such market policy by the government is referred as *state monopoly*. When a firm obeys all the rules laid down by the government and yet is able to enjoy the market supremacy then such situation is termed as *government granted monopoly*. A market in which, for any relevant level of industry output, the total cost incurred by a single firm producing that output is less than the combined total cost that two or more firms would incur if they divided the output among themselves, is termed as *natural monopoly*. A monopoly that exists in a limited geographical area, for example, cable TV companies may have monopolies within a city or an airline may have a monopoly over some routes, is termed as the *local monopoly*. A monopoly firm whose prices and production rates are controlled by a government entity such as electric utility companies, telephone companies, etc. is termed as *regulated monopoly*.

Because of the lack of competition, monopolist will make an economic profit which will attract other firms to enter the market. There must be some barriers to entry to make the market monopolistic. They are the factors that allow an incumbent firm to earn positive economic profits while making it unprofitable for the newcomers to enter the industry. For example:

(a) *Structural barriers to entry*: They are the barriers to entry that exist when incumbent firms have cost or demand advantage that would make it unattractive for a new firm to enter the industry. The interaction of economies of scale and market demand that gives rise to a natural monopoly market is an example of a structural barrier to entry.

(b) *Legal barriers to entry*: This is a situation where a law prevents other firms from entering the market to sell a product.

(c) *Patents*: A patent gives the inventor of a product a monopoly in producing and selling that product for a limited amount of time. It is a tool that governments use to promote innovation, as firms should be more willing to create new products if they know they shall have monopoly power over those products.

(d) *Strategic barriers to entry*: These are the barriers that result when an incumbent firm takes explicit steps to deter entry. A firm will aggressively defend its market against encroachment by new entrants.

(e) *Natural barriers to entry*: Foreign firms cannot enter the market because either the startup costs are too high, or the cost structure of the market gives an advantage to the largest firm. Most of the public utility falls in this category.

In the real world, pure monopoly is as rare as perfect competition. Local public utility industries approximate it. In spite of the fact, that pure monopoly is an extremely rare phenomenon, the principles of pure monopoly provide an important tool for analysing the problems of pricing, output and resource allocation. First, they are very useful for analysing the problems of industries approaching pure monopoly. Secondly, they along with their modifications are useful for studying industries operating under oligopolistic and monopolistic conditions.

Assumptions underlying the monopoly market:

(a) There is a single seller who controls the entire market which consists a large number of buyers.

(b) The marginal cost of production is constant, and the monopolist knows this cost.

(c) The monopolist has perfect information about the market demand at each price.

(d) There is no substitute for the product produced by the monopolist.

(e) There is only one firm consisting the industry.

(f) There is barrier to the entry of a new firm.

(g) The only aim of the firm is to maximise profit and hence super normal profit cannot be ruled out.

(h) Firm in the monopoly is price maker instead of price taker.

(i) The monopolist may not discriminate among buyers, but must offer the same price to all.

Costs of Production

It is assumed that the monopolistic seller of product is a purely competitive buyer of inputs and as such his purchases of inputs do not influence the prices of inputs. When this assumption is made, the cost concepts formulated in the last chapter for pure competition become applicable to pure monopoly also.

Revenues

Pure monopoly differs from pure competition in regard to the sale of product. Under pure competition, a producer can sell as much as he likes at the ruling market price and as such his marginal revenue and price are equal. The monopolist, in contrast, faces the market demand curve for his product and, therefore, every increase in the quantity sold would be followed by a decline in the price of the product. Thus, while a competitive firm faces a horizontal demand curve, the monopolist faces a downward sloping demand curve. For understanding the behaviour of a monopolistic, it is very essential to realise the significance of the downward slope of his demand curve. This is because the nature of his marginal and total revenue curves depends upon the demand curve facing him. A decline in price (or average revenue) leads to a greater decline in marginal revenue because the sale of an additional unit results in a decline in price not only of this unit but of previous units also. Marginal revenue declines faster than price and may become zero or even negative while the price is still above zero.

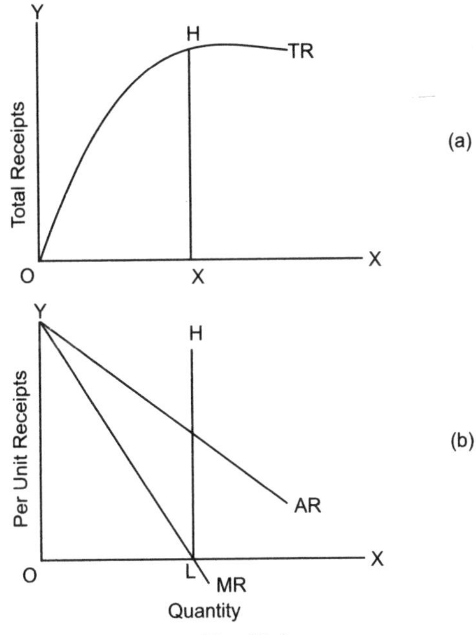

Fig. 18.1

Figure 18.1(a) shows the relationship between the marginal revenue and average revenue curves. Since under monopoly average revenue must continue to decline, the marginal revenue always lies below the average revenue. Figure 18.1(b) depicts the shape of the total revenue curve. While the quantity axis of both the figures are drawn on the same scale, the vertical axis of Fig. 18.1(a) is relatively compressed. The monopoly total revenue curve is always convex to the horizontal axis because total revenue increases at a declining rate. Since the total revenue increases at a declining rate, it must cease increasing at some point. In the figure this happens when the output is OL at which marginal revenue is zero.

Mathematical Representation of the Demand and Revenue of a Monopolist

Let us consider the demand function of the monopolist firm is linear and is given by

$$X = \alpha_0^* - \alpha_1^* P \qquad \text{(i)}$$

Here we have considered that all the factors, such as, income, tastes, price of other goods which affect demand are constant. Any change these factors will shift the demand curve.

The slope of the demand function is given by

$$\frac{dX}{dP} = -\alpha_1^* \qquad \text{(ii)}$$

Price elasticity of demand is given as

$$e_P = \frac{dX}{dP} \cdot \frac{P}{X} = -\alpha_1^* \cdot \frac{P}{X} \qquad \text{(iii)}$$

Total revenue of the monopolist is given as

$$R = P.\,X \qquad \text{(iv)}$$

From equation (i) we can find the expression for P as

$$P = \frac{\alpha_0^*}{\alpha_1^*} - \frac{1}{\alpha_1^*} X \qquad \text{(v)}$$

Let us consider $\frac{\alpha_0^*}{\alpha_1^*} = \alpha_0$ and $\frac{1}{\alpha_1^*} = \alpha_1$ then the price equation can be written as

$$P = \alpha_0 - \alpha_1 X \qquad \text{(vi)}$$

Therefore, revenue is

$$R = P.\,X = (\alpha_0 - \alpha_1 X)X$$

$$= \alpha_0 X - \alpha_1 X^2 \qquad \text{(vii)}$$

Average revenue of the monopolist is

$$AR = \frac{R}{X} = \frac{PX}{X} = P \qquad \text{(viii)}$$

Thus, the demand curve can also be given by the AR curve.

The marginal revenue is given by

$$\frac{dR}{dX} = \frac{d(\alpha_0 X - \alpha_1 X^2)}{dX} = \alpha_0 - 2\alpha_1 X \qquad \text{(ix)}$$

Thus, we see that the MR is a straight line with the same intercept as the demand curve, but twice as steep.

P and MR is related as

$$R = PX$$

$$MR = \frac{dR}{dX} = P + X \cdot \frac{dP}{dX}$$

Or,
$$P = MR - X\frac{dP}{dX} \qquad \text{(x)}$$

Since the term $X \cdot \frac{dP}{dX}$ is positive due to $\frac{dP}{dX} > 0$

Hence, P > MR.

Now let us find the relationship between MR and price elasticity e.

We have
$$MR = \frac{dR}{dX} = P + X \cdot \frac{dP}{dX}$$

The price elasticity of demand is given by

$$e_P = -\frac{dX}{dP} \cdot \frac{P}{X}$$

Or ,
$$\frac{1}{e_P} = -\frac{dP}{dX} \cdot \frac{X}{P}$$

Or,
$$\frac{dP}{dX} = -\frac{1}{e_P} \cdot \frac{P}{X} \qquad \text{(xi)}$$

Thus, we get

$$MR = P + X\left(-\frac{1}{e_P} \cdot \frac{P}{X}\right)$$

Or, $$MR = P\left(1 - \frac{1}{e_P}\right) \qquad \text{(xii)}$$

Hence, this is the required expression showing the relationship between MR and price elasticity.

Short-run Period

Profit Maximisation: Total Revenue and Cost Curves

When the firm aims at profit maximisation, the basic principles governing price and output under monopoly are the same as those determining price and output under pure competition. The profits of the monopolist, like that of the competitive firm, would be maximised at that level of output at which the difference between his total revenue and total cost is the greatest.

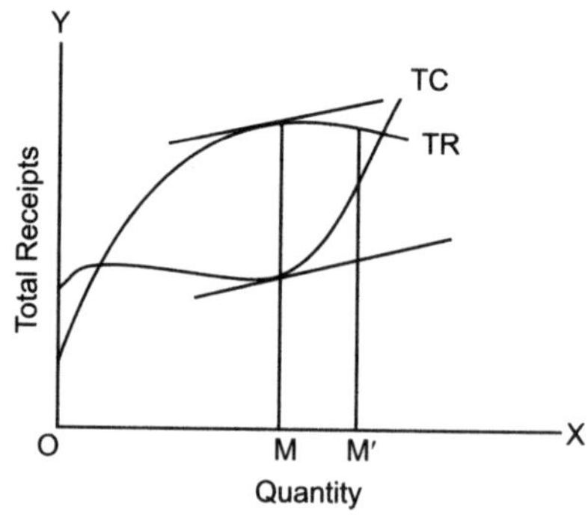

Fig. 18.2

In Fig. 18.2, the profits of the monopolist are maximum when he produces an output OM. The difference between total revenue and total cost curves would be greatest at that level of output at which their slopes are equal, or in other words, at which the tangents to the curves are parallel. As the slope of the total cost curve is marginal cost and that of the total revenue is marginal revenue, the profits are maximised at that level of output at which the marginal revenue is equal to the marginal cost.

Profit Maximisation: Per Unit Curves

The profits of the monopolist, as seen above, are maximum at that level of output at which his marginal revenue is equal to his short-run marginal cost. This condition of equilibrium under monopoly is the same as under competition. The difference between the two situations is that while under competition price is equal to marginal revenue, under competition the price is higher than marginal revenue. Under monopoly, since price is always higher than marginal revenue, it must also be higher than the equilibrium marginal revenue.

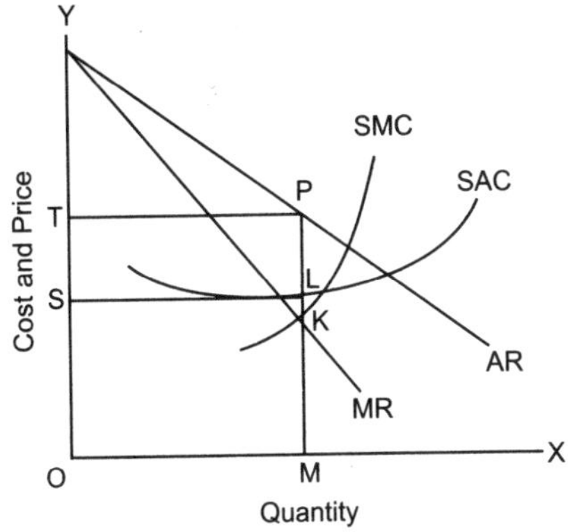

Fig. 18.3

In Fig. 18.3, marginal revenue is equal to short-run marginal cost at the output OM. At this level of output, the demand situation is such that the consumers are willing to pay a price equal to OT per unit. The difference between this price and the corresponding short-run average cost of production represents the excess profit per unit of output. The total monopoly profits (i.e. SLPT) would equal total output (i.e. OM = SL) multiplied by the difference between the equilibrium price and the corresponding short-run average cost or production (i.e. LP).

There often prevails a misconception that the monopolist always makes profits. This, however, need not necessarily be so. Whether or not the monopolist makes profits, in fact, depends upon the relationship between the market demand curve faced by him and his cost conditions. The monopolist, like the purely competitive firm, may incur losses in the short-run if his entire short-run average cost lies above his average revenue curve.

In Fig. 18.4, the equilibrium output is OM at which marginal revenue is equal to short-run marginal cost. At this output, the monopoly price ML, as determined by demand conditions, does not cover the entire corresponding short-run average cost MP. It covers only the average variable cost ML which is shown by tangency between the average revenue curve and the average variable cost curve at point L. Thus, the monopolist suffers a loss equal to LP per unit of output. The total loss of the monopolist (SLPT) is equal to the total output (OM = SL) multiplied by the difference between the equilibrium price and the corresponding short-run average cost of production (LP). In the figure, L is the shut down point for the monopolist. If the demand conditions are such as result in a price below ML, the monopolist will temporarily cease production.

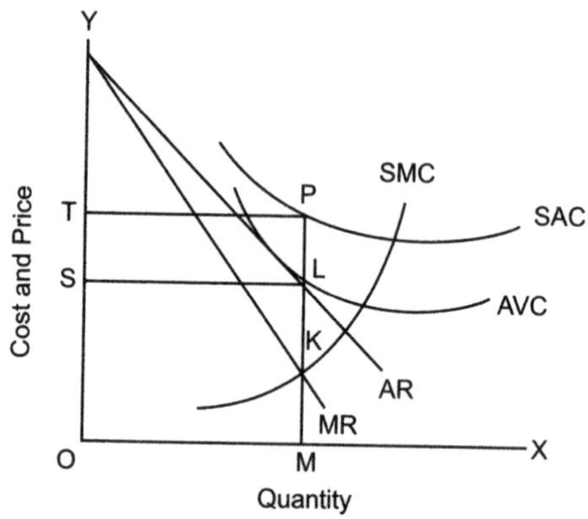

Fig. 18.4

Another misconception which often prevails is that the demand curve faced by a monopolist is inelastic. In fact, most of the demand curves, excepting those faced by the purely competitive firms, range from highly elastic towards their upper ends to highly inelastic towards their lower ends. As such, most of the demand curves cannot be called either elastic or inelastic. They are normally both, depending upon the portion of the demand curve under consideration. If the monopolist has any costs of production, the output that maximises his profits will always lie within the elastic sector of his demand curve. Since the marginal cost is always positive, at the output at which marginal cost equals marginal revenue, the marginal revenue must also be positive. But the marginal revenue would be positive only when the elasticity of demand is greater than one.

Mathematical Derivation of the Equilibrium of the Monopolist

Let us consider the demand function as

$$X = q(P) \qquad \text{(i)}$$

From the demand function we can find for P as

$$P = f_1(X)$$

And the cost function can be given by

$$C = f_2(X)$$

The profit function of the monopolist can be written as

$$\Pi = R - C$$

The only aim of the monopolist is to maximise its profit.

First order condition of profit maximisation:

$$\frac{\partial \Pi}{\partial X} = 0$$

$$\frac{\partial \Pi}{\partial X} = \frac{\partial R}{\partial X} - \frac{\partial C}{\partial X} = 0$$

Or, $$\frac{\partial R}{\partial X} = \frac{\partial C}{\partial X}$$

Thus, we have

$$MR = MC$$

Second order condition of profit maximisation:

$$\frac{\partial^2 \Pi}{\partial X^2} < 0$$

$$\frac{\partial^2 \Pi}{\partial X^2} = \frac{\partial^2 R}{\partial X^2} - \frac{\partial^2 C}{\partial X^2} < 0$$

Or, $$\frac{\partial^2 R}{\partial X^2} < \frac{\partial^2 C}{\partial X^2}$$

i.e. [Slope of MR] < [Slope of MC]

By fulfilling the above two conditions the monopolist maximises his short-run profit.

Long-run Period

In the long-run, the monopolist can adjust the size of his plant to a long-run change in demand. This is true in case of a purely competitive firm also. But the difference between monopoly and pure competition is that under monopoly, the entry of new firms being ruled out, excess profits can exist even in the long-run.

Further, in the long-run, a purely competitive firm must build an optimum-sized plant and also operate it at the optimum rate; it is only then that the profits would be eliminated and long-term equilibrium established. A monopolist will, however, build the optimum plant only if his marginal revenue curve cuts his long-run cost curve at its lowest point.

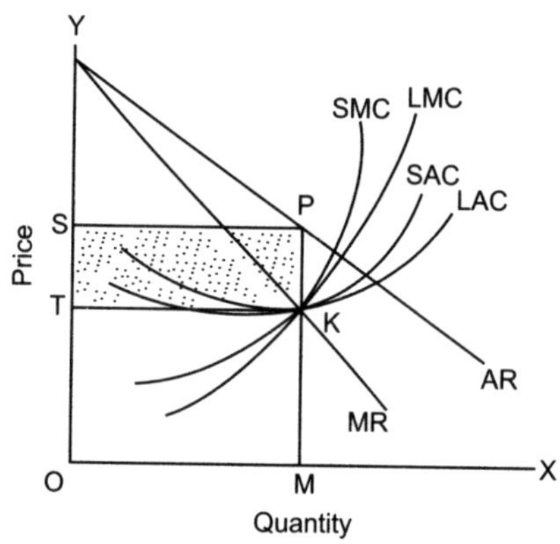

Fig. 18.5

In Fig. 18.5, the marginal revenue curve cuts the long-run average cost, short-run average cost, long-run marginal cost and short-run marginal cost curves at their lowest point K and, therefore, the monopolist employs the optimum-sized plant and also operates it at the optimum rate. In case the marginal revenue curve cuts the long-run average cost curve to the left of point K, the monopolist will build a plant smaller than the optimum-sized one and also operate it at less than the optimum rate. In contrast, if the marginal revenue curve cuts the long-run average cost curve at a point to the right of point K, the monopolist will build a plant larger than the optimum-sized one and also operate it at above the optimum rate. Under monopoly excess profits can exist even in the long-run. The dotted area TKPS in the figure represents excess profits.

Multiplant Monopolist

In the earlier section of this chapter we have analysed the monopoly having single plant. But now we shall consider a monopolist who produces a homogeneous product in different plants. For simplicity we shall consider only two plants. Let the monopolist operates in two plants having different cost structure. Here the monopolist faces two problems:

(a) How much output to produce and at what price to sell it to get maximum profit?

(b) How to allocate the production of optimal output between the two plants?

Since the cost structure of the different plants and the market demand are known, we can compute the total MC curve of the monopolist by the horizontal summation of the MC curves of the individual plants.

i.e. $$MC = MC_1 + MC_2$$

The ultimate aim of the monopolist is to maximise his profit. To fulfill his aim he will utilise each plant up to the level at which the marginal costs are equal to each other and to the common marginal revenue.

i.e. $$MR = MC_1 = MC_2$$

If the MC in one plant is lower than the MC of the second plant, the monopoly would increase his profit by increasing the production in first plant and decreasing it in the second plant until the above condition is fulfilled.

Let us consider the following market demand and the cost structure of the plants:

$$P = f(X) = f(X_1 + X_2)$$
$$C_1 = f_1(X_1)$$
$$C_2 = f_2(X_2)$$

where X_1 and X_2 are the products in two different plants and C_1 and C_2 are the cost functions of the respective plants.

$$\Pi = R - C_1 - C_2$$

Firsts order condition for profit maximisation:

Let us consider the first plant.

$$\frac{\partial \Pi}{\partial X_1} = 0$$

i.e. $$\frac{\partial \Pi}{\partial X_1} = \frac{\partial R}{\partial X_1} - \frac{\partial C_1}{\partial X_1} = 0$$

or, $$\frac{\partial R}{\partial X_1} = \frac{\partial C_1}{\partial X_1}$$

Hence, $$MR_1 = MC_1$$

Now consider the 2nd plant.

$$\frac{\partial \Pi}{\partial X_2} = 0$$

i.e. $$\frac{\partial \Pi}{\partial X_2} = \frac{\partial R}{\partial X_2} - \frac{\partial C_2}{\partial X_2} = 0$$

or, $$\frac{\partial R}{\partial X_2} = \frac{\partial C_2}{\partial X_2}$$

Hence, $$MR_2 = MC_2$$

But $$MR_1 = MR_2 = MR$$

Therefore,

$$MR = \frac{\partial C_1}{\partial X_1} = MC_1$$

And $$MR = \frac{\partial C_2}{\partial X_2} = MC_2$$

Thus, $$MR = MC_1 = MC_2$$

Second order condition of profit maximisation:

The second order condition for profit maximisation requires that the MC in each plant must be increasing more rapidly than the MR of the industry.

i.e. $$\frac{\partial^2 R}{\partial X^2} < \frac{\partial^2 C_1}{\partial X_1^2}$$

and $$\frac{\partial^2 R}{\partial X^2} < \frac{\partial^2 C_2}{\partial X_2^2}$$

Monopoly Equilibrium and Competitive Equilibrium

In the last chapter we studied the equilibrium of a purely competitive firm and industry. In this chapter, we have analysed the equilibrium under monopoly. We are now equipped to proceed with a comparative study of the equilibrium under competitive conditions and under monopoly. The only similarity between the two is that both the purely competitive firm and the monopolist are in equilibrium at the level of the output at which the marginal revenue is equal to the marginal cost. But there are important differences between them which are briefly explained below.

In the first place, while under perfect competition price is equal to marginal cost at the equilibrium output, it is higher than the marginal cost under monopoly equilibrium. A purely competitive firm faces a horizontal demand curve and as such marginal revenue curve coincides with the average revenue curve at all levels of output. At the equilibrium level of output, therefore, the marginal cost equals not only the marginal revenue but also the average revenue or the price. In contrast, the demand curve facing the monopolist slopes downwards and as such marginal revenue is less than price at all levels of output. Since at the equilibrium level of output marginal cost is equal to marginal revenue, the former would necessarily lie below the price.

Secondly, while under perfect competition equilibrium is possible only when the marginal cost curve is rising at the point of equilibrium, under monopoly, the firm can be in equilibrium whether the marginal cost curve is rising, declining or remaining constant at the equilibrium output. This is because the second order condition of equilibrium, i.e. the marginal cost curve must intersect the marginal revenue curve at the equilibrium point from below, can be satisfied under monopoly in all the three cases, namely when marginal cost curve is rising, declining or remaining constant, while under perfect competition this condition is satisfied only when the marginal cost is rising. Under perfect competition, as the marginal revenue curve takes the shape of a horizontal straight line, marginal cost curve can intersect the marginal revenue curve from below only when the marginal cost curve is rising. Under monopoly, in contrast, since the marginal revenue curve is declining, the marginal cost curve can intersect the marginal revenue curve whether the marginal cost curve is rising, declining or remaining constant. The three equilibria of the monopolist are shown in Fig. 18.6(a), (b) and (c).

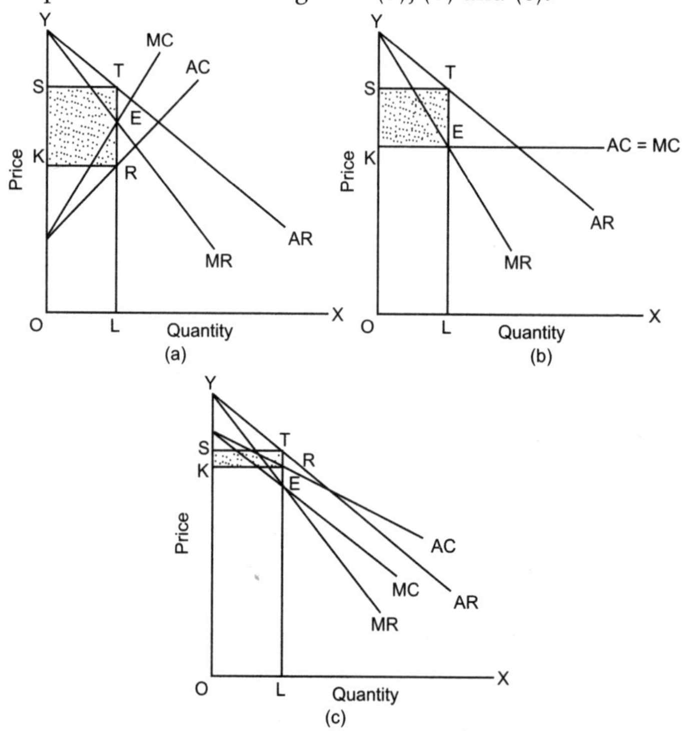

Fig. 18.6

Figure 18.6(a) depicts monopoly equilibrium when the marginal cost curve is rising at the equilibrium level of output. Figure 18.6(b) illustrates monopoly equilibrium when the marginal cost curve is constant at the equilibrium output. Figure 18.6(c) shows monopoly equilibrium when the marginal cost is declining at the equilibrium output. In all the three cases, the monopolist is in equilibrium at the point E where his marginal revenue is equal to the marginal cost and produces an output OL. In all the three cases, LT is monopoly price and the monopoly profits are represented by the dotted area.

Thirdly, while a perfectly competitive firm is in long-run equilibrium at the lowest point of the long-run average cost curve, the monopolist is generally in equilibrium at a level of output at which the average cost is still falling and has not yet reached its lowest point. In other words, in the long-run, while a perfectly competitive firm is of the optimum size, the size of the monopolist firm may be smaller than the optimum one. Under perfect competition, as the average revenue and marginal revenue remain constant, it is profitable for the firm to increase production till the average cost is declining. In contrast, under monopoly, since the average as well as marginal revenue declines with every expansion in production, it may not be profitable for the monopolist to carry production to the level at which the average cost of production is the lowest.

Fourthly, in the long-run, while a competitive firm cannot earn more than normal profits, the monopolist may enjoy super-normal profits. Under perfect competition, as we have already seen, the firm is in long-run equilibrium when its AC = MC = MR = AR. When average cost is equal to average revenue, the firm enjoys only normal profits which are included in the average cost of production. In contrast, as we have already seen, the monopolist can be in equilibrium at an output at which his average revenue is greater than his average cost and hence he can earn super-normal profits.

Fifthly, while a monopolist can charge different prices for the same product from different customers, depending upon the elasticity of their demand, the same is not possible for a competitive producer. In a perfectly competitive market, an individual firm faces a perfectly elastic demand curve. Hence, if it tries to charge a slightly higher price from some buyers, they would at once shift to some other firm and buy the product at the ruling market price. In contrast, under monopoly, since there is only one seller, if he charges a higher price from some buyers, it is not possible for them to turn to some other seller.

Sixthly, assuming uniform cost conditions under perfect competition and monopoly, the price would be higher and output smaller under monopoly than under perfect competition. Suppose a number of firms are producing a homogeneous product under perfectly competitive conditions so that no single firm is in a position to influence the price of the product. Under these conditions, the price and output of the product would be determined by the intersection of the demand and supply curves for the product. Now let us assume that all these firms combine together and form a monopoly. It is assumed that the combination of the competitive firms into monopoly does not lead to any internal or external economies and, therefore, no change occurs in the cost or supply conditions. Now, under monopoly, the price and output are determined at the level where the marginal cost equals marginal revenue. Figure 18.7 shows the determination of price and output under perfect competition and monopoly.

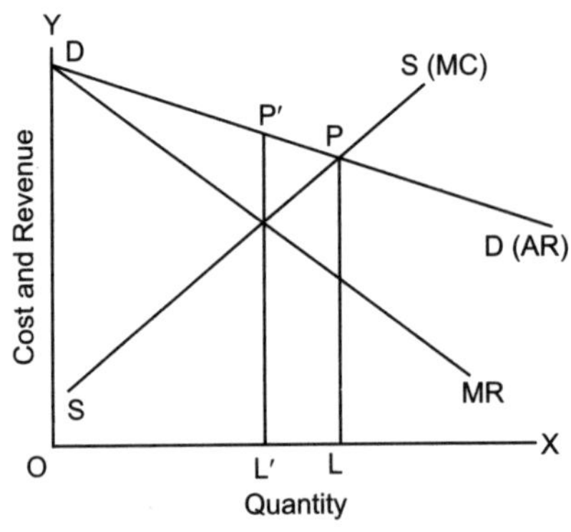

Fig. 18.7

DD and SS represent demand and supply curves respectively of the perfectly competitive industry. They intersect each other at point P. At this point, the perfectly competitive industry produces an output equal to OL and the price is equal to LP. MR represents the marginal revenue curve corresponding to the demand curve DD. The curve SS, which is the supply curve of the perfectly competitive industry, is the marginal cost curve under monopoly. The monopolist's marginal revenue curve (MR) and marginal cost curve (SS) intersect each other at point P′. At this point the monopolist's output is OL′ and price is L′P′. This shows that under monopoly the output is smaller and price higher than under perfectly competitive conditions.

Now the question arises as to whether the cost conditions would remain unchanged when several competitive firms combine into a monopoly. In other words, the question is, would there accrue certain economics when the small plants of the perfectly competitive firms are replaced by the large-sized plant of the monopolist. There are two opinions on this issue. One opinion is that the amalgamation of small firms into a monopoly would lead to sever economies arising from greater scope for division of labour, bulk buying of raw materials and machinery, organisation of sales on a large scale leading to smaller advertising costs, better credit in the money market avoidance of cross freights between one part of the market and another, etc. These economies would bring down the marginal cost curve of the monopolist. If the economies are quite important and lead to substantial decline in the cost curve, it is quite possible that under monopoly the output may be larger and price smaller than under perfect competition.

The other view is held by Mrs. Joan Robinson who believes that perfect competition brings in all the economies which monopoly can introduce. She points out that the economies mentioned above arise when the comparison is between monopoly output and output under imperfect competition and not under perfect competition. "In a perfect market, competitive advertising would be unnecessary. If a very small reduction in price by one competitor would secure an indefinitely large increase in sales, it would be folly to spend money on advertisement.... If the cost of production of individual plants could be lowered by specialisation, specialisation would come about in a perfect market. Suppose, for instance, that there are ten rolling mills, each of which keeps a set of rolls for making ten sizes of steel rails, and that none are used to capacity. A monopolist could allot to each mill one size, and save the expense involved by frequent changes and by maintaining surplus rolls. But in a perfect market any mill which specialised on a certain size could produce that size more cheaply than the rest, capture the whole market in that size, and force the other mills to specialise in the remaining sizes. This process would continue until each mill produced one size only, and the same result would come about under monopoly. In a perfect market lateral disintegration of this type would be carried to the point at which there is no further economies to be had from specialisation. Similarly, if there are economies from specialising upon particular processes in manufacture, vertical disintegration would come about under perfect competition.... If a large-scale organisation can deal more efficiently with the output of the whole industry than the separate sales departments of the separate firms, under perfect competition a system of independent merchants would grow up and an optimum sized sales unit would deal with the output of a number of producing firms. If there is a waste of transport cost because a more distant firm sells in a part of the market which could be more cheaply served by a firm nearer to it, perfect competition would ensure that this waste was eliminated, and each buyer would be served by the firm which could serve him most cheaply. In short, perfect competition would bring about all the economies which monopoly could introduce".[1]

Price Discrimination

In some cases, the monopolist may find it possible and profitable to divide the market for his product in two or more parts and charge a different price for the same product in different parts of the market.

Essential Conditions for Price Discrimination

In the first place, price discrimination is possible only when there exists a monopoly or imperfect competition. A seller can divide and keep the market into separate parts only when he operates under monopoly or imperfect competition. In an imperfectly competitive market, the customers do not shift from one market to the other because of ignorance and inertia. In a perfectly competitive market, price discrimination would not be possible even if the market can be divided into different parts. Under perfect competition, the demand would be perfectly elastic in each part of the market and every seller would like to sell his entire output in that part of the market where the highest price can be obtained. Such an attempt on the part of all sellers would bring the price down to the competitive level and the result would be a single price in the entire market.

Secondly, price discrimination is possible only when the elasticity of demand is different in different parts of the market at a single monopoly price. When the elasticity of demand differs in different markets, the monopolist would be able to charge a higher price in the market where the demand is less elastic and a lower price in the market where the demand is more elastic.

Thirdly, price discrimination would be possible only when different markets are separated from each other in such a way that the goods sold by the monopolist in the cheaper market cannot be resold in the dearer market, and also the customers cannot transfer themselves into the cheaper markets to obtain the benefit of the lower price.

Price discrimination is very likely to take place when a single seller is not subject to close competition or when there is an agreement between rival sellers. The most common case is the sale of direct personal services which cannot be transferred from one market to another. The doctors, for instance, usually charge a higher fee from rich persons and a lower fee from poor persons. This practice is maintained by a tradition among doctors and would break down if they start competing among themselves by underbidding each other in the fees charged to rich patients.

Price discrimination is possible when the markets in which the monopolist is selling are separated from each other geographically or by tariff barriers so that substantial costs are involved in moving goods from the cheaper to the dearer market. Sometimes the monopolist sells goods abroad at a price lower than the price at which the same goods are sold in the domestic market. This type of discrimination is known as 'dumping'. If the transportation costs are quite high, they may prevent the dumped goods from coming back to the country of origin. The same would be the effect of high tariff barriers.

Price discrimination may occur when different groups of people require the same service in connection with clearly differentiated commodities. The railways, for instance, can charge different rates for the transportation of coal and steel. The steel cannot be converted into coal for taking benefit of a lower rate applicable to coal.

There also exists a sort of rather haphazard discrimination when the goods sold are made-to-order. In this case one individual buyer has no means to know the price which is being charged from another buyer for a similar commodity.

Even when there exists no natural barrier between different groups of customers, the monopolist may adopt several devices to divide the market so as to make discrimination possible. He may sell the same commodity under different names and labels which induce the rich and snobbish buyers to distinguish themselves from the poor buyers. Thus, the market is broken up and the monopolist is able to sell more or less the same product at different prices. This device of breaking up the market also safeguards the monopolist from criticisms of according unequal treatment to different groups of buyers.

Degrees of Price Discrimination

Prof. A.C. Pigou in his book *Economics of Welfare* distinguishes between three types of price discrimination, viz. (i) price discrimination of the first degree, (ii) price discrimination of the second degree, and (iii) price discrimination of the third degree.

Price Discrimination of First Degree

Price discrimination of the first degree means that the monopolist charges a different price for all the different units of a commodity in such a way that the price exacted for each unit is equal to the demand price for it so that no consumer's surplus is left with any buyer. This type of discrimination is called *perfect discrimination* by Mrs. Joan Robinson. Price discrimination of the first degree assumes that the monopolist knows the maximum amount of money which each consumer would be willing to pay for a unit of the commodity rather than going without it. Thus, the price per unit charged to each buyer indicates the average utility of the quantity which he purchases. The simplest kind of the first degree discrimination is when each consumer buys only one unit of the commodity from the monopolist. The monopolist charges to each consumer the maximum price which he would be willing to pay rather than going without the commodity. In case the buyers need more than one unit, he fixes a price so high for the entire quantity sold to each buyer that his entire consumer surplus is squeezed out.

Under discrimination of the first degree, the monopolist would charge as money prices as ordinates can be drawn from the demand curve or as there are degrees of the demand curve. In Fig. 18.8, DD represents the composite demand curve of all the buyers and is the average revenue curve to the simple monopolist.

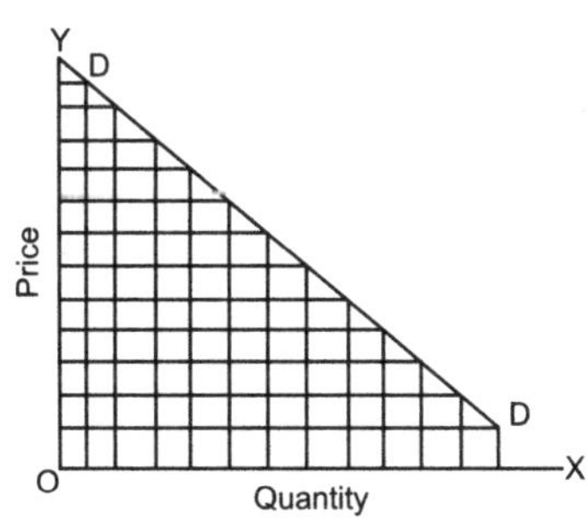

Fig. 18.8

Under simple monopoly, the MR curve lies below the AR curve but under perfect price discrimination, the average revenue curve becomes the marginal revenue curve because each unit of the commodity is sold at a different price.

It may be pointed out that such extreme discrimination is rarely possible in actual practice. It may take place only when there are a few buyers and the monopolist is shrewed enough to know the maximum price which each buyer would be wiling to pay.

Price Discrimination of Second Degree

Price discrimination of second degree means that the monopolist is able to charge several separate prices in such a way that all units with a demand price higher than X are sold at a price X, all units with a demand price below X and above Y at a price Y and so on. Under this type of price discrimination, the buyers are divided into different groups and a different price is charged from each group which is the lowest demand price of that group. This type of price discrimination is possible when each individual buyer's demand for the commodity is perfectly inelastic below and above a certain price. Under this type of price discrimination, the monopolist squeezes out only a part and not whole of the consumer's surplus. The total revenue of the monopolist is larger than that which he obtains when a uniform price is charged. Discrimination of the second degree is usually practiced when there are several consumers with different tastes and different incomes. An outstanding example of such price discrimination is the supply of electric power by the government or a private company. Figure 18.9 shows that the government can obtain a larger amount of total revenue by practising discrimination than that would have obtained had it charged a uniform price.

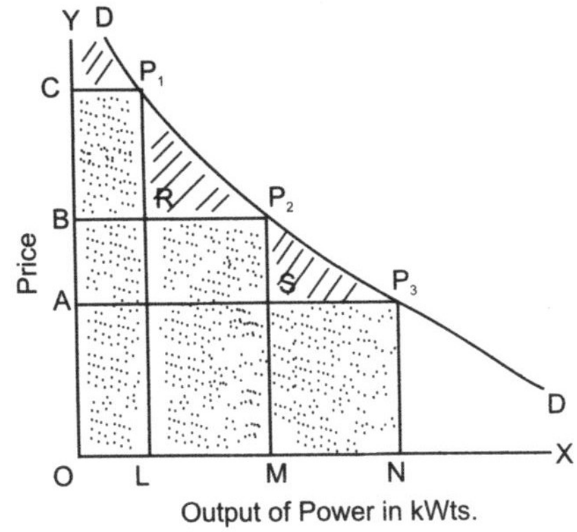

Fig. 18.9

The curve DD indicates the various volumes of demand for electric power, at different prices. A price LP_1 per kWt. is charged upto OL units of power. The price is lowered to MP_2 per kWt. for the next LM units of power consumed. Similarly the price is lowered to NP_3 for the next MN units of power consumed. By charging different prices for different unit slabs, the government obtains total revenue equal to OLP_1C + LMP_2R + MNP_3S. In contrast, had the government charged a uniform price NP_3 per kWt., its total revenue would have been only ONP_3A which is much smaller than total revenue obtained by government by charging different prices for different unit slabs. The shaded area in the figure shows the consumer's surplus still left with the consumers.

Price Discrimination of Third Degree

Discrimination of the third degree means that the monopolist divides the buyers of his commodity or service into two or more groups and charges a different price to each group. The price charged to each group need not be the lowest demand price of that group. The price charged to each group depends upon the quantity sold to that group and the demand conditions of that group. A common example of this type of discrimination is the sale of electric power at a higher price for household consumption and at a lower price for industrial purposes. Price discrimination of the third degree is the most common and usually more practicable of the three types of price discrimination mentioned above. The analysis of price discrimination given below relates to this type of discrimination.

Equilibrium Under Price Discrimination

Assuming that the monopolist is in a position to practice price discrimination between different markets, the question arises as to what would be the optimum output of the monopolist which when distributed among different markets and sold at different prices would yield maximum net monopoly revenue. Since the monopolist aims at maximising his profits, how could he attain this objective when faced with several markets instead of one? When the monopolist sells in a single market, his profits would be maximised by producing and selling that quantity of output at which his marginal cost equals marginal revenue. In the same way, under discriminating monopoly, the monopolist would maximise his profits if he sells in each market the quantity at which his marginal cost equals marginal revenue. He would, of course, charge a different price for the commodity in each market, depending upon the elasticity of demand in that market. Under discriminating monopoly, the marginal revenue, however, would tend to be equal in different market. So long as the marginal revenue is different in different markets, the monopolist can increase his profits by transferring his sales from the markets where the marginal revenue is lower to those where it is higher. When the monopolist sells less in the former markets, his marginal revenue would rise in those markets. Similarly, when he sells more in the latter markets, his marginal revenue would decline in those markets. Ultimately, the marginal revenue would become equal in all the markets. Thus, under discriminatory monopoly, while the prices will be different in different markets owing to differences in the elasticity of demand, the marginal revenue will be equal in all the markets.

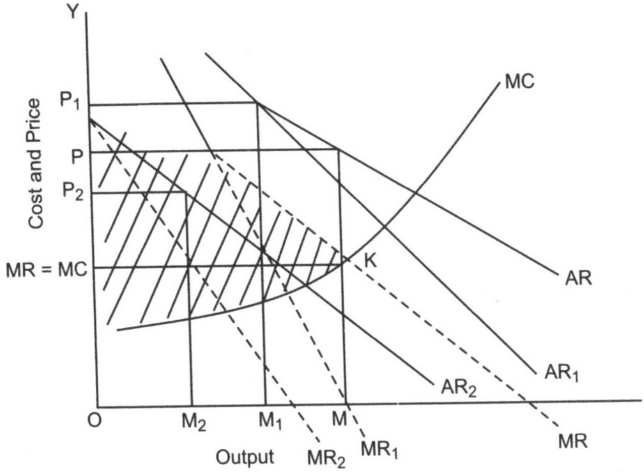

Fig. 18.10

Figure 18.10 shows the determination of price and output under discriminatory monopoly. The monopolist sells his output in two markets, 1 and 2. The demand is more elastic in market 2 than in market 1. AR_1 represents the average revenue curve in market 1 and MR_1 the corresponding marginal revenue curve. AR_2 shows the average revenue curve in market 2 and MR_2 the corresponding marginal revenue curve. AR shows the aggregate average revenue curve obtained by lateral summation of AR_1 and AR_2 curves. MC represents the marginal cost curve. The monopolist's output is determined by the intersection of his marginal cost curve with the aggregate marginal revenue curve. This total output consists of the quantities sold in the two markets, in each of which marginal revenue is equal to the marginal cost of the entire output. The price in each market is the demand price for the output sold there. The total output produced is OM and is equal to OM_1 + OM_2. MK is the marginal cost of the output OM. Quantity OM_1 is sold in market 1 at price M_1P_1 and quantity OM_2 is sold in market 2 at price M_2P_2. The shaded area shows the monopoly revenue, which is equal to the area lying under the aggregate marginal revenue curve (total revenue) minus the area lying under the marginal cost curve (total costs).

In the figure, the marginal cost is rising, but whether marginal cost is rising, constant, or declining, the output will be determined by the point at which the aggregate marginal revenue curve intersects the marginal cost curve and the quantity sold in each market will be the quantity for which marginal revenue is equal to the marginal cost of the entire output.

The proposition that the monopolist will charge a higher price in the market, where demand is less elastic and a lower price where the demand is more elastic, can also be proved algebraically. We have seen that in order to maximise his profits, the monopolist divides his sales into different markets in such a manner that the marginal revenue is equal in all the markets. Let us suppose there are only two markets, 1 and 2. Since the monopolist aims at equating his marginal revenues in the two markets.

$$MR_1 = MR_2$$

We know that $MR = AR\left(1 - \frac{1}{e}\right)$

Therefore, $AR_1\left(1 - \frac{1}{e_1}\right) = AR_2\left(1 - \frac{1}{e_2}\right)$

We also know that AR = P

Therefore, $P_1\left(1 - \frac{1}{e_1}\right) = P_2\left(1 - \frac{1}{e_2}\right)$

If e_1 equals e_2, P_1 would equal P_2. In other words, when the elasticity of demand is equal in the two markets, the monopolist would charge a uniform price in the two markets. If the elasticity of demand is higher in market 1 than in market 2, i.e. $e_1 > e_2$, $\left(1 - \frac{1}{e_1}\right)$ would be greater than $\left(1 - \frac{1}{e_2}\right)$.

Hence, P_2 would be higher than P_1.

Mathematical Derivation

The total demand of the monopolist is

$$P = f(X)$$

Let us suppose that the demand curves of the two price discriminating markets are

$$P_1 = f_1(X_1) \qquad \text{and} \qquad P_2 = f_2(X_2)$$

The cost of the firm is given by

$$C = f(X) = f(X_1 + X_2)$$

Profit of the monopolist is given by

$$\Pi = R_1 + R_2 - C$$

R_1 and R_2 are the total revenue in the two markets.

First order condition of the profit maximisation:

$$\frac{\partial \Pi}{\partial X_1} = 0 \qquad \text{and} \qquad \frac{\partial \Pi}{\partial X_2} = 0$$

Or,

$$\frac{\partial \Pi}{\partial X_1} = \frac{\partial R_1}{\partial X_1} - \frac{\partial C}{\partial X_1} = 0$$

and

$$\frac{\partial \Pi}{\partial X_2} = \frac{\partial R_2}{\partial X_2} - \frac{\partial C}{\partial X_2} = 0$$

Or,

$$\frac{\partial R_1}{\partial X_1} = \frac{\partial C}{\partial X_1} \qquad \text{and} \qquad \frac{\partial R_2}{\partial X_2} = \frac{\partial C}{\partial X_2}$$

Hence,

$$MR_1 = MC_1 \qquad \text{and} \qquad MR_2 = MC_2$$

But

$$MC_1 = MC_2 = MC = \frac{dC}{dX}$$

Therefore, we have

$$MC = MR_1 = MR_2$$

Second order condition of the profit maximisation:

This condition of profit maximisation requires that the MR in each market should be increasing less rapidly than the MC of the total output.

i.e. $$\frac{\partial^2 R_1}{\partial X_1^2} < \frac{\partial^2 C}{\partial X^2} \quad \text{and} \quad \frac{\partial^2 R_2}{\partial X_2^2} < \frac{\partial^2 C}{\partial X^2}$$

Comparison Between Simple Monopoly Output and Discriminating Monopoly Output

We now proceed to discuss the comparison between monopoly output when a single price is charged for a commodity (i.e. simple monopoly output) and the monopoly output when different prices are charged in different markets (discriminating monopoly output). There is no single rule in regard to the effect of price discrimination on output. The introduction of price discrimination may lead to a larger, smaller, or the same output depending upon the various conditions.

In case the simple monopoly output is small, the power of charging discriminatory prices may have no effect at all on the volume of output. It may happen that above a certain price there are buyers only in one market, and if the simple monopoly price is so high that only members of the stronger market will buy, it is possible that the power of charging discriminatory prices will be ineffective simple because the marginal revenue in the weaker market is too small to make it worthwhile for the discriminating monopolist to sell any output there. In such a case no quantity is sold in the weaker market either under discrimination or under simple monopoly and the entire quantity is sold in the stronger market. Thus, there would be only a single price and the possibility of charging different prices would not make any difference.

Within the limits in which only the stronger market is served, the possibility of charging discriminating prices will not affect the monopoly price or output. But as soon as the marginal revenue in the stronger market is equal to the highest price at which any output would be bought in the weaker market, it would become profitable for the discriminating monopolist to sell some output in the weaker market also. Introduction of discriminatory prices in this case would lead to an output larger than that which would be produced under simply monopoly. The increase in output would be less than, equal to, or greater than the quantity of the commodity sold in the weaker market according to whether the marginal cost is rising, constant, or declining.

In case it is profitable to fix the simple monopoly price at a level at which the buyers of the weaker market can also buy, the commodity will be sold in both the markets under simple monopoly as well as under discriminatory monopoly. If at the simple monopoly price the elasticities of demand are different in the two markets, the marginal revenue would be higher in the market where the demand is less elastic than that in the market where the demand is more elastic. When discrimination becomes possible, it would be profitable for the monopolist to reduce output and raise price in the less elastic market and increase output and lower price in the more elastic market till the marginal revenue is equalised in the two markets. Thus, introduction of discriminatory prices results in a reduction in output in one market and an expansion in output in the other market. Whether the aggregate output in the two markets under discriminatory monopoly would be greater or smaller than that under simple monopoly would depend upon whether the more elastic of the demand curves in the separate markets is more or less concave than the less elastic demand curve. The aggregate output would remain unchanged if the demand curves are straight lines or if the concavities of the demand curves are equal. This can be proved from Fig. 18.11.[2]

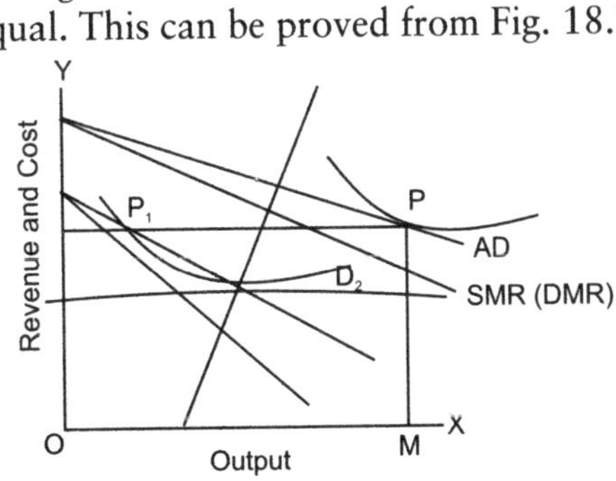

Fig. 18.11

Let MP be the simple monopoly price and OM the simple monopoly output which consists of outputs OM_1 and OM_2 sold in the two different markets. Let AP be the tangent to the aggregate demand curve (AD) at point P. Draw perpendicular to the Y-axis to cut it at F and to intersect the two separate demand curves (D_1 and D_2) at P_1 and P_2. Let the tangents to D_1 and D_2 at P_1 and P_2 intersect the Y-axis at A_1 and A_2. Let AC, AC_1 and AC_2 be the correspondents to the demand curves at P, P_1 and P_2 cutting the perpendiculars to X-axis through P, P_1 and P_2 in C, C_1 and C_2. The aggregate demand curve (AD) is obtained by summing the separate demand curves (D_1 and D_2) and similarly the tangent AP represents the lateral summation of tangents A_1P_1 and A_2P_2. It follows that AC (the correspondent to the aggregate demand curve at P) is the sum of two correspondents A_1C_1 and A_2C_2 because at any ordinate the abscissa of each correspondent is half the abscissa of the tangent. Thus, for the ordinate OF, A_1C_1 bisects FP_1 and A_2C_2 bisects FP_2 and AC bisects FP. But FP is the sum of FP_1 and FP_2. The same is the case for any other ordinate. Therefore, AC is equal to the lateral summation of A_1C_1 and A_2C_2. Now draw BC perpendicular to the Y-axis to intersect P_1M_1 and P_2M_2 at H_1 and H_2 and to intersect A_1C_1 and A_2C_2 at G_1 and G_2. Now it can be proved that H_1G_1 is equal to H_2G_2.

Because $BH_1 = FP_1$, $BH_2 = FP_2$, and $BC = FP$

Therefore, $BH_1 + BH_2 = FP_1 + FP_2 = FP$ because AD is the lateral summation of D_1 and D_2

Therefore, $BH_1 + BH_2 = BC$

But $BG_1 + BG_2 = BC$ because AC is the lateral summation of A_1C_1 and A_2C_2.

Therefore, $H_1G_1 - G_2H_2 = 0$

It follows from above that if the demand curves are straight lines, so that they coincide with their tangents, the output under discriminatory monopoly would be equal to that under simple monopoly. When the monopolist is in a position to charge discriminatory prices and equates the marginal revenue in each market, given by curves MR_1 and MR_2 (which in this case coincide with A_1G_1 and A_2G_2), with the marginal cost of the aggregate output (which is equal to the marginal revenue, MC, of the simple monopolist), he would increase output in one market from OM_1 or BH_1 to BG_1 and reduce it in the other from OM_2 or BH_2 to BG_2 by equal quantities, H_1G_1 and G_2H_2 and hence the aggregate output remains unaltered.

When the demand curves are straight lines, since the aggregate output is the same under discriminatory monopoly as under simple monopoly, it does not make any difference whether the marginal cost is rising, declining, or constant. The introduction of discrimination does not alter the aggregate output and the marginal cost; it changes only the prices and outputs in individual markets and the profits of the monopolist.

Let us now analyse the case where the demand curves are not straight lines. If the demand curve of one market is concave, as is D_1 in Fig. 18.11, its marginal revenue curve, MR_1, would intersect FP to the left of the correspondent and as it passes through C it must intersect BC outside H_1G_1. It follows that when the more elastic demand curve is concave, as in the figure, the increase in output in the separate market resulting from the introduction of discrimination would be larger than when the demand curve is a straight line. Similarly when the less elastic demand curve is concave, the decline in output would be greater than when the demand curve is a straight line. In case the demand curve is convex, as is D_2 in the figure, the marginal revenue curve would intersect BC between G_2 and H_2 and the increase or reduction in output in the separate market will be less than for a straight line.

From above analysis it follows that if the more elastic demand curve is concave and the less elastic demand curve is a straight line or convex, the increase in output in the market in which output is increased will be larger than the reduction in output in the other market and as such the aggregate output would be larger under discriminatory monopoly than under simple monopoly. In contrast, if the less elastic demand curve is concave, and the more elastic a straight line or convex, the aggregate output would be smaller under discriminatory monopoly than under simple monopoly. In case both the demand curves are concave or both convex, the result would depend upon whether or not the concavity of the more elastic demand curve is more than that of the less elastic demand curve. If the concavities of the two demand curves are equal, the introduction of discrimination will not alter the aggregate volume of output. The straight line demand curves represent a special case of the two demand curves being of equal concavity.

The analysis was so far based on the assumption that the introduction of discrimination leaves the marginal cost unchanged. In fact, this assumption would not hold good in cases in which the introduction of discrimination results in a change in the volume of aggregate output. If the increase in output resulting from discrimination leads to an increase in the marginal cost, the increase in output would be carried less far. Similarly, if the discrimination leads to a reduction in output, the reduction would be carried less far if the marginal cost is declining. But the change in marginal cost cannot be so larger as to prevent the change in output because if it were so the change in marginal cost would no occur. Further, in case the marginal cost is declining, the increase in output resulting from discrimination will be enhanced; and if the marginal cost is rising, the decline in output would be enhanced. If the increase in output owing to price discrimination is sufficiently large and if the marginal cost declining sufficiently fast, the introduction of discrimination may lower the price in both the markets.

The Price Elasticity of Demand and the Discriminating Monopoly

The market with the lower elasticity of demand will have higher price and it will be lower in the market with higher elasticity of demand. The equality of MR does not mean the equality of prices in the two markets so long as the elasticities of demand are different in the two markets.

Let P_1 and P_2 be the prices and e_1 and e_2 be the absolute values of the elasticities of demand in the two markets respectively. Then,

$$MR_1 = P_1\left(1 - \frac{1}{e_1}\right)$$

$$MR_2 = P_2\left(1 - \frac{1}{e_2}\right)$$

And, $$MR_1 = MR_2$$

Therefore,

$$P_1\left(1 - \frac{1}{e_1}\right) = P_2\left(1 - \frac{1}{e_2}\right)$$

Or $$\frac{P_1}{P_2} = \frac{\left(1 - \frac{1}{e_2}\right)}{\left(1 - \frac{1}{e_1}\right)}$$

If $e_1 = e_2$ the ratio of prices is equal to unity, i.e.

$$\frac{P_1}{P_2} = 1$$

Hence, $$P_1 = P_2$$

It implies that price discrimination is not possible when both the market have same price elasticities.

If $|e_1| > |e_2|$, then we have

$$\left(1 - \frac{1}{e_1}\right) > \left(1 - \frac{1}{e_2}\right)$$

Thus, MRs will be equal if

$$P_1 < P_2$$

This implies that the market with the higher price elasticity will have the lower price. Hence, the price discrimination is profitable if the monopolists are able to sub-divide the consumer into a large number of groups with different demand elasticities.

Price Discrimination—Harmful or Beneficial to Society

We are now in a position to analyse as to whether price discrimination is harmful or beneficial to the buyers and to the society as a whole. In the first place, since average revenue is larger under discriminatory monopoly than under simple monopoly, in some cases it may not be profitable to produce the commodity at all unless price discrimination could be practised. If the average cost curve for a commodity lies above the demand curve for it throughout its length, it will not be profitable to produce the commodity under a single-price system. But if the average cost curve, though above the demand curve lies at some point below the average revenue curve, it would be possible to make a profit and produce some output if discriminatory prices could be charged. "It may happen, for instance, that a railway could not be built, or a country doctor would not set up in practice, if discrimination were forbidden. It is clearly desirable that price discrimination should be permitted in such cases, for the average revenue of the monopolist cannot be greater than average utility to the consumers. If the average revenue is greater than average cost, average utility will also be greater, and the investment will lead to a gain to society.[3]

When some output would be produced even in the absence of discrimination, introduction of discrimination would benefit those buyers for whom the price is reduced and harm those for whom the price is raised. In view of the difficulties involved in comparing the gains of one group against the losses of the other group, it is difficult to pass a definite judgement as to whether or not discrimination would be beneficial for all the buyers taken together. But if the buyers in the more elastic market, for whom the price is reduced are poorer than the buyers in the more elastic market, and it is assumed that the same amount of money has more value for the poor than for the rich, the price discrimination would be considered beneficial for the buyers in general.

But if the less elastic market is at home and the more elastic market abroad, the foreign customers would be charged a lower price and a higher price would be charged to the domestic customers. Foreign demand being more elastic, however, a greater quantity be sold abroad at a lower price, which means a larger income and employment at home. Further if the production of the commodity in question is subject to law of decreasing cost, sale of a larger output abroad may mean larger economies of scale and hence lower costs and prices in the domestic market also.

From the point of view of the society as a whole, it is difficult to say with certainty as to whether price discrimination is beneficial or not. It is obviously wasteful, from the point of view of the society as a whole, if the commodity in question fails to be produced upto the point where its marginal utility (as indicated by its demand price) is equal to its marginal cost. Under simple monopoly, however, marginal revenue is equal to marginal cost and as such monopoly output is undesirably restricted. Discriminatory monopoly, therefore, is superior to simple monopoly in all cases in which it leads to an increase in output and as we have already seen such cases are likely to be more common. Against this advantage, however, we must set the fact that price discrimination leads to a maldistribution of resources as between different uses. Before we can say whether discrimination is beneficial or not, we have to weigh the advantage from a larger output against the disadvantage resulting from a maldistribution of resources as between different uses. In cases in which the discriminatory monopoly may lead to a decline in output, it is injurious on both the counts.

Measurement of Degree of Monopoly Power

We have already seen that a monopolist is in a position to influence the price and output in the industry in question. The degree of monopoly power is indicated by the extent of influence which the monopolist can exercise on price and output. In other words, it indicates the extent of competition which affects the seller in determining his policy in regard to the price and output of his product and the differentiation of his product by quality and service. In short, it means the extent of deviation from the competitive behaviour.

Several methods have been suggested to measure the degree of monopoly power in an industry. One of the methods measures the extent of monopoly power by relationship between marginal cost and price. Under perfect competition, MR (Marginal Revenue) = MC (Marginal Cost) = AR (Average Revenue) = P (Price). Under monopoly, MR = MC but MR > AR or P. Thus, an important difference between monopoly and competition is that while under competition MC = P, under monopoly MC > P. The monopoly power, therefore, can be measured by the extent to which MC deviates from P.

Lerner measures degree of monopoly by the formula:

$$\text{Monopoly Power} = \frac{P - MC}{P} \qquad \text{(i)}$$

where P stand for price and MC for marginal cost.

Under perfect competition, P = MC (ii)

From equations (i) and (ii) we obtain

$$\frac{MC - MC}{P} = \frac{0}{P} = 0$$

In other words, the monopoly power is zero under perfect competition. The larger the gap between price and marginal cost, the greater would be the degree of monopoly power.

The monopolist's attempt to increase his profits by raising the price may, however, be counteracted by a decline in his sales as a consequence of the rise in price. The degree of monopoly power, therefore, is measured in terms of the elasticity of demand and the formula is

$$\text{Degree of Monopoly Power (DMP)} = \frac{E(P - MC)}{P} \qquad \text{(i)}$$

The profits are maximised when MC = MR (ii)

Substituting equation (ii) in equation (i) we get

$$DMP = \frac{E(P - MR)}{P} \qquad \text{(iii)}$$

We have already seen $$MR = P \cdot \frac{E-1}{E} \qquad \text{(iv)}$$

Substituting equation (iv) in equation (iii) we get

$$DMP = \frac{E\left(P - P\dfrac{E-1}{E}\right)}{P} = \frac{1}{E}$$

The above formula shows that the degree of monopoly power is the inverse of price elasticity of demand. The lower is the price elasticity of demand, the greater is the degree of monopoly power and vice versa.

Limitations of Lerner's Measure

In the first place, monopoly power does not exclusively depend upon the difference between price and cost. It also depends upon the restriction of output by the monopolist. The difference between price and cost may be larger, if the demand for the commodity in question is less elastic. The reduction in output in this case would, however, be small. Lerner formula does not take into consideration the influence of the monopolist on the volume of output. Secondly, Lerner's formula cannot measure non-price competition under monopolistic competition and differentiated oligopoly. A firm selling a differentiated product may have a high degree of monopoly not because of price variation but because of non-price competition. A firm may be able to expand the demand for its product by changing its quality and by intensifying its selling effort. Thirdly, the major drawback in Lerner's measure is that it does not attach any definite coefficient of elasticity to the degree of monopoly power.

Triffin's Measure

Triffin measures monopoly power in terms of cross elasticity of demand. Cross elasticity tells us how change in the price of one commodity affects the demand for another commodity. The higher the cross elasticity of demand, the lower would be the monopoly power and vice versa. If the cross elasticity of demand between the product of a firm and those of other firms is zero, the reciprocal of cross elasticity would be infinity and hence the firm would enjoy absolute monopoly power.

Triffin's measure of monopoly power also suffers from several shortcomings. In the first place, it is not possible to find out a definite coefficient of cross elasticity of demand for any product.

Bain's Measure

Prof. J.S. Bain measures the degree of monopoly power by the size of super normal profits. Under perfect competition, in the long-run, a firm can earn only normal profits. In case there are any other supernormal profits, they are competed away by the entry of new firms and the expansion of the existing firms in the industry. It is only under monopoly that supernormal profits can exist because the entry of new firms is ruled out. As such the degree of monopoly power can be measured by the size of supernormal profits. The strongest the monopolist's position, the larger would be the size of the supernormal profits.

Bain's measure of monopoly power also suffers from several shortcomings. In the first place, it is difficult to determine the net income of a firm. It is very difficult to accurately determine the extent of amortisation of the cost of fixed factors. Secondly, all profits accruing to a firm are not monopoly profits. Under competition as well as under monopoly, the firms often earn windfall profits because of certain changes in demand and cost conditions. To determine pure monopoly profits, windfall profits must, therefore, be deducted from total net profits.

NOTES

1. Joan Robinson, *The Economics of Imperfect Competition* (London, 1954), pp. 167-68.
2. *Ibid.*, pp. 190-95.
3. *Ibid.*, pp. 203-04.